Final Cut Pro

EFFICIENT EDITING

Final Cut Pro

EFFICIENT EDITING

SMART, QUICK, AND EFFECTIVE VIDEO EDITING
WITH FCP 10.5

Iain Anderson

BIRMINGHAM—MUMBAI

Final Cut Pro: Efficient Editing

Iain Anderson

Copyright © 2020 Packt Publishing

Commissioning Editor: Pavan Ramchandani
Acquisition Editor: Apurv Desai
Senior Editor: Sofi Rogers
Content Development Editor: Rakhi Patel
Technical Editor: Deepesh Patel
Copy Editor: Safis Editing
Project Coordinator: Kinjal Bari
Proofreader: Safis Editing
Indexer: Manju Arasan
Production Designer: Nilesh Mohite

First published: October 2020

Production reference: 3081220

Published by Packt Publishing Ltd.
Livery Place
35 Livery Street
Birmingham
B3 2PB, UK.

ISBN 978-1-83921-324-3

WWW.PACKT.COM

This book is dedicated to my delightful wife Nic and my awesome daughter Hazel for putting up with me for more than 20 years and 13 years respectively.

— Iain Anderson

Packt>

CONTRIBUTORS

ABOUT THE AUTHOR

Iain Anderson is a trainer and freelance editor based in Brisbane, Australia. Among other things, Iain is an Apple Certified Trainer in Final Cut Pro, a lead trainer for macProVideo.com, a tutorial creator for coremelt.com, a videographer, an editor, an animator, a writer, a designer, and occasionally a coder of Apple Watch and iPad apps. In the past, he's created animations and live videos for Microsoft, virtual islands in Second Life for governments, and screensavers for fun. Find him at iain-anderson.com and @funwithstuff on Twitter.

ABOUT THE REVIEWERS

Kevin Luk is an editor, colorist, and VFX artist based in Melbourne. His television work includes the *Neighbours* spin-off *Erinsborough High* (on Channel 5 in the UK and the 10 Network in Australia) and the children's action-adventure *The Legend of Burnout Barry* (ABC).

He's also worked extensively on short-form projects including actor/musician Guy Pearce's music video for his track *What Makes You Think* and the AACTA- and SPA-nominated short film *Rebooted*, which has screened at major festivals including Annecy, Clermont-Ferrand, and the Austin Film Festival.

Kevin is a regular collaborator with LateNite Films, where Final Cut is the standard. Beyond software, VFX, and color grading, Kevin remains true to his passions in stories, characters, and the moments between the cuts.

Chris Hocking has been working in the entertainment industry for over two decades, starting in animatronics and lighting design, before moving into the world of film and television. He was previously the post-production Supervisor at Melbourne's award-winning editing house The Butchery and finishing house The Refinery, before co-founding LateNite Films.

Twice nominated by Screen Producers Australia for Breakthrough Production Company of the Year, LateNite Films' work has been nominated for AACTA, SPA, ADG, AWG, and ARIA awards, and has been screened in competitions at major local and international festivals.

He is also the creator of CommandPost, an open source automation tool used by thousands of Final Cut Pro professionals all around the world.

TABLE OF CONTENTS

3 BRING IT IN: IMPORTING YOUR FOOTAGE

4 SORT IT OUT: REVIEWING AND KEYWORDING

5 CHOOSE YOUR FAVORITES: SELECTING, RATING, AND SEARCHING

7 COVER IT UP: CONNECTIONS, CUTAWAYS, AND STORYLINES

8 NEATEN THE EDGES: TRIMMING TECHNIQUES

9 CONSIDER YOUR OPTIONS: MULTICAM, REPLACING, AND AUDITIONS

10 EXPLORE A LITTLE: COMPOUND CLIPS AND TIMELINE TRICKS

SECTION 3: FINISHING AND EXPORTING   359

11 PLAY WITH LIGHT: COLOR CORRECTION AND GRADING

12 REFINE AND SMOOTH: VIDEO PROPERTIES AND EFFECTS

13 BLEND AND WARP: VIDEO TRANSITIONS AND RETIMING

16 YOU'RE DONE: EXPORTING YOUR EDIT AND FINISHING UP

PREFACE

Final Cut Pro is Apple's flagship non-linear editing application, used by both professionals and independent editors alike. Featuring the Magnetic Timeline, advanced organizing tools, professional titling and effects, industry-leading multicam, and powerful finishing tools, it runs on any modern Mac.

This book is up to date with all the latest features included in the 10.5 release.

To stay up-to-date with future releases of Final Cut Pro, visit http:// fcpefficientediting.com/ for fresh information about new features or changes.

WHO THIS BOOK IS FOR

Anyone who'd like to learn how to edit video in Final Cut Pro is welcome here. If you're new to editing, terrific, and if you're an old hand, you're welcome too.

WHAT THIS BOOK COVERS

PART 1: IMPORTING AND ORGANIZING

Chapter 1, Quick Start: An Introduction to FCP
This chapter presents an overview of the workflow and an introduction to the book.

Chapter 2, Before the Edit: Production Tips
Learn about the technical details and on-set strategies.

Chapter 3, Bring It In: Importing Your Footage
We'll consider different importing techniques and media management tips

Chapter 4, Sort It Out: Reviewing and Keywording
Watch and tag your clips smartly.

Chapter 5, Choose Your Favorites: Selecting, Rating, and Searching
We'll consider how to go about marking the best and worst clips, and finding them again.

PART 2: ROUGH CUT TO FINE CUT

Chapter 6, Build the Spine of the Story: Quick Assembly
Create a project and assemble your media inside it.

Chapter 7, Cover It Up: Connections, Cutaways, and Storylines
We'll explore connections, storylines, and other key Magnetic Timeline skills.

Chapter 8, Neaten the Edges: Trimming Techniques
Slip, slide, roll, and soften your edits.

Chapter 9, Consider Your Options: Multicam, Replacing, and Auditions
Switch one shot for another with clever workflows.

Chapter 10, Explore a Little: Compound Clips and Timeline Tricks
Learn some fancy workarounds and advanced techniques.

PART 3: FINISHING AND EXPORTING

Chapter 11, Play with Light: Color Correction and Grading
We'll cover everything to do with exposure, saturation, contrast, and balance.

Chapter 12, Refine and Smooth: Video Properties and Effects
We'll learn about scaling, cropping, animating, and changing video in all sorts of ways.

Chapter 13, Blend and Warp: Video Transitions and Retiming
This chapter covers creating a bridge between clips, and speed-ramping others.

Chapter 14, Boost the Signal: Audio Sweetening
Making the audio sound as good as the video looks.

Chapter 15, A Few Words: Titles and Generators
We'll consider a few words about titles, backgrounds, and captions.

Chapter 16, You're Done: Exporting your Edit and Finishing Up
Export your video in a few different ways.

TO GET THE MOST OUT OF THIS BOOK

Readers will need basic familiarity with using a Mac, and an installed copy of Final Cut Pro or the free trial. While you don't need to have any editing experience to read this book, basic familiarity with the process will help. If you're an experienced editor, remember what you know about the art of editing, but don't be tied down by existing methods — Final Cut Pro takes a new approach and it's best approached with an open mind.

It's recommended that you have access to a camera or at least an iPhone so you can shoot your own footage, but it's possible to work with stock footage too.

The screenshots in this book are consistent with the public version of Final Cut Pro 10.5 as of November 2020, using macOS 10.15 Catalina. If you're using a later version of macOS (for example, macOS 11 Big Sur or later), you may notice some minor differences in the appearance of the user interface. We intend to update this book for future releases of Final Cut Pro and macOS, but if you're using newer software than is covered here, you may see some differences.

CONVENTIONS USED

There are a number of text conventions used throughout this book.

`Code in text`: Indicates code words in text, database table names, folder names, filenames, file extensions, pathnames, dummy URLs, user input, and Twitter handles. Here is an example: "Name your workspace `Audio`."

Bold: Indicates a new term, an important word, or words that you see onscreen. For example, words in menus or dialog boxes appear in the text like this. Here is an example: "Choose **Match** from the **EQ** menu or **Match Audio** from the **Audio Enhancements** menu." Some terms which have special meaning in Final Cut Pro, including **Library**, **Event** and **Project**, have also been capitalized to avoid confusion.

> TIPS OR IMPORTANT NOTES
> **Appear like this.**

GET IN TOUCH

Feedback from our readers is always welcome.

General feedback: If you have questions about any aspect of this book, mention the book title in the subject of your message and email us at customercare@packtpub.com.

Errata: Although we have taken every care to ensure the accuracy of our content, mistakes do happen. If you have found a mistake in this book, we would be grateful if you would report this to us. Please visit www.packtpub.com/support/errata, selecting your book, clicking on the Errata Submission Form link, and entering the details.

Piracy: If you come across any illegal copies of our works in any form on the Internet, we would be grateful if you would provide us with the location address or website name. Please contact us at copyright@packt.com with a link to the material.

If you are interested in becoming an author: If there is a topic that you have expertise in and you are interested in either writing or contributing to a book, please visit authors.packtpub.com.

REVIEWS

Please leave a review. Once you have read and used this book, why not leave a review on the site that you purchased it from? Potential readers can then see and use your unbiased opinion to make purchase decisions, we at Packt can understand what you think about our products, and our authors can see your feedback on their book. Thank you!

For more information about Packt, please visit packt.com.

SECTION 1: IMPORTING AND ORGANIZING

In this section, you will understand what we are trying to achieve, in terms of bringing the footage in and organizing it for an efficient editing process.

This section comprises the following chapters:

- Chapter 1, Quick Start: An Introduction to FCP
- Chapter 2, Before the Edit: Production Tips
- Chapter 3, Bring It In: Importing Your Footage
- Chapter 4, Sort It Out: Reviewing and Keywording
- Chapter 5, Choose Your Favorites: Selecting, Rating, and Searching

1 QUICK START:
AN INTRODUCTION TO FCP

"FCP X was built for the future as we saw it developing — more cameras, much more footage, reliance on metadata, the need to simplify complex and technical tasks to focus on creativity. You can see that this imagined future is exactly where we are right now."

— Steve Bayes, Final Cut Pro X and ProRes Product Manager, 2010–2018

After 10 years as a video editor in the 1980s, Steve became the first certified instructor for the Avid Media Composer and eventually the Principal Product Designer. In 2006 he became Apple's Senior Product Manager for FCP. From 2010 he product managed the development and release of the ProRes video codec and FCP X, including the almost 30 subsequent releases. Steve retired from Apple in 2018 and continues to consult and invest in developing new technology for film and video.

(www.thestevebayes.com)

Welcome. In this book, you'll learn how to use Apple's flagship non-linear editing application, Final Cut Pro, from a standing start — and it's going to be fun. As I won't be assuming that you already know how to edit, this chapter will guide you through a few of the fundamentals of editing, give you a broad overview of the interface, show you how the editing workflow functions, and give you a few tips on what kind of hardware will help you down the track.

Video editing is a huge field, and there are many, many ways to proceed, either on your own or as part of the wider industry. You'll hear many opinions on best practices, and, indeed, not all of those opinions will agree with the advice I'll give you here. And that's fine! Wherever there are conflicting opinions, I'll do my best to explain why I'm making my specific recommendations, and you can feel free to go a different way if you have different needs. It's all good.

Before I get into the details of Final Cut Pro — frequently abbreviated to FCP — I'd like to take you on a quick tour of video editing more broadly. You can tell a story with any software, but the technical details do matter, and a lot has changed. This book has been completely updated for the 10.5 release, where Final Cut Pro X became Final Cut Pro. All the recently introduced features will be pointed out throughout the book so that existing users can easily discover them.

This chapter will cover the following main topics:

- A brief history of editing
- Interface basics
- An editing workflow overview
- Hardware recommendations

By the end of this chapter, you'll have a great understanding of what the app is about, what this book's about, the editing process that you'll learn, and the gear you'll need to put it into practice.

A BRIEF HISTORY OF EDITING

Cinema has been around for a little over 100 years, and for a long time, the editing process was straightforward. Each frame of film was a single image on a continuous strip of celluloid, and, to combine multiple shots in a sequence, the film was physically cut and then taped to another piece of film. Every cut took real physical effort and time, and revisiting your earlier edits could be difficult, expensive, or impossible, depending on when the decision was made. And then, the arrival of video in the 1980s made it more accessible, but also worse.

Tape-based editing meant that an editor didn't have to physically cut film, and because it made the process much cheaper, an entire generation of teenagers could explore movie making on a budget. However, images recorded on magnetic tape cannot be easily reordered. To rearrange shots A-B-C to B-A-C means offloading the whole sequence to a second tape, then placing them back on the original tape in a different order, and often with a degree of quality loss. Linear editing surely democratized the industry, but it came at a cost.

Computer-based non-linear editing changed it all for the better, giving editors the low cost of tapes, the ability to change the image without chemicals, far easier access to special effects, and, thankfully, the return of easy clip reordering. Today, this is normal and natural, and a new video editor need not consider how things used to be done. Still, most **Non-Linear Editing** applications (**NLEs**) work in a way that's driven by the tape-based metaphors of the past. For example, the common **Overwrite** and **Insert** operations come straight from video tape decks.

While there's nothing inherently wrong with these operations (and, indeed, they exist in FCP), they come from a paradigm with a heavy emphasis on tracks, and a linear timeline structure. Just as with tape, nothing moves unless you explicitly tell it to. These linear methods make sense if you grew up with them, but there are better ways today. While many other NLEs have incorporated concepts such as *ripple edits* while retaining a default linear timeline, FCP defaults to a non-linear **Magnetic Timeline**.

If you're new to editing, you'll be totally fine: it makes sense. But if you've edited with another NLE, you might struggle as you try to mash the square peg of your existing knowledge into the round hole of the Magnetic Timeline. While you can make it work, it's going to be much easier to pretend you know nothing, and start afresh.

This is easier said than done, and in the wider professional video world, the traditional paradigm is still dominant for many reasons. Firstly, most high-end productions still use the first computer-based editing app their editors learned: Avid Media Composer. It's deeply embedded into many expensive workflows, it works, and change would cost money. Secondly, there's a large pool of people who already know how to edit, and many of them would rather not relearn the basics; fair enough. Thirdly, FCP X (back when it had an X) was missing key features at a poorly received launch, and public perception takes a long, long time to change.

Does it matter if you use the same software as most production companies? Well, if your goal is to get a job at a production house, maybe. But if your goal is to make great videos for yourself or for your clients, not at all. Apple aimed for the non-traditional video editor, and while I'm sure they'd love more professionals to take another look, they've made many FCP users happy so far.

If you'd like to learn more about the launch of FCP X, please watch the excellent film *Off The Tracks* by Brad Olsen. There's a free version and a longer paid version on offer at offthetracksmovie.com, and it's absolutely worth your time. (Not just because I'm in it!)

But enough background: that's how we got here. Let's take a bird's-eye view of FCP and see how things tick.

INTERFACE BASICS

Here's a quick screenshot of the main window in FCP. On the left, I have several libraries open in the Browser, where a few media clips can be seen. The **Timeline** is showing a music video I worked on, and you can see a drone shot visible in the **Viewer**. The **Effects** pane and **Audio Meters** are open in the bottom right, and the **Inspector** is showing **Color Wheels** in the top right, as you can see here:

Figure 1.1: The main window, with several panes open

The interface is quite changeable. You can choose which panes you want to see, and how much space they each take up. There are several floating windows too, but let's go over the basics first.

OVERVIEW

Most of the time you spend in FCP will be working in a single window. While additional windows will be shown to adjust preferences, import media, and export, the editing process is largely a single-window experience. Within this single window there are several panes, each of which can be resized by dragging its edges and can have its contents adjusted, by using menus and dropdowns. (If your workspace looks very different from these images, press ⌘0 to reset it to **Default**).

First, look to the top left of the screenshot here:

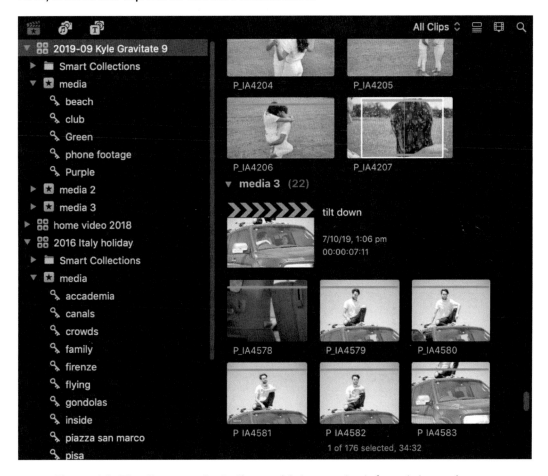

Figure 1.2: The Browser, including a sidebar to the left and the main area
to the right

This area is called the Browser, and it's where you locate, organize, tag, and choose your footage. It's where you locate photos, music, and sound effects, and where you look through pre-designed title and background templates. All up, it's where you find things you want to include in your edit, and it's where we'll spend the first part of this book, *Importing and Organizing*.

Central to all operations is the **Viewer**, a place to view video, which is shown in the following screenshot:

1080p HD 25p, Stereo   Storyboard v 17   72% ⌄   View ⌄

00:02:19:13

Figure 1.3: The Viewer, surrounded by properties, details,
menu, buttons, and a timecode display

This could be a clip from the browser that you're considering, a frame from your current timeline, or it could show more: video scopes to judge color, angles in a multicam clip, or additional controls for effects or titles. You'll use the **Viewer** in just about every part of this book.

To the bottom of the screen is the **Timeline** — your current edit, as can be seen in the following screenshot:

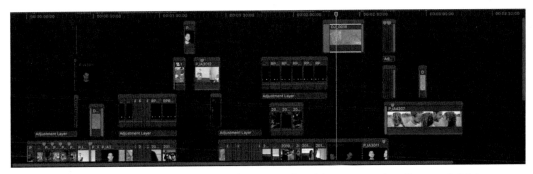

Figure 1.4: Part of the timeline for a music video; your timelines might be simpler, or more complex

This is where clips are arranged in sequence, reordered, and placed above or below other clips. It's where you trim, roll, slip, and slide your edits; where clips are replaced; where speeds are changed; where markers are set; and much more. It's where the "magic" happens, and it's where we'll spend Part 2 of this book, *Rough Cut to Fine Cut*.

To the right of the screen is the **Inspector** — a place to change all kinds of properties, as illustrated in the following screenshot:

Figure 1.5: The Inspector has many faces; these are the Color Wheels in the Color tab

Usually, you'd use this to adjust one or more clips in the timeline, changing color, or size, or volume, or the video effects you've applied. However, you'll probably use this earlier in the process too, to inspect or modify the properties of a clip in the browser, and for other operations too. We'll spend a lot of time here in *Part 3* of this book, *Finishing and Exporting*.

With the basics covered, let's take a slightly deeper look at some of the specific areas in the interface. (While you can simply follow along with the screenshots here, if you'd like to click on your own copy of FCP, you'll need to have some footage already imported and a timeline open.)

IN THE CENTRAL BAR

In the center of the screen, at the top of the Timeline panel, is a bar with several icons and a few words, as illustrated in the following screenshot:

Figure 1.6: These buttons and menus live on the left of the main gray central bar

From left to right, you'll first see the word **Index**, which opens the **Timeline Index** and lets you navigate and refine the display of your timeline. More on that in *Chapter 10*, *Explore a Little: Compound Clips and Timeline Tricks*.

Next are *four editing buttons* that let you copy footage from the browser above to the timeline below. When you hover over these buttons, each shows a shortcut key that you could press instead of clicking on the button, and that's often a better way. To the right of these buttons, there's a **Tools** pop-up menu, currently showing an arrow. Yes — these tools are helpful, and we'll explore them in *Chapter 6*, *Build the Spine of the Story: Quick Assembly*, *Chapter 7*, *Cover it Up: Connections, Cutaways, and Storylines*, and *Chapter 8*, *Neaten the Edges: Trimming Techniques* of this book.

In the center of the screen, there's a title and a menu next to a duration or a timecode, surrounded by two arrows, as can be seen in the following screenshot:

Figure 1.7: There's an arrow to go back to the previous timeline, a name, a menu, a timecode display, and an arrow to go forward

The name and time code tell you which Project you're currently working on and where you've parked the playhead within it, while the arrows allow you to jump to other recent Projects or to step back out of nested items, such as Compound Clips.

New in 10.4.9, the menu lets you duplicate your current Project, change its properties, and more.

Moving to the right, several toggle switches are lit in blue if they're on and white if they're off, as can be seen in the following screenshot:

Figure 1.8: These buttons, to the right of the main gray bar, provide toggle switches and display options

The first four are **Skimming**, **Audio Skimming**, **Solo**, and **Snapping**. These let you control some of the finer points of timeline editing.

Next along is a filmstrip icon — the **Clip Appearance** menu — which lets you change how the timeline appears: how far you have zoomed in, how much space audio and video are allocated, how tall clips are, and so forth:

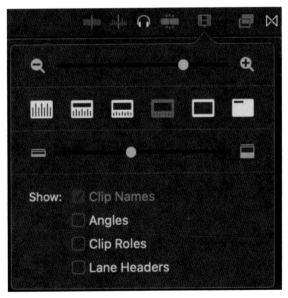

Figure 1.9: This popup lets you control the appearance of clips on your timeline — use ⌘minus and ⌘plus for zoom, and ⇧⌘minus and ⇧⌘plus for clip height

You'll see a similar clip appearance icon to the right of the Browser, and a slightly different icon when you bring up **Video Scopes**. They'll always give you display options for that part of the interface.

Finally, the **Effects** and **Transitions** buttons to the far right of the main gray bar will show or hide an additional browser when clicked, letting you access a range of ways to change how a clip looks, sounds, or changes over the course of an edit. And that's the central bar.

IN THE BROWSER

Back up in the Browser, you'll see buttons and menus on the left and right, as follows:

Figure 1.10: The toggles, menus, and buttons in the Browser will change what you see here

On the left, the first icon represents **Libraries**, where you'll find your footage; the second icon takes you to **Photos and Audio**, and the third icon displays **Titles** (for showing text) and **Generators** (for creating backgrounds and filler content). In each of these areas, you'll see higher-level categories in a sidebar to the left and actual content on the right, but you can hide or show the sidebar with an extra click on the currently selected icon.

Moving across, you'll see a different selection of icons and menus that are different for each of the **Libraries**, **Photos and Audio**, and **Titles and Generators** areas. In general, these allow you to search and control your current view, and we'll look at them in more detail throughout the book.

IN THE VIEWER PANE

The **Viewer** pane includes several pieces of information and important controls, and is shown in the following screenshot:

Figure 1.11: The top of the Viewer shows information above and to the left, and menus to the right

At the top left, you'll see the resolution and frame rate of whatever thing you're playing back, and at the top center, you'll see its name. To the top right, you'll see two menus, the first of which controls how big the video appears on screen (usually set to **Fit** to the space available), and the **View** menu to the far right lets you show additional panes and overlays, and adjust playback settings.

At the bottom left of the **Viewer**, three drop-down menus give you access to onscreen controls that you can adjust in the **Viewer**, as shown in the following screenshot:

Figure 1.12: Menus on the left; buttons and display controls below and to the right

The first offers **Transform**, **Crop**, and **Distort**: to resize, rotate, crop, and stretch the video directly — though we'll see in *Part 3, Finishing and Exporting* that you can also find these controls in the **Inspector**. Next along is a drop-down menu with a selection of color-correction and audio enhancements, and the third icon lets you retime video in a variety of ways: speeding up, slowing down, freezing time, and changing speed over time.

In the bottom center of the **Viewer**, on the left of a small group of numbers and icons, you'll see a **play/pause** button; it also indicates if looping is active. Next is a timecode readout, showing the current hour, minute, second, and frame of the clip or timeline playing back. To the right of the timecode you'll see mini **Audio Meters**, but this small icon can be clicked to show a much larger version, down to the right of the timeline. Finally, in the bottom right of the **Viewer**, you'll see an icon to enter fullscreen video playback. (Press **Escape** to leave this mode).

OTHER IMPORTANT WINDOWS AND CONTROLS

At the very top of the main window, just below the standard Mac menu bar to the left, you'll see the standard circular "traffic light" window controls, as illustrated in the following screenshot:

Figure 1.13: Close, minimize, resize/fullscreen; Import, Keywords, Background Tasks, and Extensions

Pressing the green button enters fullscreen mode, which is helpful if you prefer to focus on a single app at a time, but is less helpful if you want to see multiple apps at once. It also hides the traffic light controls, but you can hover at the top of the screen to show them, or simply press **Escape** to leave.

Next to the traffic lights you'll see three (or perhaps four) buttons, each of which spawns an additional window. They handle importing footage, creating and assigning keywords, and displaying the progress of background tasks, and the fourth (optional) button shows workflow extensions — if you have any installed. These allow third-party developers to integrate with FCP for more advanced workflows.

The menu bar gives quick access to some additional important windows. Choose **Final Cut Pro > Preferences** to bring up the **Preferences** window, where you can change a few important settings regarding warnings, background rendering, and more, as illustrated in the following screenshot:

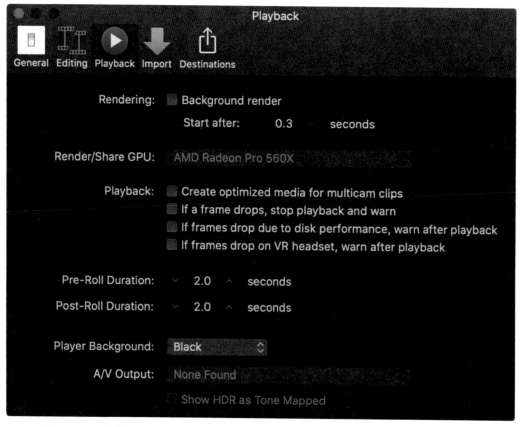

Figure 1.14: The surprisingly spartan Preferences window, with just five sections along the top

Choose **Final Cut Pro** > **Commands** > **Customize** to bring up the **Command Editor**, where you can discover and assign keyboard shortcuts, as illustrated in the following screenshot:

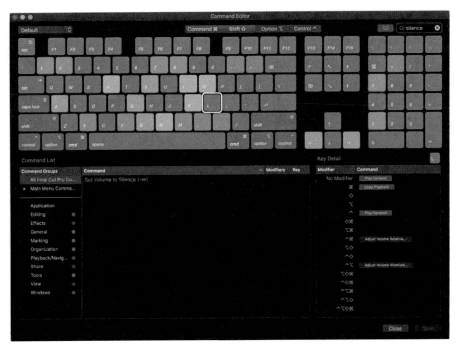

Figure 1.15: The Command Editor provides an excellent way to create your own shortcuts

Importantly, modifier keys such as **Command (⌘)**, **Option (⌥)**, **Control (^)**, and **Shift (⇧)** are *not* required when creating shortcuts, though they can of course be used. This means that the **0** key alone could be assigned to a command just as easily as **⇧0** or **⌥0**.

Throughout this book, symbols are used for the modifier keys instead of names. While keyboards vary in different regions, no matter what your keyboard looks like, the symbols are what you'll see in the menus, so you'll need to learn them. To recap, these are the modifier keys:

- **Command: ⌘**
- **Option: ⌥**
- **Control: ^**
- **Shift: ⇧**

With the modifier keys in mind, you can use the **Command Editor** window to discover shortcuts, as follows:

- To discover a shortcut, simply *click a key in the onscreen keyboard*, and you'll see which commands that key maps to — when using any combination of modifier keys — in the bottom-right part of the window.

This is useful when you're exploring the program, and want to find the function attached to a recently-pressed key. To make new shortcuts, there are a few more steps, as follows:

1. To create a shortcut, first search for the command in the top-right search field to see matching commands at the bottom of the window.

   For example, you could search for **silence**, and you'll see the single command **Set Volume to Silence (-∞)** in the lower part of the window.

2. Next, click your desired modifier keys above the keyboard, then drag the command to the key you want to assign it to. (Alternatively, you can type the shortcut key instead. Zero is a perfect key for the Silence command above.)

3. If this is the first shortcut you've made, make a copy of the command set, and give it a new name.

4. Finally, verify that the command has been assigned, by checking below or below left.

   Command sets (collections of shortcuts) can be chosen, imported, exported, and managed with the menu at the top left of this floating window.

5. When you're done, press **Save** and **Close**.

CONTROLLING THE MAIN WINDOW

While any additional windows can be opened, closed, resized, and positioned freely, you'll have to use a slightly different technique to resize, show, or hide the panes in the main window.

To resize two panes, you need to hover over the thin line between them, as seen between the Browser and the Viewer, or at the top of the gray bar above the **Timeline**, until you see a resize cursor, as illustrated in the following screenshot:

Figure 1.16: The resize cursor appears when your cursor is in just the right spot

You can then click and drag to resize multiple panes together. The panes themselves can also be toggled on or off with the buttons shown in the following screenshot:

Figure 1.17: These controls appear in the top-right and toggle parts of the interface on or off, except for the rightmost Share button

To show or hide an entire pane, click one of the icons at the top right of the interface. There are three buttons here that control the visibility of the **Browser**, **Timeline**, and **Inspector** respectively, and they're visible when the icons show blue. Note that one of the **Browser** and **Timeline** panes must remain visible, and that the **Viewer** cannot be hidden.

If you have an independent external display connected, you'll see an additional button and drop-down menu to the left of these three buttons. Push the button, and the external display will show just one pane: the **Timeline**, **Viewer**, or **Browser**.

Happily, you won't have to manage all these panes manually, because you can store and recall as many layouts as you wish. Here's how:

1. Choose **Window > Workspaces > Color & Effects** to see this in action.

   The browser is hidden, four scopes are shown with the **Viewer**, and the **Inspector** and **Effects** pane are visible.

2. Choose **Window > Workspaces > Organize** to hide the **Timeline** and scopes, leaving you with a big **Browser** pane ideal for organization.

3. After applying your own tweaks, use **Window > Workspaces > Save Workspace as** to store your own layout.

4. Choose **Window > Workspaces > Default** to return to the standard set of interface panes.

Custom layouts can be recalled from the same **Window > Workspaces** submenu. This will be revisited later in the book.

Under **Window > Show in Workspace**, you'll see commands and shortcuts to show or hide any part of the interface, including two I haven't mentioned yet: the **Event Viewer** and the **Comparison Viewer**. These are both optional and will be discussed later in the book.

Finally — because it's the only button left — is **Share**. Located in the very top-right corner of the main window, this lets you export your finished Project. But that's a little way off! Before we move on, if you're using a laptop, you might also have a Touch Bar, and that's worth a look too.

THE TOUCH BAR

Apple's current Pro laptops all include a Touch Bar at the top of the keyboard, as have most of their Pro laptops since 2016. It replaces the **F1-F12** keys normally found above the number keys with a touchscreen offering custom buttons and sliders for the current app, and Final Cut Pro takes great advantage of this. The options available also change as you move between different parts of the app:

Figure 1.18: Click on the Timeline pane to see these general-purpose buttons

While you browse, you can switch between views and clear selections. While you edit, you can switch tools, use trim commands, play around with the edit, or even show an overview of your entire timeline:

Figure 1.19: This timeline view is a great way to move around and zoom in on part of your edit

When you tap the audio button, you can also change volume, add fades, or silence a clip:

Figure 1.20: Audio controls in the Touch Bar, including volume changes and fades

While none of these are essential, they're all really nice to have. If you don't have a Touch Bar on your Mac, you can still assign keyboard shortcuts for quick access to these features, and if you want to push your Touch Bar to do even more, then you'll want to explore the third-party app Command Post (commandpost.io).

Where to next? A quick overview of the editing workflow.

AN EDITING WORKFLOW OVERVIEW

At the very highest level, every editing job is the same. You shoot — or somebody else shoots — some footage, which is then copied to your system and backed up for safety. You choose the best parts of the best clips, and then arrange them in sequence. You trim and re-arrange, tweak color and audio, and then add titles. You gain approval from the client (who could be you), and then you make further changes. When everyone's happy, you export the final file. The file is uploaded, or otherwise sent to its destination. The original files are then archived to make room for future jobs or kept for further editing. Sounds simple, right? It can be, but often isn't. There are several complicating factors, but it's easy to keep it simple — and that's what I'd recommend for many first-time editors.

TERMINOLOGY

FCP uses some unique terms, but here is a quick summary:

- A **Library** holds all the data for a job.
- Each **Library** contains one or more **Events**.
- Each **Event** contains **Clips** and/or **Projects**.

Importantly, a **Project** is an edited sequence of clips that forms the final output — a timeline, if you prefer. I like to use the term *job* when talking about a high-level task, such as a collection of finished videos for a client.

Clips and **Projects** live in **Events**, and **Events** live in a **Library**. You can open multiple Libraries at the same time, but to recap, here's a handy diagram of just one:

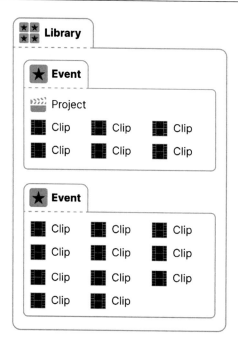

Figure 1.21: A simplified diagram that shows Clips and Projects inside Events, inside a Library

If you've edited before, you might be expecting some other terminology, such as *bin* or *sequence*, and those concepts do carry across. A *sequence* is a **Project**, and a *bin* is a collection of clips that can be exactly re-created with a **Keyword Collection**.

Depending on your personal preferences, there are many ways to work with the Library/Event structure. My following recommendation is simple:

- Create a new **Library** for each job you do for a client, with **File** > **New** > **Library**.

While it's possible to keep everything in a single Library, it will soon become very large indeed — slow, and hard to back up. Ongoing jobs such as home video can be controlled by creating a new dedicated Library every year, or every month.

When you create a new Library, you'll be immediately asked where you want to save it, and the answer is: on *a fast drive with plenty of space*. (More on this in *Chapter 3, Bring It In: Importing your Footage*.)

And Events? When a Library is created, *a new Event is automatically created* inside the Library, *named with today's date* in your system's date format. You can simply use this Event to hold everything, but for more complex jobs, you might create additional Events, to hold different groups of clips or different Projects (timelines). One way I like to work is to create a new Event for each day in a multi-day shoot, and I like to keep my Projects (timelines) together in another Event. Short jobs just need one Event, while bigger jobs benefit from more. But there are many ways to work, and you can change your mind down the track.

WORKFLOW

This book is structured the same way as most edits, and you can use your own footage alongside it if you wish. Not every edit will go in exactly this order, but many will be pretty close, and this is a great way to explore the program if you're not sure how to get going. Use this outline as a starting point, and change it up as needed. We'll start the process (and the book) with:

PART 1: IMPORTING AND ORGANIZING

CHAPTER 1: QUICK START: AN INTRODUCTION TO FCP

You're reading this now!

CHAPTER 2: BEFORE THE EDIT: PRODUCTION TIPS

You need to make sure you shoot in the right formats, with the right cameras, and shoot the right things to make an edit work. This is the only chapter in the book that's not strictly about FCP, but it's still important.

CHAPTER 3: BRING IT IN: IMPORTING YOUR FOOTAGE

No matter how many Events you decide to use, you'll want to import your footage. This should be easy but there are a few different ways to work, and you'll hear strong opinions about which way is best.

Next, you'll sync up clips shot with multiple devices that recorded the same scene at the same time, such as two or three cameras, or an audio recorder and video camera. If you used good practices on set (*Chapter 2, Before the Edit: Production Tips*) then this will be straightforward.

CHAPTER 4: SORT IT OUT: REVIEWING AND KEYWORDING

First, you'll watch what you've shot, or have been given, and there are a number of good ways to do that. After or during that process, you'll *organize your footage* using **Keywords**, putting them in "virtual buckets" for easier retrieval later on.

CHAPTER 5: CHOOSE YOUR FAVORITES: SELECTING, RATING, AND SEARCHING

After keywords come **Favorites**, which mark the best parts, and possibly **Rejecting**, to mark the parts you won't use. Marking up your clips here is a far more useful method than the traditional technique of making timeline-based collections of clips you like, because your choices are permanently recorded and searchable, and you can instantly refer back to them way down the track. This is a trick that only FCP can really offer, and it's a fantastic way of working.

The next part of of the process (and, again, the book) is editing:

PART 2: ROUGH CUT TO FINE CUT

CHAPTER 6: BUILD THE SPINE OF THE STORY: QUICK ASSEMBLY

With all the clips organized, you finally make a **Project**, matching the technical requirements (frame rate and resolution) of what you want to deliver. Those may be the same settings you shot with, though if they're different it's not the end of the world.

With a view on the organized footage, you'll build up a rough cut, getting the best parts of the best clips in order on a timeline, until it all sounds good. Maybe you'll drag and drop; maybe you'll use keyboard shortcuts; but you'll definitely use a few basic edits to trim, cut, rearrange, and delete your clips.

CHAPTER 7: COVER IT UP: CONNECTIONS, CUTAWAYS, AND STORYLINES

Now, you'll get a little fancier, disguising edits, adding clips above or below other clips, using the B-roll you shot to make your edit feel more complete, moving clips around, and fleshing it all out. You might use **Storylines** to group connected clips together, and you might use three-point editing if you want to be precise.

CHAPTER 8: NEATEN THE EDGES: TRIMMING TECHNIQUES

Further finesse your edit, to make sure every frame is needed and is in exactly the right place. Slip, slide, and roll your edits, and use the precision editor if you wish. Soften any audio edits that need it, expand and collapse audio, and use plenty of shortcuts.

CHAPTER 9: CONSIDER YOUR OPTIONS: MULTICAM, REPLACING, AND AUDITIONS

This chapter discusses how to deal with Multicam media in the most efficient way. With or without Multicam, you'll learn how to revisit your earlier choices, switch clips out for other clips, swap one music track for another, and generally try to make the edit even better.

CHAPTER 10: EXPLORE A LITTLE: COMPOUND CLIPS AND TIMELINE TRICKS

If you're wanting to try something fancier, such as treating a group of clips as a single clip, or you're becoming frustrated with the magnetic timeline for some reason, this is where you discover how the **Timeline Index** works, how to lift and merge, and how to use the **Position** tool. With luck and good planning, you won't need to relink media, but this chapter has some tips on that too.

With the edit locked (or nearly locked?) it's time for:

PART 3: FINISHING AND EXPORTING

CHAPTER 11: PLAY WITH LIGHT: COLOR CORRECTION AND GRADING

First, you'll fix basic color issues such as white balance and exposure, and then perform shot-to-shot matching. Next, you'll add curves if you want to change contrast, and use color or shape masks to selectively brighten, darken, or change the color of part of the frame. You might also use adjustment layers to quickly change many clips at once.

CHAPTER 12: REFINE AND SMOOTH: VIDEO PROPERTIES AND EFFECTS

If some of your clips need a further tweak, you'll adjust their properties to move, scale, crop and apply effects now, and maybe even animate those properties. If a shot is too shaky, you can stabilize; if it's too soft, you can sharpen, and if there's something else you'd like to fix, there's an effect for that too.

CHAPTER 13: BLEND AND WARP: VIDEO TRANSITIONS AND RETIMING

Transitions help to soften the transition between two clips, and here, you'll learn all about how to apply and adjust them. Simplicity is often a good idea with transitions, but maybe subtlety isn't your thing and you'd like to go crazy — it's all good. Perhaps you're also experimenting with high-speed footage and you want to add some speed ramping, or even just pause it? Now's the time.

CHAPTER 14: BOOST THE SIGNAL: AUDIO SWEETENING

Video sorted? Don't forget audio. Adjust the volume for each clip to get things roughly in the right spot, apply automatic enhancements if you need to, and then add whatever audio effects are going to improve the overall sound. Viewers don't forgive bad sound, so don't skip this step.

CHAPTER 15: A FEW WORDS: TITLES AND GENERATORS

Adding titles to introduce an entire video or your speakers, or simply to deliver a message, can fill in gaps that your subjects didn't, and can also give your work a cohesive overall look that helps it to stand out. Generators are a good idea if you need custom backgrounds. With the edit nearly complete, this is also the time to add captions, to make your videos more accessible and searchable.

CHAPTER 16: YOU'RE DONE: EXPORTING YOUR EDIT AND FINISHING UP

Export your video in a few different ways, then send it to your client or direct to a video-sharing service. Or, maybe you might need to send an editable Project to someone else — that's fine too. When you're really, finally done with this job, archive its Library to some other storage medium.

That really is just about it. Anything this book doesn't cover in detail can be found in Apple's official user guide, and many other links will be provided along the way.

HARDWARE RECOMMENDATIONS

As a final note for this introductory chapter, it's worth looking at your computer: what do you need? Technology will continue to advance, so I'll keep this broad, but FCP can work on anything from a low-end laptop to a fully upgraded Mac Pro worth more than most cars. What do you need?

A MAC

This one is obvious, since FCP doesn't run on Windows, but what kind? There are many options, but the most obvious question is *laptop or desktop?*, and the answer is simple. Laptop if you need portability, or desktop for better speed, easier expansion, and a bigger screen.

An important factor for video editing is the graphics power on offer, and while only larger laptop and higher-end desktops currently offer high-powered graphics, the transition to Apple silicon may change this. Any Mac can deal with almost any job, but the higher the resolution you want to work with, and the more effects that you want to be able to add, the more money you should spend. A good mid-range desktop is the 27" iMac, and the best laptop is a 16" MacBook Pro, but you can spend more money or less, and still be happy.

ACTIVE MEDIA STORAGE

You'll need enough fast storage to hold as many jobs as possible, because you'll be shooting and storing a lot of footage. There are several options, as follows:

- **Solid-State Drives (SSDs)** are very fast, can be moved or dropped while in use, but are still somewhat expensive. The fastest Thunderbolt drives are more expensive than slightly slower **Universal Serial Bus (USB)** drives. If you can afford them, and you don't need to store a lot of jobs at once, get a few of these. They might be your only choice if you work with really demanding media.

- **Spinning hard disks** are big and cheap, but not hugely fast, and somewhat fragile. Available in portable and desktop versions, a desktop hard drive is larger and requires independent power, but is faster, usually cheaper, and potentially much larger. Get a few of these if you're on a budget.

- Between these two options is a **RAID (Redundant Array of Independent Disks)** in which multiple drives (usually spinning disks) are combined to make a larger storage volume. A RAID usually includes redundancy, to partly protect against drive failure. RAID enclosures aren't cheap, but they're cheaper than SSDs, faster and more reliable than a single disk, and potentially larger than either. Get this if you regularly need to access a lot of jobs.

But hang on a second. Your Mac has a very fast SSD inside — can't you just use that? Yes — you can. Many experienced editors will tell you no, but that's partly because it used to be a very bad idea. Back when computers were slow, using the system disk could mean that an import or export operation failed when the operating system suddenly needed to access the same drive as your media. Modern SSDs are much, much faster and the same rules don't apply. The only concern is that of space, and for that reason alone, an external SSD is often a better idea.

BACKUP STORAGE

Backup is critical, because any device can fail at any moment. Losing a hard drive is an inevitability, but losing the files on that drive is not — if you have a backup. (I've seen people knock over hard drives and lose thousands of photos in an instant; don't let this happen to you.) So, how do you back things up? Here are a few suggestions:

- **Time Machine** is a built-in feature on macOS that takes a copy of your entire system hard drive every hour, keeping past versions accessible. All you need is a regular spinning hard drive, and to say "Yes" when you first plug it in. (You might also need to use the built-in **Disk Utility** app to format it as "HFS+ (Journaled)" first.)

- **Online backup** (such as Backblaze) is an excellent option if you have fast upload speed because every direct-connected drive can be copied without you having to lift a finger, and at a reasonable price. Depending on the provider, you may need to plug in all your media drives regularly, but this is a good solution for current work at least.

DISPLAYS

An external display will give you a much better editing experience, giving you more space for all your work and potentially a big screen to view your final edit. Ideally, a **4K (UHD) monitor** will let you see every pixel in 4K footage, and you'll find a range of cheaper and more expensive options. Choose an **In-Plane Switching (IPS)** screen for color consistency and wider viewing angles, and a **High Dynamic Range (HDR)** and/or wide gamut screen if you plan to work with those kinds of footage. (If you're not sure what they are, I'll talk about it in *Chapter 11, Play with Light: Color Correction and Grading.*)

AUDIO

Self-powered monitor speakers are an excellent idea, allowing you to hear the details in the sound you're mixing. PreSonus Eris and KRK Rokit are popular choices. Remember, though, that many people will be listening on regular computer speakers, and you'll want to make sure your work sounds good on them too.

If you're planning on recording your own voiceovers, you'll want a **USB-connected microphone** of some kind, and there's a huge variety of microphones and audio interfaces available. One tip is that some audio recorders (including some from Zoom and RØDE) can also function as USB microphones — two devices for the price of one.

MEDIA CARD READER

If you're shooting on a "real" camera, you'll need to be able to import footage from its media cards, which could be **Secure Digital (SD)**, **CompactFlash (CF)**, or something more exotic. While iMacs have SD readers built in, no other Macs do, so pick up a fast card reader if you need one. Note that some brands perform better than others when paired with matching readers — check the fine print.

MISCELLANEOUS USB GEAR

If you want to get fancy, you can use additional hardware (such as **Musical Instrument Digital Interface (MIDI)** controllers) with additional free software (such as CommandPost) to augment your editing experience. I really like using a MIDI controller for color grading, but this is definitely an optional extra.

ANYTHING ELSE?

The world of camera gear is endless, but after the shoot, your footage and a Mac are all you really need. Edit at a desk, in the field, or on a couch if you like — but stretch regularly, and make sure to keep your body comfortable and healthy by following ergonomic guidelines. You'll appreciate a good desk and a good chair every day.

SUMMARY

FCP really tries to make things look simple — and for many editors, it can be. There's a ton of power hidden behind the scenes but you don't have to use every feature available, and the editing process can be pretty straightforward if you follow a few rules.

Now that you know what the editing process involves and how this application can help you achieve it, you're well on your way. You should understand the basics of the interface now, and though it might appear simple, there's a lot of complexity behind the scenes. You know what hardware you want in an ideal world, but just about any Mac will do while you're learning. Ready to go? Almost!

To keep everything running smoothly, a little planning and prior knowledge is needed to make sure the right content is captured in the right format. And that's in *Chapter 2, Before the Edit: Production Tips*.

REVIEW QUESTIONS

1. What's the name of the area where you collect and organize your media?
2. What's bigger, a Library or a Project?
3. What do you put in a Project?
4. Where do you change most settings about a clip?
5. What's the name of the area where you play back video?
6. Where do you find buttons to show or hide part of the interface?
7. Can you store media files on your internal hard drive?
8. Which chapter covers color correction?

9. Where can you change or add shortcut keys?

10. What kind of timeline does Final Cut Pro use?

REVIEW ANSWERS

1. The Browser.

2. A Library. Libraries contain Events, and Events can contain clips and/or Projects.

3. A Project contains your finished edit — it's a sequence, or a timeline.

4. The Inspector.

5. The Viewer.

6. In the top right corner, just to the left of the Share button.

7. Yes, you can, but you might run out of space.

8. *Chapter 11, Play with Light: Color Correction and Grading.*

9. The **Command Editor**, found at **Final Cut Pro** > **Commands** > **Customize**.

10. A magnetic timeline (no tracks).

2 BEFORE THE EDIT:
PRODUCTION TIPS

"With Final Cut Pro, I appreciate how the "how" of the edit gets out of the way so quickly, so I can explore the creativity in the "what" of the edit. Editing is much less tiring in Final Cut because it is so much more enjoyable."

—Alex "4D" Gollner, Final Cut Pro plugin maker
Alex4D.com

This chapter, unlike the other chapters in this book, isn't directly about **Final Cut Pro (FCP)**. Instead, it deals with many of the technical and camera-based details that you *should* know and the basics that you *must* know — codecs, shot types, data rates, and more. Technical details are important, regardless of whether you're shooting your own video or you're working with a separate operator, *because you'll know what to ask for.*

> IMPORTANT NOTE
> If you've been in the industry for a while or you have no plans to ever shoot a video of your own, feel free to skim quickly over this chapter. This book is designed to be useful for a wide audience, and so this chapter is full of details that new editors and shooters need to know. Experienced editors will probably know most of these important details already, so if that's you, speed-read your way to *Chapter 3*, *Bring It In: Importing Your Footage*.

There's plenty of detail here, but this chapter is not a complete preproduction guide. The preproduction process has many stages, and before you open FCP, you should at least have an idea of what you're trying to make. The more detailed your idea, the better you'll be able to execute it. However, as there isn't space to cover the non-technical details of writing a script, drawing a storyboard, managing a crew, and wrapping cables to avoid tripping over them, this chapter talks about the following:

- Getting the settings right
- Choosing a camera
- Shooting the right shots
- Working with multiple cameras and audio recorders
- Managing everything on set

The goal of this chapter is to provide a technical primer for shooters and for the editors who have to work with them. If you're not 100% confident with frame rates, resolutions, shutter speed, banding, types of cameras and accessories, what B-roll is, and what types of shots you'll need to produce a great edit, this chapter is for you.

GETTING THE SETTINGS RIGHT

Resolution, codecs, white balance, and other image controls are critical to capturing not just a good-looking image, but one that can be easily edited and manipulated. Technical settings are key, regardless of what kind of camera you use, so even if you don't plan on shooting a video yourself, these are the tech specs you'll need to know.

RESOLUTION

Video is essentially a series of still images, and each frame has a horizontal and a vertical dimension in pixels. Common resolutions use abbreviations, including the following:

- **Ultra HD (UHD**, commonly referred to as 4K): 3840 × 2160
- **1080p**: 1920 × 1080
- **720p**: 1280 × 720

To visualize those numbers, here's a diagram:

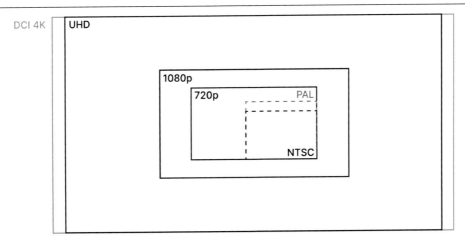

Figure 2.1: Several common resolutions you might shoot and deliver

While it's true that 3840 is a little less than 4000 (4K), there's not much in it. Some cinema purists use a size of 4096 × 2160, one of the official "DCI 4K" sizes, but it's intended for cinemas and leaves black bars at the top and bottom of a 16:9 display. For the purposes of this discussion, when I say 4K, I'm actually referring to UHD.

What should you shoot, then? Today, I always shoot in UHD and recommend that you do the same. But will people notice the extra detail over 1080p? Some will. It's true that people sit at a fair distance from their TVs, and the limitations of our eyes mean that some of the detail in a 4K image at that distance can be lost. Most phone-based viewers won't see the extra detail either; small screens, slow networks, and limited resolutions all limit what you can deliver.

Yet, even if most of your audience is using a phone, it's a mistake to only plan for that lowest common denominator. Computer users with high-resolution monitors — every iMac user and many others — sit close enough to their monitors to see the extra detail easily. Aim higher than the baseline and you'll make even the fussiest clients happy. This shouldn't slow you down, either. While some other editing applications struggle to edit 4K without stuttering, a relatively modern iMac running FCP will do just fine.

There's another big reason to shoot in 4K, though. I shoot 4K for jobs that I know I will be delivering to a client at 1080p, or even 720p. Why? Shooting in a format bigger than you need — called **oversampling** — lets you safely zoom in to show just a small part of the captured image in the final video. This means that final control over framing passes from the camera operator to the editor, giving you lots of extra options and making every shot more flexible.

Still, if your camera doesn't shoot 4K well, shooting 1080p can be totally fine. If you plan to deliver 1080p, just don't zoom (much) during editing and you'll be OK. A general rule is to never go above 120%.

PORTRAIT OR LANDSCAPE?

If you only ever plan on delivering to a vertical orientation, then you can shoot that way too. But for 99% of jobs, you should shoot in landscape — especially on a phone. If your client will be shooting footage on their own phone, be sure to ask them to shoot in landscape because most people will shoot in portrait without thinking twice:

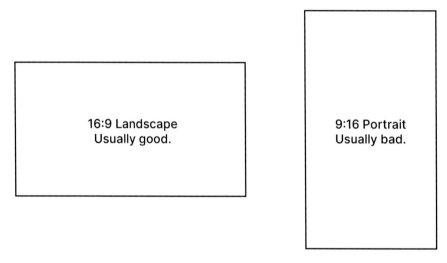

Figure 2.2: Hold your phone like it's a TV!

Computers and TVs use landscape orientation, and if you shoot portrait, your work will only ever look good on a phone. But also remember that the frame you shoot may be re-cropped and repurposed. Many kinds of commercial work are delivered in multiple aspect ratios, so bear that in mind when you shoot.

One good strategy is to use a "common top," where you frame a normal amount of space between your subject's head and the top of the frame. When you present that footage in different aspect ratios, simply put the top of the clip at the top of the frame and let the other edges of the frame change as they need to.

In summary, then — take a few steps back to zoom out, frame with a regular gap above the head, shoot in landscape, and record in high resolution, and you can use that footage for any kind of delivery.

FRAME RATE

If it is at all possible, shoot in the same frame rate that you want to deliver. For a "cinematic" look, you'll want to shoot at 24 or 25 **frames per second (fps)**, although 29.97 fps is widely used too. Why these specific numbers?

A video image is updated a certain number of times per second, and that number is different for TV signals in different parts of the world for historical reasons related to electricity. Here are some guidelines:

- In 110–120 V countries, such as the US, Canada, and elsewhere, 29.97 fps is used.
- In 240–250 V countries, such as most of Europe (including the UK), Australia, and New Zealand, 25 fps is used.
- In the international world of feature films and high-quality TV, 24 fps is the norm, although 23.98 fps is often used as it makes for easier conversion to US TV standards.

Does it matter which one you use if you're delivering online? Not much. But if you're delivering to TV or cinema, then it definitely matters, and you'll need to examine the delivery requirements carefully.

> IMPORTANT NOTE
>
> You might also have to deal with interlaced delivery (1080i) rather than progressive (1080p), but interlaced video today is only requested for TV broadcasts. Shoot and deliver in progressive formats, unless the client explicitly asks for interlaced delivery.

It's also possible to record at moderately high frame rates, such as 50 or 60 fps, or even higher. While these frame rates do deliver smoother motion, most viewers find that videos shot in these modes look a little fake, unnatural, or cheap when played back at that speed, and so these higher frame rates are rarely seen outside of sports and gaming videos. Rather, these higher frame rates are more commonly used to give the option of slow motion, captured at a high speed, but played back at a slower speed:

Figure 2.3: This splash (and, in fact, this whole shoot) was recorded at 50 fps to give slo-mo options

If you record at 60 fps, you can then slow it down on the timeline, showing every frame you shot for a speed of 42% on a 25 fps timeline or 50% on a 30 fps timeline. This is referred to as **Automatic Speed** in FCP, and it's very handy. But this is just an option — footage shot at a moderately high frame rate doesn't have to be slowed down. It's entirely possible to use this footage in real time instead by skipping frames on playback. Many shooters use these moderately high frame rates for B-roll (explained soon) to give more options during editing.

Be aware that as you increase the frame rate, especially to higher numbers, the camera has to work harder, and you may have to compromise resolution as a result. Check your camera because there's often a distinction between "regular" frame rates, up to 60 fps, and "high-speed" frame rates, which can go much higher at a lower resolution, lower quality, and/or without audio. Whatever frame rate you shoot at, you should be consistent. While it's quite easy to incorporate slow-motion footage shot at any speed, your regular footage should all use the same frame rate — probably 24, 25, or 30 fps. Mixing similar frame rates can cause visible stutters (due to skipped or duplicated frames) and it's something to avoid if at all possible.

SHUTTER SPEED

A separate but related issue is shutter speed, how many times per second an image is captured, which is expressed as a fraction of a second, such as 1/50 or 1/200. As a rule of thumb, to give your footage a natural motion blur, you should try to double your frame rate to determine the "ideal" shutter speed denominator:

- 1/48 or 1/50 for 24 fps
- 1/50 for 25 fps
- 1/60 for 30 fps

If you shoot at a significantly faster shutter speed, such as 1/100 or 1/200, the natural motion blur of 1/50 or 1/60 will be lost, and anything in motion will look a little "choppy" as a result. Conversely, if you shoot at a significantly slower speed, such as 1/25 or 1/30, everything in motion will look a little blurry.

It's important to note that this rule (known as the **180° shutter rule**) does not apply to higher frame rates simply because any objects in motion will barely move between frames — there's hardly any blur to be had! If there's very little movement in the shot, there's not much blur in that either.

BANDING

However, there's another reason why these frame rates are popular, and it goes beyond a natural-looking blur. If you shoot at frame rates that aren't an even multiple of your lighting source, you might record **banding**, which is lines that are continuously moving down your image. Why? The answer gets a little messy, but it's for a similar reason to frame rate. Here's an extreme example:

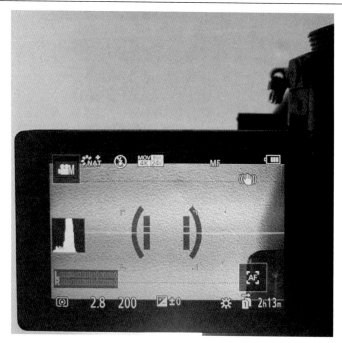

Figure 2.4: This blank wall shows extreme banding when a 1/200 shutter speed is used

Your electricity supply is based on alternating power, which cycles at 60 Hz in North and South America and western Japan, and 50 Hz in Europe, Australasia, and eastern Japan. Many light sources cycle at the lighting frequency found in your country, and if your shutter speed doesn't match the frequency of your lighting source, your camera won't capture the light evenly. Instead, it will catch a little more in one part of a frame than the rest, leaving a dark band that moves from frame to frame. Sometimes, these problems are subtle, but often they're not, and it's critical to get this right for your camera.

This issue has led many people to conclude that the frame rate must be 25 fps in Europe and 30 fps in North America, but the frame rate can in fact be different. It's the shutter speed that controls banding, and even in 50 Hz countries, if your main light source is from a projector or large TV refreshing at 60 Hz, you'll need to adjust your shutter speed to 1/60. (Note that some special lights and some computer monitors refresh at unusual frequencies, and some cameras have special modes to deal with this issue.)

Extra care is needed for high frame rates above 60 Hz. Shooting at extreme frame rates requires a really high shutter speed, and therefore, you'll need to use a light source that doesn't refresh itself at these low rates. Some professional lights are suitable, but the great ball of light in the sky always works well.

WHITE BALANCE

Before you shoot in a new location, it's important to set a custom white balance, ideally with a gray card positioned where your subject will be. Different light sources give different color to a scene, and if you don't get this right, your subjects will look "wrong" — too blue, green, orange, or yellow. This can be corrected to some degree in the edit, but it's not always the easiest task.

IMPORTANT NOTE:

Don't use auto white balance unless you have no choice! Auto white balance can drift in the middle of a shot and be very hard to correct, while an incorrect manual white balance will be consistently wrong and is more easily fixed.

The time before a shoot can often be used to set and store a custom white balance, and fancier cameras can store multiple custom white balance settings, such as the 1/2/3/4 setting shown here:

Figure 2.5: The Panasonic GH5 white balance menu

If your camera doesn't have custom white balance options, you'll at least be able to choose from a range of presets, including daylight, fluorescent light, tungsten, and more. Choosing one of these will at least give you a consistent place to work from.

CODECS

Almost all cameras record in a compressed format and some are more heavily compressed than others. While it might seem useful to be able to record files in a smaller space, the more you compress a video, the lower the quality will be. Finding that sweet spot between a video that takes up too much space and a video that falls apart can be tricky, and not all cameras give you many options here.

Most compressed videos today use a compression method (codec) called **H.264**, although H.265 (also known as HEVC) is becoming more popular. Support for HEVC (at the time of writing) is less mature; only recent Macs with a T2 chip can decode HEVC easily. Higher-end cameras might offer other options, such as ProRes, ProRes RAW, and Blackmagic RAW. While all of these formats do increase the quality, they take up significantly more space.

For example, a Panasonic GH5 records at a data rate of 100 **Megabits per Second (Mbps)** at 4K at 24/25/30 fps, or 150 Mbps for 4K at 50/60 fps, alongside many other options. Here's what that looks like:

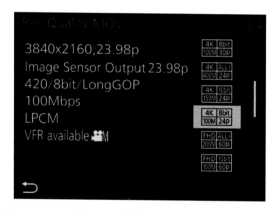

Figure 2.6: So many options — delve into the menus of your camera and test the settings out

The data rate for ProRes at the same resolutions and frame rates ranges from 470-589 Mbps, much, much higher than typical H.264 and HEVC codecs. These increased data rates require a much faster and larger recording device, typically an SSD rather than an SD card. You'll want to find a balance between quality and file size that suits your job's needs; read reviews, download files, and do the math to figure out how much space you'll need.

Lastly, it's very important to know that not all cameras compress video in the same way. H.264 from one camera can be easy to deal with, while footage from another camera stutters on playback. If it is at all possible, download some original footage from a camera you're planning on using to make sure it works well in your workflow. Expect new codecs and workflow changes in the future — standards do shift over time.

CONTAINERS

Video data is encoded using a particular codec and is then stored in a container, usually a file with a `.mp4` or `.mov` file extension. *A container is not a codec*, however; H.264 can be found inside many different types of containers, and a `.mp4` file might contain video data in one of many different codecs. Still, you'll probably be fine; just look at the extension at the end of the filename to see which kind(s) your camera makes.

However, there are cameras out there that don't produce single contained video files at all. The AVCHD format, for example, spreads important data out on separate files across different subfolders, meaning you can't simply copy a file from an SD card and have a single video clip. Instead, the video data needs to be rewrapped inside a container format that FCP can use by importing directly from the SD card. Other cameras do contain their clips in single files (yay!), but they restart their file numbering on every card (boo!), leaving you to manage multiple files with identical names.

Where possible, I prefer to avoid AVCHD and other fussy container formats. A standalone video clip with a unique name using a standard codec is the gold standard, and plenty of cameras make files like this. If you're choosing the camera, don't bend over backward to support one that makes your life difficult.

REVIEW — GETTING ALL THE SETTINGS RIGHT

Let's combine all of these settings:

- Ideally, you'll be shooting in 4K to H.264 or HEVC in a `.mp4` or `.mov` container at a data rate of around 100 Mbps or higher.
- You'll use a gray card to set the white balance for each location you shoot in.
- If you're in Europe or Australasia, you'll probably mostly shoot at 25 fps with a 1/50 shutter speed.
- In North and South America and most of Asia, you'll probably mostly shoot at 24 fps or 30 fps with 1/50 or 1/60 shutter speed.

- You might choose to use a moderately high shutter speed (50 or 60 fps) for B-roll shots, to allow for 50% slow motion.
- You'll change the shutter speed for high frame rates or if you see banding.

That's it — you've set your camera up for files that FCP will import easily and that will cut well together. Now, you just need to master aperture, ISO, color profiles, and everything else that your camera offers! As much as I'd like to discuss all of these variables, it's beyond the scope of the book, and I can only advise you to keep the ISO low to avoid noise, keep your subject correctly exposed, shoot with a low f-stop if you want blurry backgrounds, and if you want to keep things simple, use a color profile that's close to what you want to deliver. But what kind of camera will give you these controls? Read on!

CHOOSING A CAMERA

Camera operators are utterly spoilt for choice these days. While there will never be a perfect camera for everyone, you will be able to find something that works for you that's also in your budget. This is an ever-changing field, and specific camera advice will be quickly outdated, so I'm focusing here on general advice only. Remember that the adage mostly holds true: you can choose any two from **fast**, **cheap**, and **good**.

AN IPHONE (OR ANY OTHER MOBILE PHONE)

Yes, you can absolutely shoot videos on your iPhone, and according to most reviews, an iPhone does a better job of video than most Android phones do. An iPhone will also be easier to use with your Mac, and it even includes iMovie, so you can start an edit on your iPhone, then transition it to FCP on your Mac. The dynamic range (from shadows to highlights in a single shot) is huge, so you can film in more places. Image stabilization means the image shouldn't be too shaky. And it's always in your pocket! So far, so good. You can also add accessories, such as this ioGrapher case, if you want to tripod-mount it and add a microphone:

Figure 2.7: There are many ways to mount a phone on a tripod; this is
a good one

However, even though an iPhone can deliver 4K, it has several limitations. First, the built-in **Camera** app can only shoot at 24, 30, or 60 fps, but not the 25 fps you'd probably prefer in Europe or Australasia. A third-party app, such as Filmic Pro or ProCamera, can set this frame rate, along with many other controls, but you still won't have as many direct options as on a real camera.

Also, you can't zoom far without losing quality, and the picture tends to be a bit noisy and soft, especially in low light. File management is less convenient too because everything's internal; you can't just swap out a memory card if you're running out of space or swap out a battery if it's running low.

Lastly, shooting on a phone probably won't impress paying clients, as silly as that may seem. Perception is reality for a lot of people, and if you turn up to a paid gig with the same camera that your client owns, they could perceive you as an amateur. That isn't fair; phones today shoot better video than most cameras from a few years ago, but it's still what happens. This will, eventually, change.

So, it's convenient, but it could struggle in difficult situations and it doesn't impress clients.

A DSLR OR MIRRORLESS CAMERA

This is the current sweet spot for most new videographers. Canon, Nikon, Sony, Panasonic, and Fujifilm are the five main companies making mid-range to high-end video-capable cameras with interchangeable lenses. Some cameras are better at autofocusing during video recording than others. Some offer a more pleasing color profile than others. Some have amazing sensor-based image stabilization. All of them should give you a better image than any phone out there, and the better ones will let you plug in external microphones and headphones, too. Here's my GH5 with a wireless **lavalier (lapel** or **lav)** microphone receiver attached, at a jaunty angle:

Figure 2.8: A GH5 with an Olympus lens and a RØDE Wireless GO lapel mic

Overall, these cameras create files that are easy enough to work with. They can shoot 4K, many accessories are available, they are reliable, and they come in many price categories. Larger sensors and faster lenses (which let in more light) make it easier to throw the background out of focus, an effect that many people associate with "professional" shots. A blurred background (from a fast aperture, rather than faked) is one of the key image characteristics that lifts a "real camera" above the "everything-in-focus" look of a phone.

Some of these cameras have limitations (especially in 4K) relating to their continuous recording time, whether they can capture the entire image area or just a cropped part of it, and the data rates that they allow you to use. Another common limitation relates to frame rates — my Panasonic GH5 can switch to a huge variety of frame rates, but my cheaper, older Panasonic G7 is region-locked, stuck at 25 fps, and limited to half an hour maximum recording length.

Importantly, most of these cameras give you full control over shutter speed, aperture, and other image properties, plus there are more advanced controls on higher-end cameras. The ability to use manual controls is one of the key features of a professional camera and allows you to get the shot in difficult shooting conditions where a fully automatic camera would make a bad call.

You'll find a number of opinions out there, and your needs may well be different from other people's. Read as many reviews as you can, and download some sample files and test them out in FCP before committing to a particular system. If you start spending a lot of money on lenses, you could be stuck using that system for several years.

A HIGH-END CAMERA

If you decide to seriously invest in a camera, you might look to a high-end Sony, Panasonic, or Canon, a Blackmagic camera, or perhaps even a RED or ARRI. These cameras produce a lovely image that's very flexible and easily adjusted, but they require *more care, more accessories, and more resources* in post-production. Because they're built for a set, these cameras can be heavy, chew through batteries, make huge video files, and be harder to learn and use. Most also don't include image stabilization, so you'll need additional support gear for stable moving shots.

But what you can sometimes lose in ease of use, you get back in raw resolution, color detail, and dynamic range. Your camera will also look expensive on set and in the edit bay, and it is indeed expensive. It's a camera for a professional crew on a professional set and will certainly impress clients:

Figure 2.9: A photo of a RED RAVEN camera by Bruno Masseo via Pexels.com

Regarding formats, most can record to ProRes (which is easy to work with) or more exotic formats (which are harder to work with), so if you receive footage from one of these cameras, you might need additional software to view its files. If you decide that you really need the look that a high-end camera gives you, FCP can handle it (8K and beyond), but know that this power comes with limitations.

AN ACTION CAMERA OR DRONE

At a variety of price points, you'll find pocketable cameras that incorporate a gimbal (such as DJI Osmo Pocket), as well as blocky cameras that you can mount to a car, helmet, surfboard, or ski pole (such as GoPro and many others) and drones of all shapes and sizes. Typically, these cameras have several options for resolution and frame rate, but you can't change lenses and you might not even have a screen; everything's on auto:

Figure 2.10: This DJI Spark drone is a cheap way to find out if flying cameras are for you

The strength of these devices is in getting shots from crazy perspectives that you would otherwise have missed, which is valuable. However, they shouldn't be your primary camera, because fully automatic settings will inevitably fail eventually, focusing on the wrong thing, under- or over-exposing, or messing up the white balance. If you need manual controls, look elsewhere.

Typically, the files you get from these cameras are fairly small; they look OK, but not great, and they'll probably have a wide-angle look. Drones have the same benefits and drawbacks, except that their lenses are not usually so wide, and (of course!) they can fly. If they're legal where you are, they're great for very specific purposes — perhaps for introductory shots flying over a building — but not so good for interviews.

A 360° CAMERA

These cameras typically use two lenses (and sometimes more) to record the entire scene around the camera. Here's an Insta360 ONE X, with the second lens just visible at the back:

Figure 2.11: An Insta360 ONE X, seen from the side

The images from the two cameras are stitched together to create an "equirectangular" video, showing the entire scene around them. While it's possible to deliver this 360° footage to a headset, allowing the viewer to look around freely, it's probably more common to use 360° footage in a regular video-editing project. In that workflow, the editor chooses where the camera will look, and you deliver it to a regular display.

The great joy of 360° is that *you never miss the shot because you're facing the wrong way* — just spin it around in the timeline. However, there's some crossover here between the Action and the 360° categories; you can't easily control what's happening on the camera and you will usually end up in the shot yourself, certainly if you're holding the camera. I love mine, and while it's terrific for family holidays, it's unlikely to crack the mainstream any time soon.

AUDIO EQUIPMENT

This area is huge, and I'll keep it brief. Your camera will have a microphone built into it, but it won't be very good. The *best audio is recorded from as close to your subject as possible*, and you could capture that with a boom microphone pointed directly at them (if you have a person to hold it) or with a **lapel** microphone that they wear. You can record audio directly into a camera (which is easier, but with potential quality loss) or into an external recorder (which is slightly more work, but with potentially higher quality):

Figure 2.12: The Zoom H5 is a four-track recorder that accepts XLR and a minijack, with a built-in stereo mic

Professional gear has three huge advantages over cheap gear: *it sounds better, it has less noise, and it's more reliable*. But beware — more expensive gear will only get better sound if it's used correctly. If you're a one-person operator, you probably can't keep a boom mic pointed in exactly the right direction while operating a camera, so consider using a good lapel mic instead. For ease of operation, wireless lapel mics that include the mic on a clip-on transmitter are far, far easier to set up than a traditional setup that runs wires under a subject's clothes.

Different environments require different approaches, and recording good sound is important. Having several kinds of microphones with you lets you use them all at once, then find out which sounds best in the editing bay. However, when you record your audio, always, always plug in a pair of headphones (and wear them!) to make sure you're recording a clear signal.

OTHER ACCESSORIES

Cameras are often supplemented with support gear, such as tripods, gimbals, body straps, mounts, cages, and handles. Add these as you need them, but don't go crazy. **Gear Acquisition Syndrome (GAS)** is a real addiction, and it's an expensive one. Heavier cameras need more expensive support gear, too.

Lighting is hugely important, and if you can't add your own lights, you'll need to learn how to position your subject to maximize available light. As with microphones, you'll need different lights for different purposes, such as small, camera-mounted lights, larger lights that live on stands, and more. You'll find plenty of advice online; start with a quick search for "three-point lighting" and learn as you go.

REVIEW — CHOOSING A CAMERA AND AUDIO EQUIPMENT

Armed with all that information, what are you going to buy? Your budget will guide you, and you'll probably start on the lower end, building up to something more expensive over time. As a starting point, consider the following:

- Use your phone to start. Put all the quality options to maximum, use it for a couple of test jobs, see if you're happy with it, and assess its flaws.
- If your phone isn't good enough for what you need, get a good mirrorless camera, with a capable zoom and at least one prime lens for low-light and blurred backgrounds. Make sure the camera has a microphone and a headphone jack.
- Get a microphone or wireless lapel system that you can plug into your camera.
- Get a solid video tripod that lets you pan and tilt smoothly.

Once you've mastered that setup and you're looking for more, consider the following:

- Get an audio recorder that works with your microphones (such as an XLR or minijack). You can use this as a backup or primary audio source.
- Get another camera for dual-camera shoots and backup purposes. This should be the same brand as your primary camera and should record in the same formats, but could be a cheaper model.
- Get some lights and learn how to use them well.
- Get an action camera, a 360° camera, or a drone to provide different kinds of shots to add variety to your edit.
- Buy a gimbal if you need to capture smooth walking or running movements.

- If or when you hit the limits of what your camera can do, consider moving up to a more professional camera and/or lenses with proper manual focus control:

Figure 2.13: Not all lenses allow proper manual focus, but this "clutch" focus ring does

That's it for a starting point. If you're planning on shooting videos yourself, it's a good checklist to use, and if you're working with others, it's a good checklist of questions you should be asking them. Not every job requires all this gear — I've worked on many jobs where audio is unimportant and I can't add lights — but every videographer needs at least a basic kit. With that kit, what should they capture?

SHOOTING THE RIGHT SHOTS

Whatever kind of camera you end up with, you will need to capture a variety of shots to make the edit run smoothly. If you've planned well, you'll go into a shoot with a list of shots that you need to capture, and it's very satisfying to tick them off as you go.

The shots you need will vary from shoot to shoot, but it's rare that you can simply capture a subject once from a single angle and be done. Nearly always, you'll want to capture two different kinds of footage: A-roll and B-roll.

A-ROLL

This is simply *the primary video that you need to capture*. If people speak on camera or to a camera, that's A-roll:

Figure 2.14: A subject talking on camera? That's A-roll (from Brad Olsen's
Off the Tracks)

In dramas, a scene where people are talking is A-roll, and in a corporate piece, the interviews are A-roll. This is the spine of the story — the driving message keeping the viewer's attention — and it can be captured on one or more cameras:

Figure 2.15: A subject on camera, but not talking? That's probably not A-roll
(from Brad Olsen's Off the Tracks)

The term A-roll isn't widely used today, but it's still a useful descriptive term for your primary story-telling footage. Yet without A-roll, we wouldn't have...

B-ROLL

This is *a secondary video that illustrates or augments the A-roll*. In a corporate video, if a CEO is talking about how proud they are of their new website, then the B-roll could be a shot of someone using that website on a phone or computer:

Figure 2.16: A related keyboard shot that you could use to cover an edit? That's B-roll (from Brad Olsen's Off the Tracks)

In an interview, maybe you have a close-up of the interviewee's hands moving, doing their normal tasks around the office, or an over-the-shoulder shot from behind the interviewer. B-roll can also include shots in the location of an interview to use at the beginning of a piece to set the scene:

Figure 2.17: A scene-setting wide shot? That's also B-roll (from Brad Olsen's Off the Tracks)

How much B-roll do you need? Lots. *A handy rule for B-roll is 5 × 5 × 5*, which means that for each subject, you should capture 5-second shots from 5 different angles at 5 different focal lengths. In the edit, you will need the flexibility that these shots will give you, and viewers will notice if you simply repeat the same shots or the same angles. *A camera operator can't shoot enough B-roll, and an editor never wants less.*

MOVEMENT

B-roll can be **static**, a fixed shot from a tripod, or **moving**, which could be hand-held, or a pan, tilt, or dolly on a tripod, slider or gimbal. Slow, subtle movements can be used as a way to bring life to an otherwise static shot, but there's no shame in using a tripod. Where possible, I try to *capture both static and moving options together*:

1. Start recording while static.

2. Wait for 5 seconds (hold on to your shot).

3. Pan or tilt smoothly to a second position.

4. Finally, wait for another 5 seconds (hold on to your shot again).

5. Stop recording.

This gives me flexibility in the edit because I can use the static first part or the static second part if I need a still shot, or I can use the movement between, with or without the start or end of that movement. Static shots and moving shots don't always work well next to one another, so give yourself a selection of both types and ways to move between them. If you're shooting with a hand-held device, keep your movements slow and intentional:

Figure 2.18: With a gimbal, your hand can go way out to the side, but the camera stays rock solid

As you shoot, visualize how it's going to look in the edit, and *shoot footage to be edited*. You'll do a better job as a shooter if you know how editing works, and it's easier to edit footage that was shot with editing in mind.

FOCUS PULLING

If you don't have a good tripod or the environment isn't big enough to allow movement, you can try to get fancy without moving by using a focus pull (also known as a rack focus). This requires a real lens with manual focus, and the process is simple:

Figure 2.19: Focusing from the back to the front

Start with a foreground subject in focus, wait for a few seconds, then smoothly shift the focus to an object in the background. Wait for a few seconds, then come back the other way. Repeat if you missed the focus. This provides movement without physically moving.

DIFFERENT PERSPECTIVES

B-roll is your chance to bring interesting shots to your edit, so experiment with low angles, high angles, or cameras mounted on an object in the shot. Use high frame rates for dedicated slow-motion shots that need it. Consider using a moderately high frame rate (50 or 60 fps) for all B-roll footage to allow you to choose between normal and 50% speed in the edit:

Figure 2.20: This slow-motion close-up of beer being poured is a great scene setter

Use macro lenses for extreme close-ups or drones for a bird's-eye view. The reason why most general snapshots look the same these days is not that they're all shot on phones, but that they're mostly shot from eye height looking straight out. Get down, up, close, and far away, and you'll bring a variety that your clients weren't expecting.

FRAMING

In both A-roll and B-roll, the composition of the frame is important, and your approach to this will depend on whether you're oversampling (for example, shooting 4K for a 1080p deliverable) or not. If you're shooting in the same resolution that you want to deliver, you'll have to frame things pretty accurately on set and learn the terminology, such as medium shot, close-up, and so on:

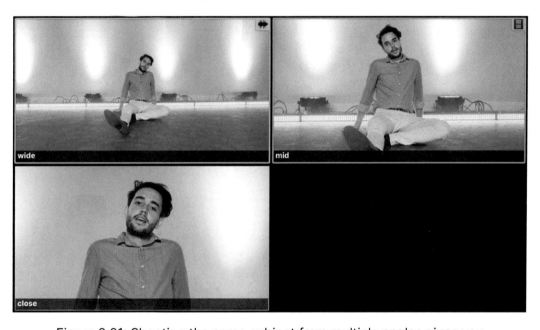

Figure 2.21: Shooting the same subject from multiple angles gives you editing choices

However, if you have extra resolution to play with, you should shoot a wider scene than normal and make the final crop in the edit suite. This gives you the freedom to zoom in on a subject for emphasis or zoom out to make room for a title next to your subject. It will also help if your client suddenly requests a deliverable in a new aspect ratio, such as square (1:1) or vertical (9:16):

Figure 2.22: Shoot the top shot in high resolution and you can crop to either of the other two frames

You'll find many guides for composition out there, but the "rule of thirds" is a good one to bear in mind, and it is probably built into your camera. Here's an iPhone screen:

Figure 2.23: The rule of thirds can be enabled in Settings, under Camera

Over your frame, imagine (or turn on!) a grid that breaks the screen up into three parts vertically and horizontally. When composing, place interesting things (such as a subject's eyes) at the intersection of these lines, 1/3 and 2/3 of the way across and down the screen.

REVIEW — SHOOTING THE RIGHT SHOTS

Within A-roll and B-roll, you've got many ways to compose your shots, and many ways to move your camera about. If you're shooting yourself, it's easy to start simply and build up from there. After all, if you've got the basics covered, you can safely experiment with unusual angles and shots that don't work every time. Even if you'd prefer to stay firmly in the editing bay, now you know what to ask your collaborators for.

Next, you'll find out what to do when a single device isn't enough.

WORKING WITH MULTIPLE CAMERAS AND AUDIO RECORDERS

While a single camera is often all you need, shooting with multiple cameras brings many benefits and can be especially useful during live events when you simply can't ask your subjects to give you another take. A second camera also works as a backup should your main camera have an issue, such as a failed battery, being out of focus, or if someone's standing in front of it:

Figure 2.24: Two angles with a similar focal length, but from different perspectives

The second angle isn't just a backup; you want the two (or more) angles to provide different perspectives because there's not a lot of benefit in two cameras capturing similar content. Angles that are too similar don't work well in the edit either. Two sequential shots that show almost the same thing are called a *jump cut*, and while their use has become more common, it's something that is best avoided if you have the option. While your angles need to be different, they also need to avoid capturing other camera operators in the same shot, and that often makes using three cameras a tricky proposition.

Another factor to consider is "crossing the line." Imagine that you're filming an interview between two people (**A** and **B**) facing each other in front of you — **A** on the left and **B** on the right:

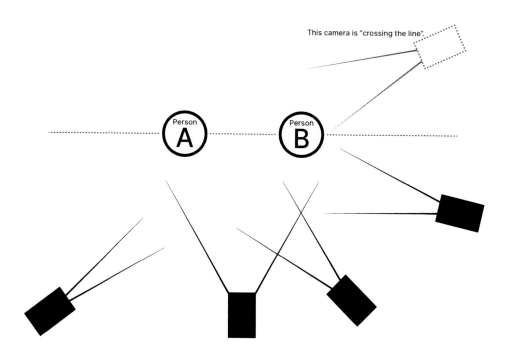

Figure 2.25: Keep your cameras on the same side of your subjects to avoid crossing the line

Any cameras you use should be placed on the same side of the two subjects to maintain that "**A**, **B**" order from left to right. If you cross the line, putting a camera behind them, they'd be shown in a "**B**, **A**" order, which is visually jarring to the viewer.

Always remember that *FCP can automatically sync your footage based on the audio recorded by all cameras and audio recorders.* As we will discuss in the next chapter, similar audio waveforms can be matched up, so you want to make sure that all the devices are recording roughly the same audio. If cameras and mics are placed a long way from one another, the different audio tracks won't have much in common and syncing can fail. If possible, ask your subjects to clap loudly on camera (or use a traditional clapperboard, yell, or use an air horn) to make your life much easier in the editing bay.

Let's consider a few examples of when using multiple cameras is useful.

CONFERENCE PRESENTATIONS

Conferences can be recorded and then shared. Be careful to use cameras that can safely record for long periods of time, and bring enough storage media and batteries!

Video devices should record:

- A wide angle to capture the presentation alongside the presenter
- A tighter angle to capture the presenter alone

Audio devices should include:

- A lapel mic for the current presenter
- A recorder capturing a feed from the sound desk
- A backup recorder on the lectern

Each camera can be exposed appropriately and the best of each combined in a picture-in-picture output. If it's possible to obtain the presentations directly, that's ideal, but some presenters will highlight parts of the screen with a laser pointer, so you really do have to film it as well.

INTERVIEWS

Shooting an interview with multiple cameras gives you extra perspectives of the subject or can allow the interviewer to become part of the story. Any of these angles could be useful:

Video devices should record:

- A normal "head and shoulders" primary angle of the interviewee
- A wider angle of the interviewee positioned 30° from the primary angle
- A normal angle of the interviewer, if they're important
- A wider angle of both the interviewer and interviewee

Audio devices should include:

- Lapel mics on each participant
- A backup recording

These guidelines apply for a single interviewee, but you may want to use additional devices for more than one interviewee. Don't forget your B-roll!

PHYSICAL MOVEMENT

When recording educational videos of people performing physical actions — such as lifting, moving their bodies, sitting down, or dancing — it can be very helpful to see them from multiple angles at once. Resetting cameras takes time, so ask your subject to turn to show the two most important angles in any movement.

Video devices should record:

- A front-on angle
- A side-on angle at 90° from the first angle

Audio devices should include:

- A lapel mic on an on-screen or off-screen narrator, although you might replace this during editing

When framing, remember to capture the entire person if that's important, and always ask a subject matter expert to verify that the important actions are being captured.

WEDDINGS AND LIVE EVENTS

Many live events have predictable key moments that need to be captured, and for a wedding, they would include exchanging rings, vows, walking down the aisle, speeches, dances, presentations, and impromptu interviews. Prepare to capture all the key moments and be ready for anything else.

Video devices should record:

- A focused angle of all the key shots
- A backup angle from a different position
- A wider-angle shot to give context and crowd reactions

Audio devices should include:

- A recorder capturing a desk feed
- Lapel mics for anyone important
- Camera-mounted mics for ambiance and a backup

Reliable equipment and a quick response are critical, because you're not in charge here. As ever, you'll still need B-roll.

REVIEW — WORKING WITH MULTIPLE CAMERAS AND AUDIO RECORDERS

Multiple cameras are vital for a lot of jobs, but they do require more attention and care. If you're just getting started and those lists of equipment sound daunting, that's OK — just don't take on a wedding as your first paying job! There are many simpler jobs for which a single camera is plenty, and you should start there, as complexity brings risk. Be sure to practice multi-camera setups alone before you try to do it in front of a client, and build a network of other camera and sound professionals to work with; don't try to do everything yourself.

As a shooter, you want to make sure you get all the shots the editor needs, and as an editor, you don't want to be left to rescue a shoot gone wrong. Multi-camera shoots are a great way to increase flexibility and protect against problems, but even in a single-camera shoot, there are a few small details to pay attention to, and you'll learn them next.

MANAGING EVERYTHING ON SET

You've picked a camera and audio recorders, everything's charged, and you know what kinds of shots to capture — what next?

Most importantly, if you're working with more than one device, be sure to synchronize the clocks (to the second!) on all of the devices before you record anything. This will make the syncing process far easier, and you'd be surprised at how quickly cameras and recorders can drift from the correct time.

If you've bought a camera that lets you customize the names of the files it produces, set up each camera to make files with different names. My A and B cameras make files that start with `P_IA` and `P_IB` to make life easy, and a shooting colleague uses `P1RC` and `P2RC`. With or without this feature, label the physical media cards so that you don't get confused about which card is which:

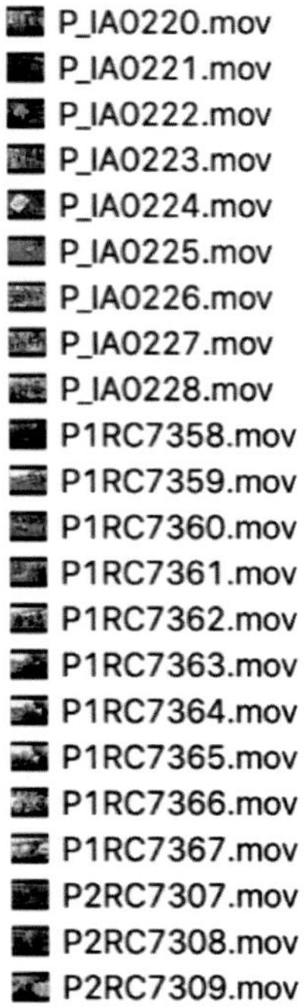

P_IA0220.mov
P_IA0221.mov
P_IA0222.mov
P_IA0223.mov
P_IA0224.mov
P_IA0225.mov
P_IA0226.mov
P_IA0227.mov
P_IA0228.mov
P1RC7358.mov
P1RC7359.mov
P1RC7360.mov
P1RC7361.mov
P1RC7362.mov
P1RC7363.mov
P1RC7364.mov
P1RC7365.mov
P1RC7366.mov
P1RC7367.mov
P2RC7307.mov
P2RC7308.mov
P2RC7309.mov

Figure 2.26: No duplicate names here, and I can tell at a glance which camera each clip was shot on

Some cameras have two card slots, and this can be a lifesaver if you're recording to both slots at once as a guard against faulty SD cards. Alternatively, you can record different kinds of media to each card (which is good if you're shooting photos as well as video) or simply fill up the second card once the first is full. That's less safe, but it means you never run out of space; you can swap the card that's not currently in use while the other card records. This is a dangerous operation, though. If you accidentally eject the wrong card, your current clip, no matter how long it is, could be entirely corrupted and unusable. Use this with great caution.

Similar caution is needed around using mains power rather than batteries with your cameras and recorders. If you have to connect main power via the usual battery compartment and the power is somehow interrupted, you can lose your entire current clip. Batteries will eventually run out, but they are significantly safer.

A final question — should you shoot as well as edit? On a smaller production, shooting the video you're going to edit can be a big time-saver because you'll know what you want, you'll remember what you shot, and you'll have a much easier time when reviewing the footage. You'll also get to know the kinds of shots you need to capture.

Editors and camera operators can do their own jobs better if they each know how the other job works.

However, larger budgets mean more specialization, and on larger productions, some editors actually prefer not to be involved in the shoot at all. That's because a crew might spend hours getting a perfect shot, and they can become emotionally attached to that shot in the edit. In contrast, an editor who wasn't there can choose to use that shot — or throw it away — on its own merits. If you're doing both jobs yourself, remember that *most of what you shoot will probably be thrown away*, and that's OK.

REVIEW — MANAGING EVERYTHING ON SET

These details seem small, but ignoring them can have serious conquences. If it's not easy to know which camera a file came from, it can be lost. If one file has the same name as another file, it can be mistaken for it, or even overwritten by accident. Battery failure is real, and cables can be tripped over; all you can do is your best. Get to know how the set works, even if you aren't always there, and you'll be a better editor.

SUMMARY

If you're just starting out with your first edit, I hope this chapter hasn't overloaded your brain. There's a lot to take in and plenty of mistakes to be made. If you prefer to stay in the edit bay, I hope this chapter has given you some insight into what a videographer has to consider, and you won't feel left out the next time you find yourself talking to someone about cameras, resolutions, codecs, or shutter speed. You'll also know what to request or shoot yourself — *lots of B-roll, at different angles, with movement and without, and from unique perspectives*.

OK, that's enough for now. If you can, go out and shoot something, and grab lots of B-roll. If you can't, head to a free online video source, such as pexels.com, to download as many clips as you can. Armed with your clips, return for the next chapter: *Chapter 3, Bring It In: Importing Your Footage*. We're jumping into FCP and not looking back.

REVIEW QUESTIONS

1. Which is bigger, UHD or DCI 4K?
2. Is it always easy to play back H.264 footage?
3. What are some advantages of more expensive audio equipment?
4. What's the old adage involving "fast, cheap, and good"?
5. What's a way to capture static and moving shots in the same clip?
6. What's a piece of equipment that helps you capture smooth walking or running shots?
7. How does Final Cut Pro usually synchronize multicam footage?
8. How do you use the rule of thirds?
9. What usually happens to most footage that's shot?
10. How much B-roll do you need to shoot?

REVIEW ANSWERS

1. DCI 4K — DCI 4K (4096×2160) is slightly wider than UHD (3840×2160).
2. No, it depends on the camera, the specific type of footage it is, and your Mac's speed.
3. In general, more expensive audio equipment sounds better, has lower noise, and is more reliable.
4. You can have any two of fast, cheap, and good — but not all three.
5. Start static, wait 5 seconds, move the camera, stop moving, wait 5 seconds, stop recording.
6. A gimbal.
7. By matching audio from each camera or audio recorder (though other options are available too).
8. Position interesting things at the intersections of the grid lines.
9. It's thrown away (and that's OK).
10. Lots.

3 BRING IT IN:
IMPORTING YOUR FOOTAGE

"The browser isn't about the glamor, but it's full of good ideas, like your accountant."

— Mike Matzdorff, father, editor, author, writer/director, post-production trailblazer, and cohost of Unauthorized FCPX

miguma.com

Now that you have a grasp of the basics of the user interface and you know how to get good shots, I'll show you how a good edit should begin — by bringing your media into the app. You'll understand your options for media management, how to set up a new Library, the subtle differences between different kinds of import operations, all about transcoding and proxies, how to sync up multiple cameras and dual-system audio, and the basics of Roles.

Roles are a feature that's unique to **Final Cut Pro (FCP)**. Applying and using them early can make the editing process easier in a number of ways, by giving you color-coding in the timeline, and enabling powerful audio editing techniques late in the process. Roles are also vital for audio turnaround on larger Projects.

Specifically, this chapter covers the following topics:

- Creating a Library (in the right place)
- Understanding original, optimized, and proxy footage
- Importing media in different ways
- Syncing media from multiple devices
- Understanding and applying Roles

By the end of this chapter, you'll know how to start any job in FCP and how to import and prepare your media for editing. This may end up being a simple process, but it's good to know about the more complex possibilities, too.

CREATING A LIBRARY (IN THE RIGHT PLACE)

Everything you do in FCP is stored somewhere in a **Library**. Events live in a Library, and everything else lives in an Event: video and audio clips, your edited Projects, photos, and music you've used — the lot. If you follow the most basic workflow, this can be a simple process, but there are reasons why you might want to go down a more complex path.

CREATING AND NAMING A LIBRARY

1. Choose **File** > **New** > **Library**.
2. Give your Library a sensible name, corresponding to the entire job it represents.

A good name might be derived from a simple rule, such as `Year-Month ClientNameJobName`, producing `2020-01 SuperCo Internal Messaging`. The reason why I prefer to use a numeric year-month format (`YYYY-MM`, part of ISO 8601) at the start of Library names is that it alphabetizes correctly as you add more and more Libraries to the same folder. Bad names will make Libraries hard to find, so avoid giving no name or a generic name, such as the following:

- `Untitled`
- `Untitled2`
- `VideoProject`
- `TEMP`
- `Edit v1`

Once you've got a good name, save your Library on a fast drive with *plenty of space*.

As mentioned in *Chapter 1, Quick Start: An Introduction to FCP*, this could be an SSD, a RAID, or another drive. While an external drive is preferred, an internal drive is OK if it's got plenty of space. Why does this matter? Because, by default, *all of the media you import to your Library will be copied inside it*. That will take a lot of space, potentially hundreds of **Gigabytes (GB)**, and running out of space will stop you in your tracks.

Now that you have a Library, you'll also have an **Event** — it will have been created automatically and named for today's date. I prefer to click on this default Event first and rename it `media`, but if today's date is relevant, feel free to leave it as it is. You can create as many Events as you wish, and you can move clips and Projects between Events simply by dragging them around. Create a new Library for each independent job because a single monolithic Library will eventually grow too large.

DECIDING WHERE TO STORE MEDIA

Although *media files are stored inside a Library* by default, if you've ever changed this option, it will have been changed for any new Libraries as well — so, it's worth double-checking. Here's the simple process to do so:

1. Click once on the name of the Library in the browser.
2. Look in the **Inspector** window on the right-hand side of the interface to find **Library Properties**:

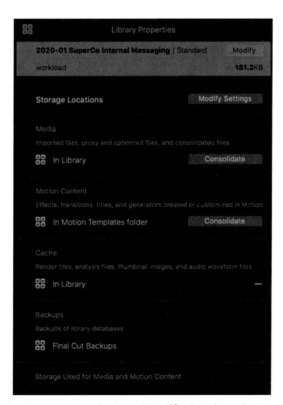

Figure 3.1: In the Inspector window, Modify Settings is the button you're looking for

3. At the top of these settings, next to **Storage Locations**, click on the **Modify Settings** button (not **Modify**).

A sheet will slide down from the top of the main window:

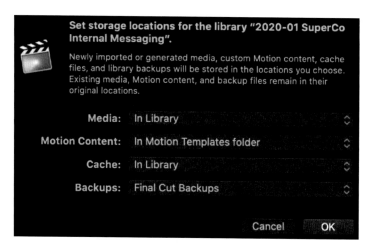

Figure 3.2: Modify Settings allows you to change the storage location of all of these items

4. The **In Library** option should be selected for **Media** although the menu will let you choose an external folder on any connected drive.

In Library (think of this as *self-contained*) is the option I strongly recommend, especially to new editors. It's dead simple, nearly foolproof, and very easy to move around. A **self-contained Library** on an external drive can be opened on any other Mac with FCP then opened up with no issues due to missing media.

If you store your media in a folder outside a Library, you gain access to more advanced collaborative workflows, but it can also create headaches. First, you now have two things to move around — a Library without media and the media itself. If you want to move to a different Mac, you have to move both of these, and you might need to reconnect your media on that second Mac. This process can be easy, but often it's not. Remember from *Chapter 2, Before the Edit: Production Tips*, how some cameras like to repeat the same filenames on different SD cards? This is a potential hassle that's worth avoiding.

The other storage locations here govern the location of other important assets:

- **Motion Content** includes the effects, transitions, titles, and generators used in your edits.

The default option, **In Motion Templates folder**, means that **Motion Content** must be installed on your Mac. Normally, that's fine because a wide range of motion-made content is included with FCP. However, if you were to use a custom or third-party title, then move this Library to another Mac, the title would be missing because it's only stored in the `Motion Templates` folder on the original Mac.

To avoid this problem, you can switch the **Motion Content** storage location to **In Library**, and then choose **File > Consolidate Motion Content**. This means that any motion-made content will be stored directly in the Library and will be available on any other Mac that opens this Library. Be aware that more complex commercial plugins will need to be fully installed on each Mac that they're used on, but this will take care of most custom titles, generators, effects, and transitions.

- **Cache** includes render files, analysis files, thumbnail images, and audio waveform files, and while this can take up a bit of space, it's normally best left inside the Library.

It's important to note that if you change any of these storage locations, you are changing the settings for future Libraries you create. Also, existing media in the current Library will not automatically be moved to a new location, so if there is any media in the Library, it's usually best to follow up with a **Consolidate** operation to keep it all together:

1. Click on the Library's icon in the browser to select it.

   Clicking on a Library's icon is safest, although clicking on the name usually works too. (Be aware that if a Library is already selected, a second click on its name will rename it.)

2. Choose **File > Consolidate Library Media...**:

Figure 3.3: The File menu when a Library (rather than an Event) is selected

The **Consolidate** process pops up an additional dialog box, confirming what types of media you want to include:

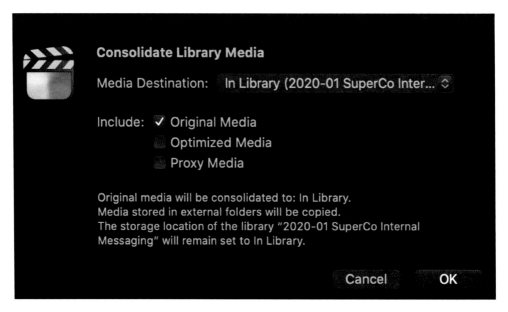

Figure 3.4: You can choose to consolidate any or all of these media types

The quick approach is to simply check the kinds of media you want to include and let FCP do its job. Note that if you attempt to consolidate media types that don't exist, FCP will now (as of version 10.4.9) offer to create them for you. Don't just tick all the boxes! Still, if you've used these media types, you'll want to copy them. However, before we explore the details of optimized and proxy media, let's have a quick recap.

REVIEW — CREATING A LIBRARY (IN THE RIGHT PLACE)

The simplest approach is as follows:

1. Create a Library with a sensible name, one for each job you do.
2. Save your Library on a fast storage device with plenty of space.
3. Store media inside the Library.

In more advanced workflows, you might store your media outside the Library, and that's OK, too. If that's your choice, just remember that you'll need to manage your media with a little more care.

UNDERSTANDING ORIGINAL, OPTIMIZED, AND PROXY FOOTAGE

You will recall from *Chapter 2, Before the Edit: Production Tips*, that different cameras record in different codecs and at different data rates. A few typical cameras with their resolutions, codecs, and data rates, respectively, are as follows:

- iPhone — 1080p, HEVC, 30 fps: **8 Mbps** or **1 MB/s**
- iPhone — UHD 4K, HEVC, 24 fps: **18 Mbps** or **2.25 MB/s**
- iPhone — UHD 4K, H.264, 24 fps: **36 Mbps** or **4.5 MB/s**
- GH5 — UHD 4K, H.264, 24/25/30 fps 8-bit: **100 Mbps** or **12.5 MB/s**
- GH5 — UHD 4K, H.264, 24/25/30 fps 10-bit: **150 Mbps** or **18.75 MB/s**
- GH5 — 4992×3744, HEVC, 24/25/30 fps: **200 Mbps** or **25 MB/s**
- Canon EOS C200 — H.264, UHD 4K, 24/25/30 fps 8-bit: **150 Mbps** or **18.75 MB/s**
- Canon EOS C200 — Canon Cinema RAW Light, DCI 4K, 24/25/30 fps 12-bit: **1,000 Mbps** or **125 MB/s**

As you can see, data rates vary widely, even on a single camera. The iPhone data rates are pretty low, which means details are sometimes lost in the compression process. If this could be an issue — and it probably is! — choose a third-party video recording app that allows higher data rates, or use a "real" camera instead. Broadly speaking, higher data rates will give a higher quality image and take up more space.

The data rate isn't the only variable, however. Modern compression methods, such as HEVC, are more efficient than older ones, such as H.264; that's why Apple uses half the data rate for HEVC recording. However, that efficiency comes at a cost in that it's more difficult to decode, which is also true for some exotic flavors of H.264. For example, 10-bit files from a GH5 are much harder to work with than 8-bit files, Canon RAW Light is demanding even on high-end hardware, and GoPro footage isn't as smooth as Canon DSLR footage. Many Macs have additional HEVC-decoding hardware (the T2 chip), so your mileage will vary there, too.

The good news is that most common formats recorded by most common cameras are easy for FCP to decode. *You can work with most footage natively*, without any extra processing. As stated in *Chapter 2, Before the Edit: Production Tips*, I'd strongly recommend testing original media from a camera before you buy it to make sure you can work with it easily. Your reward is the following simple workflow:

1. Import the original media.
2. Edit.
3. Export.

However, if you didn't choose the camera and your Mac is struggling to handle one or more clips, you can **transcode** them, making an additional **optimized** copy of some or all of the files in the ProRes 422 codec.

UNDERSTANDING OPTIMIZED MEDIA (PRORES 422)

ProRes 422 is an Apple-designed "mezzanine" codec that is relatively large, high-quality, and easy to edit. While most compressed camera codecs are **inter-frame**, describing their image data in relation to previous frames or even frames coming up soon, ProRes is an **intra-frame** codec, like a series of still images that don't refer to one another. This is less efficient and takes up more space, but it's much simpler for your Mac to work with. How much more space are we talking about?

Well, while ProRes 422 is actually just one codec in a family of others (including ProRes 422 Proxy, ProRes 422 LT, ProRes 422, ProRes 422 HQ, ProRes 4444, and ProRes 4444 XQ), optimized footage uses the "vanilla" ProRes 422 codec. Regardless of the original camera, ProRes uses around the following amounts of data:

- ProRes 422 — 1080p, 24 fps: **117 Mbps** or **14.6 MB/s**
- ProRes 422 — UHD 4K, 24 fps: **471 Mbps** or **58.9 MB/s**

ProRes 422 data rates are far higher than most camera-original data rates, but that's probably OK for smaller jobs. Optimized media will be stored in the Library, along with the original media, and as the original media is not deleted, you will need plenty of space. If you have that space, there's just one extra step in your workflow:

1. Import the original media.
2. Transcode some or all of the media to optimized media (ProRes 422).
3. Edit.
4. Export.

For longer jobs, optimized media might require terabytes of space that you don't have, and you might need to use a different approach: proxies.

UNDERSTANDING PROXY MEDIA

While optimized files are a full-quality replacement for original media, proxy files are a medium-quality (and often lower-resolution) option that is only intended for use during the editing process. It'll look softer and possibly less pretty than you'd like, but that's fine while you're editing. Proxy media is quick to work with, and it doesn't take up nearly as much space as optimized media does. Previously, ProRes Proxy was the only way to go, at a data rate like this:

- ProRes Proxy — 1080p, 24fps: **36 Mbps** or **4.5 MB/s**

From 10.4.9 onward, you can choose to use the small, efficient H.264 codec, at the resolution of your choice. If you want to save a ton of space, you can use a frame size as small as 12.5% of the original file. It's still fast, and the process is much the same, but these files will be much smaller than a full- or half-size ProRes Proxy:

- H.264 — 1080p, 24fps: **7.8 Mbps** or **1 MB/s**
- H.264 — 540p, 24fps: **3 Mbps** or **0.375 MB/s**

Note that if proxies have been created and you want to change their resolution or codec, you'll have to delete them (with **File** > **Delete Generated Library Files** or **File** > **Delete Generated Clip Files**) before recreating them at a different size.

GENERATING TRANSCODED MEDIA

If you wish, transcoding (to optimized or proxy) can be performed on every file you import:

1. Go to **Final Cut Pro** > **Preferences**.
2. Choose the **Import** icon at the top of the **Preferences** dialog:

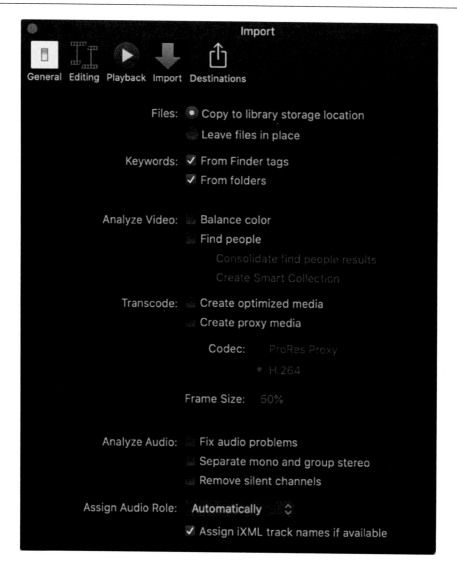

Figure 3.5: The Import dialog

3. Under **Transcode**, select the **Create optimized media** and/or **Create proxy media** checkboxes (and a proxy codec and size if needed) as desired.

Note that checking these options will also check the matching buttons in the **Import** window, coming up soon.

Another option, if most files play well in their original format, is to transcode some files on request:

1. In the browser, select the files that you wish to convert.

2. Right-click and then choose **Transcode Media**.

3. In the dialog that appears, select one or more of the checkboxes (and a proxy codec and size if needed) then press **OK**:

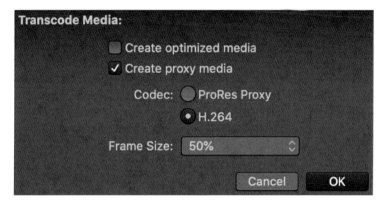

Figure 3.6: Here, only optimized media will be created

Most kinds of original media can be optimized, but ProRes, HDV, and DV footage cannot. MP3 audio files are converted into uncompressed formats automatically on import, so you can't optimize them manually either.

VIEWING PROXY MEDIA

If you create proxy files, you also have to choose to view them. You can choose to view **Optimized/Original** files exclusively, proxy files exclusively with **Proxy Only**, or use **Proxy Preferred** (new in 10.4.9) to show proxy if available, and the original or optimized file if the proxy isn't available or hasn't yet been created. That last option is what you want while you're editing with proxies, and when you're done with the edit and before you export, switch back to the original quality media.

To the workflow, then — if you can't work with the original media and an optimized version would be too big, this is the best way forward:

1. Import the original media.

2. Transcode the media into a proxy format.

3. In the Viewer's **View** menu, switch to viewing **Proxy Preferred**.

4. Edit with proxy media.

5. In the Viewer's **View** menu, switch back to viewing **Optimized/Original**.

6. Export with the optimized/original media.

Proxy workflows can save a lot of space, but if you view proxy media, that's what you'll export. Always remember to switch back to **Optimized/Original** before sharing — though you'll be warned if you don't.

REVIEW — UNDERSTANDING ORIGINAL, OPTIMIZED, AND PROXY FOOTAGE

Let's take a quick recap of the recommended workflows:

- Use original media if possible.

- If the original media is too slow, generate optimized media if you have sufficient space, then edit and export with it.

- If the original media is too slow and optimized media would be too big, generate proxy media, switch to viewing **Proxy Preferred** during editing, and switch back to **Optimized/Original** before exporting.

My personal preference is to shoot with cameras that I can work with natively. Transcoding takes time and space, and if you can combine the right camera with a modern Mac, you'll rarely need to do it. When I do use formats that don't play back smoothly, transcoding a few files isn't a big deal. If you're using higher-end cameras or collaborating, proxy files are likely to be part of the mix, and that's OK. There's room in this industry for all kinds of workflows.

IMPORTING MEDIA IN DIFFERENT WAYS

While it's not instantly obvious, there are a couple of ways to import files into FCP, with subtle differences between them. Some cameras can only be imported while others produce files that can be dragged and dropped instead, and it's good to be aware of the benefits of each approach. First off, let's keep it simple, with the giant, obvious, built-in **Import** feature, and then we'll come back to the more freeform drag and drop alternative.

THE IMPORT WINDOW

A simple import is a great way to get started, and it can be accessed in three ways:

- Firstly, by going to **File** > **Import**.
- Alternatively, by clicking on the downward-facing arrow **Import Media** button in the top-left in the bar at the top of the interface:

Figure 3.7: In full-screen mode, the Import button will be alone in the very top-left corner

- Lastly, if an Event is empty, click on the **Import Media** button in the middle of the browser pane:

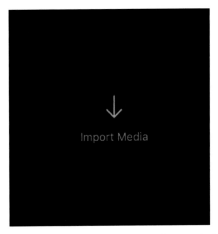

Figure 3.8: This button disappears after the first clip has been imported

All of these options open up the **Import** window, which allows you to import files from connected devices, including the following:

- Connected iPhones
- Your Mac's built-in webcam, if it has one
- SD cards and other media storage cards
- Attached hard drives where files have been copied
- Camera archives, where media storage cards have been duplicated

Here's what the **Import** window looks like with an SD card from a Panasonic camera inserted and an iPhone connected and unlocked:

Figure 3.9: The Import window, with drives on the left, options on the right, and files in the middle

In the top-left corner of the window, you'll see connected cameras and SD cards, and below that, you'll see the connected hard drives and favorite locations. Clicking on one of these displays the device or folder's media in the center pane of the window.

In the bottom-right corner of that central pane are two buttons, which control how the videos are shown:

Figure 3.10: The toggle button on the left indicates what you'll get if you click it, not the current state

The left button is a toggle between two options: the **Filmstrip** view and the **List** view.

The right-hand side filmstrip icon shows the **Clip Appearance and Filtering** popup with a couple of checkboxes, and in the **Filmstrip** view, sliders are also shown to govern the size of the clips and the length of time that each thumbnail represents:

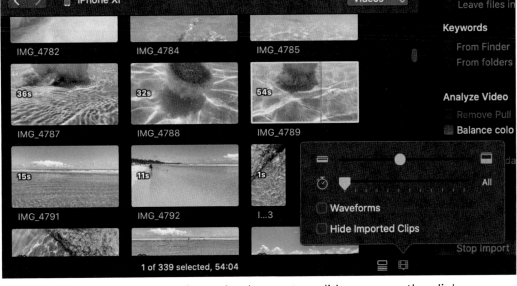

Figure 3.11: In Filmstrip mode, the top two sliders govern the clip's height and width

These two views are also used in the browser and are worth examining. The **Filmstrip** view, when zoomed in, can show every frame of a video at a glance:

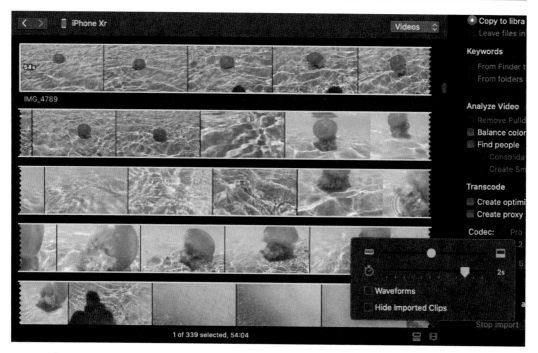

Figure 3.12: 2 seconds per thumbnail shows you how the jellyfish moves around throughout the clip

By setting the menu to **2s**, each thumbnail frame in the filmstrip shows a frame representing 2 seconds of video, and, of course, this thumbnail duration can be adjusted either way. Without this feature, you'd have to view the clip manually at high speed, watching for the subject (a jellyfish, in this case) to appear in the frame.

This is a huge timesaver for many kinds of footage and in fact, this filmstrip-based approach was created by Randy Ubillos (the creator of the original version of Premiere, the original FCP, iMovie, and FCP) after scrubbing through long diving videos looking for sharks.

The **List** view shows a more traditional column-based browser, with just a single selected clip's filmstrip above it. The length of the clip is set by the width of the pane, and so the thumbnail duration can't be adjusted in this mode. The **List** view is most useful in two scenarios — when the thumbnails don't change much, as in an interview, or when you want to view or sort by more information about the clips, such as the date or duration:

Figure 3.13: The List view, which is ideal when you want to see metadata such as the date and duration

Column headers can be clicked on to sort by that criterion, and right-clicking on a column header allows the columns to be customized. But there will be more on that in the next chapter.

Both the **Filmstrip** view and the **List** view include a **Viewer** at the top of the pane, with the current frame visible. A video can be played back with the button at the bottom of the Viewer here, but it's easiest just to press the spacebar to play or pause.

These concepts are repeated, with a similar interface, in the browser. As I'll be showing you that in the next chapter, I'll keep things simple for now. With a few exceptions, I only use the **Import** window to discover which clips I'm going to import, and the usual answer is *all of them*. You will be able to do a much better job of sorting, selecting, and deleting once you've imported your clips, so don't spend too long here. Instead, follow these steps to select the clips you want to import:

1. Choose the **Filmstrip** view or **List** view with the toggle button.

2. Use the **Clip Appearance and Filtering** menu or the columns to adjust or sort the view.

3. Click once on the first clip you want to import.

4. Hold the ⇧ key, then click once on the last clip that you want to import.

5. If you can quickly see that there are clips you don't want, such as a brief accidental recording, hold the ⌘ key and click once on each of those clips to remove them from the selection.

6. Similarly, if you can see additional unselected clips that you do want to import, hold the ⌘ key and click once on each of those clips to add them to the selection.

Great! You've selected all of the clips you want to import. But don't press the **Import** button yet — we need to *check the settings in the right-hand pane first*. They should look something like this:

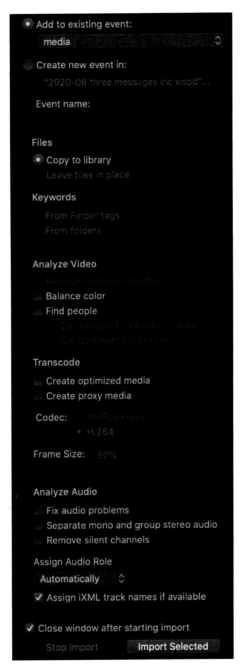

Figure 3.14: The right-hand side of the Import dialog governs many settings

At the top, you can use a drop-down menu to choose which Event, in any currently open Library, you'd like to import the footage to. If you'd like to create a new Event, you can do that instead by clicking on **Create new event in:** and choosing a Library from the menu.

Below that, you'll see a critical choice: **Copy to library** or **Leave files in place**. This is a separate setting to **Media Storage Location**, which we discussed earlier, but **Leave files in place** has a similar outcome: the media is left outside the Library and is not copied or moved at all. If you're new to FCP, don't use this option — it's for more advanced workflows:

Figure 3.15: The choice to leave files in place is not available if you're importing from a phone or a camera

Luckily, you can't go wrong if you're importing from a device that FCP thinks is a camera. When you import from an iPhone or a media card, the files must be copied (for safety and speed reasons) and can't be left in place. Note that **Leave files in place** will be available if you're importing from a regular hard drive, but don't choose it yet.

Audio Roles are important and are covered later in this chapter, as well as later in this book. For now, simply leave these options at their defaults.

Transcoding, as discussed earlier, can be applied by checking one or both of the following checkboxes in the pane. If you know that you need to use optimized or proxy media, go ahead and click whichever option applies, but if you don't know that for sure, leave them both unchecked.

Similarly, I recommend leaving the **Analyze** and **Fix** checkboxes unchecked as well. If you do want to automatically organize clips and/or apply quick auto-fixes, then you can do that later.

Note that changes to any of these settings are persistent; the matching **Import** pane in **Preferences** will reflect any changes made in the **Import** window.

When you have these settings as you want them, look to the bottom of the window and you will see an **Import Selected** button (if you have selected one or more clips) or **Import All** (if you have selected nothing). Click on the **Import Selected** or **Import All** button to begin the import process:

Figure 3.16: You'll see Import All with nothing selected, or Import Selected
with any clips selected

If **Close window after starting import** is chosen, the **Import** window will disappear, and normally this is fine. If you want to import from several different locations at once, however, you can uncheck this box, choose the next batch of clips, and then close the window yourself.

As soon as the import begins, all the clips chosen in the **Import** window will be instantly shown in the browser. They haven't actually been copied yet although (amazingly!) they can be played back, reviewed, and organized. However, for maximum efficiency, it's best to allow the import process to finish before viewing the videos. If you scrub through clips that haven't yet been copied, you'll slow down or even pause the copying process.

In the browser, clips that are being copied, or are about to be copied, will display an icon in the bottom-left corner:

Figure 3.17: During the import process, you'll see icons appear, spin to
completion, and then disappear

The following are the icons that appear when the clips are being copied:

- No icon (as in the first clip) indicates that the clip has finished copying to the Library.

- A circular clock icon (as in the second clip) indicates that the clip is currently being copied, and the progress of the clock indicates how far along it is.

- An empty gray circle icon (as in the other clips) indicates that a clip has not yet been copied, but is in the queue.

Note that a circular dashed icon in the top-left corner of a thumbnail indicates that this clip was recorded at a high frame rate, enabling high-quality slow motion.

A similar clock icon indicating the progress of the whole import is shown in the top-left corner of the interface:

Figure 3.18: The clock icon here will become a checkmark when the import is complete

Pressing this button opens up a separate **Background Tasks** window, showing more information about not just the Import process, but also any additional analysis or transcoding options that were selected:

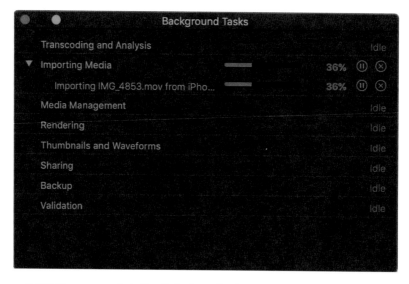

Figure 3.19: For more detail, click the disclosure triangle to the left of any active section

This window will also be informative during the **Share/Export** process, which is discussed in the final chapter of this book.

When the import is complete, which could take anywhere from a few seconds to many minutes, a notification will appear in the top-right corner of the display. If you know you don't need to import anything else from this device, click **Eject**:

Figure 3.20: Notifications appear in the top-right corner of the macOS interface

Before you physically remove an SD card, also verify that it's no longer visible in the Finder; otherwise, you'll be warned about safely ejecting volumes. Ejecting a phone with media that hasn't yet been fully imported might also cause FCP to crash.

So far, so simple. However, there's another method for importing your media that doesn't have to be complex and enables some additional workflows.

IMPORTING VIA DRAG AND DROP

You don't have to use the **Import** window at all. Instead, *it's possible — and safe — to drag and drop media* files directly from the Finder into FCP. However, this is only a recommended workflow if you are working with a camera that creates self-contained files, such as .mov, .mp4, and even .r3d. As discussed in *Chapter 2, Before the Edit: Production Tips*, if your camera uses the AVCHD format, then you should use the **Import** window instead. Common DSLR and mirrorless cameras create self-contained files, and I prefer to use drag and drop most of the time.

To import this way, it's vital to open **Preferences** and set the options in the **Import** pane first, because those are the settings that are used when you drag and drop to import. For now, do the following:

1. Go to **Final Cut Pro > Preferences**, then choose the **Import** pane.
2. Make sure **Copy to library storage location** is chosen:

Figure 3.21: The Preferences pane uses a more compact layout for these Import options

3. Now, find and select the files you want to import using the Finder:

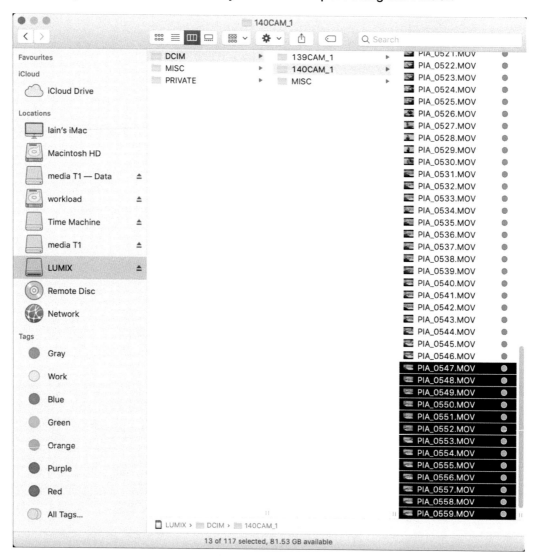

Figure 3.22: In the Finder, I've applied colored tags to clips imported in separate batches

4. Finally, drag these clips to the FCP window *directly to an Event* (not a Library). If you have already selected an Event (not a Library), you can also drag to the larger browser area to the right of the Event names.

So, why import this way? Simply, it can be more convenient to open and find clips using the Finder. If you know that you want to import everything you've just shot like I do, you don't need the extra viewing power of the **Import** window. Also, if you can see the clips you want to import in the Finder, there's no need to find those clips again through the **Import** window — just throw them in. For better or worse, drag and drop also skips over any subtle file rewrapping operations that FCP might perform when using the **Import** window.

This method also allows some very nice workflows if you're importing to a laptop while in the field, including some great ways to make sure you never skip a clip. In the preceding screenshot, you can see that I've added tags (blue and orange dots) to selected clips. My recommended workflow is as follows:

1. Select any new clips by clicking on the first clip and then ⇧-**clicking** the last.

2. Right-click and apply a colored tag to these clips. If this isn't the first import, choose a different color.

3. Drag and drop these clips to FCP.

Working with tags has several benefits:

- You won't miss a clip when importing the next batch — the previous clips are already color-coded.

- With the default **Import** options, the color tags will become keywords that can be renamed. Keywords are discussed in the next chapter and are very useful.

- If you're working with a second camera, you can use the tags to differentiate between multiple cameras, scenes, or types of shots — anything you like.

Next up, we will look at managing storage space.

MANAGING STORAGE SPACE

With or without tags, any files you import will be copied to the Library storage location that you chose earlier. If **In Library** is chosen, then they'll be stored in whatever drive the Library is in. Importantly, the Library now contains all of the files you need, and the original copies of those files are no longer needed or referenced.

To be clear, if you import directly from a camera media card into a Library using FCP, the process is extremely simple, works well, and there is no unnecessary duplication. This is the way I prefer to work, and the way I recommend most people to work.

However, some people prefer to maintain more direct control over video files in the Finder. Without access to FCP in the field, an operator might just copy the camera's media to a hard drive, then give you the files on a portable hard drive. That's OK — treat that portable hard drive like a media card, and import the files directly from it.

The one benefit of this workflow is that if the files have been organized into folders and/or subfolders within them, these will become Keywords on the clips. This can be a helpful starting point, but the capabilities of Keywords can go way beyond folders. As mentioned earlier, Keywords are discussed in the next chapter.

However, *don't just copy the media files to your main working drive first*! If you copy video files to your main working drive and then import them to a Library on that same drive, you're duplicating the media and wasting space. Backups are important, but duplicates need to live on separate drives to be useful.

There is a way forward that allows an editor to manually manage their media and avoid duplication, but it's dangerous. The **Leave files in place** option, found in the **Import** window and the **Import** pane of **Preferences**, doesn't copy anything but instead points to the media wherever it is on a drive. While there are definitely more advanced workflows that rely on manually managing media, if you're just learning about FCP, you should stay far away from this.

The **Leave files in place** workflow demands much more of you as an editor because you have to manage the location of the media as well as the Library. It becomes more difficult to move a Library between hard drives, and you run the risk of having to relink media down the line. In short, there's plenty that can go wrong, so *don't leave files in place without a good reason*.

A few good reasons to use the **Leave files in place** workflow are as follows:

- You're collaborating with other editors on a local server with a more complex media storage workflow.
- You're using Postlab or another collaboration solution that manages media in its own way.
- You frequently need to send a "lean" Library (without media) to another editor.

However, if you're working alone on a one-off job on a local hard drive, you'll only give yourself extra work. Trust FCP and store media in a Library.

USING CAMERA ARCHIVES

There's one more workflow that the **Import** window enables, and while most people don't need it, there are some good reasons to consider it when working with certain cameras.

When an SD card is inserted or a camera is directly connected, the bottom-left corner of the **Import** window contains a button: **Create Archive**. Pressing this brings up a dialog where you can choose where to save an exact copy of the entire file structure of a media card. This obviously takes up a lot of space and can be redundant if you have another backup strategy in place. So, if your camera records to standalone files and you use the drag and drop import method, camera archives probably aren't something you'll need. Still, they do enable a sometimes-handy workflow: reimporting missing media.

REIMPORTING MEDIA

If you cancel an import or an import fails due to a crash or a media drive being ejected, you can be left in an odd position: clips appear to be present, but the real media is still on the camera or SD card. You can tell that this has happened by checking for a small camera icon in the bottom-left corner of a clip:

Figure 3.23: If you see this camera warning, something went wrong with the import process

That's a big warning — if that card or camera is ejected, the thumbnail will show a red **Missing Camera** icon and message and the clip will be unusable:

Figure 3.24: Nobody wants to see this red background with a warning symbol

To recover from this problem, do the following:

1. Connect the camera or SD card that the media is on.
2. Go to **File** > **Import** > **Reimport from Camera/Archive**.

Most of the time, the camera is still available, and this process is straightforward. However, if the media has been erased, you've lost the clip. *Don't erase your camera cards until you're sure they've been imported safely, and they've been backed up twice.* Camera archives can be a handy backup solution for the original media, but I prefer to simply back up my entire main media drive to another local drive, and use automatic online backup for my whole system.

If you've used external media that's gone missing, the command you'll need to reconnect it is **File** > **Relink Files**. Simply keep your media inside the Library and you'll never need to do this, but you can read more about it in *Chapter 10, Explore a Little: Compound Clips and Timeline Tricks.*

IMPORTING FROM IMOVIE

If you're stepping up to FCP from iMovie, you'll be pleased to know that you can transfer your edits pretty easily. Here's how the process works on your iPhone or iPad:

1. Open iMovie, then tap once on the Project that you want to transfer.
2. Press the **Share** button at the bottom, then click on **Export Project**.
3. On the next sheet, choose a method (such as AirDrop) to get the Project to your Mac.

   AirDrop is the easiest option to use if your Mac and iOS devices are on the same Wi-Fi network and AirDrop is open in the Finder on your Mac.

4. With the Project now on your Mac, go to **File** > **Import** > **iMovie iOS Projects**, then locate the .iMovieMobile file and click on **Import**. (If you used AirDrop, this file will be in **Downloads**.)

A new Event will now be created, within which you'll see a Project and all of your media clips.

Moving from iMovie on the Mac to FCP on the same Mac is even easier:

1. Select the Event containing the clips and Project you want to move to FCP.
2. Choose **File** > **Send Event to Final Cut Pro**.

A new Event is now created in a new Library.

REVIEW — IMPORTING MEDIA IN DIFFERENT WAYS

You now know how to use the Import window, how to drag and drop, how to re-import from a Camera Archive, and how to move across from iMovie. But because it's really important, let's recap where your media files are stored.

After you create a Library, give it a sensible name, and choose where to save it, there's a simple workflow to follow:

1. Set your Library's media storage location to **In Library**.
2. Import with **Copy to library storage location** checked.

This always works, and the worst that can happen is that your Libraries can get pretty large. A power-user alternative you might never need is as follows:

1. Set a Library's media storage location to an external folder.
2. Import with **Copy to library storage location** checked.

In this scenario, FCP manages your media but copies it to a folder outside the Library. This means you have to manage multiple folders (boo!) but keeps the Library relatively small (yay!). Things can still go wrong if you're not careful, and some advanced workflows are possible. Another way is as follows:

1. Set a Library's media storage location to **In Library** or an external folder — it doesn't really matter.
2. Import with **Leave files in place** checked.

In this last workflow, you have to manage your video files completely on your own. Plenty of things can go wrong, but the most advanced workflows are possible. Whichever way you go, be conscious of your choice and stay organized. Speaking of which, if your production used more than one camera or multiple microphones, now's the time to join those files together.

SYNCING MEDIA FROM MULTIPLE DEVICES

If your production was recorded using multiple devices, either with multiple video cameras or a video camera and a separate audio recorder, you'll want to sync up any media files that belong together. If you've shot with a single camera and a separate audio device, you might choose to make a **Synchronized Clip**. But for two or more video angles or multiple audio sources, you should use a **Multicam Clip**.

The process for making either of these two clip types is similar and usually relies on similar audio being recorded on each of these devices. If this is not possible, there are other syncing methods available, including timecode, and you can always manually sync if needed. As mentioned in *Chapter 2, Before the Edit: Production Tips*, the best way to make sure that the audio works as a synchronization method is to make loud noises on camera. A loud action that is both visible and audible to all devices, such as clapping a classic clapperboard, is best.

CREATING SYNCHRONIZED CLIPS

When you just have a single audio source and a single video source, you just need to select them at the same time with a quick ⇧**-click** or ⌘**-click**:

1. Select the matching audio and video clips at the same time in the browser.

2. Right-click on one of the selected clips, then choose **Synchronize Clips...**:

Figure 3.25: Synchronizing clips is good for a single video and audio source

3. In the sheet that appears, choose these default options and press **OK**:

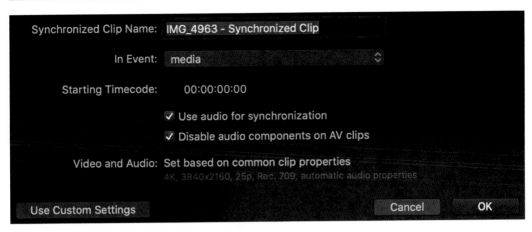

Figure 3.26: Default options will sync using audio, then mute the
camera's audio

With only a single video source, this operation is straightforward. The new Synchronized Clip will combine using the audio from the external recorder and the video from the camera, synced to the audio that the video camera recorded. If the audio is out of sync, the camera didn't record good audio. But how can you tell? Double-click on the Synchronized Clip and it will open in the **Timeline** pane.

If synced audio has been detected, *the two clips will start at different points* because one of them will have been moved to match the other. If the starting points match, that means no sync was detected or you started recording on both devices at exactly the same time (which is unlikely).

Look at the waveforms of the video and audio clips. If you can see that the audio from the video (on top) and the standalone audio (below) have the same peaks in the same places, you're done. This real-world clip is a good example, showing a slightly earlier start for the audio and clear matching peaks on both clips:

Figure 3.27: Two waveforms in sync, with one clip moved to match the other

If the two clips are out of sync, simply move the audio clip until the two waveforms match up. Zooming in (⌘**plus**) helps, as do the **comma** and **period** keys, which nudge a clip by a single frame left or right.

When you're done, you'll be able to edit with a Synchronized Clip in the same way as a regular clip — but it'll sound better. However, if you prefer, you can skip over Synchronized Clips entirely and create Multicam Clips instead.

CREATING MULTICAM CLIPS

Multicam clips combine several angles, including as many video and audio angles as you wish, into a single clip. Later in the book, in *Chapter 9, Consider Your Options: Multicam, Replacing, and Auditions*, you'll discover how to work with these files, but for now, we'll just create them.

IMPORTANT NOTE

More than anything else, decoding multiple angles of large multicam footage is likely to strain your computer, and there's a preference, on by default, to make multicam playback easier. In **Final Cut Pro** > **Preferences**, in the Playback pane, you'll see a checkbox named **Create optimized media for multicam clips**. If checked, it will create Optimized media, even if this transcoding on import was disabled. While this increases playback performance, it can also create very large files, especially for longer multicam jobs.

If you're only working with a couple of angles of H.264 footage on a moderately powerful Mac, you can probably turn this off. However, if you experience stuttering during playback, you can turn this on and wait while the Optimized media is prepared. Alternatively, transcode this media to Proxy and use a Proxy workflow instead.

For a simple multicam session with a couple of clips, the process of creating a Multicam Clip is very similar to creating a Synchronized Clip, but if any devices were stopped and started during multicam recording, you should go through a few extra steps first. At the end of the process, each audio or video device will become an "angle," and to help that along, it's a good idea to manually assign camera name or camera angle information to all of the clips you want to combine. Here's a practical example of how to apply this from a recent job of mine:

Name	Start	End	Duration	Content Created
▶ PIA_9086	13:33:03:16	14:02:37:06	00:29:33:15	22 Feb 2020 at 2:02:55 pm
▶ PIA_9087	14:02:37:06	14:24:46:21	00:22:09:15	22 Feb 2020 at 2:25:07 pm
▶ PIA_9088	14:24:46:21	14:38:22:09	00:13:35:13	22 Feb 2020 at 2:38:46 pm
▶ PIA_9089	14:38:22:09	14:52:54:13	00:14:32:04	22 Feb 2020 at 2:53:56 pm
▶ PIA_9090	14:52:54:13	14:54:32:23	00:01:38:10	22 Feb 2020 at 2:55:58 pm
▶ PIA_9091	14:54:32:23	15:47:41:14	00:53:08:16	22 Feb 2020 at 3:49:09 pm
▶ PIA_9092	15:47:41:14	16:06:17:02	00:18:35:13	22 Feb 2020 at 4:08:33 pm
▶ PIB_1019	03:13:02:03	03:42:42:11	00:29:40:08	22 Feb 2020 at 2:03:06 pm
▶ PIB_1020	03:42:42:11	04:04:48:05	00:22:05:19	22 Feb 2020 at 2:25:15 pm
▶ PIB_1021	04:04:48:05	04:33:21:08	00:28:33:03	22 Feb 2020 at 2:53:51 pm
▶ PIB_1022	04:33:21:08	04:35:32:09	00:02:11:01	22 Feb 2020 at 2:56:05 pm
▶ PIB_1023	04:35:32:09	05:28:25:04	00:52:52:20	22 Feb 2020 at 3:49:15 pm
▶ PIB_1024	05:28:25:04	05:47:27:14	00:19:02:10	22 Feb 2020 at 4:08:20 pm
▶ ZOOM0004	14:50:17:00	17:29:09:10	02:38:52:10	22 Feb 2020 at 5:29:10 pm
▶ ZOOM0037_Tr2	13:42:13:00	16:18:24:43	02:36:11:43	22 Feb 2020 at 1:42:12 pm

Figure 3.28: The names in the clips tell you which camera each file came from, but you should add a camera name or angle, too

I recorded on two video cameras (set to different filename prefixes of PIA and PIB) and two audio recorders. Each audio recorder was left to run for over 120 minutes, while the video cameras were stopped and started periodically. Pausing and restarting recording is a good idea for two reasons: it allows batteries to be changed and though one camera was connected to mains power, if the power had failed, the entire clip up to that point could have been lost. Ending a recording finalizes the current clip and protects against corruption.

With all of the clips imported into the browser and the **List** view shown, you'll see that there's a **Camera Name** column of data. That's what we want to add to, and while you can click and type directly into that column in the browser, it's easier to use the **Inspector** window. The process for this is as follows:

1. In the Browser, select all the clips from a single angle.

2. In the **Inspector** window, choose the **Info** icon (a small circle with an **i** symbol inside) to switch to the **Info** tab:

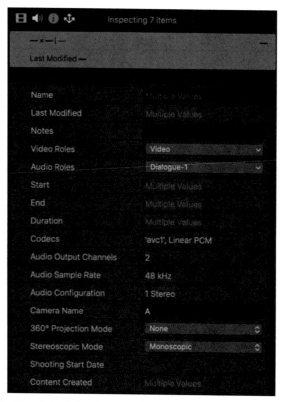

Figure 3.29: The Info tab shows all kinds of metadata, including the Camera Name

Metadata is "data about data" and the camera records lots of it, including the date of recording, the filename, and plenty more. To make it easier to view just some of the metadata, several different metadata views are available.

3. From the bottom-left corner of this pane, choose **Basic** from the menu if it's not already selected.

> IMPORTANT NOTE
>
> If you would prefer to use **Camera Angle** rather than **Camera Name**, you should switch from the **Basic** metadata view to **General** to see that field. Either is fine for our purposes here.

We're now going to add something that the camera didn't know:

4. For **Camera Name**, change the value to A, representing the "A camera," and press Return.

5. Return to the Browser and select the clips from the other camera.

6. In the **Inspector** window, for **Camera Name**, change the value to B, representing the "B camera," and press Return.

7. Repeat these steps for your other devices, such as microphones, giving each one a useful name.

You should now see something like this in the **Camera Name** column:

Name	Start	End	Duration	Content Created	Camera Name
▶ ⊞ PIA_9086	13:33:03:16	14:02:37:06	00:29:33:15	22 Feb 2020 at 2:02:55 pm	A
▶ ⊞ PIA_9087	14:02:37:06	14:24:46:21	00:22:09:15	22 Feb 2020 at 2:25:07 pm	A
▶ ⊞ PIA_9088	14:24:46:21	14:38:22:09	00:13:35:13	22 Feb 2020 at 2:38:46 pm	A
▶ ⊞ PIA_9089	14:38:22:09	14:52:54:13	00:14:32:04	22 Feb 2020 at 2:53:56 pm	A
▶ ⊞ PIA_9090	14:52:54:13	14:54:32:23	00:01:38:10	22 Feb 2020 at 2:55:58 pm	A
▶ ⊞ PIA_9091	14:54:32:23	15:47:41:14	00:53:08:16	22 Feb 2020 at 3:49:09 pm	A
▶ ⊞ PIA_9092	15:47:41:14	16:06:17:02	00:18:35:13	22 Feb 2020 at 4:08:33 pm	A
▶ ⊞ PIB_1019	03:13:02:03	03:42:42:11	00:29:40:08	22 Feb 2020 at 2:03:06 pm	B
▶ ⊞ PIB_1020	03:42:42:11	04:04:48:05	00:22:05:19	22 Feb 2020 at 2:25:15 pm	B
▶ ⊞ PIB_1021	04:04:48:05	04:33:21:08	00:28:33:03	22 Feb 2020 at 2:53:51 pm	B
▶ ⊞ PIB_1022	04:33:21:08	04:35:32:09	00:02:11:01	22 Feb 2020 at 2:56:05 pm	B
▶ ⊞ PIB_1023	04:35:32:09	05:28:25:04	00:52:52:20	22 Feb 2020 at 3:49:15 pm	B
▶ ⊞ PIB_1024	05:28:25:04	05:47:27:14	00:19:02:10	22 Feb 2020 at 4:08:20 pm	B
▶ ◀ ZOOM0004	14:50:17:00	17:29:09:10	02:38:52:10	22 Feb 2020 at 5:29:10 pm	mic2
▶ ◀ ZOOM0037_Tr2	13:42:13:00	16:18:24:43	02:36:11:43	22 Feb 2020 at 1:42:12 pm	mic1

Figure 3.30: After assigning a camera name for all the clips, look to the Camera Name column

IMPORTANT NOTE

If you use the **Import** window, the name of the SD card is used as the camera name. This isn't helpful if you use generic names for SD cards (because they will all be the same) or if you drag and drop to import (because the camera name is only assigned in the **Import** window).

Once the **Camera Name** metadata is assigned, you can create the Multicam Clip:

1. Select all of the matching audio and video clips at the same time in the browser.

2. Right-click on one of the selected clips, then choose **New Multicam Clip...**:

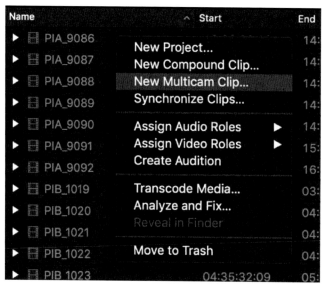

Figure 3.31: Select and then right-click to access this menu

3. In the sheet that pops up from above, click on the **Use Custom Settings** button in the bottom-left corner.

4. In the field at the top, type a name for this Multicam Clip:

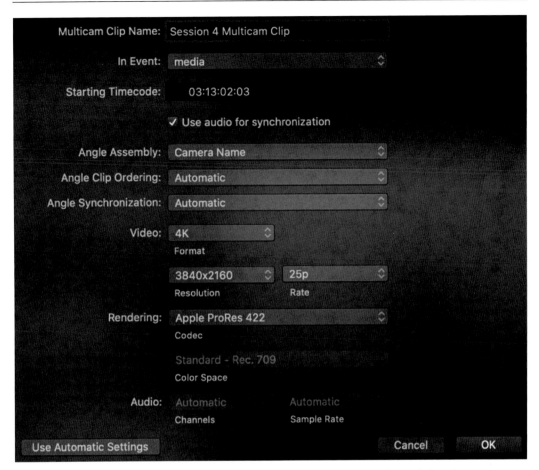

Figure 3.32: This multicam clip was the fourth session of the day

5. Make sure **Use audio for synchronization** is checked.

6. Set **Angle Assembly** to **Camera Name** (use **Camera Angle** if you assigned that instead).

7. If all of the video cameras were set to the same settings, they will be automatically detected, but if the settings don't agree, *choose a resolution and frame rate* here. (Mixed frame rates are possible but can stutter on playback. Always make sure the settings match between multiple cameras.)

8. Press **OK** to create the Multicam Clip.

Next, we will look at how to check and resync a Multicam Clip.

CHECKING AND RESYNCING A MULTICAM CLIP

As with a Synchronized Clip, if you've been careful to record good audio on every device, or at least clap a lot, the sync will go smoothly and quickly. However, you should still check:

- Double-click on a Multicam Clip to open it in the **Timeline** pane in the Angle Editor:

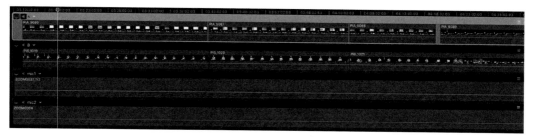

Figure 3.33: The Angle Editor shows the closest thing you'll find to "tracks" in the FCP interface

Each angle will be shown in a separate named lane. In this example, you can see that all of the angles start at slightly different times, indicating that FCP found sync. The waveforms match up, even with multiple clips in each of the two video angles. How do we check that it's exactly synced? Turn on all the audio at once and see if there's an echo. In the top-left corner of each angle, you'll see two icons. The first **TV** icon indicates the current video angle that you'll see in the Viewer; only one angle can be seen. The second **speaker** icon indicates any currently audible angles; all audible angles are heard at once. The process is as follows:

1. Click on all of the speaker icons to make all of the angles audible at once:

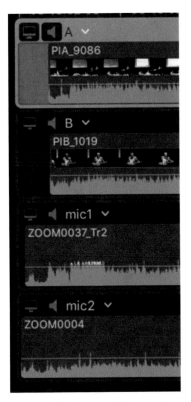

Figure 3.34: The blue speaker icons let you know whether you can hear a clip

2. Press the **spacebar** to playback everything at once.

   If anything's out of sync, you'll need to move it back.

3. As before, zoom in (⌘**plus**) to see any details, then use the comma and period keys to nudge a clip by a single frame left or right.

4. To make larger moves, the easiest way is to simply grab any clips in the wrong place and drag them sideways until the waveforms match up. (If this doesn't work, make sure you're using the **Position** tool by pressing **P**.)

   There's a subtlety here, however — hovering over a single angle will only play that angle's video and audio.

5. Hover over the timeline's ruler and press the **spacebar** to play the current video angle and all of the active audio angles.

There are additional controls hidden in a small menu to the right of each angle's name. From there, you can resync selected clips to the currently chosen video angle (the monitoring angle), but in most cases, this won't be necessary.

That's just about all you need to know about preparing multicams. This multicam Angle Editor is very handy, but it's not something you usually need to mess around with much after this initial setup phase. Instead, you'll use standard timeline controls alongside the Angle Viewer, which is discussed in a later chapter. If you do dive back in with a multicam, remember that adjusting it here will affect all instances of that multicam throughout the Library, so it is an operation to perform with caution.

REVIEW — SYNCING MEDIA FROM MULTIPLE DEVICES

Synchronized Clips are handy, but Multicam Clips are more commonly used and are more powerful. Later in this book, you'll discover how to use these container formats to perform sneaky behind-the-scenes replacements, but for now, just know that you should combine any simultaneously recorded media. Select it, right-click, create a Synchronized or Multicam Clip, double-click to edit, and resync if necessary — and that's it. The last thing on the agenda is to understand what Roles can do for you.

UNDERSTANDING AND APPLYING ROLES

Roles provide a way to categorize your video clips based on how they will be used in video or audio terms: **Music**, **Dialogue**, **Sound Effects**, **Titles**, or **Video**. You can go crazy and define your own Video and Audio Roles, or you can use the built-in Roles that I just listed. Each Role can be further split into Subroles, so a Role named **Dialogue** could have Subroles named for each of the languages you plan to support. Even more amazingly, if you have a high-end, multi-track audio recorder with iXML support, you can name its inputs on the device and they'll be mapped to Roles automatically — magic:

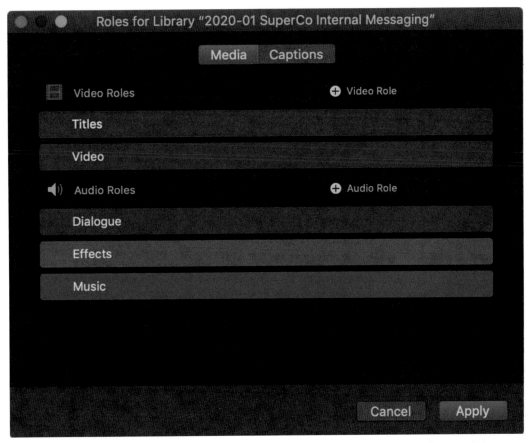

Figure 3.35: The default Roles include the basics — add more if you wish

The power of Roles is seen during the editing process, where the Roles decide the color of each clip. Audio is deemed more important than video here, and the color of a clip's Audio Role takes precedence. Therefore, if a clip has usable audio and video, it's a good idea to assign Roles based on its audio content. Any sound effects or music that you add will be tagged with the appropriate Role, but if you want to get fancy and define additional Roles, now is the time. Roles are best applied to clips before they're used in an edit.

If you have imported additional music tracks (via the import or drag-and-drop options), then you should do the following:

1. Right-click, then choose **Assign Audio Roles** > **Music**.

   Most of the clips that you have imported will be tagged as **Video** for the Video Role and **Dialogue** for the Audio Role.

2. If some of your clips will be used as sound effects or music, **assign those Audio Roles now**.

If you plan to make use of screenshots, different classes of video, such as presentation media, or special media, such as super slow motion, consider creating Roles for those categories of video, too (**Modify** > **Edit Roles** or right-click and go to **Assign Video Roles** > **Edit Roles**), and applying them to the relevant clips. Similarly, if you plan to deliver different audio mixes, you could define additional Roles or Subroles for different languages. You can choose a custom color for each Role, but Subroles share the same color.

REVIEW — UNDERSTANDING AND APPLYING ROLES

Let's take just a quick look back, as this was a short section. Consider how your Project will be exported, and if you need the flexibility to send out different versions (without dialog or titles), then you should set your Roles up now. While most clips will be correctly and automatically tagged as Video, Titles, Dialogue, Music, and Effects, complex productions should set up a few more Roles and Subroles first with **Modify** > **Edit Roles**.

Later in the process, I'll show you how to mix audio based on Roles and how to show or hide clips based on Roles. Tagging both video and audio correctly now can save a lot of tedious busywork later.

SUMMARY

Importing your footage can be very simple indeed, and it usually is for me. I create a self-contained Library on my RAID drive, then import media directly into it — but I don't usually collaborate. If I did, I would use external media, then share the media and a "lean" media-free Library with other editors. FCP will adapt to complex workflows if you need it to.

While you can manage media in a more complex way, make sure you're doing it for the right reasons. Too many editors make their jobs unnecessarily difficult, and there's no need for a solo editor to worry about where their video files are stored. They're in the Library!

Syncing up Multicams doesn't need to be hard either. While you'll doubtless encounter a tricky job from time to time, if you make sure that every camera records audio, you won't have too much trouble.

The next step, however, is crucial. With all of your media imported (and do import some media if you haven't already), your workflow moves to review and organization. Both are deeper and more powerful than they appear at first, and there's plenty to learn. Here we go!

REVIEW QUESTIONS

1. What's easier to manage in a single-person workflow, external media or internal media?

2. What date format is recommended?

3. Put these formats in order of increasing size: optimized footage, native iPhone footage, ProRes Proxy footage.

4. When should you use proxy footage?

5. Which view lets you see all your footage at a glance?

6. Can you choose **Leave files in place** when importing from a connected phone?

7. How do you apply colors to files in the Finder?

8. What does the camera icon mean on an imported clip?

9. What information should you add to a clip before making it part of a multicam clip?

10. Which of these is not a default Role: Video, Audio, Effects, Foley?

REVIEW ANSWERS

1. Internal media.

2. YYYY-MM, part of ISO 8601, because it alphabetizes correctly.

3. Native iPhone footage is smallest, then ProRes Proxy, then Optimized (ProRes 422).

4. If your Mac can't play back regular footage smoothly, and you don't want to take as much space as optimized requires.

5. Filmstrip view.

6. No.

7. Right-click and apply tags.

8. The file is still on the camera and should be reimported.

9. Camera Name or Camera Angle.

10. Foley is not a default Role.

4 SORT IT OUT:
REVIEWING AND KEYWORDING

"Deceptively uncluttered, the Final Cut Pro X interface allows me to focus on creating compelling content."
— Sean Lander, editor, producer, and shooter based in Melbourne, Australia (www.rednail.com.au)

Now that you have a Library full of footage, it's time to make sense of it. Spending time organizing your footage now means that you'll be able to make better choices later, and the larger a project is, the more you will appreciate being able to find clips easily. This chapter will show you how to review your footage in many smart ways and then how to sort out your footage using Keywords.

Don't skip or shortcut this chapter by skipping straight to editing — it's really important to understand this key process. Keywords are one of the key innovations of Final Cut Pro, and understanding how metadata can help you find the right shot is crucial. Learn it, and you'll love it.

Specifically, this chapter covers the following topics:

- Reviewing your media
- Browser view options
- Playback shortcuts
- Examining metadata
- Understanding and applying Keywords
- Searching with Keywords

By the end, you'll know how to look through all your clips efficiently, decide how they could best be categorized, and then apply those Keyword tags to your clips.

In future chapters, you'll break things down further, separating parts of clips, but for now, we'll take a high-level view. Time to start, with *reviewing*.

REVIEWING YOUR MEDIA

You probably already know that the **spacebar** performs the crucial play/pause function, but there's a lot more to reviewing media than that. Skimming is a critical skill, and the Viewer has many subtle controls too. Let's begin by finding out why you shouldn't click so much.

SKIMMING IS AWESOME

Probably the first habit that most editors need to break when shifting to FCP is that of clicking. There's simply no need to click on a clip before playing it back, and in fact, it can cause issues if that click turns into an accidental drag and changes the current selection. Instead, simply *hover your cursor over a clip's filmstrip, just before a particular moment, then press the* **spacebar**.

FCP actually has two ways to indicate a position in time: the **Playhead** and the **Skimmer**. Over a clip's filmstrip in the Browser, you'll see the following:

- The **Playhead** is a white vertical line, is positioned with a click, and stays in position when the mouse cursor moves elsewhere.

- The **Skimmer** is a red vertical line, moves with the mouse cursor, and is only visible when the cursor hovers over a clip.

- The **Skimmer** can be toggled on or off (blue means on) with this central toolbar button, or the **S** shortcut:

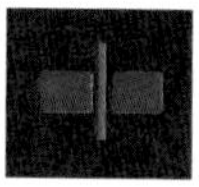

Figure 4.1: This blue icon indicates that skimming is on

- If it's present, *the Skimmer takes priority* over the Playhead.

Because the Skimmer can move through a clip as quickly as you can drag your pointer over its filmstrip, most users find the Skimmer to be very useful. The thumbnail that the cursor is currently over will change to reflect the exact frame that the cursor is over, and you'll also see the full size of the frame in the Viewer. If you don't like skimming, you can simply press **S** to disable it, but if you only have a problem with the audio, you can disable audio skimming with the next icon along, or by pressing ⇧**S**:

Figure 4.2: Skimming on, Audio Skimming off

The Skimmer is also a powerful incentive to learn common shortcuts, because if you have to click on a button to perform an action, your cursor will leave the current pane, and the Skimmer will disappear. If you don't want to learn shortcuts, you'll have to click to explicitly set the Playhead position instead.

As you skim, and as you click to position the Playhead, you'll probably be watching the Viewer, so it's time to look deeper.

EXPLORING THE VIEWER

While the Skimmer and the Playhead do visibly update a thumbnail within a clip's filmstrip, the Viewer is larger and easier to see. While it can show video in a variety of ways, for now, only a subset of these options are important, and most of them are found in the menus at the top right of the Viewer pane:

Figure 4.3: The Viewer, with the most important menus at the top right

The first menu controls the size of the video, and you'll want to use shortcuts for these operations. Click once in the Viewer to target it, then try the following:

- **⌘plus** to zoom in (technically, this is really the equals key)
- **⌘minus** to zoom out
- **⇧Z** to fit the video to the space available

This last option is persistent, so when you've chosen **Fit**, you can resize the Viewer by dragging its edges, and the video will resize to match:

Figure 4.4: When the Timeline and Inspector are hidden, there's plenty of space for a big Viewer

Normally, this **Fit** view is the best choice to make the video as large as possible, but you might prefer to view it at **100%** to see the pixels that you shot exactly. If you're using a 5K iMac, it's surprising to see just how few pixels a Full HD 1080p image takes up.

The second menu shows or hides overlays and adjusts the video quality. It has several sections, as shown in the following screenshot:

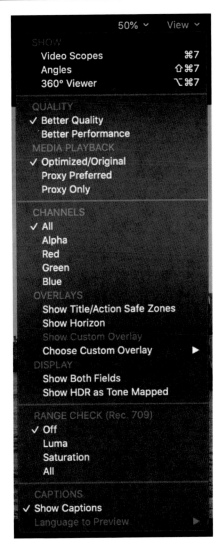

Figure 4.5: The View menu in the Viewer

In turn, they are as follows:

- **Show**, which adds or removes an additional pane to the Viewer — **Video Scopes**, **Angles** for Multicam Clips, or the **360° Viewer** for working with equirectangular footage.

- **Quality**, which lets you choose between **Better Quality** (everything you shot) and **Better Performance** (a lower-quality version that plays smoothly, but at ½ or ¼ resolution).

Start out with the **Quality** menu set to **Better Quality**, but switch to **Better Performance** if your Mac starts to stutter on playback. Stuttering means that either your hard drive is too slow (unlikely) or your computer is too slow to process this particular video clip in real time (more likely). While most common formats won't cause any issues on most Macs, if you're working with something more exotic or you're using an underpowered laptop, this could happen. You could also consider shooting with a different codec (discussed in *Chapter 2, Before the Edit: Production Tips*) or transcoding your footage (discussed in *Chapter 3, Bring It In: Importing Your Footage*) to make processing easier.

- **Media**, which lets you choose between **Optimized/Original**, **Proxy Preferred**, and **Proxy Only**.

  The first option will show **Optimized** if it's available, or **Original** (native) footage if you haven't transcoded. The second option, **Proxy Preferred**, shows proxy footage if it's available, and optimized/original if it's not. This is probably the one to go for if you're working with proxy media, because the third option, **Proxy Only**, will show a "missing media" warning for clips with no proxy available. Either way, if you do edit with proxy media, be sure to switch this back to **Optimized/Original** before exporting (though you'll be warned if you forget).

- **Channels**, which lets you see individual components of the image, including **Alpha** transparency if available. Note that proxy media doesn't include an alpha channel, so if your footage includes transparency, don't create proxy media from it.

- **Overlays**, which adds guides on top of the image to help you maintain broadcast standards, line up your titles, or get horizons straight.

- **Display**, which can show both fields in an interlaced signal and also display **High Dynamic Range** (**HDR**) data using its raw values.

- **Range Check**, which shows warnings when a video is too bright or too saturated; good to see during color correction.

- **Captions**, to choose whether captions are shown.

If you're using a second display, remember that you can use the button near the top-right corner to activate that display, then use the menu next to the button to decide what goes on it. This button/menu combo is only shown if a second display is connected and not set to mirror the first:

Figure 4.6: The button here is lit blue, indicating that a second display is active; the menu next door chooses what is shown on it

The Viewer is an obvious choice, and leaves just the Browser and Inspector (if you need it) on the first screen. Some editors prefer to use a vertical screen for the Browser instead; that works too. As well as these second display options, you can entirely dedicate a display to raw video output.

A/V OUTPUT

While it's possible to put the Viewer on a second display and enter fullscreen mode with the button in the bottom-right corner (or ⇧⌘F), there's another way to show fullscreen video. In **Final Cut Pro** > **Preferences**, under **Playback**, the last option at the bottom lets you choose an external display for **A/V Output**. Third-party external interfaces work, but any HDMI-connected display in a 4K, UHD, or 1080p resolution should work too.

> IMPORTANT NOTE
>
> This isn't a Viewer, and no overlays or quality options apply here. Instead, this is a raw video output feed, intended for high-quality dedicated output, which could be a second display or even a dedicated third display.

Here's the **Preferences** pane that holds **A/V Output**:

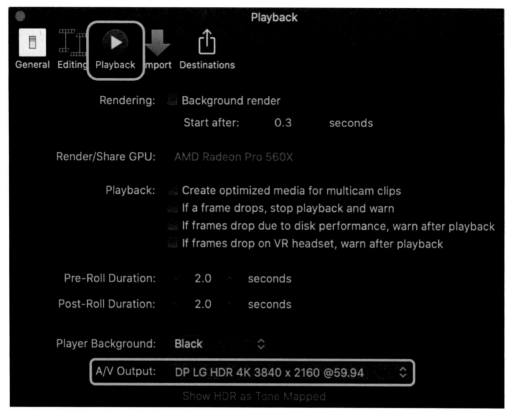

Figure 4.7: Under the Playback preferences, look for the A/V Output settings at the bottom

Once set up, **A/V Output** also needs to be activated, from **Window > A/V Output**. If you had previously put the **Viewer** on the same second display as **A/V Output**, the **Viewer** will now pop back over to the main screen, before a fullscreen output takes over that second display. This looks great, but it can be taxing on less powerful computers. You'll also still have a regular Viewer on the primary screen to show the regular overlays and controls.

REVIEW — REVIEWING YOUR MEDIA

You'll use the Viewer at almost every moment, so it's important to make sure you've got control over what it shows you. You know what the Viewer can do, and you know how to skim across your footage too. To maximize screen space, you can hide the Timeline when you don't need it, and you know how to make use of a second display too.

Now that you can see your footage clearly — how do you control what clip you're looking at? Explore the settings in the Browser.

BROWSER VIEW OPTIONS

The icons in the top-right corner of the Browser contain the same two buttons as in the Import window, along with a drop-down **Clip Filtering** menu on the left, and a search icon on the right. We'll cover all these soon:

Figure 4.8: Look for these items in the top-right corner of the Browser

As in the Import window, you'll find a **Filmstrip/List** toggle button at the top-right:

Figure 4.9: If you're in List view, the icon shows a filmstrip, and vice versa

The icon indicates *not the current state, but what you'll switch to if you click on it:*

- **List** view is ideal for visually repetitive A-roll, especially interviews, where the thumbnails aren't going to be very informative.
- **Filmstrip** view is ideal for B-roll and anything else you can visually scan.

You'll flip between these views frequently, as they're both useful in specific circumstances. Let's dig deeper.

LIST VIEW

Here's an example of a good use for **List** view, with the filmstrip lightly blurred for privacy:

Name			Start	End	Duration	Content Created	Camera Name	Notes
▶	🗋	PIA_9086	13:33:03:16	14:02:37:06	00:29:33:15	22 Feb 2020 at 2:02:55 pm	A	
▶	🗋	PIA_9087	14:02:37:06	14:24:46:21	00:22:09:15	22 Feb 2020 at 2:25:07 pm	A	
▶	🗋	PIA_9088	14:24:46:21	14:38:22:09	00:13:35:13	22 Feb 2020 at 2:38:46 pm	A	
▶	🗋	PIA_9089	14:38:22:09	14:52:54:13	00:14:32:04	22 Feb 2020 at 2:53:56 pm	A	
▶	🗋	PIA_9090	14:52:54:13	14:54:32:23	00:01:38:10	22 Feb 2020 at 2:55:58 pm	A	
▶	🗋	PIA_9091	14:54:32:23	15:47:41:14	00:53:08:16	22 Feb 2020 at 3:49:09 pm	A	
▶	🗋	PIA_9092	15:47:41:14	16:06:17:02	00:18:35:13	22 Feb 2020 at 4:08:33 pm	A	
▶	🗋	PIB_1019	03:13:02:03	03:42:42:11	00:29:40:08	22 Feb 2020 at 2:03:06 pm	B	
▶	🗋	PIB_1020	03:42:42:11	04:04:48:05	00:22:05:19	22 Feb 2020 at 2:25:15 pm	B	
▶	🗋	PIB_1021	04:04:48:05	04:33:21:08	00:28:33:03	22 Feb 2020 at 2:53:51 pm	B	
▶	🗋	PIB_1022	04:33:21:08	04:35:32:09	00:02:11:01	22 Feb 2020 at 2:56:05 pm	B	
▶	🗋	PIB_1023	04:35:32:09	05:28:25:04	00:52:52:20	22 Feb 2020 at 3:49:15 pm	B	
▶	🗋	PIB_1024	05:28:25:04	05:47:27:14	00:19:02:10	22 Feb 2020 at 4:08:20 pm	B	
▶	▦	Session 4 Multicam Clip	03:13:02:03	05:51:54:07	02:38:52:04	7 Apr 2020 at 5:04:39 pm		
▶	◀	ZOOM0004	14:50:17:00	17:29:09:10	02:38:52:10	22 Feb 2020 at 5:29:10 pm	mic2	
▶	◀	ZOOM0037_Tr2	13:42:13:00	16:18:24:43	02:36:11:43	22 Feb 2020 at 1:42:12 pm	mic1	

Figure 4.10: When you'd rather see data in columns than filmstrips,
use List view

The single filmstrip at the top isn't terribly informative, but it doesn't have to be. The camera didn't move, and though the vision is important, I won't be picking out which parts to use and not to use based on what they look like. I might use the audio waveforms, and they're visible just under the video filmstrip. The higher the peaks, the louder the noise, and you can spot where speakers changed by looking for the gaps in the waveform.

As well as situations where audio is most important, **List** view is a good place to be if you want to see common metadata, such as the clip duration or creation date, for several clips at once. The column headers at the top have many tricks:

- To sort by a column, click on the column header.

- To reverse a column's sort, click on the currently selected column header.

- To resize a column, drag the edge of its column header.

- To reorder columns, drag their column header to the left or right of other column headers.

- To show or hide a column, right-click on the column header and choose an option:

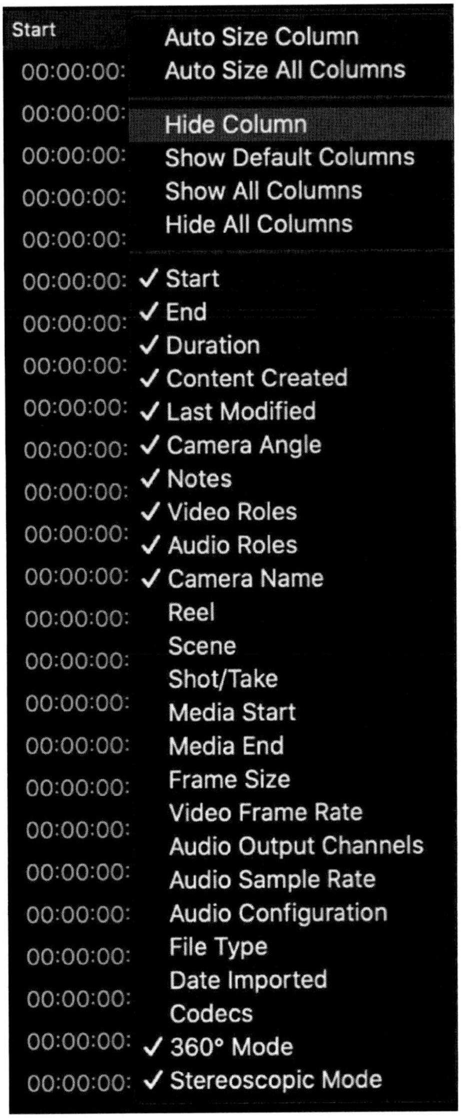

Figure 4.11: If an option is ticked in this list, that column will be visible (Last Modified is new in 10.4.9)

The **Start** and **End** columns might not be terribly useful if your camera starts every clip at a 0:00:00:00 timecode, but if your camera can use *Time of Day timecode* as mine does, these columns are more useful.

As well as sorting with, hiding, showing, and rearranging columns, you can control the view using the drop-down menu shown here at the top right of the Browser:

Figure 4.12: Browser options for List view

The **Clip Filtering** menu, currently set to the **All Clips** option, is also important, and we'll be returning to it soon.

IMPORTANT NOTE

Not all options are available in **List** view, but do note that you can group items if you want to (I usually don't) and can show or hide the audio waveforms with the checkbox near the bottom. **Continuous Playback** allows you to move from clip to clip automatically — when one clip ends, the next begins. This is handy for some things, and less handy for others.

While **List** view is great when names and numbers are important, if what you can see in a clip is more important, it's time to toggle across to **Filmstrip** view for a more visual experience.

FILMSTRIP VIEW

Here's a good example of the kind of footage best seen in **Filmstrip** view — lots of B-roll and visual shots. You can tell at a glance whether the shot is static or not or if it pans or moves along, and you can see exactly what's in it:

Figure 4.13: A Browser in Filmstrip view, showing many beach shots, with waveforms visible

Because there are no columns, the drop-down menu at the top right of the Browser shows more options in **Filmstrip** view:

Figure 4.14: The Browser options for Filmstrip view

Grouping and sorting are both here, and I prefer the options in the preceding screenshot for jobs I've shot myself. Do you need waveforms? Only if the sound is important and you're willing to sacrifice the space (and a small amount of computer power) that they require. **Continuous Playback** is useful if you want to review a number of clips at once: set it going and sit back.

Just like in the Import window, the top two sliders control the height of the video thumbnails and the duration of each individual thumbnail. You'll want to change these frequently to be able to see a greater number of clips at once or to see more frames from each clip. It's best to use shortcuts for these operations, and if you've clicked in the Browser to give it focus, they are as follows:

- **⌘plus** to zoom in (again, this is really the equals key)
- **⌘minus** to zoom out
- **⇧Z** to zoom all the way out to show a single thumbnail for each clip (the **All** setting)

Combined with skimming, these shortcuts will help you trade detail for quantity, allowing you to glance over all your footage quickly, or examine a clip more closely.

REVIEW – BROWSER VIEW OPTIONS

Between the different options for clip appearance, the **List/Filmstrip** toggle and the scale controls, you've got many different ways to see your clips. Set up your columns in **List** view however you wish, or flick across to Filmstrip mode for a birds-eye view, such as looking through all the strips of freshly processed film in a lab. Glance in the Browser at whatever size and scale you prefer, or if you want to see them in the Viewer, use the pointer to skim over your clips at whatever speed you like.

But you don't have to use the mouse for playback. Many editors prefer the keyboard, and indeed, for longer clips, it's often the best approach. In the next section, I'll show you some of the best keyboard shortcuts for playback.

PLAYBACK SHORTCUTS

The **spacebar** (play/pause) is a great shortcut to start with, and as it's the largest key on the keyboard, it's easy to hit. But you'll need to know about a few more keys too because just starting and stopping playback isn't enough. To review a lot of footage, you might need to play it back much faster than normal. Conversely, when you need to be specific about the exact frame you want, you might want to play it back much slower. All that and more is coming right up.

BASIC SHORTCUTS

J, **K**, and **L** are the three keys you should mash firmly into your brain:

- **L** plays forward.
- **K** pauses.
- **J** plays backward:

Figure 4.15: J, K, L: the keys you want to use every day

These keys work in the Viewer, in the Timeline, and even in QuickTime Player — they're probably the most important shortcuts you'll learn today. You can use these with your left or right hand, in combination with a mouse or trackpad, and be sure to leave your three fingers resting on these keys for repeated easy access. But there's more:

- Repeatedly press **J** or **L** to double the playback speed in that direction: 2x speed, 4x speed, 8x speed, and so on.
- Press the opposing playback key to jump instantly to 1x speed in the other direction.

Using these common editing keys, you can tap **L** three times to instantly play at 4x the normal speed, or tap **J** two times for double reverse playback — a good way to review footage quickly or at least to get a quick overview of it. **K** has tricks too, which are as follows:

- Hold **K** and then tap **L** to move a single frame forward.
- Hold **K** and then tap **J** to move a single frame backward.
- Hold **K** and then hold **J** or **L** to play in slow motion with slowed-down audio.

The horizontal arrow keys are important too:

- → moves forward one frame.
- ← moves back one frame.

- ⇧→ moves forward 10 frames.
- ⇧← moves back 10 frames.

Of course, **spacebar** still works to play or pause. All these keys also work with hovering, so you can hover to where you want to begin, then press **J** to play backward. If you click, rather than hover, you will also select the clip you clicked on. Finally, the vertical arrow keys can help here too:

- ↓ selects the next clip.
- ↑ selects the previous clip.

If you prefer not to use Continuous Playback, you'll be using **Up** and **Down** quite a bit. Note that these keys do select the next or previous clip, while hovering doesn't. That may seem like a small thing, but you'll see soon why it matters.

EXTENDED SHORTCUTS

To review a particular part of a clip, you can certainly hover or click just before a moment of interest, then simply play. But the following technique is often more useful:

1. Activate **Looping** with **View** > **Playback** > **Loop Playback (⌘L)**.
2. Press **⇧/** (also known as **?**, if you prefer) to **Play Around Edit**.

This is a great way to repeatedly see part of a clip as the Playhead jumps a few seconds back, plays through the selected point, and plays a few seconds forward before starting again. It's useful in an edit on the Timeline too.

If you often find yourself wanting to play at high speed, you might tire of repeatedly tapping **L** or **J**. There are some additional commands to instantly start playback at high speed forward or backward, but they're hidden: they aren't in the menus, and they don't have keys assigned. To enable them, you'll need to assign custom keyboard shortcuts:

1. Choose **Final Cut Pro** > **Commands** > **Customize** (or ⌥⌘K) to bring up the **Command Editor**:

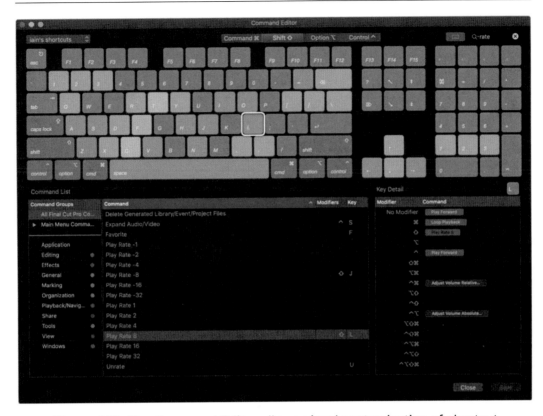

Figure 4.16: The Command Editor allows visual customization of shortcut keys and is very helpful indeed

2. In the top-right search field, type `rate`:

Figure 4.17: Look in the top-right corner to find this search field

Below, you'll now see **Play Rate -1** through **Play Rate 32** in a list of matching commands:

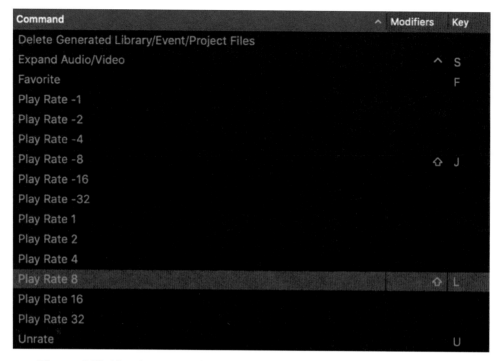

Figure 4.18: Here's everything with "rate" in its name, at the bottom of the window

3. Press the **Shift ⇧** button at the top of the window:

Figure 4.19: This bar at the top lets you see and create shortcuts that include the selected modifier keys

Don't press any additional modifier keys or click other buttons at the top as this would assign the wrong shortcuts in the following steps.

⇧J and ⇧L are currently unused, so we'll assign commands to them.

4. Drag **Play Rate -8** to the **J** key.
5. Drag **Play Rate 8** to the **L** key:

Figure 4.20: The lower-right part of the window shows what a key can do
with all the possible modifier key combinations

Try these new shortcuts out! **J** plays backward, but **⇧J** plays immediately at 8x speed backward, and **⇧L** plays at 8x forward. Keyboard customization can really make a difference to how quickly you can edit, so spend a bit of time here once you understand the app a bit more. There are additional hidden shortcuts that revolutionize the color correction process, and they're covered in *Chapter 11, Play With Light: Color Correction and Grading*.

REVIEW — PLAYBACK SHORTCUTS

The core **JKL** keys are important, but so are all the arrows, as well as the spacebar, looping, and the modifier keys too. Shortcuts, especially single-key shortcuts, can speed you up like nothing else, so force yourself to use these as much as possible. You also know how to set up your own shortcut keys, another massive time saver.

While quick playback is important, not everything can be seen at a glance. Deeper information about a clip is called metadata, and it can be very powerful. The next section tells you all about it.

EXAMINING METADATA

As mentioned in *Chapter 3, Bring It In: Importing Your Footage*, metadata is "data about data," and while it starts with the basics — the filename, creation date, frame size, and frame rate — there are hundreds of additional pieces of image data that can be explored. The columns available in **List** view are extensive, but they don't show all the information that can be stored inside a file. To see and potentially change some of this data, you'll have to use the Inspector, and we'll dig deeper this time.

METADATA IN LIST VIEW

Metadata, in terms of camera-originated data attached to media files, can be pretty boring and technical, the kind of thing that a program needs to worry about, rather than you. Maybe you don't care much about the codec or color profile of every clip. But some of this info can help you to make intelligent choices by finding files with particular characteristics.

The most commonly used metadata is available in the columns of **List** view, and sorting by any of these characteristics can help you find specific files:

- **Duration**: If you need a clip long enough to fill a certain-sized hole in your edit
- **File Type**: If you want to separate video, audio, and stills
- **Video Frame Rate**: If you want to easily find high frame-rate footage or identify frame rate mismatches
- **Frame Size**: If you want extra data to zoom in
- **Codecs**: To spot footage that could be harder to work with natively
- **Camera Name**: Useful when setting up multicams
- **Shot/Scene/Reel**: For organizing clips from larger shoots

As you will see in the menu, there are other fields available, but these are the most commonly used.

METADATA IN THE INSPECTOR

Several additional fields are not available in the columns, and you'll have to use the Inspector to reach them. Here's how to optimize your workspace for the organizing process:

1. If the Timeline is still visible, hide it by pressing the middle button at the top right of the main window:

Figure 4.21: The lighter Timeline icon here indicates that it is hidden

You don't need the Timeline while you're organizing footage. Use its screen space for a bigger Browser instead.

2. Head to the **Inspector** and press the **Info** tab icon at the top:

Figure 4.22: The Info button in blue is the one to click

3. In the bottom-left corner of the **Inspector** pane, look at the metadata menu, which will probably say **Basic** or **General**:

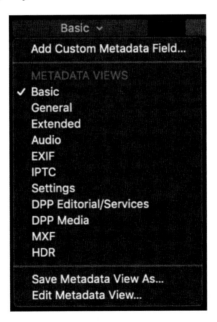

Figure 4.23: These are the default metadata views, though you can define your own

This menu controls which metadata fields are shown in the Inspector. No recording device will write data to every field, and FCP won't read all the data in every kind of file. If you wish to inspect other data that is present, choose any of the other metadata views, or make your own custom compilation with **Edit Metadata View** from the same menu. If you can't find what you're looking for, you can even create entirely new metadata fields with **Add Custom Metadata Field**.

IMPORTANT NOTE

Many cameras write metadata to record aperture, ISO, white balance, and other settings that can't usually be read or shown in the Inspector — except when working with ProRes RAW. In fact, if you use the Import feature (rather than dragging and dropping), some of this extra metadata can become inaccessible. If you want to keep and view this information, consider a third-party app called **EVR X**.

The main strength of the Inspector is not just in inspecting data, but also in changing settings and adding additional information through editable fields. Most of the interesting switches are collected in the Settings metadata view:

- **Video and Audio Roles**: To describe the kind of footage in a clip
- **360° Projection Mode**: To indicate the type of 360° footage
- **Field Dominance Override**: To adjust interlacing settings
- **Anamorphic Override**: To squish footage shot with anamorphic lenses
- **Deinterlace**: To remove unwanted interlacing
- **Color Space Override**: To force a particular color space, such as Rec. 709 or Rec. 2020
- **Camera LUT**: To automatically correct footage shot in a variety of flat "Log" formats (more on that in *Chapter 11, Play with Light: Color Correction and Grading*):

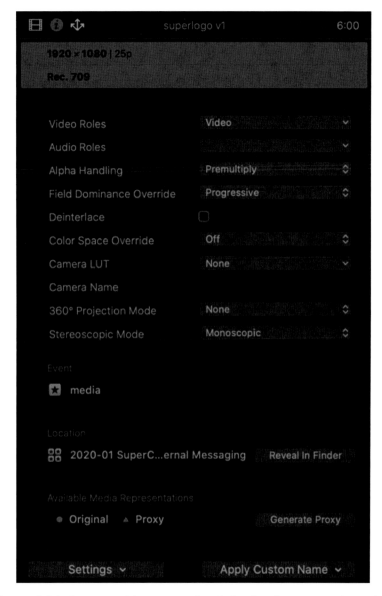

Figure 4.24: An unexciting example of the Settings metadata view

If you don't know what all these settings do, that's fine — many lucky editors will never have to deal with interlaced footage in a progressive world. But if you ever need them, this is where they live. An entire shoot can often be corrected in one click because many selected clips can be changed at once.

As well as these switches, several fields are designed to be filled in by you or (if you're lucky!) by an assistant editor:

- Switch to the **General** or **Extended** metadata views to see **Reel**, **Scene**, and **Take**, as well as the **Camera Name** and **Camera Angle** fields used in multicam workflows.

These fields are the easiest to set in bulk in the Inspector (for example, a scene's worth of clips at a time) and then viewed through **List** view.

REVIEW — EXAMINING METADATA

Whether you use the Inspector or the Browser's columns to inspect metadata, you'll find them invaluable for technical information and clip-level controls. Remember that while **List** view is convenient for common items, the different views available in the Inspector are where all the deeper details are hiding.

While clip-level metadata is informative, it doesn't describe the content of clips. A description of the content of a clip (or part of a clip) is metadata, but it's the kind of metadata you'll mostly need to add on your own — and that's done with Keywords.

UNDERSTANDING AND APPLYING KEYWORDS

The simplest way to get started with Keywords is to think of a simple one- or two-word description of your clips, something that will help you to find that clip again later. One common strategy is to focus on what's actually in the shot, such as water, trees, skies, people, or animals. Another strategy might focus on how the shots will be used: A-roll and B-roll, introductory shots, and conclusion shots. Perhaps focal length would be helpful: close up, medium shot, or long shot. There are many strategies that could succeed in different workflows and at different parts of the editing process. Yes, Keywords are metadata, but they are less about the technical aspects and more about the shot content, and they're stored in the Library, rather than on the media files themselves.

Here's the big problem with the traditional "bin" structure, which is essentially just like putting files into specific folders (and subfolders) in the Finder. You can put clips into folders or bins that approximate one of these organizational strategies, but you can't do them all at the same time. You're also out of luck if a clip could be classed as two items of the same category: a shot with water and trees, for example, or if part of a clip has water and part of it has trees.

Keywords solve all these problems because you can tag a clip with several Keywords at the same time, over its full length or just part of it. A single clip might have all these Keywords applied: water, trees, B-roll, people, long shot, and group shot. Crucially, FCP can find this clip under any of these Keywords, not just in a single subfolder in a structure — it's a fantastic system and far superior to simple bins or folders.

Before we get to the specifics, a little planning will go a long way to figure out the Keywords that will best apply to each job you do. First, think of categories (ways you might want to search for things), then think of the actual Keywords within each category. Here are some example categories with their relevant Keywords:

- **Shot content**: `water`, `trees`, `hands`, `buildings`, `abstract`, `grass`, `people`, `animals`, `boats`, `planes`, or `paper`...this really does vary a lot depending on the kind of footage you're working with.

- **Location**: `interior`, `exterior`, `stage`, `set`, `park`, `foyer`, `office`, `carpark`, `backlot`, `desert`, `lake`, or `field`

- **Script-based**: `reel`, `scene`, `shot`, `take`, or `circled`

- **Focal length**: `extreme close up`, `close up`, `medium`, `head and shoulders`, `long`, `tele`, or `over the shoulder`

- **Planned usage**: `A-roll`, `B-roll`, `introduction`, or `conclusion`

- **Rights**: `royalty-free`, `royalty-paid`, `original`, `archival`, or `stock`

- **Legal Permissions**: `release signed`, `location release signed`, `parental release signed`, or `release not required`

- **People**: `one person`, `two people`, or `group shot`

- **Selected shots**: `best`, `good`, `worst`, or `check continuity`

More importantly, you don't have to use all these strategies for every job. If you're editing a family holiday video, perhaps just a set of content Keywords are going to be most useful. For a trip to Venice, my content Keywords included `accademia`, `canals`, `crowds`, `family`, `gondolas`, `piazza san marco`, `rooftops`, `streets`, `walking`, and `water` CU (**close up**):

Figure 4.25: The content-based Keywords I ended up using for this Event,
shown as Keyword Collections

I found that I didn't need to add focal length or any other categorizations because for searching, content was enough. Don't think you need to prepare all the individual Keywords ahead of time; you can make them up as you go along. A rough plan of the categories you want to apply, and a few of the Keywords within them, will get you started.

APPLYING KEYWORDS TO CLIPS

Once you have a rough plan, it's time to add Keywords to your clips, and here's how:

1. At the top left of the interface, find and press the **Key** button to open up the **Keywords** floating window:

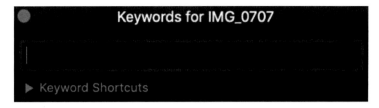

Figure 4.26: The title of the window will confirm which clip you're working on

This window can expand to show Keyword Shortcuts, but if you haven't used it before, it'll just show a single blank line. That's fine for now.

2. Click on the first clip in your **Event** to select it.

3. In the **Keywords** window, type the first Keyword that describes this clip, then press **tab**, **comma**, or **return** to finalize the Keyword:

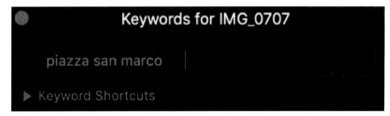

Figure 4.27: When a Keyword is finalized, it's wrapped up in a blue box

4. If you can think of another Keyword that could apply, repeat this process to add a second Keyword. They will then alphabetically sort themselves, as shown:

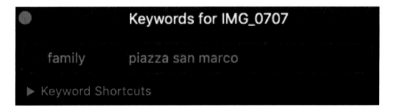

Figure 4.28: Alphabetical order will apply, no matter what order you add the Keywords

Now that you've added a couple of Keywords, you'll have also created a couple of **Keyword Shortcuts** along the way automatically. To see them, do the following:

1. Click the disclosure triangle to the left of **Keyword Shortcuts** at the bottom of the **Keywords** window to show the shortcuts:

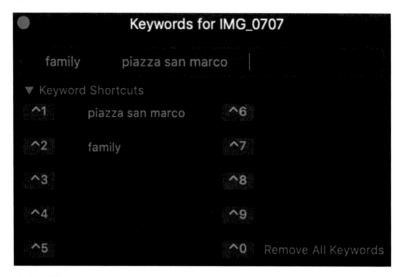

Figure 4.29: The Keyword Shortcut fields here will be empty if you've never added Keywords on this Mac

Each Keyword you apply is also added to the persistent shortcut fields below, using shortcuts using the ⌃ key and the numbers: ⌃**1** to ⌃**9**. These are remembered, so if Keywords have been added to any Library on this Mac before now, you might see other shortcuts already here.

Those shortcut fields can be edited by clicking and typing directly, but changing shortcuts doesn't affect the current clip. The Keywords for the current clip are still shown at the top of the window and that doesn't change no matter what Keywords are shown in the shortcut fields.

2. Press ↓ to move to the next clip and type new Keywords.

3. If you start typing the first letters of an existing Keyword, it will offer to autocomplete it — press **comma**, **tab**, or **return** to accept the suggestion, or keep typing something else.

4. Use the shortcut keys to apply existing Keywords. You can also click on the button next to the shortcut field if you prefer.

IMPORTANT NOTE

As you continue to assign Keywords to an entire shoot worth of shots, you might run out of shortcut slots — or they might already be taken up with previously added shortcuts. That's OK because you can edit those shortcut fields, removing less-used shortcuts and replacing them with more common ones. It's also possible to add multiple Keywords to a single shortcut if you want to. Keyword Shortcuts are also persistent, and every now and again you'll want to clear them out. Double-click on the first shortcut field to select it, then repeatedly press **delete** (to remove the current Keyword shortcut) and **tab** (to jump to the next field).

As each new Keyword is created, a **Keyword Collection** will also be created in your Event, as seen in *Figure 4.25*. Each one collects all the clips tagged with that Keyword — just click on a Keyword Collection to see all those clips together. Less obviously, Keyword Collections can also be used for assigning Keywords, like this:

1. Click the disclosure triangle to the left of an Event name to reveal all the Keyword Collections for that Event.

2. Drag a clip into an existing Keyword Collection to apply that Keyword to that clip.

If you're curious about which exact Keywords have been added to a clip, you can do one of the following:

- Open the **Keywords** window and check the top line:

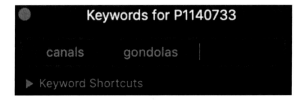

Figure 4.30: The Keywords window shows the Keywords for the current selection

- Choose **View** > **Browser** > **Skimmer Info** (**^Y**) and hover over the clip:

P1140733
canals, gondolas
01:00:14

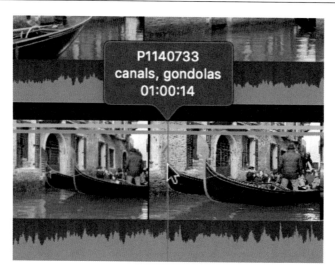

Figure 4.31: Skimmer Info shows the Keywords for the frame the cursor is over

- Switch to **List** view and click the disclosure triangle to the left of a clip name:

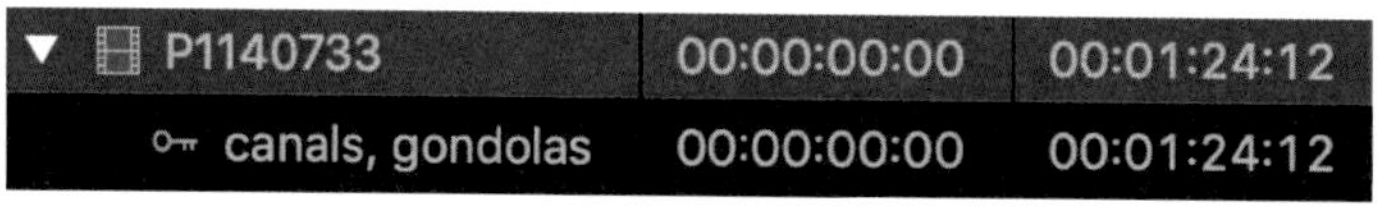

P1140733
00:00:00:00
00:01:24:12
canals, gondolas
00:00:00:00
00:01:24:12

Figure 4.32: The Keywords can be exposed in List view, but it's not as convenient as the other methods

You may also notice that clips with Keywords display a blue line across their thumbnail filmstrip. The blue line indicates that a Keyword has been added, and other colors are used to indicate other properties:

P1140733

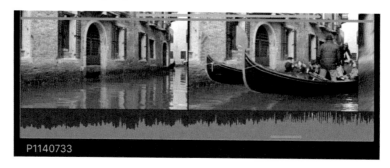

Figure 4.33: Blue means a Keyword has been applied; green and orange are coming soon!

If you want to add Keywords to everything (a good idea), you can visually scan these blue indicators to find clips that you haven't added Keywords to — but there's an even easier way of doing this.

At the top of the Browser, find the **Clip Filtering** menu, which probably says **All Clips** or **Hide Rejected**. This menu changes which clips are currently shown, hiding those which don't satisfy the criteria:

1. Choose **No Ratings or Keywords** from the **Clip Filtering** menu:

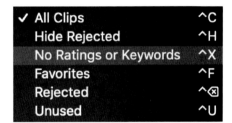

Figure 4.34: The Clip Filtering menu governs what you see in the Browser (ratings are coming soon!)

Now, you'll only see clips you haven't dealt with yet, and as you add Keywords to these clips, they will disappear from this view. It's important to realize that this will only help you add the first Keyword to each clip, and if you want to add multiple Keywords to each clip in your first pass through your clips, this will be counterproductive. When all the clips have Keywords, take the following step.

2. Choose **All Clips** from the **Clip Filtering** menu to show everything once again.

    If you now want to add additional Keywords to some of your clips, repeat the earlier steps. You can easily type additional Keywords into the **Keywords** window, use Keyword Shortcuts, or drag clips into Keyword Collections.

Here's one last super-speedy way to add Keywords:

1. In the Browser, click on the background to make sure no clips are selected.
2. Hover your cursor over a clip you want to add a Keyword to, but don't click!
3. Press a Keyword shortcut to add the matching Keyword(s) to that clip.
4. Repeat the process, hovering and then tapping a Keyword shortcut over all the remaining clips.

IMPORTANT NOTE

If you've accidentally clicked and dragged on part of a clip before applying a Keyword, only that part of the clip will have the Keyword applied. This can absolutely be a useful workflow, especially with longer clips, and we will tackle it soon. For now, if you have accidentally selected just part of a clip, you can remove a selection with ⌥X. If you've already added a Keyword to just part of a clip, you can select that Keyword instance in **List view** (under the disclosure triangle) and then delete it from the **Keyword** window.

We'll look at selecting parts of clips in *Chapter 5, Choose Your Favorites: Selecting, Rating, and Searching*. For now, let's make FCP do some work for us!

AUTOMATIC TAGGING FOR PEOPLE

While Final Cut Pro can't suggest Keywords for the content of your clips, it will tag your clips with people-related analysis Keywords to tell you how many people are visible in a shot, and what kind of composition was used to record them. To create these Keywords, do the following:

1. Select some or all of your clips that feature people by clicking on one and ⇧-**clicking** another, by ⌘-**clicking** on separate clips, or by dragging a box around several clips. (If some clips do not feature people, they'll be ignored.)

2. Right-click and then choose **Analyze and Fix**.

3. In the sheet that appears, check **Find people** and the two checkboxes underneath it, as shown:

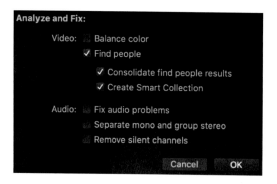

Figure 4.35: Clips can be analyzed for color, people in the shot, or audio issues

4. Click on **OK**, and wait for the process to complete by watching the circle-based progress indicator or the **Background Tasks** window:

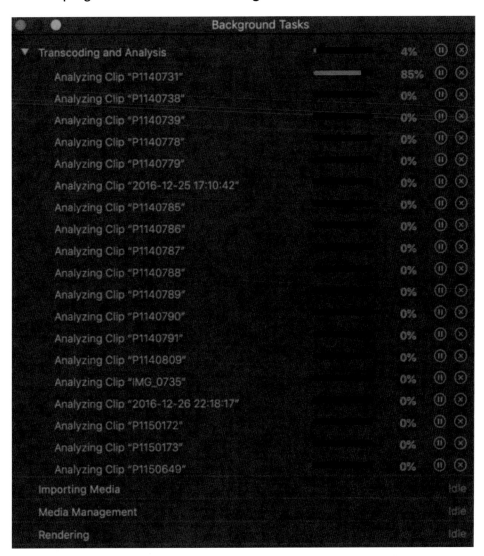

Figure 4.36: Analysis can take a while if a large number of clips are chosen — which is one reason not to do this at import time

When the analysis is complete, **Analysis Keywords** (a purple bar below the blue one) will have been applied to the clips where people have been detected. You'll also see a new folder within your Keyword Collections called **People**. Inside it, you'll see small "cog" icons, Smart Collections, which collect shots of particular types, such as **Group**, **Medium Shot**, **One Person**, and so on, as follows:

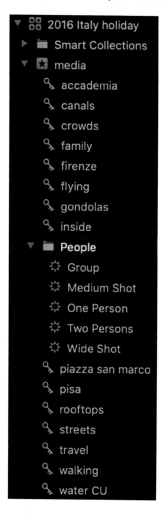

Figure 4.37: All these Keywords can be used to isolate specific kinds of shots

If you're following along with your own footage, you might get different results. Make sure to analyze different shots of people to see a variety of results. The folder is something you can also create on your own, with **File** > **New** > **Folder**. This folder isn't a bin, though: here, a folder is for organizing Keyword Collections. You can add as many folders as you wish — if you've added enough Keywords to make that worthwhile, of course.

REVIEW — UNDERSTANDING AND APPLYING KEYWORDS

Now, you know why Keywords are important, and how to add your own Keywords by typing, by using shortcuts, by dragging into Keyword Collections, and even how to get the app to add people-related Keywords for you.

Keywords are a big deal: effectively, Keywords are the difference between a carefully cataloged bookshelf and a loose pile of books on the floor. Without Keywords, you'll spend a lot of time repeatedly viewing the same media as you try to find what you're looking for, and bins or folders are just too crude to properly handle larger tasks.

But applying Keywords is only part of the story. How do you use them to quickly find the shots you need?

SEARCHING WITH KEYWORDS

Time to reap the harvest: here, you will use the Keywords you've applied to find clips easily. You'll also discover how to take this further. But first: the simple, important, magic part.

As you've seen, when you apply a Keyword (such as `gondolas`) to a clip, you're also adding it to a matching **Keyword Collection**, gathering all the clips that share the same Keyword without actually moving those clips to a separate location.

You can see the clip in the Keyword Collection, but you can also see it in the Event where it was imported, and in the Keyword Collections for any other Keywords you've added to the same clips. There's no downside here; the clip is effectively in all these places at once. Magic!

Figure 4.38: The "gondolas" Keyword Collection has anything with a gondola, and many of these clips have other Keywords applied too

Keyword Collections collect related clips just as well as folders or bins can, with the bonus that the same clip can appear in multiple Keyword Collections — a clip could have `water` and `gondolas` applied, for example. This means you can find clips *far more easily* during the editing process. Applying multiple Keywords to a single clip makes it easier to find, unlike bins or folders, which lock a clip away in a single place and can make it harder to find.

Even better, it's easy to combine the contents of multiple Keyword Collections:

1. Click on one Keyword Collection to select it, and you'll see the clips with that Keyword to the right.

2. **⌘-click** on a second Keyword Collection to also show clips with that Keyword.

This makes it easy to broaden your search, so you could find `rooftops` **OR** `canals`. But what if you want shots with `rooftops` **AND** `canals`? That's pretty easy too, but requires a different approach:

1. Click on the magnifying glass icon in the top-right corner of the Browser to drop down a search field.

   You could type in this field to locate clips with a phrase in their name, in the **Notes** field, in their Keywords, and more, but we won't. Instead, we'll take the following steps.

2. Click on the small window icon to the right of the new search field.

   This causes the **Filter** window to appear, and it's very powerful:

Figure 4.39: Filtering starts with text, but can do much more

   You can search for text in the field at the top of this window, or add additional criteria, which is what we will do.

3. In the top-right corner of the **Filter** window, press the **Plus** button, and choose **Keywords**:

Figure 4.40: Filtering by Keywords allows more complex searches

It's possible to filter by many different metadata items, but Keywords suit us here.

4. Using the controls within the **Keywords** area, uncheck all the Keywords, then check only two of your Keywords, like this:

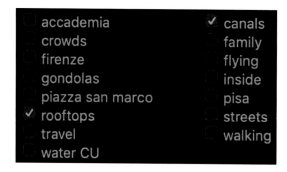

Figure 4.41: Check two of your Keywords at once

5. Change **Include Any** to **Include All** to change the `or` operation to an `and` operation, like this:

Figure 4.42: Include All rather than Include Any

6. Now, only clips with both those Keywords will appear in the view beneath it:

Figure 4.43: Include All means that only clips with both Keywords applied
will be shown

7. Finally, click on the **New Smart Collection** button at the bottom of the **Filter** window.

   A **Smart Collection** is like a saved search — it always displays clips that satisfy the specified criteria.

8. If the Smart Collection's name is selected and ready for editing, type a name and press **return**. (If you've clicked elsewhere and the selection has been lost, first select it with a single click and press **return** to start renaming it.)

The new Smart Collection will appear with Keyword Collections within your Event, and can be selected at any time to view its clips. You can't drag clips directly into a Smart Collection, though you can add Keywords or notes to make that clip match its search criteria. You can also double-click a Smart Collection to edit those criteria.

Very helpfully, each Library comes with a preset group of Smart Collections that collect all video files, audio files, Favorites (*Chapter 5, Choose Your Favorites: Selecting, Rating, and Searching*), projects (*Chapter 6, Build the Spine of the Story: Quick Assembly*), and still images. You can drag your own Smart Collections into this top-level folder if you want to search across multiple Events at the same time.

REVIEW — SEARCHING WITH KEYWORDS

Now, all that work creating and applying Keywords is worthwhile. You know how to show clips within a single Keyword Collection, and also how to search in more advanced ways for clips that satisfy multiple Keywords. Persistent Smart Collections allow you to keep a search active; Keywords go way beyond what simple bins or folders can do, and we've only scratched the surface. In the next chapter, we'll get into selecting parts of clips, but first, let's wrap things up.

SUMMARY

This chapter covered several important features. By now, you should know all kinds of shortcuts for moving around your footage instantly, know how to deal with the Viewer, how to manipulate the Browser, understand what metadata is and how to find it, and all about how to plan for, apply, and search with Keywords. If you've been working along with your own footage, and especially if you've never worked this way before, I hope you're seeing the power of Keywords for yourself. You might want to jump straight into a timeline now!

But don't start editing just yet. There's one more thing you should do first, and it's just as useful as keywording. In the next chapter, we're going to mark the best parts of our best clips as our Favorites. It's going to be great.

REVIEW QUESTIONS

1. Which line moves with the cursor, the playhead, or skimmer?

2. Where do you find the **Better Quality** and **Better Performance** playback options?

3. Which view allows you to view and rearrange columns?

4. Which of these keys does not play a clip forwards: **J**, **space**, **L**?

5. What's the shortcut to move forward ten frames?

6. Out of the three buttons to show or hide parts of the interface, which one shows or hides the Timeline pane?

7. Can you apply more than one keyword to a clip?

8. Which modifier key do you hold down to add a Keyword Shortcut?

9. Where can you find the **Anamorphic Override** option?

10. What's the shortcut to toggle skimmer info?

REVIEW ANSWERS

1. Skimmer.

2. In the **View** menu at the top right corner of the Viewer.

3. **List view**.

4. **J**, which plays backwards.

5. ⇧→ (**Shift-right arrow**).

6. The middle one out of the three.

7. Yes, you can apply as many as you want.

8. ⌃ (**Control**).

9. In the Settings metadata view in the **Info** tab in the Inspector.

10. ⌃**Y** (**Control-Y**).

5 CHOOSE YOUR FAVORITES:
SELECTING, RATING, AND SEARCHING

"I've edited on everything from a KEM table to an iPhone, and FCP X is the most enjoyable way I've ever translated ideas into edits."
— Alan Seawright is an Emmy-winning director and editor from the mountains of Utah (www.alanseawright.com)

Organizing your clips with Keywords is an important first step, but it's not the whole story. Keywords tell you roughly what each clip contains, or what it can be used for, but just as important is knowing which parts of a clip are best. Soon after you apply Keywords to entire clips, you should select the best parts and then mark them for later retrieval. Final Cut Pro makes all that easy, allowing you to define a range with an In and Out point, then apply Favorites and/or Keywords to just that clip segment. Within a short time, you'll have not only an organized view of all your clips but also an organized view of the best parts of your clips. Get this right, and the editing process becomes much easier.

This chapter includes the following topics:

- Selecting part of a clip
- Favoriting
- Rejecting
- Storing additional information
- Advanced searches

SELECTING PART OF A CLIP

To date, we've been working with entire clips — whatever the camera recorded — but editing is about selecting just the best parts. The Browser is a great place to do that because your choices will be automatically recorded. First, we'll select ranges on clips, and next, we'll rate.

The selection process has a few subtleties, so make sure you're working with clips that haven't been partly selected already, and follow these steps carefully:

1. Switch to **Filmstrip** view, not List view. (While these steps can mostly be performed in List view too, we'll use Filmstrip view here.)

2. Click on the background, which is the space between clips.

   This will deselect any clips that have been fully selected, which makes the next step simpler. To select part of a clip, it's now easy to click and drag.

3. Click on a blank, unselected area inside a clip, then drag forward to another point in that same clip, and release.

This marks an **In point** where you clicked and an **Out point** where you released, marking this part of the clip as your selection. It's also possible to drag backward to the left, in which case you'll be dragging from the Out and releasing on the In point:

Figure 5.1: The start and end of this clip aren't what I wanted, but a chunk of the middle is

Once you've marked an In and Out point on a clip, it will be remembered until a new In and Out point is marked on that same clip. This is the case even if you click on the background between clips. However, you can change the selection:

- Starting from a point outside the current selection, drag a new selection from In to Out.

The current selection can also be adjusted with the mouse:

- Drag on the edges of the current selection to move the In or Out points:

Figure 5.2: Dragging the edges of an existing selection is obvious and works, but is slow

But it's much easier to position (or reposition) a selection with two easily remembered shortcut keys. Place the playhead, skim over a clip, or simply start playback, then do the following:

- Press **I** to set an **In point** at the current skimmer or playhead position.
- Press **O** to set an **Out point** at the current skimmer or playhead position.

The **I** and **O** shortcuts are much faster than trying to pick up the edge of a selection and dragging it to the right spot, and they let you use any method (keyboard or mouse trackpad) to move through a clip. The original In and Out points are simply replaced if you tap **I** or **O** again, and you can change your mind repeatedly. You can even tap **I** or **O** while the video is playing, and combined with **JKL**'s multi-speed playback, you'll be able to mark exactly the right part of a clip very quickly, and we'll practice this soon.

Here's an illustrated sequence of how you might mark up a clip with a false start:

1. Starting with selection on a clip, press **Space** to start playback:

Figure 5.3: Playback has started, so watch the Viewer

2. After a few seconds, tap **I** to set a new In point:

Figure 5.4: Tap I to set a new In point; keep it playing

3. After a few more seconds, tap **I** again, clearing the last In point and setting a new one:

Figure 5.5: Tap I again to set another new In point; keep it playing

4. Finally, let the clip play for several more seconds, then tap **O** to set an Out point:

Figure 5.6: Tap O to set the Out point and you're done

Sometimes, you'll want to clear the current selection entirely, or clear selections on several clips at once. If selection ranges have already been created on one or more clips and you want to start over, do the following:

*   Press ⌥**X** to remove a selection from all the selected clips.

While tapping **I** or **O** is usually quickest, if you want to able to drag and release to make a new selection, always press ⌥**X** to clear the old selection first. If you don't, you'll often end up dragging the old selection instead. This is a more common issue in List view, because clicking to select a full clip there is more persistent.

> **IMPORTANT NOTE**
> It is possible to create multiple In and Out points on a single clip, but the next section of the chapter makes this largely unnecessary. Still, if you need to select an additional range on a single clip, hold ⌘ while you drag on its thumbnail.

Let's finish with a quick word about the persistence of selections. As you've no doubt found already, clicking on a clip selects it all, showing a yellow outline. Essentially, you've marked an In point at the start, and an Out point at the end. Selecting a whole clip like this is helpful if you want to add a Keyword to an entire clip, or if you want to use an entire clip in an edit, but clicking next to the clip's filmstrip in List view doesn't remove that selection.

That said, if you've selected part of a clip, clicking next to that clip doesn't remove it *in either Filmstrip or List view*. Dragging the edges of an existing selection is slow and painful, so use ⌥**X**, **I**, or **O** to select what you really want, and train yourself out of needlessly clicking, especially in List view.

REVIEW – SELECTING PART OF A CLIP

You've learned how to select with click-and-drag, and how to do it with the keyboard too — **I** and **O** are great for revising selected ranges or creating them in the first place. Remember too that if you need to start again, clear those ranges out with ⌥**X**, and avoid needless clicking because it just creates work for yourself.

But we're only halfway there. While it's true that a selection is persistent, it's still pretty fragile, and could be lost with a single keypress. How to make them more permanent? The solution is **Favorites**.

RATING AS A FAVORITE

Here, I'll show you not only how to rate parts of clips as "good," but also give you a few workflow tips that you can apply to your own content. Seeing this part of the process in action is one of the magic "wow" moments you'll encounter as you learn FCP, so don't skip it. This is simple stuff, but powerful.

A selection is temporary, so if you've selected the "good" part of a clip, you should then mark it as a Favorite so that your choice will be remembered and be easier to find later. This is done with just one key:

- Press **F** to mark the selection as a **Favorite**.

On the thumbnail, a Favorite is shown as a green line, above the blue Keyword line. If you want to mark another part of the same clip as a Favorite, that's fine — just repeat the same steps as before:

1. Press **I** to set an **In point** at the current skimmer or playhead position.

2. Press **O** to set an **Out point** at the current skimmer or playhead position.

3. Press **F** to mark the selection as a **Favorite**:

Figure 5.7: Marking your selection as a Favorite is a great way to remember it

Ideally, you'll have a selection active when you press **F**. But if no selection is active, the entire current clip will be marked as a Favorite — sometimes useful, often not. Usually, the quickest thing to do is undo (**⌘Z**), but you can also remove a Favorite by unrating it:

- Press **U** to **remove Favorites** from the selection.

Now, it's just a matter of marking everything you like as a Favorite. If you're working with a longer clip, such as an interview or longer B-roll, you'll want to scan it for potentially useful content. It'll go something like this:

1. Hover near the start of a clip, then press the **spacebar** to start playback.

2. If nothing interesting is happening, press **L** once or twice (to speed up) until something potentially interesting starts.

3. Press **J** to skim back to where the potentially interesting thing begins, then press **L** to play forward, and **I** to mark an In point.

4. Watch and listen to the video as it plays back.

5. If this section ends up being good, press **O** at the end, and then **F** to mark it as a Favorite.

6. If it's no good, don't mark a Favorite; just play forward, at high speed if necessary.

7. Repeat this process, pressing **I** to set a new In point when the next potentially interesting thing starts, then **O** and **F** at the end of that interesting thing.

8. At the end of one clip, press ↓ to move to the next clip. This will happen automatically if you use the Continuous Playback option.

There are several ways to mark Favorites, and many can work well. In general, I prefer to use the keyboard more heavily for interviews, with one hand for **J**, **K**, **L**, **I**, and **O**, and another on **F**. I'll use lots of quick **JKL** movement to get to the right In point before pressing **I**, and then watch like a hawk before pressing **O** at the Out point. With experience, you'll be able to anticipate the In and Out points by visually scanning the audio waveform to see where sentences start and end. There's no need to pause playback; just tap **I** and **O** as the video plays, and **F** before you reset the selection with the next press of **I**:

Figure 5.8: Most of the critical keys on a custom editing keyboard

For scanning visual B-roll, I usually prefer to use the mouse. With my right hand, I skim over the footage at high speed, clicking and dragging to select, while my left hand rests on **F** to mark as I go. Of course, using the Browser's Filmstrip view serves as a solid preview of a clip's content, so you'll have a good idea of where the In and Out points should go before you start. If you're working with your own Library, go ahead and mark several parts of several clips as Favorites now.

You can take your time with this process, or be less careful. While carefully marked Favorites will need less tweaking down the line, they'll take more time to create upfront. In general, I like to take my time with interviews, and I'm pretty loose with my B-roll edits. How long you spend on choosing your Favorites will depend on the edit, but do use them. You don't have to get your selections perfect, but the more work you do now, the less you'll have to do later:

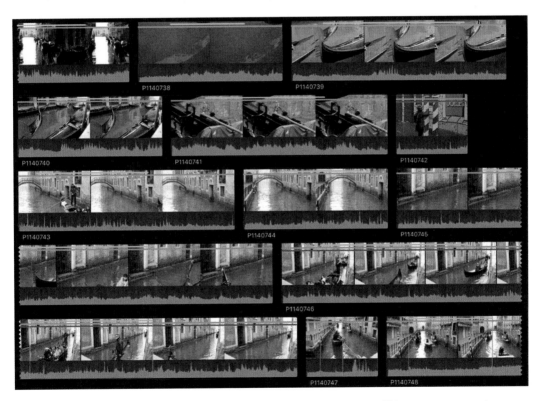

Figure 5.9: Some clips will have one Favorite, some will have more, and some will have none

OK, so you've made some green lines — so far, so good. But I promised you a "wow" moment, and here it is.

SHOWING ONLY THE FAVORITES

Your clips will now be covered in green Favorite lines, and the last selection made on each clip will still be selected in yellow. To reset the selection to one of the Favorites on a clip, you can click on its green line, which can be helpful. But it's not the best trick here. Instead, look at the top of the Browser for that **Clip Filtering** menu we used earlier, probably showing **All Clips**:

- Choose **Favorites** from this menu, or press **^F**:

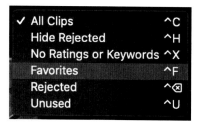

Figure 5.10: The Clip Filtering menu

Now, you're only looking at your Favorites, and everything else is hidden. Take a quick moment to let that sink in.

This is hugely helpful because you can just ignore everything you don't care about. If you've marked two parts of a single clip, then you'll see two separate clips with the same name. Keywords still work too: if you choose a **Keyword Collection** while **Favorites** is active in the **Clip Filtering** menu, then you'll see the best clips in that category. The same is also true in **Smart Collections**:

Figure 5.11: Viewing Favorites: only the best parts of the best clips remain

The less-good parts of your clips are still there if you need them — just choose **All Clips** from the **Clip Filtering** menu. It's very possible to envision your entire edit from the clips you're looking at now; all you need to do is put them in the right order. If you don't choose the right clips the first time around, you'll have easy access to a collection of the best alternatives.

REVIEW — RATING AS A FAVORITE

You've learned that Favorites are a great way to remember the best parts of your clips. **I**, **O**, and **F** are three keys you'll press a lot when you're rating the best parts of your clips, and after you add your Favorites, be sure to limit your view to **Favorites** only so that that's all you see.

If **Keywords** make a pile of books into an ordered bookshelf, **Favorites** are a collection of bookmarks drawing your attention to the best pages in every book. The **Favorites view** is like a corkboard at the front of a bookshop with a copy of all the best pages from all of those books in one place — except that everything is non-destructive, and you can change your view at any time.

While I use Favorites on almost every job I do, I don't use them on every clip. If I know that a particular segment will definitely be used, I'll simply select part of it and then immediately add it to a timeline. Favorites are used to make your decisions easier, and if a clip is important, there's no choice to be made. But, as B-roll is often changed, even if I plan to add a selected B-roll straight to a timeline, I'll press **F** first to record that clip in case I change my mind.

As awesome as they are, Favorites aren't enough for every workflow. Final Cut Pro also offers other ways to mark parts of your video, which can be useful. These ways include Rejecting, using Keywords on ranges, Markers, and notes.

RATING AS REJECTED

So far, there are two levels of "good" — the Favorite parts and the rest. But how about the "bad" parts? If you'd like to approach your rating process from the other end, you'll want to get into Rejecting, and that's what you'll learn here.

Marking part of a clip as Rejected is the opposite of marking part of a clip as a Favorite: you're saying that the selection is bad or unusable. The workflow is very similar, too:

1. With the keyboard or mouse, mark **In** and **Out** points on a clip.

2. Press the **delete** key (not forward delete) to mark that selection as **Rejected**:

P1150175

Figure 5.12: The camera was shaky at the start of this clip, so I Rejected that section

If your current Browser view is showing **All Clips**, then you'll see a red line appear on that part of the clip. A range cannot be both a Favorite and Rejected at the same time: it's one or the other, or not rated at all. Just like with Favorites, a selected area can be unrated with **U**.

There's another choice from the **Clip Filtering** menu that can be useful here: **Hide Rejected**. In this mode, you won't see red lines because those parts will be hidden entirely, and clips with Rejected sections in the middle will be split into two or more separate segments.

Marking clip segments as Rejected can be used in addition to Favorites, or instead of them if you prefer. Some editors like to Reject the clapperboard at the start and end of a clip because once that information has been used, you don't need to see it anymore. Another use is to Reject brief moments between answers in long interview clips to make each answer into an independent clip.

Personally, I don't Reject very much because I prefer to use Favorites more heavily. But if you'd prefer not to limit your view to Favorites only, consider Rejecting and using **Hide Rejected** as a happy middle ground:

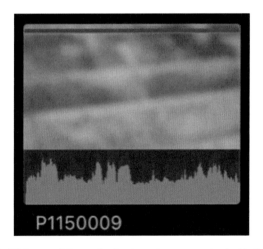

Figure 5.13: This accidental clip has been entirely Rejected, but I want it gone

One last note on really bad footage. If you encounter a clip that's entirely 100% useless — from an accidental press of the record button, for example — don't just Reject the entire clip. Instead, trash it by pressing ⌘**delete**, and the clip will be thrown away entirely. Hard drive space might be cheap, but there's no need to waste it:

Figure 5.14: This warning is the final step before a clip is deleted from a Library (and likely, the disk)

Time for a recap.

REVIEW — RATING AS REJECTED

That was fairly straightforward — if you don't like something, press **delete**, and it'll be hidden without actually being destroyed. Also, Rejecting a small part of a long clip is a nice way to break it up without picking any Favorites. Still, if a clip is totally useless, you can absolutely throw it away if you want to.

Now that you know how to rate a clip as Rejected, let's dive into the next section, where we will see different methods by which you can add notes to a clip.

STORING ADDITIONAL INFORMATION

Marking a clip segment as good or bad is powerful, but what if you want to include more substantial notes about a clip? There are several ways to do this, and while it's optional, on larger productions it's a great idea. Selective Keywords? Sure. Changing clip names or adding notes? Absolutely. Adding **Markers** to note moments in time? Done.

SELECTIVE KEYWORDS

One method is to add Keywords to specific parts of clips, rather than on entire clips. Keywords can have quite long names, and different Keywords can overlap. The process is predictable:

1. With the keyboard or mouse, mark **In** and **Out** points on a clip.
2. Use the **Keywords** window to apply a Keyword.

While this can be a handy workflow for longer, more complex clips, I usually find it's not necessary for shorter ones. Personally, I prefer to use Keywords on entire clips, and in combination with a more targeted Favorite, it's often all you need.

Adding Keywords to ranges is an option if you want another level of more targeted organization, and is more likely to be used if your operators tend to prefer longer continuous shots, potentially with several takes in a single clip. Selective Keywords are also useful when collecting related thoughts from several different clips, such as a series of interviews with different people on similar topics. You can apply Favorites as usual, but then also add a Keyword to a specific range to make a note of the subject being discussed. When all the interviews have been processed, the related sections of each interview will be gathered together in a series of Keyword Collections.

NOTES

The **Notes** field, found in the **List** view in the Browser and in the **Info** tab of the Inspector, can contain text of arbitrary length. These notes can be added to an individual clip, or even to a Favorite within a clip, and could contain notes for VFX artists, instructions from the director, or anything else. To add a note to a single clip, do the following:

- Click to the left of the **Notes** column on a clip or a Favorite, and then type your note:

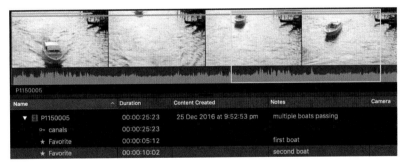

Figure 5.15: You can leave as much text in the Notes field as you wish

Alternatively, for one or more clips, do the following:

1. Select one or more clips in the Browser.

2. Open the **Inspector** and switch to the **Info** tab.

3. Switch to the **Basic**, **General**, or **Extended** metadata view using the menu in the bottom-left corner.

4. Type a note into the **Notes** field:

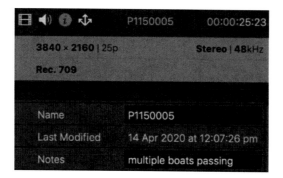

Figure 5.16: The Inspector might be an easier place to add Notes to entire clips, but not to a range

A limitation is that the Inspector can only add a note to an entire clip, not to a Favorite part of a clip. Notes aren't the only way to add general-purpose text, but they are a convenient one.

NAMES

Clip names can also hold information. While I generally recommend using the original media name as the clip name, some editors prefer to rename clips to include general text. Probably a better approach is to rename a Favorite range. Currently, each Favorite is just called **Favorite**, but it can be renamed: click once on the word **Favorite**, then press **return**, type a new name, and press **return** again to finish. If you've created multiple Favorites on the same clip, changing their names like this will help you to differentiate between them:

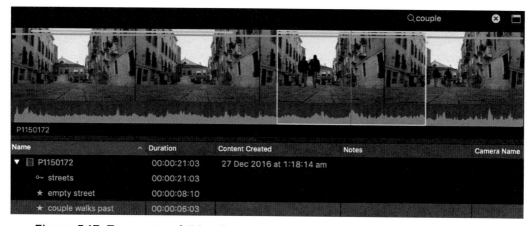

Figure 5.17: Two parts of this clip have been marked as a Favorite (the stars) but renamed, making them searchable

Now, let's move to the last method — **Markers** — which allow us to make a potentially lengthy note in a specific spot, not across a range.

MARKERS

The most specific way to add notes is to add a Marker. A Marker is attached to a particular frame, rather than a range, but its name can be long and informative. It's also possible to create different types of Markers for different functions. To create a Marker, do the following:

1. Skim to or click on a frame within a clip.

2. Press ⌥M to create a Marker and edit its name.

3. Type a name for the new Marker:

Figure 5.18: Naming a Marker

Pressing **M** alone is sufficient if you don't want to name a Marker. You could also press **M twice** to create it and then edit it, if you are careful not to move the mouse between the two keypresses. Any of these approaches make a generic Marker, and while there are two other kinds of Markers, they will be explored in *Chapter 10, Explore a Little: Compound Clips and Timeline Tricks*.

Why make a Marker? One good reason is that a Marker is easy to see in any Browser view, while Notes and Favorite names are only visible in the List view when a clip's disclosure triangle is open:

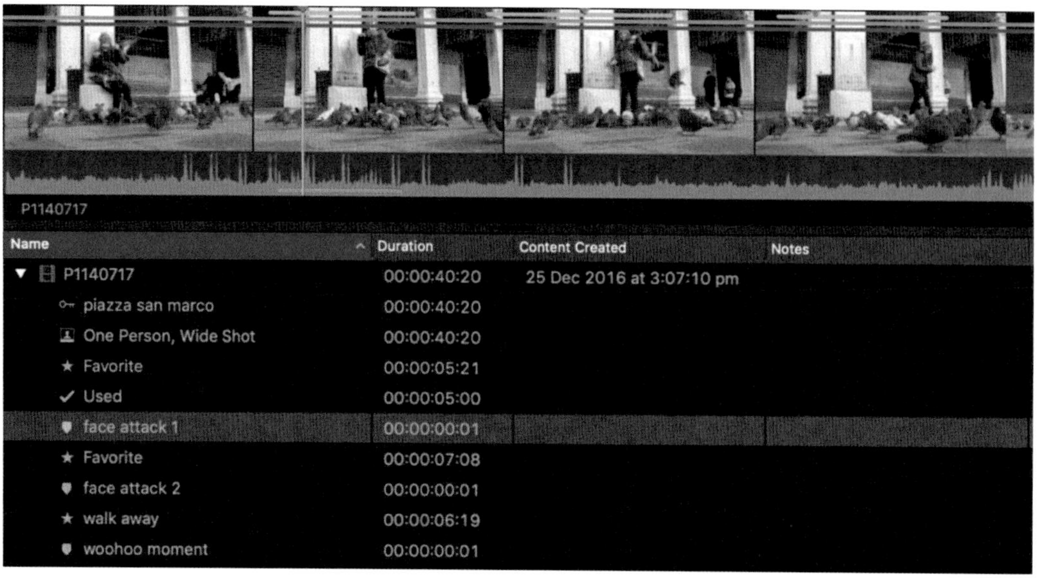

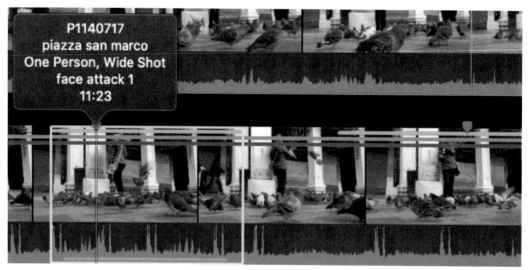

Figure 5.19: The List view lets you see all the Marker names at a glance

A Marker can be clicked on to show its name in the Skimmer Info (toggle with **^Y** if you don't see it) above your cursor, and if **Snapping** is active, then you'll hit Markers easily while you skim. **Snapping** is a feature that will be used more during the editing process, but you can press **N** to toggle it on or off at any time:

Figure 5.20: Markers visible in Filmstrip view with the Skimmer Info visible

There's no fixed workflow regarding Markers, names, or notes, so experiment to discover what works best for you.

REVIEW — STORING ADDITIONAL INFORMATION

You've learned plenty of great ways to work here, and applying Keywords to sections of clips is a useful way to step beyond even what a full-clip Keyword and a Favorite can do. If that's not what you need, you can rename a clip, rename a Favorite, add a Marker, or add some Notes. By adding text of any kind, you're making your clips easier to find, and that's going to help you when you use the search feature. As you might expect by now, it's simple at a glance, but complex if you look deeper — let's take that deeper look now.

ADVANCED SEARCHES

In a moderately sized project, you can click on a Keyword Collection to get you started, look at the Favorites, then visually scan to find the clip you remember. But on a big project, text organization is the only way to stay sane, and in this part of the book, I'll show you how to dig into searching and filtering.

In *Chapter 4, Sort it Out: Reviewing and Keywording*, I showed you how to use the **Filter** window, accessible through the magnifying glass icon at the top right of the Browser. Now that you know how to add text to your clips, the Filter window will be even more useful. To start, do the following:

1. Click on the magnifying glass icon in the top-right corner of the Browser to drop down a search field.

2. Into the search field, type a word that appears in the name of any clip or any notes field, or a name that you've given to a Favorite range or any Marker:

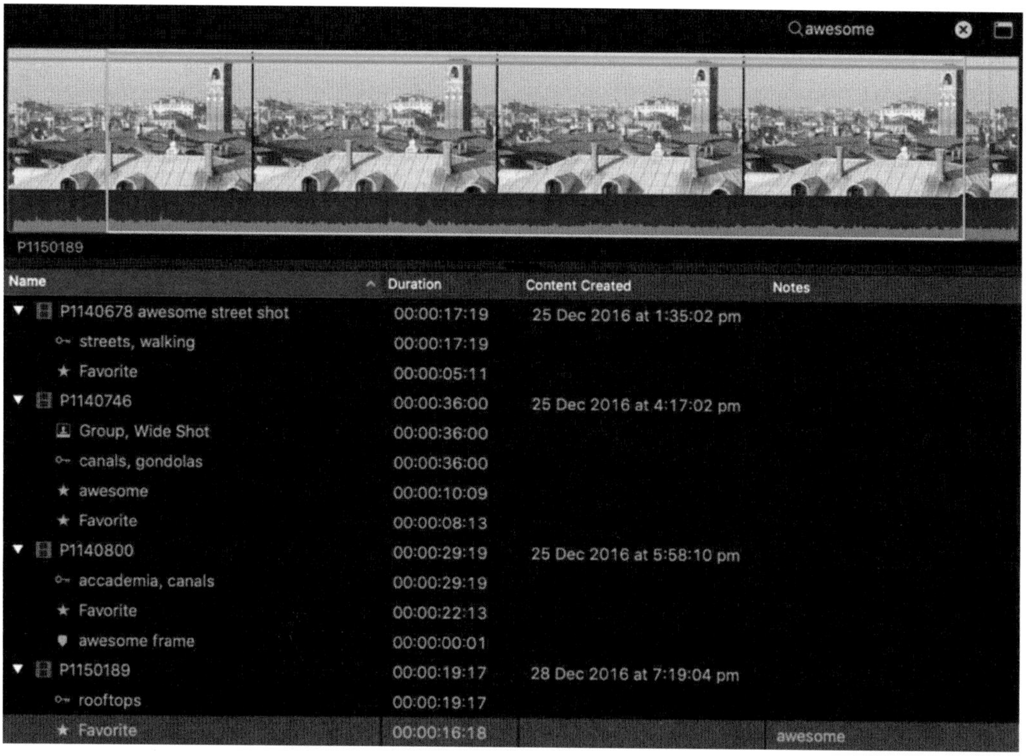

Figure 5.21: The word "awesome" can be found in Notes, clip names, Favorite names, and Markers

Within the current view, which could be a **Keyword Collection** or **Smart Collection**, you'll now only see clips that use that word somewhere. It doesn't matter which field the word is stored in:

- Click on the small window icon to the right of the new search field.

The **Filter** window will now appear, and the text field will be prepopulated with the word you chose. Just before the name, there's a menu allowing you to exclude clips with the chosen word (**Does Not Include**). You can further limit your search by including **Favorite** or **Rejected**:

- In the top-right corner of the **Filter** window, press the plus button, and choose **Ratings**.

You can now choose to show only Favorites or only Rejected clips. Because of **All** at the top left, the Rating combines with the text you searched for to constrain the results and show fewer clips. While that's probably what you want, if you want to see clips that satisfy *either Text or Rating, but not both*, you could choose **Any** instead of **All**. Then, you'll see clips that satisfy *at least one* of the criteria.

That would be good if you wanted to broaden your selection, but we want to narrow it down even further, so leave the top-left menu set to All, and then:

- Press the plus button, add **People** to the search, and choose one shot type.

Here, I'm viewing clips with **awesome** as text that are Favorites and that are of one person only:

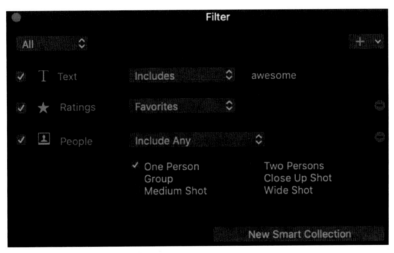

Figure 5.22: Getting more specific with text, ratings, and analysis Keywords

As before, you can save a **Smart Collection** to preserve this search for later viewing. If you continue to add Keywords, text, and ratings, then you might see more items inside this **Smart Collection** in the future.

Including those already discussed, you can filter by the following:

- **Text**, including names, Markers, notes, and more
- **Ratings**, including Favorite and Rejected regions
- **Media Type**, including **Stills**, **Video With Audio**, **Video Only**, and **Audio Only**
- **Type**, to find various special clip types, such as multicam and synchronized
- **Used Media**, to find whether a clip has been used in the current timeline — handy when you are searching for something original
- **Keywords**, to include or exclude clips with specific Keywords
- **People**, to include or exclude specific framing types or numbers of people

- **Format Info**, to search by one of several technical file characteristics
- **Date**, to search a creation or import date that is on, before, or after or a specific date, as well as in a recent timespan, such as the last week
- **Roles**, to include or exclude clips with specific roles:

Figure 5.23: You wouldn't search for everything at once, though you can

Obviously, that's a pretty comprehensive list, and you might never need all the power it offers. But if you're working on a larger project, and the director asks to see the best alternative takes of a specific line of dialogue, an open **Smart Collection** is a great way to find a shot. Tag your clips well if you want to make the best use of this.

REVIEW — ADVANCED SEARCHES

You now know that the **Filter** window can be used for a lot more than you'd first think. Larger productions can really take advantage of this, tagging all kinds of information and then finding exactly the right shot by searching for it. While Keywords on entire clips and selected ranges are probably the easiest tools to use, **Smart Collections** based on advanced searches can expose whatever you need. If you're working on a larger production, plan carefully to use this feature to its full potential.

Time for a look back at this chapter.

SUMMARY

While Keywords let you know roughly what you shot, you now know that Favorites let you focus in on the very best of what you shot. As you continue through the rest of the editing process, you'll love being able to instantly locate the best shot for any situation simply by viewing only Favorites. A huge chunk of your job is done, you don't need to repeatedly and manually search through all your clips, and you don't need to build "stringouts" either. The traditional workflow of making throwaway timelines to gather "good" clips simply can't compete with the efficiency of Keywords combined with Favorites.

For larger productions, you can see that changing clip names and adding notes, Markers, and range-based "selective" Keywords will help you (or your editorial team) to add less obvious and more subtle information to clips. With the added metadata you now know how to add, along with searching, filtering, and Smart Collections will allow you to discover the right clips when you can't just see them at a glance.

Try the Favorite approach out on a few different kinds of jobs, try Rejecting, then adding text and Markers on a few more, and you'll discover that different approaches work in different situations. If you need to get a video out in no time flat, you'll probably spend a little time on keywording and then not much at all on Favorites because you'll be editing by instinct — each clip you throw onto a Timeline has to be the right one. But longer projects will benefit from all kinds of information being added: scenes, shots, takes, multiple Favorites, Notes to help you find things, Markers to remind you of further processing, and more. Spend the time early on to save time down the track.

Next, though, it's time to make a new Project, and throw some media into it. Everything so far has been about preparing for the edit, and now it's time to jump in. Here we go!

REVIEW QUESTIONS

1. What keys can be used to mark the start and end of a range?
2. What shortcut removes the selection from all selected clips?
3. After rating some parts of your clips as Favorites, how do you see only those regions?
4. What color line is shown on a clip if you Reject all or part of it?
5. What can you use to add information to a particular frame rather than a region?
6. What is the shortcut for **Snapping**?
7. Where can you search through all text attached to a clip?
8. How can you save the results of a search?
9. Can part of a clip be marked as Rejected and Favorite at the same time?
10. Can more than one Favorite range be applied to a clip?

REVIEW ANSWERS

1. **I** and **O**.
2. **⌥X (Option-X)**.
3. Choose **Favorites** from the **Clip Filtering** menu in the Browser.
4. Red.
5. A marker.
6. **N**.
7. The search field at the top right of the Browser, or the **Filter** window.
8. Create a new **Smart Collection** in the **Filter** window.
9. No.
10. Yes, as many as you wish, though overlapping Favorite regions become a single region.

SECTION 2: ROUGH CUT TO FINE CUT

In this section, you will learn how to add media, trim and rearrange it, replace it, and manipulate more advanced timeline features in order to create an edit.

This section comprises the following chapters:

- Chapter 6, Build the Spine of the Story: Quick Assembly
- Chapter 7, Cover It Up: Connections, Cutaways, and Storylines
- Chapter 8, Neaten the Edges: Trimming Techniques
- Chapter 9, Consider Your Options: Multicam, Replacing, and Auditions
- Chapter 10, Explore a Little: Compound Clips and Timeline Tricks

6 BUILD THE SPINE OF THE STORY:
QUICK ASSEMBLY

"The organizational tools, magnetic timeline, and third-party ecosystem have made Final Cut Pro X an integral part of my editing experience on everything from corporate video, to documentaries, to feature films."
— Not to be outdone by Alan, Patrick Southern is also an Emmy award-winning editor and a Workflow Architect at Frame.io

You've got your footage imported into a Library, you've added Keywords, you've made Favorites, and you're looking at the next step: starting to put the best bits together in a sequence. Here, you'll learn how to create a new Project in which you can start your edits, and all the technical settings you need to know. As well as adding clips with shortcuts, buttons, and drag and drop, you'll learn about basic timeline operations: rearranging, trimming, breaking up, and deleting. You'll also learn how to duplicate an entire timeline.

While the steps here are easy to follow, it's possible to get frustrated if you try to fight the system and put clips far away from one another. The Magnetic Timeline has some powerful tricks, and if you're new to editing, it makes a ton of sense. That said, because of the way the Magnetic Timeline functions — closing gaps by default and using connections instead of tracks — some operations don't work exactly as experienced editors might expect them to. If that's you, don't worry! Just relax and go with the flow, rather than fighting the system. You'll still be able to get the job done, as we'll cover more advanced freeform techniques later in the book. This chapter covers the following topics:

- Creating a new Project
- Adding your media in a few different ways
- Rearranging your clips

- Basic trimming with the Magnetic Timeline
- Blading and deleting
- Duplicating Projects

At the end of this chapter, you'll have a rough cut in place — an important step in the journey toward a finished edit. That rough cut spine will be just a row of clips in a single layer, and we'll expand it, adding clips above and below the spine, in future chapters.

CREATING A NEW PROJECT

This is the part of the book where you finally get to play in a timeline, putting one clip after another and creating a story. It's important to get the technical details right, and there's plenty of that coming up soon, as well as some sneaky tricks for easy version control and weird custom Projects. But first, a terminology recap.

As you'll recall, you make a **Library** for each separate job you take on. **Libraries** hold **Events**, and **Events** hold anything smaller: **clips** and/or **Projects**. We've mostly been dealing with clips so far: importing them, keywording, selecting, and rating parts as Favorites. To put those clips in the right order and make a movie, you need to make a Project, which you can think of as your timeline, edit, or sequence. Each Project will be trimmed, finessed, finished, and shared to a final deliverable file.

Remember — the overall job is held in a **Library**, and each edit you deliver is called a **Project**. When you open up a Project, it's shown in the **Timeline** pane of the interface. When talking to clients, I tend to use the term "timeline" or "edit" to avoid confusion, because the term "Project" has other meanings outside of FCP.

Naming aside, creating a Project can be pretty simple:

1. Select the Event where you want to store a Project.
2. Go to **File > New > Project (⌘N)**.
3. With the simple **Automatic Settings** shown, give the Project a name ending in v 1 (the space is important, and you'll see why at the end of this chapter):

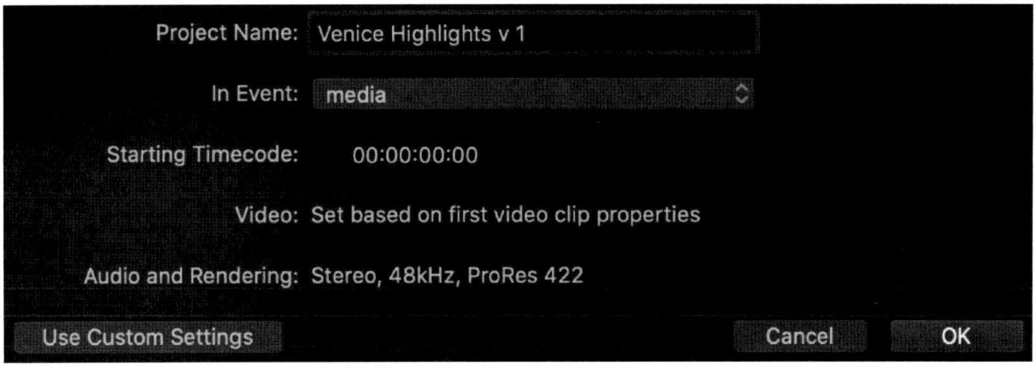

Project Name: Venice Highlights v 1

In Event: media

Starting Timecode: 00:00:00:00

Video: Set based on first video clip properties

Audio and Rendering: Stereo, 48kHz, ProRes 422

Use Custom Settings   Cancel   OK

Figure 6.1: If you see Use Custom Settings at the bottom left, you're looking at Automatic Settings

4. Click **OK** to create your first Project.

Great — you'll see a timeline appear at the bottom of the screen, and you'll also see your new Project in your Browser with a new kind of icon at the top of the list:

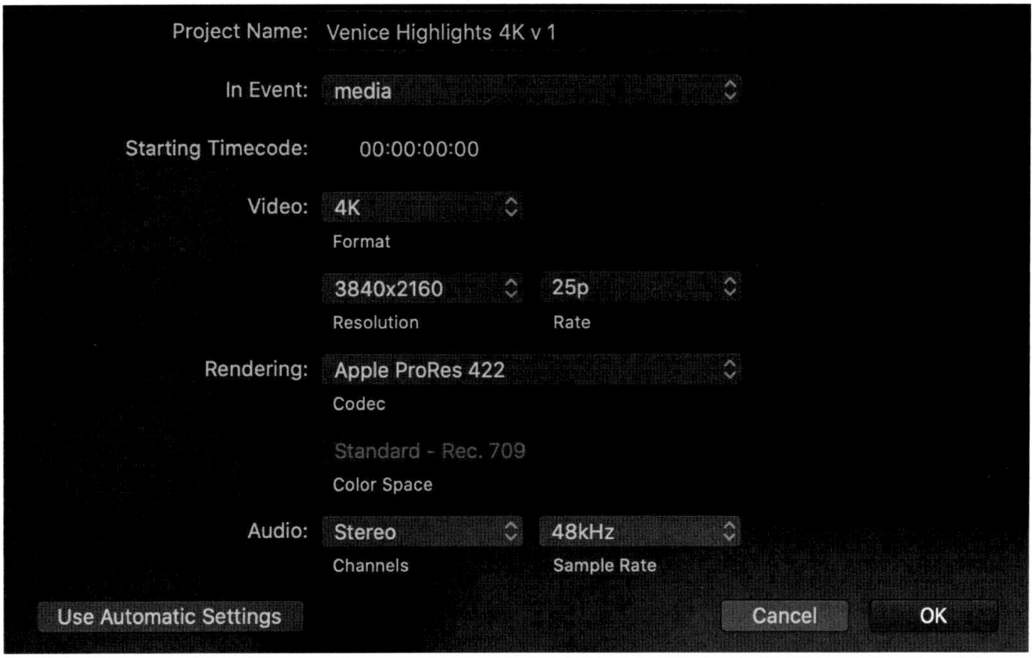

Project Name: Venice Highlights 4K v 1

In Event: media

Starting Timecode: 00:00:00:00

Video: 4K
Format

3840x2160   25p
Resolution   Rate

Rendering: Apple ProRes 422
Codec

Standard - Rec. 709
Color Space

Audio: Stereo   48kHz
Channels   Sample Rate

Use Automatic Settings   Cancel   OK

Figure 6.2: A new Project, ready for clips

If you need to rename a Project, do the following:

1. Click once on the name.

2. Press **return**, then type the new name.

Double-clicking on a Project name will open that Project, so if you want to rename it, be sure to leave a pause between clicks.

THE PERILS OF AUTOMATIC SETTINGS

By default, **Automatic Settings** defines the frame rate and resolution of the Project by matching the first clip you add to the timeline. While you'll often want to shoot and export with the same settings, that's not always the case. **Automatic Settings** can get you into trouble if you've shot footage with a variety of frame rates, or if you need to deliver to a non-standard aspect ratio, such as a square (1:1) or vertical (9:16).

For example, if you've shot most of the footage at 25p and plan to deliver that, you would also want to set your timeline to 25p. But if a client provides additional iPhone clips shot at 30p, and you add one of those clips to your timeline first, your timeline will be set to 30p. Another common trap is sprung if the first clip you add doesn't have a frame rate (such as a still image) or a resolution (such as a music track). Adding one of these clips first causes FCP to ask you what settings you'd like for your Project, forcing you to pick your settings manually after all.

Getting one of these settings wrong can be a huge issue, because a Project's frame rate cannot be changed unless it is empty; you can only copy its contents, then paste them into another Project and mess up all the edits. While a Project's resolution can be changed, if you change the aspect ratio, all your clips will be repositioned.

To avoid all these problems, I'd recommend going a step further when creating a Project:

1. Go to **File > New > Project (⌘N)** and give this Project a different name (still ending in `v 1`, as before).

2. Click on **Use Custom Settings** in the bottom-left corner to see the full set of options:

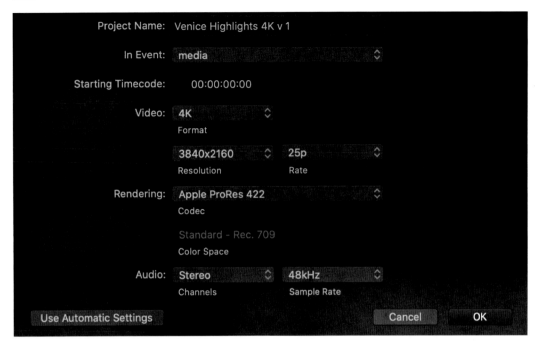

Figure 6.3: If you see Use Automatic Settings in the bottom left, you're looking at Custom Settings

These controls can be important, but what do they all mean? Read on.

CUSTOM PROJECT SETTINGS

Custom Settings lets you define exactly what resolution, frame rate, and rendering codec you want to use for this Project. You should know what you want to deliver, so getting the settings right should be simple. In most cases, you should do the following:

1. Under **Video**, choose **4K** or **1080p HD** from the first drop-down menu:

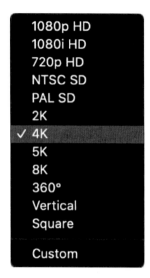

Figure 6.4: Here, I've chosen 4K, but if you want to choose 1080p HD, that's fine

2. Confirm that the first item in the second drop-down menu is selected. This will be **3840×2160** for 4K:

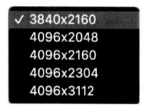

Figure 6.5: In 4K, the first resolution (also known as UHD or 2160p) is most common

Or, this will be **1920×1080** for 1080p:

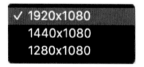

Figure 6.6: In 1080p, you'll almost always use the first resolution

3. Choose **24p**, **25p**, **30p** or something else, depending on the requirements:

Figure 6.7: Here, I've chosen 25p, although you may choose something
entirely different

You'll remember from *Chapter 2, Before the Edit: Production Tips*, that the frame rate should probably match what you've shot. If you're delivering online, it won't matter much, so long as you're consistent, but your choice might be forced by your region and your equipment. In terms of resolution, I like to deliver 4K when I can, but if the spec says 1080p, that's fine.

Rendering and **Audio** are normally fine on their default settings: **Apple ProRes 422** and **Stereo** at **48kHz**. All the other **Rendering** options are higher quality than you'll likely need, and most delivery methods can't handle surround sound. Still, you can absolutely deliver a surround mix direct from FCP if you want to, so experiment if you have the gear to play it back.

A final note: if you've jumped ahead and created a Wide Gamut Library, then you'll see options for Wide Gamut Projects here too, but that's something for *Chapter 11, Play With Light: Color Correction and Grading*.

NON-STANDARD RESOLUTIONS

If you want to deliver to a non-widescreen format, likely for social media, then you'll want to follow the specifications. Social media is unlikely to be fussy about frame rate (30fps or lower should be fine), but the aspect ratio is important. The **Video** menu here allows you to choose **Vertical**, **Square**, or **Custom**, and between them, you can do anything you like. **Vertical** and **Square** include common resolution presets for those aspect ratios, but if you need something else, choose a custom resolution, like this:

1. Under **Video**, choose **Custom** from the first drop-down menu.

2. In the two fields that appear below, type in the width and height that the specifications ask for:

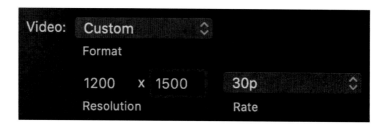

Figure 6.8: With Custom, you can choose anything you want

Those numbers are one option for an **Instagram In-Feed (4:5)** video, which specifies 600×750 or 1200×1500.

Essentially, you can make pretty much anything you need. I've delivered 2000×96 and 1536×144 videos for use on advertising boards at stadiums, and that's not the strangest thing you might be asked for. More importantly, if you need to deliver to multiple aspect ratios, such as widescreen and portrait versions of the same edit, you should account for this during the shoot by shooting wider than usual, then cropping to suit each delivery aspect ratio.

You'll find out more about cropping in *Chapter 12, Refine and Smooth: Video Properties and Effects*. You'll also find out more about duplicating your edit for multiple aspect ratio delivery in *Chapter 16, You're Done: Exporting Your Edit and Finishing Up*. Why so late in the process? Because it can make sense to have an edit in one aspect ratio entirely approved before converting it for other aspect ratios.

Note also that there are higher resolutions (5K, 6K, and 8K) in the menu, in addition to **Custom**, as well as options for creating 360° equirectangular Projects. While 8K is just regular video at a much higher resolution, the 360° video options create a Project that behaves very differently to regular video. If you've shot 360° footage that you want to deliver as 360° footage, then this is the option for you.

MOVING BETWEEN OPEN PROJECTS

If you followed all of those instructions, you'll have two Projects in your Browser, one with **Automatic Settings** and one with **Custom Settings**. They're both empty for now, but you can double-click on either one to open it, and you'll see the name of the current Project in the center of the interface, just above the timeline:

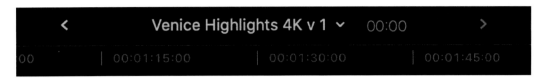

Figure 6.9: The name of the current open Project is always shown just above the timeline in the middle

To the left and right of the name are two arrows, though the right arrow might be grayed out. Those arrows let you jump to other Projects you're working on. You can do the following:

- Click on the left or right arrow to move through recently opened Projects.
- Click and hold on either arrow to see a menu with a list of recently opened Projects.

With a Project open, let's get some footage in there! At the moment, it's probably empty and looks like this:

Figure 6.10: An empty-looking Project timeline

That blank Project is about to get a lot busier, but before we fill it up, a quick recap.

REVIEW — CREATING A NEW PROJECT

You've learned how to create a new Project, and why it's best to define a Project's properties explicitly. You've considered the resolution, frame rate, and aspect ratio, and you know how to move around between Projects. Lastly, if you're planning to eventually distribute your Project in a couple of different aspect ratios, that's totally fine. *Chapter 16, You're Done: Exporting Your Edit and Finishing Up*, has more information about that. For now, just focus on editing your primary deliverable. For that, you'll need to add some clips.

ADDING YOUR MEDIA IN A FEW DIFFERENT WAYS

From *Chapter 5, Choose Your Favorites: Selecting, Rating, and Searching*, where you organized your media with **Keywords** and selected the best parts as **Favorites**, you're way ahead. Now, you'll finally learn how to add things to a timeline, creating the first stage of a rough cut. You'll learn how to add real clips (and placeholders with the keyboard and with the mouse).

To summarize, you'll be selecting each clip you want to add, one at a time or as a group, and pressing **E** to append, **W** to insert or dragging and dropping. But the process is (of course!) more subtle than that, and you'll learn why you'd want to add clips in these ways, how to fake it if you don't have your media yet, and why keyboard shortcuts are often the way to go.

APPENDING WITH A BUTTON OR SHORTCUT

On the left side of the central bar in the interface, you'll see the word **Index**, then four icons. They correspond to **Connect**, **Insert**, **Append**, and **Overwrite**:

Figure 6.11: From left to right, we have Index, Connect, Insert, Append, Overwrite, and a small menu

In *Chapter 7, Cover It Up: Connections, Cutaways, and Storylines*, I'll show you **Connect** and **Overwrite**, including how to put clips *above* one another, but we'll keep it simple for the moment. Right now, the best option is simply to **append**, because it just adds the selected clip(s) to the end of the current timeline, no matter what the Playhead or Skimmer are doing.

The slow and steady method is as follows:

1. Click on a clip to select the whole clip, or click and drag to select part of it:

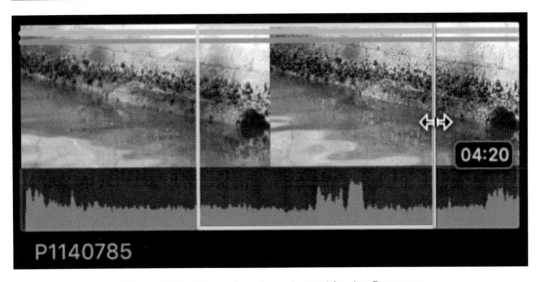

Figure 6.12: Part of a clip selected in the Browser

If you decide to select just part of a clip, you'll see the duration of your selection on the tooltip attached to the cursor. You can easily trim this later, but remember to consider the duration of a shot in the context you plan to use it.

2. Move down to the **Append** button and click it:

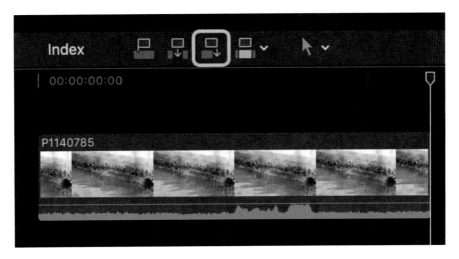

Figure 6.13: The Append button, and the clip appended to the current Project

However, you'll find it much faster to do the following:

1. Click (or click and drag) on a clip to select the whole clip (or part of it).
2. Press **E**:

Figure 6.14: Now there are two clips in the Project

But that's not the best option. You can go even faster if you have no clips selected:

1. Hover over the clip you want to add.
2. Press **E**.

This last technique only works if you've already made a selection on a clip, or if you want to add the entire clip. It's therefore best used in combination with carefully chosen Favorite ranges.

While it's easy to rearrange the clips afterward, try to add the clips in a sensible order. Hover over the first clip you want to add, press **E**, then the second press, **E**, and so on. Pretty quickly, you'll have the spine of the story in front of you. In different kinds of edits, that's going to look pretty different: perhaps it's a series of pieces to camera, which you'll cover up with B-roll later. Or perhaps it's a few moody introductory shots that you'll add music to, or a story of a character's journey. But there's not necessarily a right or wrong answer here; the goal is always to build the basics of a story. If people are speaking, it needs to sound good first, and we can cover up any issues to make it look good later — think in those terms.

Lastly, try not to get hung up on the exact timeline position of clips just yet. If you know what clip you want to be first, and you know what you want last, you can add them both now, then rearrange clips later — but don't try to create a huge blank space before that last clip. It's possible to add gaps, to force a clip to go a long way down the timeline, but resist that temptation! Just go with this "gapless" layout for now, and add gaps later if you need them.

ADDING CLIPS WITH DRAG AND DROP

Dragging and dropping is a natural way to work, and it does work pretty well:

1. Select a clip (or part of a clip) in the **Browser**:

Figure 6.15: If you hover over a selected area, the cursor changes to a hand to indicate it is draggable

2. Drag from a selected part of a clip from the **Browser** to the **Timeline**:

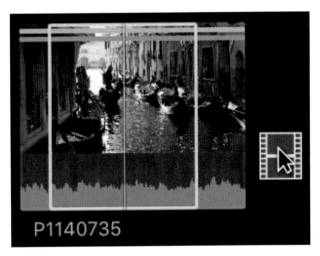

Figure 6.16: As you start dragging, a film icon appears

What happens next depends on where you release the drag operation. If you release your mouse past the last clip in the **Timeline**, it's exactly like pressing **E**, just slower:

Figure 6.17: Release the mouse after the last clip in the timeline, and it will be appended

Look out! If you drag to a spot above an existing clip, you'll be connecting a clip above another one:

Figure 6.18: Don't drag above or below other clips just yet

Don't do that yet, as it's going to be covered in *Chapter 7, Cover It Up: Connections, Cutaways, and Storylines*. (If you've done it already, **undo** with ⌘Z). Another operation to avoid for now is to drag directly on top of another clip until it shows a white highlight, like this:

Figure 6.19: Don't do this yet either — it's a Replace operation, and we'll return to it later on

But what if you end up dragging a Browser clip between two Timeline clips? That's just fine, and it's called an **insert** edit:

Figure 6.20: So long as you can see the blue outline where the clip is going to land, it's an insert edit

No clips will be broken or destroyed if you use these simple operations, and if you get anything wrong, you can always just press ⌘Z to undo, or ⇧⌘Z to redo. Everything you do is saved automatically, and every change to a Project is undoable until you quit or close the Library. While these operations are always safe, and an easy way to experiment, if you insert with a button or shortcut, you could chop up the clips on your timeline.

INSERTING WITH A BUTTON OR SHORTCUT

The second of the four icons here is the **Insert** button, and as you'd expect, it inserts a video, much like dragging a clip between two others:

Figure 6.21: As before, these are Connect, Insert, Append, and Overwrite

When you press the **Insert** button, the selected clip is placed wherever the timeline Playhead has been positioned. If you've left the Playhead between two clips, then this is just like drag and drop. But if you've left the Playhead in the middle of a clip, then that clip will be broken up into two parts — even if one of those parts is just a few frames long — and the new clip placed between:

Figure 6.22: Here, the wide P1140747 clip has been inserted in the middle of close-up P1140741, breaking it up

Breaking up a clip with an **Insert** operation is sometimes what you want to do, but since it creates a discontinuity in the original clip, it's often not quite what you wanted. Note also that if you would prefer to use the Skimmer (rather than the Playhead), then you'll be unable to press the button, and will have to use the shortcut (**W**) instead. This is because the Skimmer will disappear as your cursor leaves the timeline pane to press the button.

If you want to insert without drag and drop, and without breaking anything apart, then you'll want to master **Snapping**.

HOW TO USE SNAPPING

Snapping is a toggle, and when it's on, it forces the Skimmer and the Playhead to snap to the start or end of other clips, and to markers on clips. This will become more important in the next chapter (as it affects connected clips) but it's also important when inserting video.

Glancing to the right of the main bar, you'll see these four icons:

Figure 6.23: From left to right: Skimming on, Audio Skimming off, Solo off, and Snapping on

The fourth icon indicates **Snapping**, which has the shortcut **N**. With **N**, **Snapping** can be toggled at any time, even in the middle of a drag or an edit operation when pressing the button is impossible. You'll toggle **Snapping** often: when dragging clips about, when making trim edits, and in many other contexts.

Inserting is an occasion where we want **Snapping** on, to avoid the possibility of leaving a tiny "leftover" clip on one side of the newly inserted clip:

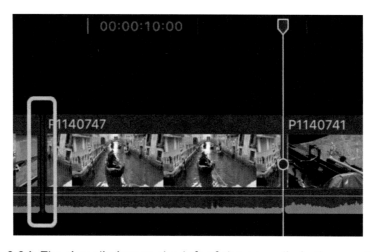

Figure 6.24: The tiny clip just to the left of the new clip is the result of not using Snapping

To place the Playhead or Skimmer exactly between two clips, follow these steps:

1. If the **Snapping** icon is white, press **N** to turn it blue (on).

2. Hover to near an existing edit point, between two clips, until the Skimmer turns yellow to indicate a snap.

3. Press **W** to insert the currently selected Browser clip:

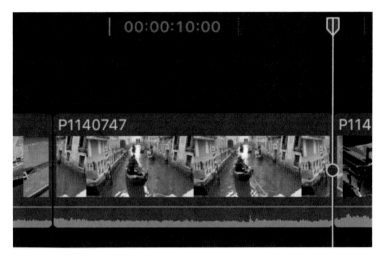

Figure 6.25: Inserted safely between two other clips

You'll have noticed the yellow Playhead and Skimmer when snap points are reached, and that's the clear clue that a snap has been found. Let's take a closer look at the Skimmer and the Playhead in the context of the Timeline.

REVISITING THE SKIMMER AND THE PLAYHEAD

In *Chapter 4, Sort It Out: Reviewing and Keywording*, we looked at the behavior of these lines in the **Browser**, but in the **Timeline**, they're a little different. Point by point, in the **Timeline**, we have the following:

- The **Playhead** is a vertical line with an arrow at the top, is positioned with a click, and stays in position when the mouse cursor moves elsewhere.

- The **Skimmer** is a vertical line with no arrow at the top, it moves with the mouse cursor, and is only visible when the cursor hovers over a clip.

- If skimming is active, the **Playhead** is white, or yellow if the **Skimmer** is on top of the Playhead.

- If skimming is not active, the **Playhead** is red, or yellow if **Snapping** is active and the Playhead is positioned on a snap point.

- The **Skimmer** is normally red, but if **Snapping** is active, it turns yellow when it's over a snap point or the Playhead.

As before, note the following:

- The **Skimmer** can be toggled on or off (blue means on) with this central toolbar button or the shortcut, **S**:

Figure 6.26: This blue icon indicates that Skimming is on

- If it's present, *the Skimmer takes priority* over the Playhead.

If those rules seem a little complex, simply remember: look for the yellow line if you want your edit to snap. Press **N** to toggle off an unwanted snap, or to toggle it on if it's not active. And definitely remember that **N** shortcut!

Before you move on in the book, take a few moments to build up a story in your edit. If you've got holiday B-roll like the examples here, assemble the clips in an order that makes sense. If you're putting together a corporate message, you might start with a quick introduction, then the pieces to the camera (or other shots) that audibly tell the story. If you're following a script, pick a good take for each shot in the script. But what if you don't have all the shots you need? No problem.

ADDING TEMPORARY CLIPS

This may seem obvious, but you can import still images just as easily as importing video files. JPEG, PNG, and PDF files all work well, and you can organize them just as easily. If stills won't cut it, perhaps you can fill some gaps with free or paid stock video sites: pexels.com is one site that has a selection of free video clips you can use even in commercial jobs. If you need some more clips to edit with, grab some now, import them, organize them, and append or insert them.

FCP also has a couple of built-in options to fill gaps, and one is literally called a **Gap** clip. To add a blank Gap to fill in space, do the following:

1. Click on or skim to the spot where you want to add a Gap.
2. Press ⌥**W** to insert a Gap:

Figure 6.27: That lighter gray clip is a Gap clip

But if you'd like to start editing before you've shot a frame of video, you'll want to use Placeholder clips. Instead of a black screen, these insert an image with silhouettes of some number of people, in a changeable scene, at a certain focal length, with optional text. The process of adding and changing these Placeholders is as follows:

1. Click on or skim to the spot where you want to add a **Placeholder**.

2. Insert a **Placeholder** with ⌥⌘W (or use **Edit > Insert Generator > Placeholder**):

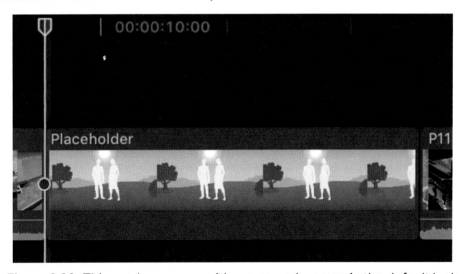

Figure 6.28: This outdoor scene with a man and woman is the default look
for a Placeholder clip

Once you've added a **Placeholder**, you can do almost anything to it, and here's how:

1. **⌥-click** on a **Placeholder** to select that clip and move the Playhead to that position.

2. If necessary, open the **Inspector** using the third window control in the top-right corner of the interface:

Figure 6.29: To show the Inspector, make sure the third icon is blue

3. In the **Inspector**, click the first icon at the top left to switch to the **Generator** pane, then change any of the settings underneath, as shown here:

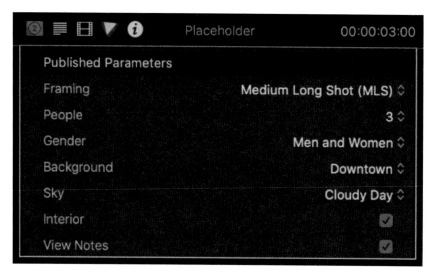

Figure 6.30: Just one possible setup for this Placeholder

4. Text is optional, but to make it visible, check the **View Notes** box at the bottom, then switch to the **Text** icon, just to the right of the **Generator** icon at the top left of the **Inspector**, and add text there:

Figure 6.31: Here's the result of those previous options

You can use these Placeholders to build up an entire editing timeline before you start shooting, and then replace these clips with the techniques you'll learn in *Chapter 9, Consider Your Options: Multicam, Replacing, and Auditions*. Here's an example of a music video that I planned out with the artist Ky. at our first meeting:

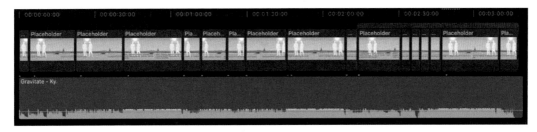

Figure 6.32: The music video for Ky.'s song Gravitate started out like this

You'll see that I didn't bother changing the appearance of each of these Placeholder clips, but I did add extensive text descriptions to each shot, and positioned the edits in the right places to work with the song. I'll show you how to add music like this soon, but for now, just work with the audio in each clip.

REVIEW — ADDING YOUR MEDIA IN A FEW DIFFERENT WAYS

By now, you should have appended a number of clips, inserted a few more, discovered **Snapping**, and added a Placeholder or two. Your timeline should be looking a bit busier; so, let's mix up those clips.

REARRANGING YOUR CLIPS

This basic part of the edit — putting things in the right order — is very important, yet deceptively simple. FCP makes it hard to get this wrong, because it's hard to break up a clip by accident, and the Magnetic Timeline means that you won't leave any gaps unless you add them on purpose.

If you're new to editing, this probably doesn't seem too strange. You're putting clips in order to tell a story, so why would you want to leave gaps in that story? It's probably a little jarring for new editors to realize that simply rearranging clips is actually not a simple operation in most other **non-linear editing systems (NLEs)**. One of the key innovations of Final Cut Pro was to make it easier for you to experiment with your edit, letting you rearrange your clips without worrying about breaking anything. If you're an experienced editor used to juggling clips up and down to avoid clip collisions across multiple tracks, you can simply relax. It's easier here.

Rearranging media is useful in all kinds of edits, so it doesn't matter if you're cutting a drama, corporate video, advertising, or a piece for an influencer on social media — flexibility is always useful. In this section, you'll learn all about moving, selecting multiple clips, and a few playback shortcuts too.

MOVING CLIPS IN THE MAGNETIC TIMELINE

Moving and reordering a single clip couldn't be easier:

1. Click on the main part of a clip (its filmstrip is ideal) and drag it left or right:

Figure 6.33: Four clips in a row — A, B, C, and A — and C has just been clicked on

2. When you see the clips rearranged to indicate their new position, release the mouse button:

Figure 6.34: The blue outline behind the dragged clip indicates where it will land after release

The tooltip shows how far in time the clip has been moved, and when you release the mouse, the clip will simply land in the new position. Feel free to experiment, as you can't really break anything.

The only way this can go wrong is if you drag too far up or down, moving the dragged clip outside the primary storyline and creating a connected clip. If you do this by accident, just press ⌘Z to undo, and we'll revisit connected clips in the next chapter.

SELECTING MULTIPLE CLIPS

If you want to move more than one clip, that's easy too — simply select more than one clip before you drag them. You can select multiple clips in a few ways:

- Starting in empty space, drag a box around multiple clips:

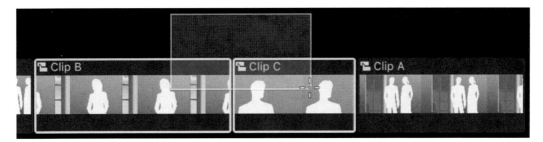

Figure 6.35: Dragging a selection over the first two clips

- To select sequential clips, click on the first clip, then ⇧-**click** the last clip:

Figure 6.36: Click on the first clip you want, then ⇧-click the last clip

- To select separate clips, click on the first clip, then **⌘-click** every other clip you want to select:

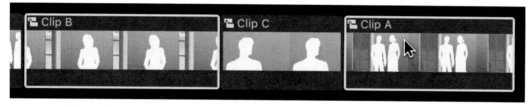

Figure 6.37: Click on the first clip you want, then ⌘-click any others

It's entirely possible to pick up and rearrange multiple clips from anywhere in the timeline in a single operation. Gaps between clips will not be maintained after dropping the clips, though the order will.

DUPLICATING CLIPS

While copy (**⌘C**) and paste (**⌘V**) do work, it's often much easier to **⌥-drag** to duplicate one or more clips. The process to duplicate a single clip is, again, very simple:

1. Hold **⌥**, then click on the main part of a clip and drag it left or right.
2. When you see the clips rearrange to indicate their new position, release:

Figure 6.38: The arrow with the green plus circle indicates duplication

While **⌥** is held, the cursor indicates that a duplicate clip will be created. Any time you want another copy of any kind of clip, just **⌥-drag**. (This also works to create copies of files in the Finder.) And yes, you can select multiple clips before ⌥**-dragging** to create duplicates of all those clips if you wish.

Why not just use good old cut, copy, and paste? Well, with these simple edits, they'd work just fine, but as you build more complex timelines, with clips connected to other clips, pasting can become a little more complicated, as you'll discover in the next chapter. However, if you want to copy between two separate timelines, drag and drop isn't possible; so, copy from one Project, switch to another, then paste.

BASIC TIMELINE SHORTCUTS

As you rearrange and duplicate your clips, you'll want to review them in context in the **Timeline**. The playback shortcuts that work in the **Browser** work well here too, but a few keys have changed. The original shortcuts you'll still want to use are as follows:

- Hover in the timeline, then press **Space** for play/pause.
- **J**, **K**, and **L** for forward and backward playback at high speed.
- ← and → to move by one frame.
- ⇧← and ⇧→ to move by 10 frames.
- ⇧**/** (or **?**) to play around the current point.

Some changed or new shortcuts that move between edit points are as follows:

- ↓ or **apostrophe (')** jumps to the first frame of the next clip.
- ↑ or **semicolon (;)** jumps to the first frame of the previous clip.

These last two shortcuts work well to let you jump around the timeline quickly, and when used with **?**, let you review any edit quickly.

REVIEW — REARRANGING YOUR CLIPS

You've learned how to select one or more clips, and how to rearrange them into the correct order. Duplicating by ⌥**-dragging** is a vital operation in all kinds of creative applications, so be sure to use that too. The review shortcuts you learned when assessing media are just as useful here. But review only takes you so far — how do you make a clip longer or shorter? You trim it.

BASIC TRIMMING WITH THE MAGNETIC TIMELINE

Trimming, at a basic level, usually involves moving the edges of a clip to see more or less of it. As with many other operations in FCP, trimming is one that starts out being very simple, but has powerful subtleties (slipping, sliding, and rolling — all to come later). For now, we'll focus on several useful ways to make a clip longer or shorter, with the mouse and with the keyboard. But first, a little check — do you have enough media?

DO YOU HAVE ENOUGH MEDIA?

Each clip on a timeline represents a link to all or part of an actual clip that was recorded. Put simply, the start and end of each clip can be adjusted to the left or right, making a clip longer or shorter. But that's only true if there's enough media to allow the edit to proceed. If you've added entire clips to your timeline, you might be using the very first or very last frame of a real clip, and each one is a hard limit past which you can't extend a clip. You can't use a frame of a video that doesn't exist:

Figure 6.39: When you drag to a clip's limit, the red out point in the Timeline and the film overlay in the Viewer indicate that there's no more media available

The good news is that in a real-world edit, you probably won't run out of media very often. Normally, an experienced videographer will start recording at least a few seconds before the action happens, and record for a few seconds after the action ends. You'll end up using some part of the middle of a clip in most circumstances, and so you won't run out of media. These spare few seconds, known as "handles," give you editing flexibility — which is especially important with transitions — so make sure to record for a little longer than you think you need.

For now, if you've skipped a few steps and thrown entire clips onto a timeline, you might want to throw the middles of a few clips on there instead, because we're about to trim clips in both directions. Once you've got a few parts of some clips on a timeline, grab your mouse and let's get started.

TRIMMING WITH THE MOUSE

When you hover over the start or end of a clip, you'll see that the cursor changes to an icon that represents the start or end of a clip, with arrows on either side to indicate movement, and a filmstrip beneath:

Figure 6.40: Here's the trimming cursor, enlarged for detail

That filmstrip points to the clip that's going to be adjusted, and also indicates that this is an operation that "ripples" — that is, it won't leave a gap. To many editors this is a Ripple trim or a Ripple edit, but here, we'll just call it a trim. To perform the edit, do the following:

1. Click and drag near the start or end of a clip on the timeline:

Figure 6.41: Dragging the in point (left edge) of this clip to the right shows a positive timecode

2. Drag left or right to move that start or end point:

Figure 6.42: Dragging the out point (right edge) of this clip to the left shows
a negative timecode

Regardless of whether you are making the clip longer or shorter, you can see what's happening in several different ways, all at once:

- First, you can look at the timeline, where the video thumbnail and audio waveform reflect what's visible and audible.

- Second, you can watch the tooltip's display of the timecode and distance moved to see just how far an edit has gone.

- Lastly, you can watch the Viewer, where a two-up display shows you the out point and neighboring in point around the edit you're adjusting. As you're only adjusting a single edit point here, one of the two frames will change while the other stays still:

Figure 6.43: In the Viewer, only the left side of this two-up display changed
as the out point of the left clip was adjusted

This two-up display is a great way to judge if two shots belong together, and also where you'll match up continuous action across two shots. The two shots just shown of *Campo San Marco* are telling different parts of the same story, of a child being swarmed by Venetian pigeons, but if neighboring shots are too similar in content, viewers (and you) will notice. For example, take the following:

Figure 6.44: These two shots are both OK on their own, but back to back, they look uncomfortably similar

When dragging edits, you may find that **Snapping** helps, but it can equally get in the way. If an edit point unhelpfully snaps to the Playhead (or anything else), just disable **Snapping** by pressing **N** during the operation. You'll also often want to focus on a single edit, to be able to drag it and see just what's going on; so (with the **Timeline** pane active), use ⌘**plus** (actually, **=**) to zoom in. To see less, zoom out with ⌘**minus**, or type ⇧**Z** to see the entire edit. ⇧⌘**plus** and ⇧⌘**minus** adjust the clip height, and all those shortcuts have visual equivalents in the **Clip Appearance** dropdown menu to the right of the gray bar. Finally, remember that using **?** is a great way to check your work (**Play Around Edit**) after trimming.

Mouse-based editing makes sense visually and is easy to understand. However, if you want to edit really quickly, the keyboard is often the fastest choice.

TRIMMING WITH THE KEYBOARD

Editing with the keyboard is effective, and if you're an experienced editor trying to nail those story beats, you'll like these:

1. Click near the start or end of a clip on the timeline to select the edit point.

2. Move that edit point one frame to the left with the **comma** key or one frame to the right with the **period** key. Use ⇧**comma** or ⇧**period** to move by 10 frames.

As simple as that is, the major downside is that there is no two-up display when you move edit points with the keyboard. That's not always a problem, though. If you're trying to clean up an edit by trimming a few frames from a sequence of clips, you'll want to know a few more keys:

- ↓ or **apostrophe (')** jumps to the first frame of the next clip.
- ↑ or **semicolon (;)** jumps to the first frame of the previous clip.
- **[** selects the out point of the clip to the left of the Playhead.
- **]** selects the in point of the clip to the right of the Playhead.

Combine those keys with **period** and **comma** to move selected edits, and you can trim many clips in just a few seconds. As great as those keys are, they're not my favorite way to trim. Read on to find out what is.

TRIMMING THE TOP AND TAIL OF A CLIP

Edits need to be tight, and clips need to become shorter far more often than they need to be longer. With that in mind, the **Trim Start** and **Trim End** commands are a great way to make clips shorter, and they can be used while the video is paused, or while it's playing:

1. Press ⌥[to use **Trim Start**, moving the in point of the current clip to the current Playhead or Skimmer.

2. Press ⌥] to **Trim End**, moving the out point of the current clip to the current Playhead or Skimmer.

IMPORTANT NOTE

If you don't like those keys, define your own with **Final Cut Pro > Command > Customize**, and remember that one-key shortcuts are easiest to hit. If you have an extended keyboard, consider defining new single-hand shortcuts for these operations, such as **F5** and **F6**. If you have a MacBook Pro, you can also use dedicated **Touch Bar** buttons for these operations.

I like to shorten B-roll collections by playing an edit through at normal speed, then pressing ⌥[when a clip should start, and ⌥] when a clip should end — but never stopping playback. To see a few edits in sequence, let's play back some video:

Figure 6.45: The Playhead is nearly at the end of P1140678

Then, Trim End is performed, which makes the first clip shorter:

Figure 6.46: P1140678 now ends at the Playhead

The Playhead continues to move forward:

Figure 6.47: The Playhead is now passing through P1140712

It does so until the next Trim Start, which shortens the current clip:

Figure 6.48: The first part of P1140712, before the Playhead, is now removed

A few seconds later, Trim Start is pressed again to make the same clip even shorter:

Figure 6.49: More of the start of the same clip (P1140712) is now removed

If that didn't click for you the first time, try it out for yourself, preferably without stopping playback, on a sequence of a few B-roll clips. If you like, you can also explore the combo command, **Trim To Playhead** (⌥\), which always trims the nearest edit point (either the start or end) to the Playhead. Trim Start and Trim End are a great way to make your edits tighter and make you a faster editor.

EXTENDING EDITS

Occasionally, you might want to make a clip longer, rather than shorter, and there is a way to do that using the keyboard and the mouse together:

1. Select an edit point on a clip.
2. Skim over a point near that edit where you want the edit point to be.
3. Press ⇧X to perform an **Extend Edit**.

What did that do? Well, if you skimmed to a point inside the clip, it's just like using Trim Start or Trim End — it made the clip shorter. But if you skimmed to a point outside the clip, the clip will become longer; it's like you've grabbed that edit point and moved it. So why not just grab it with the mouse? Well, this operation can also be done entirely with the keyboard while the video plays, so if you prefer to edit by feel, it's a good way to work.

REVIEW — BASIC TRIMMING WITH THE MAGNETIC TIMELINE

OK. Now you can add clips, move clips, and make them longer or shorter in interesting ways: with the mouse, with the keyboard, by trimming the start and end, or by extending edits. But what if a clip is just wrong? Get rid of it!

BLADING AND DELETING

Chopping things up and throwing away the bad parts is a perfectly OK way to work. A big part of an editor's job is to remove unnecessary media, and if you're feeling old school, you can cut things up just like you're playing with film. There are many ways to remove a clip, or part of a clip, and that's what this section covers. As you might expect, we'll start at the simple end of things.

DELETING CLIPS

This is pretty simple. First, you select the clip(s) you want to delete, and then you delete them. Simple enough:

1. Select a clip by clicking on it, or select multiple clips by dragging a selection by ⇧-**clicking** or ⌘-**clicking**:

Figure 6.50: A few clips selected

2. Press **delete** to remove selected clips and leave no gaps:

Figure 6.51: Those clips have now been deleted, and the gaps removed

But there's another way if you don't want these deleted clips to cause anything else to move:

1. Press ⇧**delete** or **forward delete** (⌦, only on wider keyboards) to replace selected clips with Gap clips:

Figure 6.52: ⇧delete leaves gaps, but doesn't move around anything else

While you probably won't need to worry about the movement of other clips at this early stage of an edit, it can be an important factor in a more complex timeline.

BREAKING UP A CLIP

From time to time, you need to break up a clip into a few parts, rather than trimming either end. To do that, you'll need to switch tools. For everything we've done so far, we've used the standard **Select** tool, a regular arrow, because it's the default tool from the menu to the right of the editing buttons:

Figure 6.53: The Select tool is chosen in the menu at the right

There are other tools available here, and while you can click and choose one with your mouse, it's best to simply tap the shortcut to choose the tool you need:

Figure 6.54: For the Blade tool, press B

If you tap a key, you'll switch to that tool. But if you hold a key, you'll only switch to that tool temporarily, for as long as you hold it down. Anyway, we'll take it easy for now:

1. Press **B** to switch to the **Blade** tool.

2. Click on a clip to split it into two clips at that point:

Figure 6.55: Just after clicking with the Blade tool

The new edit is indicated with a dashed line for now. It's called a **through edit** because the two frames around the edit are actually sequential. If you change your mind, through edits can be selected (with the **Select** tool) and deleted, healing the clip as if it was never bladed. Alternatively, select multiple clips and then choose **Trim > Join Clips** to remove all through edits in the selection.

On the other hand, if you move either point around a through edit, it will no longer appear dashed, as it's now just a regular edit, and no longer a through edit. (Instead, it'll probably create a jump cut when played back, and we will fix those in *Chapter 7, Cover It Up: Connections, Cutaways, and Storylines*.)

There's another way to blade that gives the same result, but without switching tools. As the video plays back, you can press ⌘B to break up the current clip at the Playhead, and the strength of this approach is that you can blade a clip while it's playing. That's certainly handy from time to time, but **Blade** (either way) shouldn't be your first choice. If you want to make a clip shorter, Trim Start and Trim End are more efficient. If you want to delete part of a clip, it's not the best for that either. The (tedious) process would be as follows:

1. Press **B** for the **Blade** tool.
2. Click to place the first split.
3. Click to place the second split.
4. Press **A** for the **Select** tool.
5. Click the new separate clip between the through edits to select it.
6. Press **Delete**.

That's slow, and you'll be glad to know that there's a much better way.

SELECTING PART OF A CLIP

So far, we've selected multiple clips, but not part of a clip or parts of multiple clips. As the **Select** tool prefers to keep clips whole, you'll need to switch to another tool for this. It's called **Range Selection**, and the shortcut is **R**:

Figure 6.56: The Range Selection tool in the menu

It's much easier to delete part of a clip with this tool with the following steps:

1. Press **R** for the **Range Selection** tool.
2. Click on the clip where you want the edit to begin, then drag left or right and release where you want it to end, on the same clip or another clip:

Figure 6.57: Here's a selection over part of a single clip

3. Press **delete**:

Figure 6.58: Here's what's left after a delete

This process makes selecting in the Timeline just like selecting in the Browser. Just like the Browser, you don't need to use the mouse at all. If you'd prefer to use the mouse, you don't even need to switch tools, and the process is even simpler:

1. Skim to the start of the edit and press **I**.
2. Skim to the end of the edit and press **O**:

Figure 6.59: This process looks exactly like using the Range Selection tool, but here I've selected part of two clips

At this point, a handy shortcut could be **/**, to play just the selected region. If you've selected part of a single clip, you can press ⌥\ to trim the selection to remove the unselected areas. But we'll get rid of the selected area instead.

3. Press **delete** to remove the selected video range:

Figure 6.60: Here's what you get after another delete

That's right — the standard **I** and **O** shortcuts work in the timeline too, and they give you a great way to select part of a clip so that you can get rid of it. As you continue through the book, you'll see other uses for selecting ranges in the timeline (such as changing audio levels); but for now, just remember to use this method instead of the clunky old **Blade**, **Blade**, **Select**, **Delete** method. When you're done, press **A** to switch back to the regular **Select** tool.

REVIEW — BLADING AND DELETING

This section covered a few important features. Deleting is straightforward, and you'll learn to know when you want to leave a gap and when you don't. Breaking up clips with the blade is a common operation for some editors and a rare one for others, but if you like it, use it. Selecting ranges is a core technique for many operations besides deleting, including audio volume changes and some editing operations, so don't ignore it.

After all that experimentation, you'll have made a lot of changes. If you decide they don't make your edit better, you can always undo them, but that only works until you quit the app. Why not make multiple different versions of your timeline so that you can step back in time whenever you want?

DUPLICATING PROJECTS

Final Cut Pro saves all the time in the background: everything you do is saved automatically as you work. The one downside is that if you were to make a crazy, experimental change and then suffer a crash, you could lose some work. For safety, it's therefore best to duplicate a Project before you make significant changes, and certainly before you begin a new round of changes based on client feedback.

These are the steps to duplicate a Project:

1. Click once in the **Browser** pane to give it focus.

2. Right-click on your current project in the Browser, then choose **Duplicate**, or press ⌘**D**. (Alternatively, in version 10.4.9 you can also use the small menu to the right of the project name in the central gray bar.)

3. Double-click this new **Project** to edit it, and check that its name is showing in the middle of the interface.

That last step is important: always immediately double-click on the new Project to make sure you're editing the newest version. If you forget, you'll continue to make changes to your old Project while the new one sits there unopened and unseen. Messy.

One more thing. The names we chose for our Projects way back at the start of the chapter allow a nice trick. If a Project name ends with a space before a final number, a duplicate of that Project will automatically increase that final number by 1. For example, `Venice Highlights v 1` will become `Venice Highlights v 2` for the duplicate Project. If you don't use a space, this trick doesn't work, so make sure to add that space before the final `1`:

Figure 6.61: Always leave a space before the final number, and always double-click after duplicating

The small menu to the right of the Project name in the central gray bar also allows you to change the properties for the current Project, but if you want to change the properties (or the name) of a *duplicate* Project, you should right-click and choose **Duplicate Project As** instead. This brings up the **Project Properties** dialog as the new duplicate is being created, and is an ideal way to create alternative aspect ratio versions of a Project. There's more on that process in *Chapter 16, You're Done: Exporting Your Edit and Finishing Up.*

You might also notice **Snapshot Project** in the right-click menu, and you can use that instead if you wish. It produces a new duplicate with a timestamp in its name, leaving you to continue editing the original Project; but personally, I prefer the simpler v 2 naming strategy. Also note that there are some important differences between **Duplicate** and **Snapshot** that will be covered later in this book:

Figure 6.62: Using Snapshot Project adds a date and time, rather than incrementing the final number

REVIEW — DUPLICATING PROJECTS

This was a short section, but it's really important. Autosave is wonderful until you need to refer to an older version of your Project that you didn't keep. Duplicating is a great solution to this problem — you can keep working safely, but if you ever need your old Project, it's a double-click away. Just always make sure to check that you're working on the newest Project, because old Projects are sometimes opened unintentionally.

SUMMARY

That probably felt like a lot. You've created a new Project with custom settings, opened it up, duplicated it a couple of times, added a heap of clips with the mouse and the keyboard, trimmed clips with the mouse and the keyboard in countless ways, rearranged clips by dragging, bladed clips apart, and deleted parts of clips before finally making a duplicate Project. All these operations are going to be your bread-and-butter tools going forward, and you'll use them on every single job.

But we're not even halfway done yet. In the next chapter, you'll learn about the wonderful world of connected clips and cutaways. They'll let you disguise your edits, smooth over problems, and make your subjects sound better. Using cutaways effectively is one of the easiest ways to make your edits more professional, so if you're keen to learn more, turn the page.

REVIEW QUESTIONS

1. Why should you add a space before a final number in a project's name?
2. What happens if you choose **Automatic Settings** for a new project, then add a still image?
3. Which operation adds a clip to the end of the primary storyline?
4. Can the **Insert** operation break up a clip on the timeline?
5. What's the shortcut to add a **Placeholder** generator?
6. What are the shortcuts for Undo and Redo?
7. Why is it useful to know the shortcut (**W**) for **Insert**?
8. What do you see in the Viewer when you drag the end of a clip?
9. How do you delete a clip and leave a gap in its place?
10. How do you break up a clip under the Playhead or Skimmer?

REVIEW ANSWERS

1. So it automatically increments when the project is duplicated.
2. You'll be asked to manually choose project properties.
3. **Append**.
4. Yes, it can.
5. ⌥⌘**W (Option-Command-W)**.
6. ⌘**Z (Command-Z)** for Undo and ⇧⌘**Z (Shift-Command-Z)** for Redo.
7. Because without the shortcut, you can't use the Skimmer to indicate the insert position.
8. A two-up display showing the edit point being dragged and the edit point next to it.
9. ⇧**delete (Shift-delete)** or **forward delete** (⌦).
10. Press ⌘**B**.

7 COVER IT UP:

CONNECTIONS, CUTAWAYS, AND STORYLINES

"If FCP X had gotten rid of tracks and made no other paradigm changes, I'd still be an acolyte. Just from that one breakthrough! But instead of stopping there, the team reimagined what non-linear editing could be at every single step, and they got so much of it right. It really is like driving a Tesla while the legacy systems are chugging along in a four-cylinder station wagon. Sure, we'll all get to the same place in the end. But us FCP X drivers are having a lot more fun on the way."

— Michael Yanovich, A.C.E.

M.Y. is a Los Angeles-based editor who works on feature films and TV shows, is a decent guitar player, and totally sucks on drums. But plays them anyway. (FilmYak.com)

We're starting to get somewhere, but there's a long way to go yet. So far, we've got some good video on the timeline, we've put it in the right order, and we've trimmed it down. But in terms of editing, what we've done is still pretty simple. While the Primary Storyline should always be the spine of the story, there are many reasons why you'd want to put clips above or below that spine.

Final Cut Pro takes a unique approach: it doesn't just place higher clips at a point in time, it connects them to clips on the Primary Storyline. While that makes many operations more flexible, it's different from the traditional track-based paradigm, and if you're an experienced editor, this is a chapter you'll want to read carefully. In detail, this chapter covers the following:

- Understanding cutaways
- Connecting clips

- Grouping connected clips in Storylines
- Controlling and overriding connections
- Three-point editing and more

By the end of this chapter, you'll be able to make more sophisticated edits, hide your edits to make the overall product smoother, and understand how Final Cut does it differently and how to place clips in particular spots. Remember: video editors are liars, and the good ones get away with it. You'll find out how, right now.

UNDERSTANDING CUTAWAYS

A **cutaway** is the term for video placed above the main story to hide edits underneath. While a person in a video probably said the words they appeared to, they probably didn't manage to say them all in the right order, without interruptions. Removing the *ums*, *ahs*, and pauses leaves visible **jump cuts**: two sequential shots with almost, but not quite, the same content. To hide the edits, an editor places a cutaway above the Primary Storyline, and while you still hear the words below, you don't see the jump cut.

How does the editor find the right clip to "cut away" to? Usually, they use B-roll that's related to the current topic. An edit has to feel justified, so you can't just put any old clip on top. This is why editors want relevant B-roll; if you don't have enough, you won't be able to cover all of the edits you want to.

Not all cutaways are B-roll, though. You might cut away to a reaction shot such as an interviewer nodding or a reverse angle of a character in a dramatic piece reacting to another. It could be a wider angle of the same scene, a close-up of an important detail, or something else. Cutaways allow timing to be adjusted beneath them, and by shifting the audience's gaze, can help you to maintain an illusion of continuity.

As well as covering up an edit, cutaways can also be used above a continuous, unedited shot to break up a shot that's been on-screen for too long or to hide something. The defining factor of a cutaway is that it sits above the Primary Storyline rather than within it.

At this point, I should note that the times, as ever, are a-changing, and jump cuts (created when part of a shot is removed and the edit is seen) are becoming more accepted in a wider range of productions. They've always been available as an occasional stylistic choice, but they've become far more mainstream over the last several years. When vlogging became popular, jump cuts were embraced wholeheartedly and since then, they've quickly spread to the rest of online video and back to mainstream TV and cinema. Don't feel that you must always disguise jump cuts, but they remain a jarring choice. Since "professional" media usually hides jump cuts, your clients may prefer if you avoid them too, but go with your gut and what the story demands.

IMPORTANT NOTE

Technically, any two sequential clips of the same subject, shot within about 30° of one another and with the subject at a similar size, will usually appear as a jump cut. If you take out the middle of a single static shot, that's very likely to cause one, but changing scale and position on one side of the edit can help.

You can also avoid cutaways and B-roll by shooting your subject from multiple simultaneous angles. Shooting two angles of the same person will keep the focus on your subject while giving you some options for avoiding jump cuts, and there's more on editing multicam media in the next chapter.

At a really high level, this is the process you'll follow for any video that's driven by someone speaking on camera:

1. Select the good clips (*Chapter 4, Sort It Out: Reviewing and Keywording*, and *Chapter 5, Choose Your Favorites: Selecting and Collecting*).

2. Put them in the right order (*Chapter 6, Build the Spine of the Story: Quick Assembly*).

3. Delete unwanted pauses and phrases, even if it leaves a jump cut (*Chapter 6, Build the Spine of the Story: Quick Assembly*).

4. Connect B-roll cutaways on top of the Primary Storyline to hide edits and cover long, boring shots (this chapter).

Most videos involve someone talking, but for anything else, you'll place clips above other clips simply when you want to cover something up or you want to stay flexible with regard to its position in time. You'll also use connected clips when you use keying (green screen) or picture-in-picture effects, but we'll return to those in *Chapter 12, Refine and Smooth: Video Effects and Transitions*. Let's now prep some footage of someone talking — it's a simple, common situation that you'll need to deal with, and it's easy to understand.

PREPARING FOR A CUTAWAY

Somewhere in your Library, you should have a shot of someone speaking. They don't have to be saying anything important for this exercise, but it helps if they've taken at least a brief pause between some of their words. The process starts simply:

1. Add a clip of someone speaking to your timeline.

   You now need to locate a part of this clip that you'd like to remove. Maybe it's an *um* in the middle of a good sentence; maybe it's a not-so-great sentence between two good ones. Maybe it's just a pause that's a little too long, a word that doesn't belong, or a stumbled word. Find it, and get ready.

2. Press **R** to switch to the **Range Selection** tool, then click, drag, and release to select the problematic part of this clip. (Alternatively, hover before and press **I**, then hover after and press **O**):

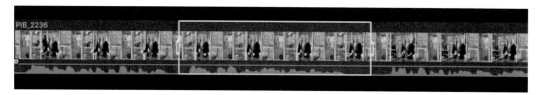

Figure 7.1: Here, I've selected a less important sentence from this continuous shot

3. With the selection active, press **delete** to remove that section, leaving two clips:

Figure 7.2: Now there are two clips, but the cut will be obvious

You've made a jump cut. Now it's time to get the edit sounding right:

1. Use the **Select** tool (and perhaps the **comma** and **period** shortcuts) to trim the Out point of clip 1 and the In point of clip 2 to make sure it sounds good.

2. Review and re-edit this cut as many times as you need, using the **?** "Play Around Edit" shortcut repeatedly.

When it sounds good, you're done: don't worry about how it looks as it's about to be covered up. Remember that you can add a cutaway above any edit, jump cut or not, and whether the two clips are from the same shots or different ones — it's all good.

REVIEW — UNDERSTANDING CUTAWAYS

Now that you know what cutaways are all about, and you've prepared your timeline with a jump cut that sounds good but looks bad, the next step is always to connect the cutaway above. Remember that you can use cutaways in other situations too, and that jump cuts are just the most common example. Still, this is a common workflow and it's worth mastering. Let's find out how to cover that edit and anything else in this new connected world.

CONNECTING CLIPS

Any time you add a clip above or below other clips, you're connecting them — forming a parent-child relationship — and this section shows you how. While you might want to connect many types of clips (B-roll, sound effects, music, or titles), the most common thing to use as cutaway footage is B-roll video, to cover an edit, and that's where we'll begin. After looking at connecting video, we'll circle back to connecting audio and music and take a slightly deeper look.

CONNECTING VISUAL B-ROLL

You shot plenty of B-roll, right? Assuming that you have the right shots and you've organized them, you'll be able to use your keywords and favorites to quickly locate a shot that illustrates something being discussed by your interviewee. Here we go:

1. Using **Keywords** and **Favorites** in the Browser, locate a relevant B-roll clip.

2. Select a 3–5 second section of this clip.

   Selecting the right part of the clip is an art — should it be static or moving? If there's motion in the shot, should you start or end on the action or show it in the middle? These are deeper content-related questions that I'll sidestep here, so just go with your gut and know you'll get better at it.

3. Hover in the **Timeline**, just before the visible jump cut:

Figure 7.3: You can see that a selection has been made in the Browser, and the Skimmer is in place in the Timeline

4. Press **Q** to connect the Browser clip above the jump cut in the timeline:

Figure 7.4: The B-roll clip has been connected above the Primary Storyline, and the browser clip has an orange line to indicate usage

So far, so good — you've connected a clip. Let's try drag and drop too:

1. Repeat the earlier steps: create another jump cut elsewhere in the timeline, then select a few seconds of a second relevant B-roll clip.

2. Drag the selected part of the clip from the Browser to above a jump cut in the **Timeline**, and drop it there:

Figure 7.5: Dragging clearly shows the duration of the dragged clip before you drop it

Drag and drop gives a nice visual preview of the length of the clip you're dragging, but using the keyboard is a little faster. Use either method or both, but you'll find that if the selected area of a clip in the Browser is small, you'll struggle to drag and drop it, and **Q** will work best.

Those two options for connecting B-roll video also work for audio, but with a few differences.

CONNECTING SOUND EFFECTS

The process of finding and then connecting sound effects is similar, especially if you've imported your own audio into your Library. Here, we'll look in a different place:

1. Click on the **Photos and Audio** icon at the top-left of the Browser.

2. Click on **Sound Effects** to access the built-in bank of sound effects and short music pieces. (Note: If these are missing, choose **Final Cut Pro > Download Additional Content** to get them for free.)

3. Select the **Final Cut Pro Sound Effects** or **iLife Sound Effects** category from the menu in the top-right.

4. Move through the list and preview one or more sound effects by pressing **Space**:

Figure 7.6: Start by clicking on the icon in the top left, then choose what to look at with the menu in the top right

There are hundreds of effects here, from explosions to wind, to telephones ringing and children laughing. It doesn't have to totally make sense in the context of your shot — squeaky toys used instead of footsteps are pretty funny. Of course, you can use your own banks of sound effects too. They can be stored in **iTunes** or the **Apple Music** app, then accessed in the list above **Sound Effects**. Alternatively, simply import audio clips from the Finder to your Library when needed.

5. When you find a sound effect appropriate for something in your timeline, with or without a jump cut, press **Q** to connect it (this adds the entire sound effect, but if you want only part of it, select it first):

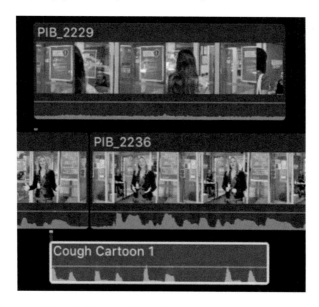

Figure 7.7: Here, a "cough" sound has been added below the main Storyline, possibly relevant in this video about health checks on entering a hospital

When you connect an audio clip, you'll see that it connects below the vision rather than above, but you'll still hear it. While you can always hear all of the clips at any point in a timeline, in general, you'll only see the highest clip in the stack. There are exceptions with regard to keying, cropping, or blending, but as the purpose of a cutaway is to cover up the clips below, it works well. Video above and audio below is a simple rule and keeps the timeline uncluttered:

Figure 7.8: Drag this line to adjust the volume of a clip

While audio will be explored more thoroughly in *Chapter 14, Boost the Signal: Audio Sweetening*, know that you can change the volume of any clip by dragging on the horizontal line running above its waveform. There's much more to it, but that's all you need for now.

CONNECTING ONLY AUDIO OR VIDEO

Often, a clip with both audio and video tracks is only partly useful. Maybe the audio portion of an interview is useful, but the video is out of focus. Maybe the vision of cars in traffic is great, but the sound is unusably distorted. You can deal with this situation in a couple of different ways: by hiding or silencing what you don't want or not adding it to the timeline in the first place. First, here's how to hide it:

- One method to mute visual B-roll so it can't be heard is to **Silence** it. The **Modify > Adjust Volume > Silence (-∞)** command is the quickest way to do this, but you could also drag the clip's volume line all of the way to the bottom of the clip (if you followed the steps in *Chapter 1, Quick Start: An Introduction to FCP*, to set up a custom shortcut, you could press **zero** now):

Figure 7.9: That top clip didn't have useful audio, so I turned it down

- To hide the video component of a clip but keep the audio, connect the clip underneath the Primary Storyline. That way, it's hidden, but you can hear it.

If you know that you never want to see the vision or hear the audio for a particular clip, there's a small menu next to the edit buttons that will change how they work:

Figure 7.10: If you choose to bring in only Video or Audio, the icons will change to reflect this

The default option of **All** brings in an entire clip, but if you choose **Video Only** or **Audio Only**, then that's all you get. With video only, there's no audio to make quieter, and with audio only, there's no image to see:

Figure 7.11: With no audio, there's no waveform at all and no volume line

However you connect your clips, and whatever kind of clips you connect, it's not just a name — Final Cut makes an explicit, visible connection between a Primary Storyline clip and a clip above or below it:

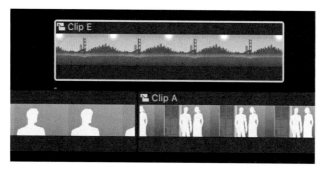

Figure 7.12: The line at the lower left of Clip E indicates which clip it's connected to

Normally these connections are small stubs, but they become visible when a clip on either side of the connection is selected. These connections aren't just for show; they change the way editing works and are worth a deeper look.

UNDERSTANDING CONNECTIONS

Probably the biggest difference between a traditional editing timeline and the FCP Magnetic Timeline is the way in which clips sit above or below other clips. In a traditional editing application, a clip's timecode is the most important factor: clips sit at a point in time, and any relationship between two clips positioned above or below one another is merely implied. Such clips can move out of sync with each other if you're not careful.

Here in FCP, clips on the Primary Storyline form the spine around which everything else is built: clips above or below are always connected to a clip on the Primary Storyline, no matter how many clips there are in the stack. When a clip with connections is moved, the connected clips also move, and when a clip with connections is deleted, the connected clips are also deleted. Logically, this makes sense: a shot of a car should be connected to a person talking about that car. It's even clearer for sound effects: a sound effect of a car backfiring belongs to a specific time within a shot of a car. Music behaves a little differently though.

WORKING WITH MUSIC

The process of connecting a music clip is much the same as connecting any other clip: find a clip, select all or part of it, then connect it with **Q**. Therefore, to add background music for an entire edit, you'd connect that clip at the very start of a timeline. That makes a connection to the first clip on the Primary Storyline: perhaps a regular video clip or even a Gap clip. But be wary, because this can become complex, and this timeline isn't unusual:

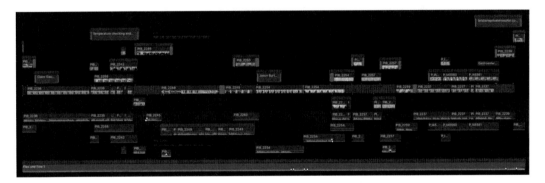

Figure 7.13: Here's a real-world finished job, with plenty of connected clips, and music connected at the start

A music clip can be quite long, a few minutes or so, and like any connected clip, it can only have a single connection point. Here's the issue: even though the music may drive an edit, later edit points aren't explicitly connected to specific points in the music. They can't be, as each clip has only one connection point. For background music that doesn't interact with the edit, this isn't a problem at all — move your edits around as much as you like and it'll work well. But if you want the whole edit to be driven by the music, don't move the initial clip where the audio is connected.

Moving that first video clip (or Gap clip) would shift the music in time throughout the whole edit. Any implied sync moments, where a later edit works with the music at that time, would be lost — this includes edits placed on beats and lip-synced performances. To avoid problems, you'll want to apply any ripple trim edits to only the last couple of clips you've added, working from left to right in the Primary Storyline. Any edits earlier on the timeline would change the sync relationship between later clips and their accompanying music. Also, deleting that first video clip would be disastrous because the audio would disappear with it.

While none of these sync problems are unique to FCP, connections and the Magnetic Timeline can make the process of editing a music video a little different from other types of jobs. Because many of the video clips in a music video should be explicitly connected to specific, different points in the audio, one reasonable approach is to place the audio track on the Primary Storyline and then to connect all video above it:

Figure 7.14: This music video (Gravitate by Ky.) uses several connected Storylines above a music track in the Primary Storyline

Later on, once you have more of a handle on how things work, you might try a hybrid approach with audio connected to a primary clip as usual, and that's fine too. Music videos remain a special case, and in most other types of edits, you'll enjoy the local clip-based sync that connections enable.

But there's something a little different with clips that aren't on the Primary Storyline. Connected clips can still be moved and can be trimmed by dragging their edges, but if you pay close attention, the cursor you'll see when trimming is a little different from trimming Primary Storyline clips.

TRIMMING CONNECTED CLIPS

Hovering over the edges of a connected clip, you'll see that while the cursor shows the end or beginning of a clip, it doesn't show the filmstrip below that points to the clip being adjusted:

Figure 7.15: There's no filmstrip on the cursor when you trim an independently connected clip

That part of the icon indicated that a ripple operation was taking place, affecting other clips in the timeline. There's no filmstrip here because trimming a connected clip doesn't affect anything else — every connected clip is independent:

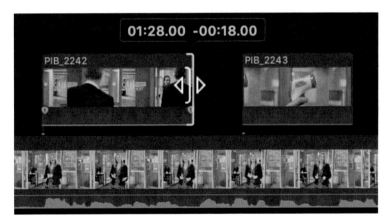

Figure 7.16: Rather than closing the gap, trimming the Out point of the first clip creates a gap

If a clip is extended in time to overlap another clip, the other clip simply moves out of the way. Try it now in your own timeline:

Figure 7.17: Extending a connected clip doesn't erase anything else — other connected clips just move up or down

In the **Viewer**, you'll only see the clip that's highest in the stack at a point in time, and if the wrong clip is on top, you can drag clips directly up or down to change the stacking order. (A quick tip: hold ⇧ as you move a clip up or down to avoid also moving it in time.)

REVIEW — CONNECTING CLIPS

That was a big section. From learning about cutaways to adding video above, adding audio below, learning how connections work, considering music, then trimming... connections are powerful and used in all but the simplest of edits. Still, connected clips don't really interact with one another: when you move a connected clip up, down, left, or right, it's the only thing that moves. Other nearby connected clips stay exactly where they're already connected and aren't pushed around. What if you want other connected clips to move around, rippling and rearranging like clips on the Primary Storyline? There's a solution: Storylines.

GROUPING CONNECTED CLIPS IN STORYLINES

Connected clips are great, but as they're totally independent, they can feel somewhat limited, and grouping two or more clips together in a gray box is the solution. To use the ripple-trim and rearranging magic of the Magnetic Timeline on connected clips, you'll need to wrap one or more clips up into a **Storyline**, and here's the process:

1. Select multiple nearby connected clips by dragging a selection box around them:

Figure 7.18: Each of these connected clips has its own connection line

2. Press **⌘G** to place those clips inside a **Storyline** (the **Create Storyline** command is in the **Clip** menu):

Figure 7.19: These two selected clips have been placed in a Storyline with a single connection line

You'll see that the selected clips are placed within a gray box — that's the **Storyline**. While each of the clips was previously connected to separate Primary Storyline clips, there's now only one connection to the Storyline. The entire Storyline functions like a group and can be moved in time by selecting it, then dragging it or using the **comma** and **period** nudging shortcuts. And critically, rearranging and trimming clips inside a Storyline works just like it does on the Primary Storyline:

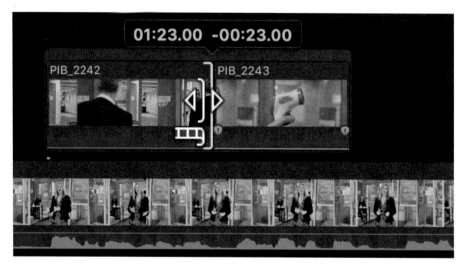

Figure 7.20: Trimming the end of the first connected clip now closes gaps

Storylines give you the power of the Magnetic Timeline with the flexibility of connections. They're great for visual B-roll where more than one clip is appropriate: place a few connected B-roll clips in a Storyline (perhaps above one or more jump cuts) to allow easier editing.

They are also great for audio editing, even if you start with just a single clip inside one. If you place music or a longer voiceover in a Storyline, you can use the **Range Selection** tool to select anything you don't want, then press **delete** to close gaps automatically. Conversely, if you do want Gap clips in a Storyline (and you can make one with ⇧**delete**), they can be extended in time to increase the length of a pause.

IMPORTANT NOTE

Though we will come back to **transitions** much later in this book, if you add a transition to a connected clip (for example, a **Dissolve** with ⌘**T**), then you'll automatically create a Storyline because transitions require them.

There's another sneaky way to make a Storyline. If you drag a clip next to another connected clip, then hold **G** as you release, you'll see it snap in place into a newly created Storyline that holds both clips. Nice.

The process of dragging a box to select multiple clips has a subtlety that's especially important with Storylines. If you drag sideways through a Storyline, you'll select the clips within it:

Figure 7.21: Dragging sideways through a Storyline selects the clips within it

However, if you drag vertically through a Storyline, you'll select the Storyline itself:

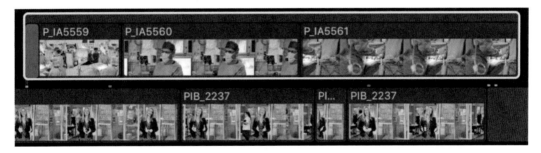

Figure 7.22: Dragging vertically selects the Storyline and not the clips inside

The difference is important because you'll need to select clips (not a Storyline) if you want to adjust their properties in the Inspector, and you'll want to select the Storyline (not the clips) if you want to move the entire Storyline. It's not hard to get used to, but it is subtle.

Finally, if you don't want one or more clips to be in a Storyline any more, just drag them upward and out of the gray enclosing box. Any remaining clips inside the Storyline will rearrange to close any gaps created, and if the last clip is removed, the Storyline will disappear. Note that you won't be able to drag a transition outside its Storyline because transitions can only exist within Storylines.

REVIEW – GROUPING CONNECTED CLIPS IN STORYLINES

Storylines are a great feature, and you'll pop clips in and out of them as you work through an edit. Grouping clips in Storylines is a key way to gain the gap-closing magnetic benefits of the Primary Storyline with the freedom of connected clips, and mastering them will be important as you build more complex edits. Connections from clips and Storylines to clips on the Primary Storyline are a big part of what makes editing in FCP so fluid.

However, those connections can sometimes cause trouble. If something goes wrong, you'll need to know how to force a clip to stay put. Let's find out how.

CONTROLLING AND OVERRIDING CONNECTIONS

Normally, when you move a Primary Storyline clip around, any connected clips will move too. That's because the clip-to-clip connection is usually the most important, and it's what FCP tries to maintain. Sometimes, though, you want to keep a connected clip exactly where it is, and this section will show you a couple of techniques to do that.

First, if you want to connect a clip at a different point, hold ⌥⌘ and click on the connected clip. The connection will now be shifted to the clicked point in time, connecting to the clip on the Primary Storyline at that timecode. The same applies to Storylines, but you'll have to hold ⌥⌘ and click in the gray bar just above the clips instead:

Figure 7.23: Here, the connection has been moved to the second clip in the Primary Storyline rather than the first

Moving connections like this lets you change which Primary Storyline clip "owns" a connected clip. As connected items are moved or deleted when a Primary Storyline clip is moved or deleted, this lets you decide which primary clips control those connected clips. For example, consider this timeline:

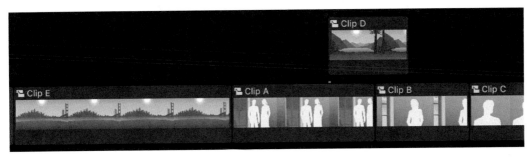

Figure 7.24: Clip D is connected to Clip A

If you want to delete **Clip A** but keep **Clip D** connected in place, you could first attach **Clip D** to a clip that follows **Clip A**:

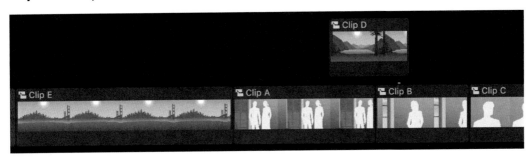

Figure 7.25: After repositioning, Clip D is now connected to Clip B

Clip A can now be deleted safely. However, the connected **Clip D** will still move in time if its new "parent" **Clip B** moves after the deletion of **Clip A**:

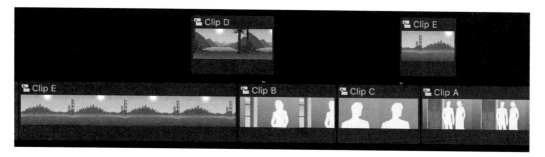

Figure 7.26: Clip A has been deleted, and Clip D now overlaps the previous Clip E

If that's not what you wanted, you have a few options:

- Reposition connected clips to a point preceding (not following) the clip you're about to delete. This isn't always possible.

- Use ⇧**delete** instead of **delete** to replace a clip with a Gap clip. The connected clips remain in the same spot with the same connection points:

Figure 7.27: Use ⇧delete to replace a clip with a Gap and keep all other clips where they are

- Use the **Replace** or **Replace from Start** feature to exchange one clip for another rather than deleting it. Replacing is covered in *Chapter 9, Consider Your Options: Multicam, Replacing, and Auditions.*

- Use the **Position** tool to overwrite Primary Storyline clips without affecting clips connected to that region. This is likely to affect timeline behavior in a more substantial way and so might not be appropriate. This is covered in *Chapter 10, Explore a Little: Compound Clips and Timeline Tricks.*

There's one more solution that warrants deeper discussion:

- Hold down the ` key (*grave*, on the same key as ~ or *tilde*) to temporarily override connections on primary clips you're rearranging or deleting.

When holding `, you'll see an additional icon appear on your cursor:

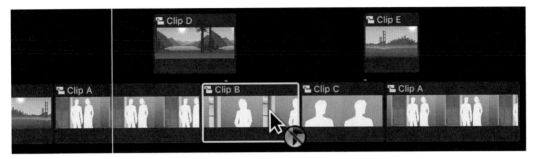

Figure 7.28: With ` held down, Clip B is moved

The "override connections" mode is an important toggle: any clips connected to the clip you're moving or deleting will stay where they are as if they weren't connected at all:

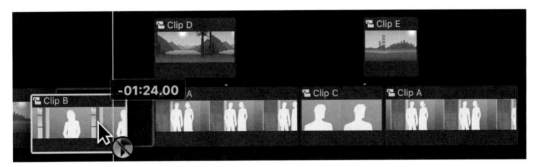

Figure 7.29: When Clip B is dropped before Clip A, connected Clip D doesn't move

However, any clips connected to other Primary Storyline clips might still move around if their parents move as a result of the rearrangement or deletion:

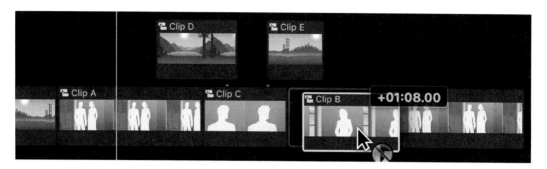

Figure 7.30: Starting from the earlier timeline, Clip B is moved later in the timeline past Clip C, and Clip E moves along with Clip C

That's normally just fine because you don't want to mess up an entire timeline worth of clip relationships, but the first time your connected clips jumble on top of one another, it may feel jarring. In the real world, this isn't normally much of a problem; you'd need to reposition the connected B-roll clips anyway.

If you ever find yourself confused by what's going on, or a clip moves when you didn't expect, just Undo (⌘Z) and try again a different way. You'll also find that Replacing a clip is often a cleaner approach compared to deleting an old clip and then adding a new one — but more on replacing later.

REVIEW — CONTROLLING AND OVERRIDING CONNECTIONS

While it's possible to stumble through an edit without it, you've learned how to reposition a connection with a quick ⌥⌘-click, and that can be very helpful. Overriding a connection with ` is similarly important, and you've learned about other options too. Connections can occasionally be complex, but their benefits are worth a little juggling from time to time.

Next, you'll learn about a more precise way to work, where you explicitly define the region in a timeline where you'll add a clip.

THREE-POINT EDITING AND MORE

You may not have considered it, but most edits are defined in terms of the source clip (which part of a clip you want to use) rather than the timeline (where do you want the clip to go). However, it's possible to prioritize the timeline instead, and this is sometimes called "three-point editing," because technically, at least three points are defined every time you add a clip. It's a traditional method, and here, you'll learn about how to mark part of the timeline to receive a clip and how to connect or overwrite a clip to that region.

So far, we've added connected clips in a somewhat haphazard, less controlled way, by selecting a few seconds of a clip and then pressing **Q**. That means that the three points are the In (1) and Out (2) on a Browser clip, plus an In (3) point on the timeline.

But you can flip that "source clip dominance" around by explicitly placing two of those points on the timeline. To connect a new clip in a specific region, do the following:

1. In the Browser, skim over a clip you'd like to connect at a point you'd like to start from, and press **I** to mark an In point.

2. In the timeline, skim to a point where you want to add the connected clip, and press **I** to mark an In point.

3. Skim to where you want to end the connected clip.

4. Press **O** to mark an Out point:

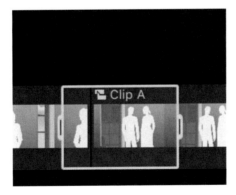

Figure 7.31: On the timeline, make sure you have an In and Out selected

5. Press **Q** to connect the selected clip:

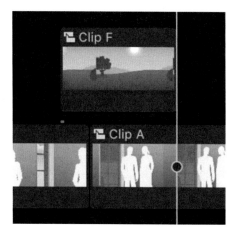

Figure 7.32: After connecting, the region selected on the timeline defines
the duration of the source clip

If the source clip has enough media to fill the selected region of the timeline, a clip will be connected to just that region. It'll start from the In point you chose in the Browser, and run for the length you chose in the timeline, but the Out point in the Browser (chosen or implied) will be ignored. The Skimmer is also ignored, if present.

If you're viewing **Favorites**, **Hide Rejected**, or a **Keyword Collection**, be aware that hidden parts of your source clip might be used if the selected timeline duration needs more content than the visible display currently shows — if more media is available, it will be used. Should the source clip really be too short, you'll be presented with an error, and if you proceed, you'll be given as much media as there is available.

BACKTIMING

From time to time, it can be more important what's at the end of a connected clip rather than the beginning, and there's a solution for that too. Instead of picking an In point in the Browser, press **O** to pick an Out point. And instead of pressing **Q** to connect, press **⇧Q** to perform a backtimed connect. This option places the Out point from the Browser clip at the Out point in the **Timeline**, then uses as much media before that point as the timeline region requires.

Both the regular and backtimed three-point edits are useful if you're an editor who likes precision, but if you'd prefer to just throw it in and trim it later, it's up to you.

OVERWRITING

There's one more feature to look at here. Though it's not prominent, it's one of the two primary methods of editing in traditional non-linear editing apps and the fourth of the four editing buttons: **Overwrite**, which puts video at a specific point on the Primary Storyline:

Figure 7.33: Overwrite is button #4 here, but in the original FCP X 10.0, it didn't have a button at all

It's possible to Overwrite with two points on a source clip and a third on the timeline, but it's more common to put two on the timeline, as before:

1. In the Browser, skim over a clip you'd like to connect, at a point you'd like to start from, and press **I** to mark an In point (or **O** to mark an Out point).

2. On the timeline, skim to a point where you want to add the connected clip, and press **I** to mark an In point.

3. Skim to where you want to end the connected clip.

4. Press **O** to mark an Out point.

5. Press **D** to Overwrite the selected clip, or **⇧D** to Overwrite with backtiming (from the Out point back):

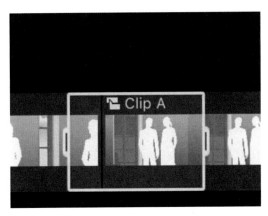 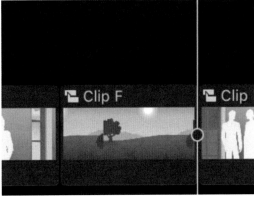

Figure 7.34: Before and after an Overwrite operation using three-point editing

What's different? This isn't a connection above the Primary Storyline but a replacement of the clips currently on the Primary Storyline. This is not an easily reversible operation, and any clips or regions within the selection will be entirely overwritten. Why do this? Well, I confess that I almost never do. If you want to use the Primary Storyline rather than connecting clips, then I can see the appeal, but I find connecting a clip above does what I want and lets any audio from the primary be heard.

One exception: you might want to Overwrite a clip into a connected Storyline. That's possible, but you'll have to select the Storyline (not a clip within the Storyline) before you press **D** or **⇧D**. Again, that's not something I usually do, as I prefer to Replace — but that's coming up in the next chapter. Lastly, let's clarify copy and paste.

COPY AND PASTE

Copy and paste are key operations in many applications, and while they're here too, connections can complicate matters just a little. If you copy a connected clip, it'll stay connected when you paste it, which makes sense. And if you copy a Primary Storyline clip, it'll paste to the Primary Storyline, performing an Insert operation and potentially breaking up a clip under the Skimmer. All of that makes sense.

If, however, you want to copy from the Primary Storyline and then paste as a connected clip, you'll need to use **Edit** > **Paste as Connected Clip** (**⌥V**) instead of a regular paste. There's no complementary operation to "paste as primary" but it's easy to do a regular paste and then drag it into the Primary Storyline if that's what you want.

REVIEW — THREE-POINT EDITING AND MORE

You've learned how to perform a few more traditional edits in this more modern timeline, and some of them are just as useful now as they have been for decades, even if you might not overwrite as often as an editor from 10 years ago. Defining the part of the timeline where a clip should go is a perfectly sensible way to work, and backtiming is a great answer when the end of a clip is more important than the start. Copy and paste flexibility is also important for that time when you need to connect a clip that was once part of the Primary Storyline.

It's possible to ignore these commands and just nudge and trim everything into place, but you'll get a certain satisfaction from a clip that just slots perfectly into place. Do explore these operations and see whether they work for you, and if not — no problem.

Let's wrap it all up.

SUMMARY

While some of the concepts in this chapter are simple, others are a little on the tricky side. I've long said that "a good user interface makes simple things easy and hard things possible," and the unfortunate side-effect of connecting clips to other clips is that can add complexity.

While it's true that the same complexity isn't present in a track-based editing paradigm, connections allow you to move a single clip in the Primary Storyline, move its connections automatically, and be sure that all other connected clips will stay connected to their parents too. The unique parent-child connection here means that a connected clip always belongs to a parent, but that parent isn't dragged around if its child moves. It's not a locked group with both clips in charge; the primary clip is always the spine of the story.

Without connections, the lack of parent-child clip-to-clip linking means that it can be easy to lose sync between two items, or for one clip to wipe out another when they end up on the same track at the same time: *Track Tetris* is a real issue in most **Non-Linear Editors (NLEs)**. This never happens in FCP, and if the trade-off is a little complexity around connections, I'm happy to take it.

In *Chapter 10, Explore a Little: Compound Clips and Timeline Tricks*, I'll show you a few more ways to boss around the Magnetic Timeline, but you won't need them yet. Keep the spine of the story on the Primary Storyline with any cutaways connected above, use Storylines for a sequence of cutaways, and connect any background music in a Storyline below. If something goes weird, **⌘Z** it away, and drag and drop will save the day.

Rearranging, trimming, and covering up clips will take you a long way, but a few extra tools will make things much easier. Next up, because this isn't iMovie, it's time to explore some of the more advanced trimming options.

REVIEW QUESTIONS

1. What is a cutaway usually used for?

2. What kind of clip is usually used for a cutaway?

3. What happens when you hover over the timeline and press **Q**?

4. What's different about connecting audio as compared to video?

5. If you bring in a clip without audio, what is visually missing in the timeline?

6. What is not shown on the trim cursor when trimming the edge of a connected clip?

7. What can be used to group connected clips so they can be easily rearranged?

8. How do you reposition a connection point?

9. What key can you hold down to override connections?

10. What is it called when the Out point of a source clip has priority in an edit rather than the In point?

REVIEW ANSWERS

1. It's used for covering up an edit underneath it.

2. B-roll is used.

3. The selected clip (or part of a clip) is connected to that point.

4. Audio connects below while video connects above. (Video can be moved below the Primary Storyline, but audio cannot be moved above the Primary Storyline.)

5. Its waveform is missing.

6. The filmstrip isn't shown, which would indicate a ripple edit.

7. Storylines can be used.

8. You do so by using ⌥⌘-click (**Option-Command-click**) on the connected clip or Storyline.

9. You hold down ` (grave) on the same key as ~ (tilde).

10. It's called backtiming.

8 NEATEN THE EDGES:
TRIMMING TECHNIQUES

"With FCP X, I was able to establish my own filmmaking and editing business in remote outback Queensland, to create and share the unique stories of the people of the bush."

— Kirstie Davison, MaRiKi Media
Kirstie is a videographer and editor based in Blackall,
Queensland, Australia. (www.marikimedia.com)

Following the book so far, you've been moving clips around in time, chopping them up, selecting and deleting, and hopefully getting a bit more confident. Probably the single most common operation you've done so far is a basic trim on a single edit point. Simple one-point trimming is certainly a useful operation, and you can make a clip longer or shorter with the keyboard or the mouse. But a one-point trim doesn't always do enough.

In this chapter, you'll discover several ways to adjust not one, but two edit points at the same time. This chapter covers the following topics:

- Rolling an edit
- Slipping and Sliding clips
- Softening audio with split edits (J- and L-cuts)
- Editing numerically and with the Precision Editor

By the end of this chapter, you'll understand when and how to use the **Trim** tool and you'll be able to make subtle edits that don't cause a ripple effect all along the timeline. You'll be able to use a different part of a source clip with a single flick, and move the edit point between two clips. You'll also learn how to soften your edits by cutting audio and video separately, how to edit with numbers, and how to use the Precision Editor, a special mode that exposes the media behind each edit.

Before we begin, a quick word on the best ways to switch between tools. Most of these edits are enabled by the **Trim** tool (**T**) that's found in the regular tool menu, and you'll be toggling between it and the regular **Select** tool (**A**) from here on. Use the keys!

The tool menu can be seen in the following screenshot:

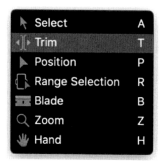

Figure 8.1: The tool menu is found on the central gray bar

As with all the tool shortcuts, you can use keys as a persistent switch, or a temporary one, as follows:

- To switch to the **Trim** tool persistently (that is, until you switch to another tool), just press the **T** key and let it go.

- To switch to the **Trim** tool temporarily, hold down the **T** key, perform your trimming operations, and then release the **T** key.

If you're using the "temporary" strategy, your previously selected tool will be selected once you release the key. This technique works with all of the tool shortcuts. For now, we'll start out with the regular **Select** tool, so press **A** to switch to that for a quick discussion about trimming, before we jump to Rolling. To work along with the book, use regular clips rather than Multicam Clips for now, because (as you'll see in the next chapter) trimming functions differently with multicams.

Shortcuts sorted — great. Onward!

ROLLING AN EDIT

While a regular trim adjusts an In point or an Out point on a clip, a Roll edit adjusts the Out point on one clip and the In point on the next clip at the same time, by the same duration. While it works best on two neighboring clips in the Primary Storyline, it can also work on two clips in a connected storyline, or even on two independently connected clips that have no gap between them.

Why would you want to do that? Because it lets you trade one clip's length against another *without causing a ripple down the timeline*. The first clip gets longer while the second clip gets shorter, and no other clips move at all. This is a key point, so let's quickly recap on how a regular trim works.

UNDERSTANDING A REGULAR TRIM EDIT

To see the ripple edits that regular trims cause, here's a timeline before a regular one-point trim operation (using the **Select** tool) with a single Out point selected:

Figure 8.2: The Select tool dragging an Out point

And now, as that Out point is dragged, later clips are being rippled down the timeline, as you can see:

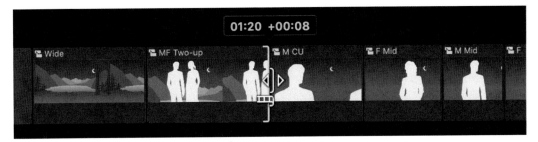

Figure 8.3: As the Out point moves right, other clips are pushed away

If the In point had been selected instead, the previous clip would have moved forward to fill the gap, as illustrated in the following screenshot:

Figure 8.4: Dragging the In point to the right makes the clip shorter, but no gap is made

You've performed both of these operations a few times already, but if you're not confident, feel free to practice. You'll be able to see the two-up display in the **Viewer** change as you do this, but only one side of the display will change; after all, you're only adjusting one edit point. When you're clear, read on.

PERFORMING A ROLL EDIT

Because one point isn't always enough, let's now try using a Roll edit to adjust two points, as follows:

1. Press **T** to switch to the **Trim** tool.

2. Hover over the point between two clips, and you'll see the cursor shown here:

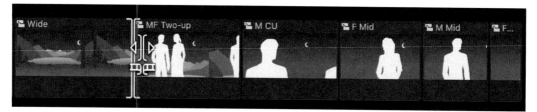

Figure 8.5: Neighboring Out and In points are selected together

Unlike the regular trimming cursor, which has one in or out indicator and one filmstrip, the Roll cursor shows both an Out point and neighboring In point, plus two filmstrips, indicating that two edit points will be adjusted.

3. Click and drag left or right to perform a Roll edit, as illustrated in the following screenshot:

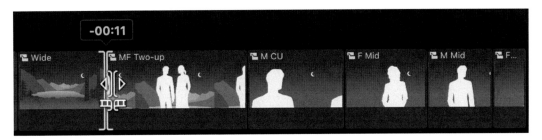

Figure 8.6: Both points move to the left, and overall timeline duration
is constant

This time, you'll see both frames in the two-up display in the **Viewer** changing. You'll also notice that the overall length of the timeline stays the same and that no other clips are affected in any way. The Roll operation is therefore extremely helpful when you're getting closer to the end of an edit and you don't want to move things around anymore.

As you might expect, you can only Roll a clip as far as the media allows. If you drag all the way to the start or end of a clip, you'll see a red clip edge that stops you moving any further, as illustrated in the following screenshot:

Figure 8.7: Red edge? You're out of media

While you probably won't have any trouble triggering the Roll operation, the **Trim** tool still actually allows you to perform a regular one-point trim operation — you just have to be more specific about where you place the mouse. As you move toward the center of where two edits meet, the cursor switches to indicate a two-point Roll, but if you move a little further toward either side, the cursor will change back to indicate a regular one-point trim. As ever, if you get it wrong, a quick ⌘**Z** will fix things up. In general, I find that if I want a regular one-point trim, I'll just press **A** to switch to the **Select** tool rather than fiddling with the **Trim** tool to find the right spot.

USING KEYBOARD SHORTCUTS TO ROLL

Unsurprisingly, you can Roll with the keyboard as well as with the mouse, and the process is as you'd expect. Here's a hybrid method using both together:

1. Press **T** to select the **Trim** tool, and hover between two clips (above the neighboring out and in points).

2. With the **Roll** cursor showing, click the edit to select both points at once.

3. Press **comma** to move both points one frame to the left, or **period** to move both points one frame to the right.

4. Press ⇧**comma** to move both points 10 frames to the left, or ⇧**period** to move both points 10 frames to the right.

These shortcuts are fantastic for making minor tweaks to an edit, and a couple of frames can make all the difference in a scene. Remember to check your work by using **Play Around Edit** (⇧/ or **?**) after you adjust. (For the moment, we'll adjust video and audio together, but we'll split them up soon.)

For the truly mouse-averse, there's no need to select with the mouse at all. You'll remember the following shortcuts from *Chapter 6, Build the Spine of the Story: Quick Assembly*:

- ↓ or **apostrophe (')** jumps to the first frame of the next clip
- ↑ or **semicolon (;)** jumps to the first frame of the previous clip
- **[** selects the Out point of the clip to the left of the playhead
- **]** selects the In point of the clip to the right of the playhead

To select two points for a Roll edit, you'll need one more key, as follows:

- **** selects both Out and In points around the playhead

The **** key is to the right of **[** and **]** on Australian and North American keyboards, and just below and to the right on UK keyboards, so it's physically nearby. It's entirely up to you if you prefer a hybrid mouse/keyboard approach or the keyboard-only way instead, but if you would prefer to hover with the mouse and then switch to the keyboard, be sure to activate **Snapping (N)**.

REVIEW — ROLLING AN EDIT

Trading one clip against another is a vital step toward more subtle edits. If you're happy with the overall length of a sequence, but one clip is a little long and the next is a little short, you need to know how to Roll. But that's not the only trick that the **Trim** tool can do: it can also Slip and Slide.

SLIPPING AND SLIDING CLIPS

These two operations both adjust two edit points, but they don't move the outgoing Out point on Clip A and the incoming In point on Clip B. Instead, a **Slip** adjusts both the In and Out points on a single clip, like this:

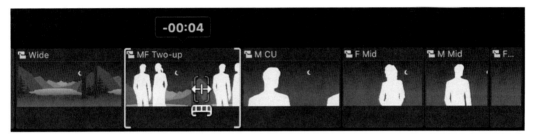

Figure 8.8: Using the Trim tool on the body of a clip (not the edges) creates a Slip

The less common **Slide** operation adjusts the Out point before a clip and the In point after a clip, as illustrated in the following screenshot:

Figure 8.9: Using the Trim tool on the body of a clip while holding ⌥ creates a Slide

That probably won't make a lot of sense without some good examples, so let's dig into those in more detail.

USING A SLIP EDIT

This is easier to do than to explain, so add a clip with obvious movement to help you to follow along. Here, I've added part of a clip to the timeline: a shot of a boat moving from left to right. The shot starts with the boat fully in frame, but ends completely out of shot to the right, as illustrated in the following screenshot:

Figure 8.10: The sequential thumbnails tell the story of a boat moving
left to right

If you're working with your own media, make sure you're only using part of a clip, and preferably a part of the clip somewhere in the middle. A handy tool here is to select a timeline clip, then press ⇧F to **Reveal in Browser**, which shows the original Browser clip. (This is a *match frame* operation, if you're an old hand.) In the Browser, you can see the whole source clip selected, and if you've enabled **View** > **Browser** > **Used Media Ranges**, you can also see an orange line underneath the section of the clip currently in use, like this:

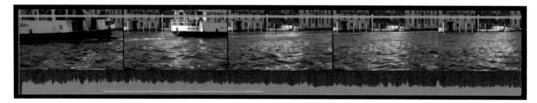

Figure 8.11: As seen in the Browser, with the orange line indicating
Used media

Understanding the link between a clip in the timeline and the source clip in the Browser will be useful in these next steps:

- With the **Trim** tool (**T**) selected, click on the middle of a clip (not near the left or right edges) and drag sideways to perform a Slip edit, as illustrated in the following screenshot:

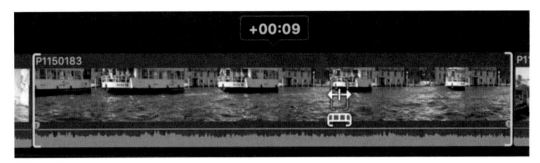

Figure 8.12: The two highlighted edit points are being adjusted

The moving filmstrips make this a natural operation. If you drag to the left, you'll use a later part of the clip, and if you drag to the right, you'll use an earlier part of the clip. You can tell what's happening by watching the filmstrip thumbnails, and the Viewer will show you the clip's new In point and Out point as you drag.

Here, I've dragged to the left, to use the later part of the clip. As the boat is moving from left to right, the shot starts with the boat about to leave the frame, and finishes at some point after the boat has left the frame. While I hold the mouse button, the Viewer looks like this:

Figure 8.13: The Viewer's two-up display shows the changing In and Out points on the clip

After releasing the mouse, in the Browser, you can see the orange line is now later in the clip, as illustrated in the following screenshot:

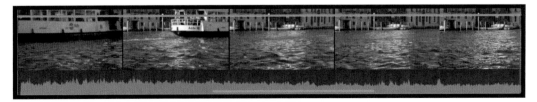

Figure 8.14: The orange line indicates which part of the media is used

Conversely, if I were to drag on the clip to the right with the **Trim** tool, I'd Slip the clip earlier and eventually run out of media, as you can see:

Figure 8.15: The filmstrip on the two-up display indicates the end of the media

The filmstrip on the left edge indicates that I'm at the very start of the clip and have run out of media. I can also see that from the red clip edge in the timeline, as illustrated:

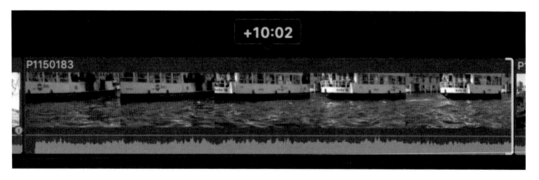

Figure 8.16: When you Slip all the way to the start of the clip, you'll see a red left edge

And after releasing the mouse, the Browser tells the same story:

Figure 8.17: With the clip slipped this far back, the boat never leaves the frame

There's a handy analogy here. Think of a clip on the timeline as a window that lets you see part of its whole source clip. The Slip operation lets you grab the whole source clip and move it backward and forward to reveal a different part of it. Rolling and one-point ripple-trim operations change the edges of this "window", but Slip doesn't — the timeline clip stays the same length, and you just use a different part of it.

Another handy example might help. Let's say you need to use a 4-second shot of a posed group of children. You've picked out a section of the shot in the middle that looks good. However, the client spots that near the end of the shot, one of the kids makes a rude gesture. You could fix this by switching to the **Trim** tool and dragging to the right, Slipping to an earlier part of the clip, and sending that gesture sailing into oblivion past the Out point.

You'll need extra media to be able to Slip. Unsurprisingly, if you were to use an entire source clip on the Timeline, dragging with the Trim tool simply won't work. Both clip edges will be red, because there's no extra media to reveal or hide. (In the preceding clip, it's a shame I didn't start recording a few seconds earlier, because it could have been helpful to catch the boat entering the frame as well as leaving it. Editors love options.)

OK. You can now Roll and Slip. But there's one more trick to the **Trim** tool.

USING A SLIDE EDIT

You can think of a Slide edit as a Roll with a clip in the middle. When you Slide, you move the dragged clip to the left or right, but the clip you're dragging only moves in time, and its contents stay the same. The Out point of the previous clip and the In point of the next clip are both changed, as if those two clips are rolling neighbors. The clip in the middle is repositioned within the timeline, but otherwise it's unchanged. So, how do you do it? Here's how:

- With the **Trim** tool (**T**) selected, hold ⌥ and click on the middle of a clip (not near the left or right edges) and drag sideways to perform a Slide edit:

Figure 8.18: With the Trim tool active, ⌥-dragging the second clip

Here, I'm ⌥-**dragging** the second clip, meaning that the Wide clip before and the close-up clip after are adjusted in a Slide operation. For many editors, this isn't a very common task because it actually crosses over neatly into a common operation with connected clips. If the active clip in this example were above the other clips — a connected clip rather than a Primary Storyline clip — then moving the clip left or right would give the same results as Sliding on the Primary Storyline. It would look something like this:

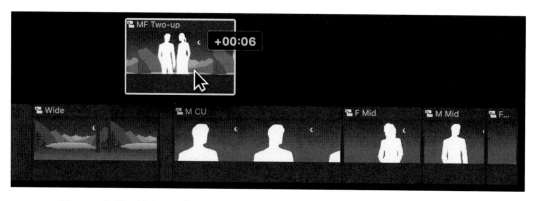

Figure 8.19: With a clip connected above, moving it sideways is a lot like sliding

Indeed, if I know I'm going to shift a clip around in time to get it just right, I'd connect it above, and so I don't Slide very often at all. But if you do Slide, you'll see a two-up display in the **Viewer**, just as you do with Roll and Slip. There's no two-up display when you move a connected clip. Another reason to choose to Slide is that it simplifies your timeline, keeping the number of vertical clips to a minimum. While one or two layers of connected clips aren't a problem, an edit is easier to understand at a glance if it's simple, and it also means you don't need as much screen space to see your entire timeline.

As with Roll and Slip, there's no two-up display for nudging with the **comma** and **period** keys. But you'll need the mouse at some point: there's no keyboard shortcut that can prepare a clip for a Slip or Slide nudging operation. To prepare for a keyboard-based Slip or Slide, you'll have to press **T** to switch to the **Trim** tool, and then do the following:

- **Click** on the middle of a clip to prepare for a Slip operation
- ⌥-**click** on the middle of a clip to prepare for a Slide operation

Only then can you use **comma** and **period**, with or without ⇧, to Slip or Slide by 1 or 10 frames.

REVIEW — SLIPPING AND SLIDING CLIPS

Slipping and sliding are crucial in that they enable you to make subtle edits without changing the overall timeline length. When you've built a complex timeline, you don't want to mess it all up to make an edit, and these tools mean you don't have to.

All these techniques you've learned, including trimming with the regular **Select** tool and with the **Trim** tool, and whether you're using the mouse or the keyboard, are going to be much more useful once you start considering how they can be used with audio. Although FCP does join video and audio components together in a single clip, it's actually very easy to trim a clip's audio independently, and that's what the next section is all about.

SOFTENING AUDIO WITH SPLIT EDITS (J- AND L-CUTS)

Way back at the rough-cut stage, the emphasis was on making an edit sound good, and then to hide the edits with B-roll. That's still a great way to work, but **split audio edits** allow you to trim the audio and video components of a clip at different points from one another, allowing you to hear a speaker before you see them (J-cut) or hear them after you see them (L-cut).

Cutting the audio and the video separately softens the edit, and (crucially) it's not something that's easy to do with simpler editing software. Using this technique will lift the quality of your edits, even if the client isn't quite sure why. You can see an illustration of this here:

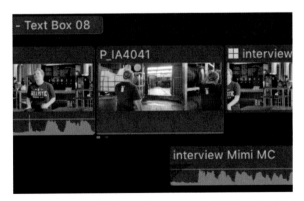

Figure 8.20: The rightmost clip here has expanded audio that starts before the video does — a J-cut

In this section, you'll learn how to expand and collapse audio, and some of the things you should avoid. You'll also learn how to blend audio from clip to clip, and how to fade audio in and out. First off, how to separate audio from video the right way.

EXPANDING AND COLLAPSING AUDIO

A clip in FCP can contain audio, video, or both, and unlike most other **non-linear editing systems** (**NLEs**), it treats them as a single, united clip. That means that it's pretty hard to send anything out of sync — the audio will always line up with the video. In a traditional workflow, audio and video tracks start out stuck together but are easy to separate, and some new FCP users might think that detaching the audio component entirely is a good way to emulate that. No, it isn't.

Don't detach audio, unless you have a really good reason. The **Detach Audio** command is there, under the **Clip** menu, but it's rarely the right way to go because it makes it far too easy to move a clip's audio out of sync. If the detached clip started life on the Primary Storyline, you're left with a video clip and a connected audio clip, which is OK, but it's trivially easy to move a connected clip. It's much worse if the detached clip was a connected clip, because you now have two separate clips connected to the same Primary Storyline clip, and you'll have to remember to select, move, and edit them together. Ugh all round.

Instead, to separate the audio component of a clip temporarily, do the following:

- Double-click on a clip's audio waveform in the timeline, or choose **Clip** > **Expand Audio**

When you expand audio like this, the audio part of a clip (the visible waveform) jumps down from the video. If this is the first time a clip has been expanded, the video and audio edges will be aligned, but they can all now be edited — trimmed or Rolled — separately. Trimming and Rolling is the key to softening edits. An example of an expanded audio clip can be seen in the following screenshot:

Figure 8.21: The audio on these clips hasn't been detached, but it has been expanded

Let's start with a practical example of how to create a J-cut. You'll need some kind of interview or presentation shot — someone speaking on camera. Take the following steps:

1. Find a clip of someone speaking, select a region where the person is speaking, and place it in the Primary Storyline, as illustrated in the following screenshot:

Figure 8.22: Here's a suitable interview piece, with waveforms showing speech

You can spot the point where someone starts speaking by looking at the waveforms: taller means louder.

2. Find a b-roll clip that would be a suitable way to lead in to the first shot.

A suitable b-roll could include a shot of that person walking or talking to another person, or whatever they're talking about.

3. Place the b-roll clip before the speaking clip in the Primary Storyline, as illustrated in the following screenshot:

Figure 8.23: Here's a shot of this expert brewer's workplace, a suitable introduction

4. Double-click the audio waveform of the speaking clip to expand its audio.

At this point, you might be tempted to drag the audio In point of the speaking clip to the left, extending it underneath the first clip. Unfortunately, this just makes the clip's audio start earlier, and since you've already chosen the right audio, this would add some unwanted audio (noise, silence, or extra dialogue) to the start of the clip. Instead, proceed as follows.

5. Drag the video In point of the speaking clip to the right, to make it start later.

This does what you want. It moves the start of the audio back to under the first b-roll clip, and the person can now be heard before you see them. Zooming in for detail, you can see the following:

Figure 8.24: Drag the left video edge of the speaking clip to the right, and you'll create a J-cut

Technically, this is similar to connecting the b-roll clip above the Primary Storyline, but in practice, this is a much easier thing to manage. The Primary Storyline drives the edit, and you often want clips of people speaking to drive the edit. Expanding audio like this allows the right clips to be in charge, but still allows you to finesse the transitions between clips. There are many good reasons to want the audio of a clip to extend beyond its normal clip boundaries, and this is a good way to do it, as illustrated in the following screenshot:

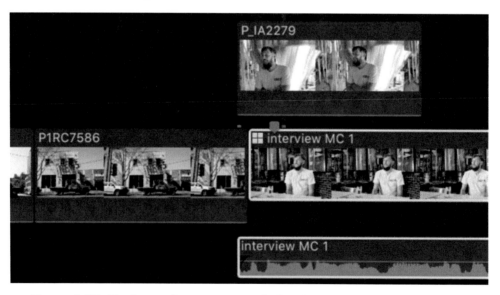

Figure 8.25: Placing a silent connected clip above the start of a speaker gives a similar result

An L-cut is much the same, but backward: you'd expand audio, then drag the Out point of a "talking" clip to the left, to let a following b-roll clip sit on top of the audio from the first one. This is a less common technique but is still useful, and it's illustrated in the following screenshot:

Figure 8.26: This is what an L-cut looks like

If you want to visually reunite expanded audio components, you can — through a feature called **Collapse Audio**. To use this, proceed as follows:

- Double-click on a clip's audio waveform in the timeline, or choose **Clip > Collapse Audio**

Note that collapsing audio doesn't change how anything sounds, but it can look like a little odd. If the audio component of a clip doesn't overlap with its companion video, it will be hidden after collapsing. Here's an example of expanded audio that started and finished before the video component:

Figure 8.27: Here's a clip with a J-cut at the start, and audio that finishes early

After collapsing the audio, this is the result:

Figure 8.28: The sample clip after audio is collapsed will look different in the timeline but sound the same

Collapsed audio might be invisible, but it can still be heard, and for that reason, I tend to leave audio expanded if its length has been adjusted. Expanded audio will always keep its current length, so if you adjust the video component of a clip, nothing happens. However, a collapsed clip will remember any offset that its audio start and end points had while expanded, and any offset will be maintained if you trim the clip's unified start or end points after collapsing. This can mean that you would hear a different part of the clip, which may or may not be an issue.

If you're confused just where the audio is and want to expand everything, select the whole timeline (**⌘A**) and use the shortcut (**^S**) to perform **Clip** > **Expand Audio** for all clips at once. Conversely, repeat the **^S** shortcut to **Collapse Audio** for all clips if you want to simplify. (There are additional tricks regarding separating audio clips into their separate components, and we'll return to them later in the book.)

As well as enabling J-cuts and L-cuts, expanding audio also allows you to create audio fades between two clips, and it's certainly the method that gives you the most control. Read on!

OVERLAPPING AUDIO EDIT POINTS

When you've taken out part of a clip of a person talking or want to run two clips of different people together, you'll probably want to slightly overlap the audio of the two clips to avoid problems. If there's a gap between the two clips, there can be an audible dip in volume as the background noise disappears, but with an overlap, this simply won't happen. Of course, some clips are easier to edit than others, and you'll experience many different issues in different jobs. Have a look at the following screenshot:

Figure 8.29: The selected waveform region is "ah, you know", which can
be removed

Overlapping two edits is often necessary to smooth out the edges of words, especially if you're having to extract good words that were said right next to bad words. If you've taken out a few extraneous words (an "um," an "ah," or more) from a single person's speech to create a tighter soundbite, you should find this process fairly simple, and it's been made easier with *a new feature in 10.4.9*:

1. Use the **Range Selection** tool to select the unwanted part of a clip.
2. Press **delete** to remove it.
3. Select both clips at once, then press ⌥T (or **Modify > Adjust Audio Fades > Crossfade**) to add a **Crossfade**.

The clip's **fade handles** are now activated, and the two clips are overlapped by a duration set in **Preferences**, under **Editing**. That might be enough; you can play it back to see whether it sounds good. From there, you can adjust the results with a more manual process if you wish:

1. Expand the audio on each of the audio waveforms.
2. Trim the audio components to include exactly the sections you want to use.
3. Trim the video components to adjust the timing and how the audio clips overlap.
4. Connect a B-roll cutaway above to disguise the jump cut.

Don't be dishonest, but also don't be afraid to make a speaker sound smoother or more professional. Tweak as much as you want to — the cutaway hides all that mess. Edits like this are common:

Figure 8.30: Without that deleted phrase, everything sounds smoother
— but remember to cover the jump cut

With or without a **Crossfade**, you can access and adjust those built-in fade handles on any audio clip. How? Read on.

FADING AUDIO EDITS

As you've seen, adding a Crossfade exposes a clip's fade handles, but every audio edge contains the same built-in fade handles. They allow you to fade that audio in or out and are a vital part of making audio edits seamless. Audio fades are also a good way to create a smooth transition between one music track and another.

To access a clip's fade handles:

1. Hover over the left or right edge of an audio waveform until you see a teardrop.

   Hovering over this teardrop shows a cursor with two separated black arrows pointing left and right, as illustrated in the following screenshot:

Figure 8.31: This is the teardrop you're looking for; audio can be expanded
or collapsed

2. Click on the teardrop and drag it toward the middle of the clip, until you reach the desired duration (if the clip's edge moves, **Undo** and try again), as illustrated in the following screenshot:

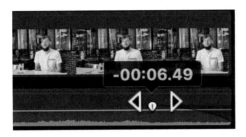

Figure 8.32: The fade on the Out point here helps the audio
smoothly fade away

You should use fades on almost every audio edit, to make sure that every audio clip starts in silence and ends in silence. If an audio clip cuts in the middle of a noise, you can sometimes hear a click or a pop as the audio cuts in. To make applying audio fades easier, you can apply shortcuts (with **Final Cut Pro > Commands > Customize**, ⌥⌘K) to the following otherwise hidden commands:

- **Apply Audio Fades**
- **Remove Audio Fades**
- **Toggle Audio Fade In**
- **Toggle Audio Fade Out**

These commands use the default **Audio Fade** length, which, alongside the **Crossfade** length, you can define in **Preferences**, in the **Editing** pane. Either or both of these can be set to a very short duration if you wish, as illustrated in the following screenshot:

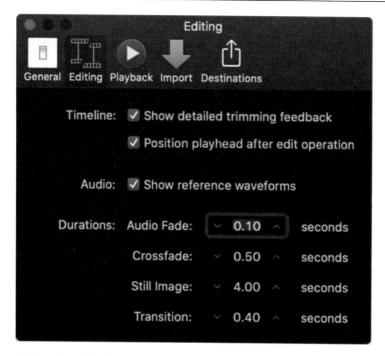

Figure 8.33: The Editing pane in Preferences, where you can define the Audio Fade and Crossfade duration

While the handles are the same on each clip, a Crossfade defaults to the **S-curve** fade style, and a standard clip's edges will default to **+3dB**. You can choose your own style with a right-click on the handle:

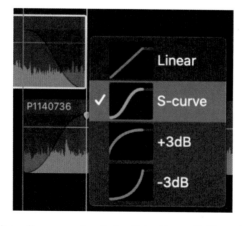

Figure 8.34: Fade handles usually default to the +3dB style, but a Crossfade defaults to S-curve

So how long should a fade handle last for? The only hard and fast rule is "as long as it sounds good," but truly, this is context-dependent. Normally, I keep fades fairly short as a rule, but when I'm blending two clips together, I just make sure that there's some kind of overlap between tracks to avoid an awkward silence. Even if you regard yourself as a visual editor first, don't be afraid to dip your toes into audio.

A fade-in should look like this:

Figure 8.35: A quick fade-in, even shorter than this, is often enough

Experiment: add some foley effects and atmosphere from the **Sound Effects** library, and keep playing until you're happy. Because sound effects use a different Role, you'll notice they are shown in a different color:

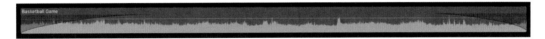

Figure 8.36: This "Basketball Game" sound effect comes with FCP, and if you need to fake a crowd, it's not bad

You'll find that the more elements you have in the mix, the easier it is to disguise the start or finish of any one element. Don't forget to adjust the relative volume of clips by dragging their volume line up and down, and there's a lot more detail on audio coming up in *Chapter 14, Boost the Signal: Audio Sweetening.*

FADING MUSIC FOR BEAT-MATCHING

Music can benefit from a slightly different technique, including fades that might be quick or last several seconds. Sometimes you need to change tempo quickly, and elsewhere you'll need a pretty hard cut, exploding into the next scene with a visible and audible bang. Here's a nice trick if you need to repeat a piece of music that's too short:

1. Put the connected audio clip into a storyline.
2. **⌥-drag** it within the storyline to duplicate it.

3. Trim the In point on the second clip to remove any introductory sections and reach a similar-sounding point in the music, as illustrated in the following screenshot:

Figure 8.37: The introduction is significantly quieter on this clip and on many others, so trim it away

4. **Expand Audio** on both clips by double-clicking the audio waveform.

    The following sneaky trick works even though the clips have no visual component.

5. Use the timeline's appearance menu (it looks like a filmstrip) to make the waveforms larger to see the beats, as illustrated in the following screenshot:

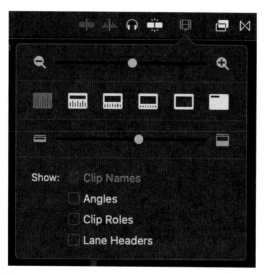

Figure 8.38: These are the settings you want for a larger, audio-only timeline display

The top slider here controls the overall zoom; the second set of icons control what is shown in each clip filmstrip (choose the leftmost icon for audio waveforms only); and the slider below the icons controls clip height. Next, do the following:

6. Reduce the length of either or both video edges to overlap the peaks in the two sequential audio tracks, as illustrated in the following screenshot:

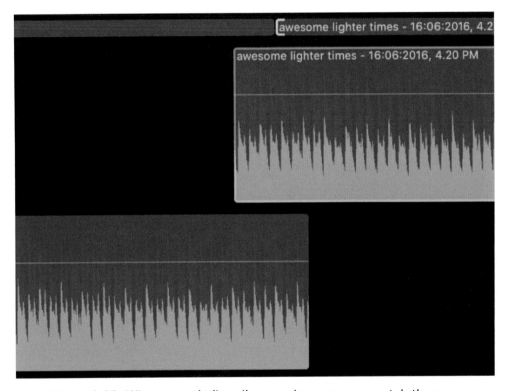

Figure 8.39: When two similar clips overlap, you can match them up

Again, this works, even though there's no video component.

7. Then, zoom in, and then trim off unwanted audio by adjusting the audio edges.

8. Use the **Trim** tool to Slip the second audio clip until the beats in the waveforms match up exactly.

Note that a Slip operation on expanded audio in a storyline clip or any audio in a freely connected clip will move by subframes. As this is far smaller than a frame, you have fine control when matching beats, as shown here:

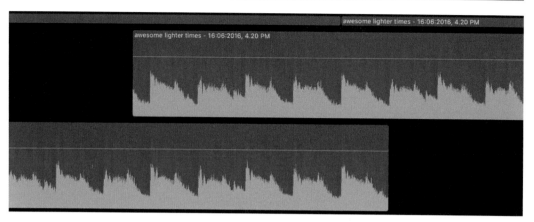

Figure 8.40: Here's the overlapping area, synced in time with a subtle Slip, though that section is now louder

9. Add fades to transition between the two tracks, as shown here:

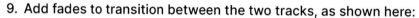

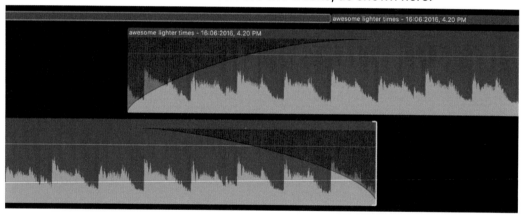

Figure 8.41: Beat-matched and faded for a seamless music repeat

Multiple music clips can be beat-matched pretty easily this way, and this approach is far more flexible than just fading one clip out and another clip in. Sound effects don't need the same treatment as they can usually sit independently, but remember to use only the part of a sound effect that you need (sometimes they're quite long), and do fade them out when they're no longer wanted.

All kinds of trims, audio, and video, can be performed with the mouse, or with the **comma** and **period** nudging shortcuts, though they move by a full frame. If you want to perform audio subframe Slip edits with the keyboard, use ⌥**comma** and ⌥**period**, and add ⇧ if you want to go faster.

REVIEW — SOFTENING AUDIO WITH SPLIT EDITS (J- AND L-CUTS)

We started out by dragging the mouse to edit a single edge of a united video/audio clip, but it's more complex now, and that's a good thing. Split edits are one of the easiest ways to up your production values, and in an era where simple phone-based editing is becoming more common, if you can use a more advanced technique to tell a story in a better way, you'll stand out for the right reasons.

There are still more ways to work if you want to move a clip or an edit by a specific number of frames, or if you want to cut in a more defined, careful way. That's up next.

EDITING NUMERICALLY AND WITH THE PRECISION EDITOR

Not every editor will want to be precise; editing is, after all, an art more than it is a science. But from time to time, it can be useful to set the length of a clip (or all your clips) to a specific value, and if a client asks for "a second more on that clip", it's great to be able to achieve it in a click and four quick keystrokes (**+, 1, period, return**). The techniques you'll learn here cover editing with numbers, setting duration precisely, and looking deeper with the Precision Editor.

TRIMMING USING NUMBERS

While the **comma** and **period** shortcuts move a selected edit point (or clip) by a single frame, you can use **plus** and **minus** with timecodes to move by any amount. To illustrate how to respond to the client who asks for "a second more," follow these steps:

1. Select an Out point on one of your clips, as follows:

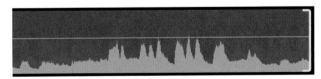

Figure 8.42: "One more second of barnyard noises"

You could do this by simply clicking on the Out point, or by moving the playhead to that point with keys, then selecting it with the **]** shortcut. While **]** selects the Out point, use **[** to select the In point, or **** to select both for a Roll edit.

2. Type **+100**, then **return**, which will result in the following timecode display:

Figure 8.43: The timecode display under the viewer will
change when you type the "+"

Movements to the right use a **plus**, and to the left use a **minus**. Timecode entry is interpreted differently, depending on how many characters you type, as follows:

- If you enter one or two digits, you're talking in frames.
- If you enter three or four digits, the first two digits are seconds and the last two are frames.
- If you enter five or six digits, the first two digits are minutes, the next two are seconds, and the last two are frames.
- If you enter a period (.), it counts as two zeros: "00".
- If you enter a number greater than the number of units available (such as 80 frames or 65 seconds), then the extra amount is converted to the next unit up.

In the timecode display underneath the Viewer, you'll see the result calculate itself as you type. Here are a few examples:

- **+215** = move the selected edit point 2 seconds and 15 frames to the right
- **+265** = move the selected edit point 4 seconds and 15 frames to the right (in a 25 **frames per second** (FPS) timeline, where 2 seconds and 65 frames = 4 seconds + 15 frames)
- **-50** = move the selected edit point 50 frames to the left (just over or just under two seconds, depending on the frame rate)
- **-2.** = move the selected edit point 2 seconds to the left (in any frame rate)
- **+5..** = move the selected edit point 5 minutes to the right

Depending on which edit point you select, either plus or minus could make a clip longer or shorter. In points moving to the left make a clip longer, as do Out points moving to the right. Roll edits, of course, make one clip longer while another gets shorter, so select the edit point(s) however you wish, and then type away. Have a look at the following screenshot:

Figure 8.44: "Let's cut from the music to the barn yard noises three
and a half seconds sooner"

Moving a clip rather than an edit works in exactly the same way, but beware. Connected clips can move freely, but if you move a Primary Storyline clip with numbers, you'll be performing a Slide operation, stealing time from one clip and giving it to the clip on the other side.

No matter what you want to move, you can use the following general-purpose precision workflow:

1. Select an edit point on one of your clips with the **Select** tool, select two edit points with the **Trim** tool, or select a whole clip.

2. Type **plus** or **minus**, then a timecode, then **return**.

It's also possible to define the duration of a clip using numbers.

SETTING CLIP DURATION

What if your client asks for a clip to be not "a second longer" but "exactly 4 seconds"? That's easy, but you'll need to use something other than **plus** or **minus**. The command is **Modify** > **Change Duration** but you'll use **^D**. To set duration, do the following:

1. Select one or more clips.

2. Type **^D**, then a timecode (without **^**), then **return**. This will result in the following timecode display:

Figure 8.45: The timecode readout under the Viewer changes to show the
new duration; this is "2." or "200"

Here are some examples, remembering that you only hold ^ while pressing **D**, and you'll need to press **return** at the end of each one:

- **^D4.** = make the selected clip 4 seconds long, an absolute change
- **^D+2.** = make the selected clip 2 seconds longer, a relative change
- **^D1** = make the selected clip 1 frame long — handy for time-lapses or animation sequences

Have a look at the following screenshot:

Figure 8.46: All these clips were set to a duration of two seconds,
the quickest holiday video ever

Extending that a little further, you can very quickly fill a timeline with videos or stills of a certain length by selecting all the clips at once, and then do the following:

1. Press **E** to append to the Timeline.
2. Click on the **Timeline** pane.
3. Press ⌘**A** to select all clips at once.
4. Press **^D3.** to set all clips to 3 seconds long.
5. Press ⌘**T** to add the default **Dissolve** transition between all these clips, as illustrated in the following screenshot:

Figure 8.47: The same clips as earlier, now 3 seconds long
with fades between them

We'll return to transitions in *Chapter 12, Refine and Smooth: Video Effects and Transitions*, but this is a good taster.

MOVING TO A SPECIFIC TIMECODE

If you want to jump to a specific timecode on the timeline it's a similar process, but you'll need to activate the **Move Playhead Position** command before typing that timecode. The shortcut is **^P**, and should be followed immediately by a timecode in seconds and frames.

If this is something you do often, I'd recommend assigning an alternative key for this command. In **Final Cut Pro** > **Commands** > **Customize**, you can search for "move playhead" in the top-right search field, then drag that command to any unused key. The **clear** key on the number pad of extended keyboards is unused, right next to all those convenient number keys, and if you assign it, you'll see this:

Figure 8.48: Assigning this command to the "clear" key looks like this

The main reason you'd want to jump to a specific timecode is if you're given a paper edit with time references for changes. While best practice is to assign To Do Markers to track changes (coming up in *Chapter 10, Explore a Little: Compound Clips and Timeline Tricks*), if you're not going to add Markers, always remember to work from the end of a change list to the start, or you'll invalidate later timecodes with the first ripple edit you perform.

One last handy way to perform edits precisely is in a different mode entirely — the Precision Editor.

USING THE PRECISION EDITOR

This separate editing mode provides a way to focus on just one edit at a time, to see how much additional media is available for the current edit, and to perform trims and Roll edits in existing and new ways. To enter this mode, simply double-click on an edit in your timeline, and to leave, press **Escape**.

The timeline now splits in two, with a line of gray boxes indicating Primary Storyline edits in the middle of the screen. One edit is active at a time, and earlier clips are shown above while later clips are shown below. You can switch to different edits in your timeline by clicking on them or by using the following shortcuts: **semicolon** or ↑ to go back, **apostrophe** or ↓ to go forward. Have a look at the following screenshot:

Figure 8.49: Zooming out to see a wider timeline with several edit points

Dragging on the gray boxes in the center of the current point performs a Roll edit, but in this mode, you can see what you'll be revealing because you can see the filmstrips for the unused parts of the prior and upcoming clips, as illustrated in the following screenshot:

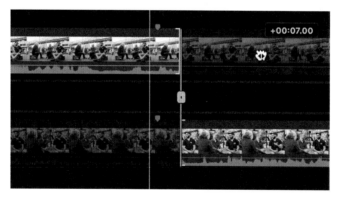

Figure 8.50: Drag the filmstrip, the edit points, or the gray box to perform an edit

If you move the mouse up to access an Out point or down to access an In point, you can click and drag it left or right to perform a regular trim. Two less obvious ways to trim are to *drag on either side of the upper or lower filmstrip* to move the In or Out point, or even just *click on the filmstrip* to set that point as the new In or Out point. And all the nudging (**comma, period**), edge-selecting (**[,], **), **Trim Start**, **Trim End**, and **Play Around Edit** (⌥[, ⌥], ⇧/) shortcuts work here too. Have a look at the following screenshot:

Figure 8.51: Click and drag on the central gray box for a Roll edit — it'll turn yellow

While some people simply never use this mode, it's a great way to visually verify every edit in your timeline. Also, if you're reviewing an edit with a client who really wants to know which media lies unseen, this is a great way to show them you're making the right choices. Still, if you don't like it, don't use it.

REVIEW — EDITING NUMERICALLY AND WITH THE PRECISION EDITOR

Precision editing helps you achieve precise results. Whether you use it yourself to quickly give a series of clips the same duration, or use it with clients so that they understand why an edit can only be the way it is, you'll probably want to use these techniques pretty regularly. The keyboard-based tricks have an added benefit: while most onlookers can understand what's happening when you adjust clips with your cursor, using the keyboard's precision adjustments makes you look like a wizard. To you, the program will simply get out of the way, and you'll be working at the speed of thought.

SUMMARY

Hopefully, this chapter has opened your eyes a little to what a modern editing program can do. If you've come from iMovie, this is probably the point where you realized just how much more power you have here. Rolling, Slipping, advanced keyboard trimming, and number-based edits are just some of the features you've now learned, and mastering these will give you new solutions to the problems you'll encounter as an editor.

The next chapter expands your options further, showing you how to work with multicam footage, how to replace one clip with another, and how to use the unique Auditions feature to give you additional flexibility — especially handy with clients who don't know what they want yet. Options ahoy: read on.

REVIEW QUESTIONS

1. What does a Roll operation do?

2. If you drag an In point to the left with the **Select** tool, does the clip get longer or shorter?

3. What does a red clip edge in the timeline mean?

4. What are the nudging shortcuts that adjust an edit by a single frame?

5. Which modifier key can be added to the nudging shortcuts to make them move by 10 frames?

6. If you Slip a clip, does the overall timeline length change?

7. What does an orange line on a clip mean?

8. Which terms indicate an audio edit that's been offset from a video edit?

9. Can you Slip connected audio by less than a frame?

10. If you select an edit point and type **+9**, what happens?

REVIEW ANSWERS

1. A Roll edit makes one clip longer and its neighboring clip shorter by the same amount.

2. Longer, if media is available.

3. There is no more media available on this clip.

4. **Comma** and **Period**.

5. ⇧ **(Shift).**

6. No.

7. That media is in use in the current project.

8. J-cut and L-cut.

9. Yes, by subframes.

10. That edit point moves to the right by nine frames, assuming there is sufficient media available.

9 CONSIDER YOUR OPTIONS:
MULTICAM, REPLACING, AND AUDITIONS

"Moving from a traditional NLE to Final Cut Pro X gave me the freedom to think like an artist instead of an engineer."
— *Gabriel Spaulding, Video Editor, ACE Enterprizes*
aceenterprizes.com

This chapter is all about switching one shot for another, whether you're switching angles, switching takes, or switching to something entirely different. The editing techniques vary, but the outcome is the same: making the best edit you can by using the best shot available for any particular moment. A shot you choose might be great, but if the client prefers another, you'll want to know how to switch in that new shot with the least pain. There are simple and smart ways to work, and if you shot your footage with multiple cameras, you'll approach things in an entirely different way.

This chapter will show you the best ways to work with Multicam, and many techniques for how to explore your options with or without Multicam. You'll find out how to test a new shot, as well as how to replace a clip more permanently. You'll also find out how to keep multiple options in a single spot in the timeline with Auditions. To summarize, in this chapter, we'll cover the following topics:

- Working with Multicam media
- Exchanging one clip with another
- Creating and using Auditions

To begin, we'll be diving into the world of Multicam footage. Historically, many TV and film productions have used just a single camera: perfecting the lighting for that one angle, then moving the camera and lighting before the cast repeats their performance. With Multicam, your subjects need to only perform once, but the cameras are far more likely to catch one another in shot — let alone lighting — so positioning is more restrictive. While not every production can or should record with multiple devices, Multicam techniques can be invaluable for capturing live events, interviews, and improvised narrative performances. Personally, I love it, so here we go!

WORKING WITH MULTICAM MEDIA

While *Chapter 2, Before the Edit: Production Tips*, discussed how to shoot with multiple cameras and audio recorders, and *Chapter 3, Bring It In: Importing Your Footage*, showed you how to synchronize all that footage into Multicam Clips, we haven't looked at how to edit it yet — and there are a few differences compared to regular footage. This section will take you through the process of editing with Multicam footage, including switching angles, controlling which component of a clip is switched, and some of the smaller changes that Multicam brings.

UNDERSTANDING MULTICAM FOOTAGE

As discussed earlier, a Multicam Clip combines multiple angles together, synced in time. When you edit a Multicam Clip, you can choose which angle you want to see at any point, and which you want to hear:

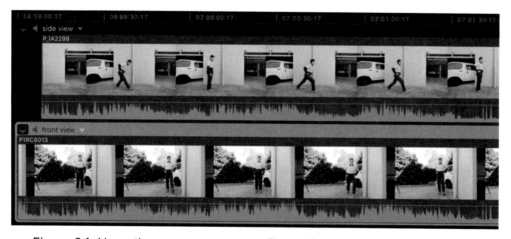

Figure 9.1: Here, the same person was filmed from two angles at once, to demonstrate stretching

You can run the clip continuously, showing exactly what was recorded, or remove unwanted sections:

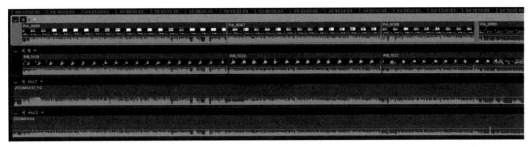

Figure 9.2: Part of a day-long Multicam shoot with two video angles and two additional microphones

While Multicam Clips are usually created with footage from multiple cameras and audio recorders working simultaneously, that's not the only way to obtain Multicam footage. When a musician lip syncs to a recorded audio track, multiple sequential shots (in the same location or in multiple locations) can be synced as separate Multicam angles:

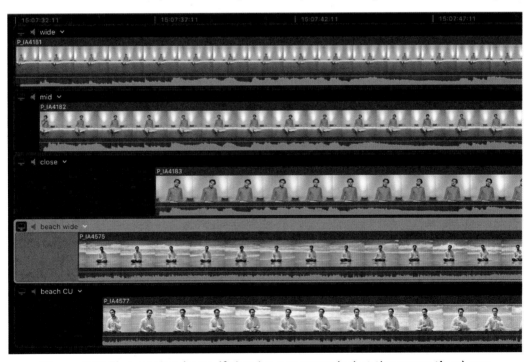

Figure 9.3: Five angles (even if they're not recorded at the same time) can be synced in a Multicam as a way to present options

Similarly, you could sync up a screen recording of a presentation being given and a video of the presenter delivering that presentation. If you're using audio to sync all the clips together, just make sure that every camera is recording audio, and it'll go smoothly. Refer back to *Chapter 3, Bring It In: Importing Your Footage*, for more information.

Enough talk — time to play! If you haven't already imported and synced up some Multicam footage, go ahead and do that now. Any phone and any other camera will be good enough to practice with, though if you can use matched cameras with matched settings, you'll have an easier time. *Chapter 2, Before the Edit: Production Tips*, provided some tips on this, but just make sure that you can see and hear the same things through every camera. Hit record on all your devices, speak a few sentences, and that'll do.

With the footage in hand, here's the process you should have already followed:

1. Import your source clips.
2. Create a Multicam Clip and use the **Angle Editor** to check the sync.

These steps are listed in the *Syncing media from multiple devices* section of *Chapter 3, Bring It In: Importing Your Footage*.

> IMPORTANT NOTE
>
> You only need the **Angle Editor** to make changes inside the Multicam — to correctly sync, make clip-wide changes to color or positioning, or manipulate the angles. To edit the finished clip, you'll need to place the entire Multicam Clip into a regular Project and cut it there.

With your Multicam Clips ready to edit, it's simple to get started:

1. Select a Multicam Clip from the **Browser** tab and mark In and Out points as usual (select most of it).
2. Open or create a Project and append your Multicam Clip to the timeline with **E**.

To get the most out of Multicam Clips, you'll want to choose the best audio channel, and then show the **Angle Viewer**, which displays all your angles alongside the main **Viewer**. Let's choose the best audio first.

PREPARING TO EDIT WITH THE ANGLE VIEWER

The most common scenario for Multicam editing is that you have a single good audio source and multiple video sources to choose from. Any other audio tracks have done their job by helping to sync up the other video tracks, so they weren't useless by any means. But we can start by choosing the right audio track. Let's get started:

1. Right-click on the Multicam Clip on the timeline. Then, choose **Active Audio Angle** and then the name of the correct track:

Figure 9.4: Who had the best audio recording?

If you've named your angles appropriately, this should be easy, but if not, you'll need to listen to find the best one.

2. Display the **Angle Viewer** by pressing ⇧⌘7:

Figure 9.5: After displaying the Angle Viewer, you can resize it and the Viewer by dragging their edges

This command can also be found in the Viewer's **View** menu, as **Angles**. The Viewer pane now splits to show 2, 4, 9, or 16 angles to the left of the main

Viewer. You're more likely to experience issues if you display a large number of angles here. To change how many angles you can see at once, simply go to the **Settings** menu.

3. Choose **2 Angles** or **4 Angles** from the **Settings** menu at the top-right of the **Angle Viewer**:

Figure 9.6: Choose the number of angles you want to see from the Settings menu

You usually only need to show video angles, so if you've got two video angles and an audio-only angle, two angles would be enough. Here, I can only see four of the five angles in this Multicam, and it's possible to switch to another bank of four angles using the icons at the bottom center of the Angle Viewer.

The most important option here is to the top-left, though.

4. Click on the second of the three icons to the top left of the **Angle Viewer**:

Figure 9.7: Choose video and audio, video-only, or audio-only switching

This toggle switch now indicates that when you switch angles, you'll only switch the video angle, so the audio will remain on the angle you chose earlier (when you right-clicked and chose an audio angle). It's absolutely possible to switch audio angles (or both audio and video) if you prefer, but this will depend on how many good audio sources you have. How do you choose the best audio?

- If you're interviewing one person or nobody at all, whichever mic sounds best wins.
- If you're interviewing two people, switch to the best audio source(s) for each person as they speak.

It's also possible to hear multiple audio angles at once; we'll discuss this in *Chapter 14, Boost the Signal: Audio Sweetening*. For now, let's just switch video angles.

SWITCHING ANGLES

Now that you've set everything up, it's time to try a live editing session, as if you're a vision mixer at a live event. Hover over the start of your Project's timeline and tap the **spacebar** to start playback. Then, as it plays, do either of the following:

- Click inside the **Angle Viewer** to cut and switch to a new angle.
- Press keys **1**, **2**, **3**... through **9** to cut and switch to that numbered angle:

Figure 9.8: Soon, you'll have something like this, where you've cut between several angles

While choosing angles, you can pause, rewind, or play at a faster speed. There's no need to work in real time, and you can skim to any point and tap a number key if you wish. Most simple Multicams use two video angles, so you'll be pressing **1**, **2**, **1**, **2** a lot. Every cut you add is marked with a through edit, which is a dashed line through the clip. With experience, you'll find that there are many ways to place edits, and you might switch angles for a number of reasons:

- There's no choice: A camera was obscured or not recording at that point.
- Variety: The current angle has been on screen for too long.
- Content: It's the best angle to show this particular piece of content.
- Editing: Cutting from one angle to another to disguise a jump cut.

There are also specific considerations about exactly when an edit should be placed:

- In a pause between sentences, which also allows pauses to be reduced
- Near where your subject blinks, which gives a natural edit point
- To attract attention for emphasis, just before an important point

With your first angle choices made, it's time to clean it up.

REPLACING AND EDITING EXISTING ANGLES

If you've got the cuts in the right places, terrific! If you've added a cut in error, you can select it with a click, and then press **delete** to get rid of it. If you just want to move the cut, you can perform a **Roll** edit, but you don't need to switch to the **Trim** tool. *The Select tool will automatically perform a Roll edit when used with Multicam Clips*:

Figure 9.9: Clicking and dragging on any edit point to Roll it with the Select tool

What if you do need to remove some part of the clip? You've got various options here:

- Switch to the **Trim** tool (**T**), move to the edge of a clip, and then click and drag to perform a regular one-point ripple trim edit:

Figure 9.10: Using the Trim tool to perform regular ripple trim edits on Multicam Clips

- Switch to the **Range Selection** tool (**R**) and select and **Delete** part of the clip:

Figure 9.11: The Range Selection tool can still select parts of clips
for deletion

Removing part of a Multicam Clip means that the edits around it are no longer "through" edits, and will no longer be indicated by a dashed line:

Figure 9.12: Through edits are dashed and indicate angle changes; no
dashes means content was removed

Lastly, what if you've simply chosen the wrong angle for a particular part of the clip? You can change any existing angles, within any region, without adding new cuts. While playing or hovering, do either of the following:

- ⌥**-click** in the **Angle Viewer** to switch the current clip to a new angle.
- Press ⌥**1**, ⌥**2**, ⌥**3**... through ⌥**9** to switch the current clip to a new angle.

Personally, I always use the keys – clicking is too slow, and it's the only way to work while hovering over the timeline. But there's one more option that's important here.

EDITING INSIDE A MULTICAM ANGLE

The nature of Multicam footage is that the recordings are sometimes quite long, and that means that you can apply changes to an entire angle at once. Though this will become more useful after *Chapter 11, Play with Light: Color Correction and Grading,* if you need to make any changes to an entire Multicam angle at once, you can simply do the following:

1. Double-click on a Multicam Clip to jump inside the **Angle Editor**.

2. Make changes (for example, audio volume) to a particular angle.

3. Click once on the leftward arrow to the left of the center bar to return to your Project:

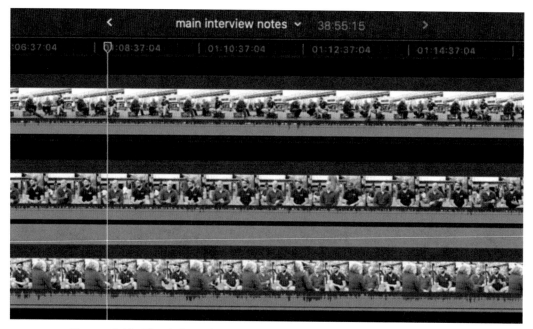

Figure 9.13: The left-pointing arrow is the key to jumping back to your Project

This operation changes every instance of that angle with the Multicam Clip in the timeline, and it's therefore the best way to make global adjustments. Remember to look at the icons to the top left of each angle to know which angle is seen and which angles are heard:

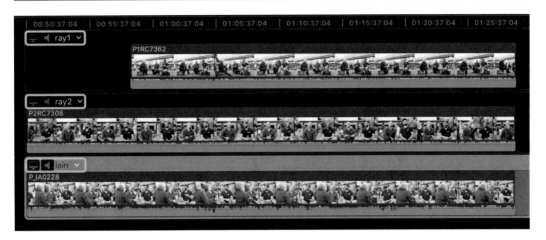

Figure 9.14: Inside the Angle Editor, I can see and hear the angle "iain," and also hear the angle "ray1"

If you're making visual changes in the Inspector (more in *Chapter 11, Play with Light: Color Correction and Grading*) then be sure to click on the **TV** icon to the left of an angle's name, to make sure you're viewing the angle you've selected. You can hear more than one angle at once, but you'll only see one at a time.

A strong recommendation is to always do as much basic correction (to color, audio, and cropping) within the Multicam angles, and not at the timeline level. Consistency in color correction is easier when the Angle Viewer is showing you all angles at once, and you'll be able to match up all the angles pretty quickly. Overall, it'll be far easier, far more consistent, and can even avoid some issues with audio plug-ins that behave differently on short clips when compared to long ones.

REVIEW — WORKING WITH MULTICAM MEDIA

Multicam is an awesome way to work, but remember that it's not the only trick you've got; you can still use regular B-roll as connected cutaway clips above a Multicam Clip. All the other techniques you've learned still work perfectly well, it's just that you've got extra options now. Prepare your Multicam Clips, show the **Angle Viewer**, cut and switch angles to get started, then switch angles without cutting to change your mind, dip inside the **Angle Editor** to make changes at a lower level, and jump back up to move the edit points wherever you want. Lovely.

But hey — if your production didn't shoot with multiple cameras, that's OK too — read on to learn simple (and smart) techniques for exchanging one shot with another.

EXCHANGING ONE CLIP WITH ANOTHER

Multicam angles are a delightful luxury, but even without them, you've got more flexibility than you might think. If, for example, you prefer one reaction shot to another, it doesn't matter if that reaction was reacting to those exact words at that exact time — it can be from any take, as long as nobody's lips are seen moving incorrectly. If you can see someone's lips moving to words you can't hear, or see lips not moving when you can hear they should be, you're pretty much locked into the matching audio for that shot.

> ### IMPORTANT NOTE
> Once you realize this, you'll see that reaction shots are frequently "cheated" in this way. An editor will often end up choosing the best reaction shot, and if you can see the head movements of a person actually speaking, you'll notice that the words they're saying probably aren't quite in sync, or worse, are from a completely different part of their conversation.

It's far less of a challenge to switch out one B-roll shot for another, and a client may have perfectly good reasons why a shot you like is actually no good at all. A smart editor keeps alternatives at hand, and here, you'll find two ways to try out an alternative clip. There's the simple, more temporary way, and the smarter, more official way. Later, we look at another technique that gives you the best of both worlds, but let's start with the simple option first.

SHOWING OR HIDING A CLIP

Toggling a clip on and off is a basic technique, and likely one you'd use in an everyday situation, such as when you want to test out a new silent B-roll shot to replace another. Quite simply, you do the following:

1. Select a new B-roll shot in your Browser that you're considering as a replacement.

2. Hover over the start of the B-roll shot in your timeline that you want to replace.

3. Press **Q** to place the replacement clip on top of the existing clip.

4. Play the section through:

Figure 9.15: Adding a new B-roll clip above an existing clip does hide it, but this is fragile

Simply placing one clip over another will hide it, but it won't remove any audio, and it's a dangerous situation – what if the top clip is a frame short, and you see it pop through? For safety, you should hide the clip you don't want by pressing **V** to toggle a clip on or off, both visibly and audibly. Hidden clips are darkened and grayed out but still present. Disabled clips can be re-enabled with another press of **V**, and even while disabled, they can occupy space in the Primary Storyline and in secondary storylines.

5. Press **V** to toggle visibility for the selected clip.
6. Play the section through again:

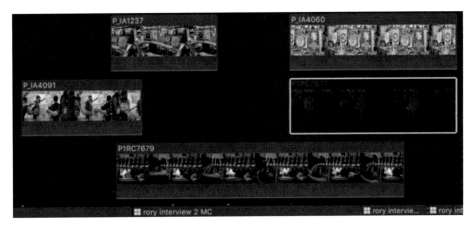

Figure 9.16: The older B-roll clip is now hidden and inaudible

With your choice made, you can delete whichever clip you like least, or keep the alternate choice hidden and give your client the final word. To switch back to the original B-roll choice, do the following:

1. Select the top clip and press **V** to hide it.
2. Select the bottom clip and press **V** to show it.

The nice thing about this technique is that it's obvious; there's a clear visual reminder in the timeline that's there's a disabled clip at a certain point, and this alone can prompt you (or your client) to take another look:

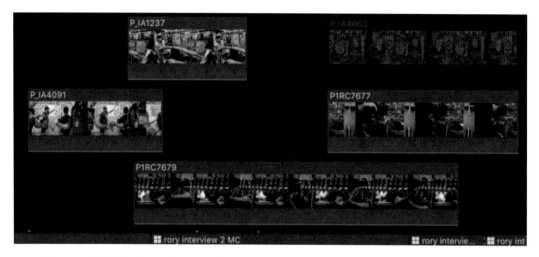

Figure 9.17: Back to the way it was, but with an additional choice available

Because a disabled B-roll clip is totally independent, it doesn't necessarily have to be the same length as any other clips, nor does it need to start at the same point. Be sure that any new clips you've placed on top start exactly at or slightly before the start point of any older clips below it; otherwise, you'll see a flash frame of the lower clip in your final output.

IMPORTANT NOTE

An additional technique is to move alternate clips *underneath* the Primary Storyline rather than above. I've sometimes used this to store spare clips near their original source position while keeping the top area clear, and I also disable these clips to reduce their visual footprint.

When the final choice has been made, you can simply leave the replacement clip visible above and (if you want) disable the old clip below. If you're sure you don't need it, and if it's not going to cause any other changes to your timeline, you could simply delete the old clip. With independent connected clips, there's no problem, but with Primary or connected Storylines, deleting a clip could lead to trouble:

- If the deleted clip is on the Primary Storyline and has clips connected to it, those connected clips could be deleted.

- If the deleted clip is in a connected Storyline, other clips in the Storyline could move.

- If the replacement clip is longer than the deleted clip, other clips could move:

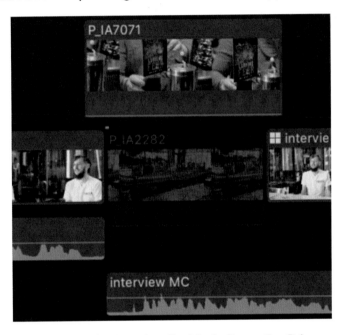

Figure 9.18: Deleting the disabled clip on the Primary
Storyline here would cause ripple mayhem

It's true that simple has its benefits, but it also has its flaws. Even if you use toggling visibility as a quick check, you'll want to use another, more permanent technique to permanently exchange one clip for another. This is known as replacing.

REPLACING CLIPS

This technique doesn't give your client options — it simply switches one clip out for another. You'd use this once you've made a decision; that is, when you know that one shot needs to go and you have the replacement handy. There are several ways to replace a clip, but here's a simple starting point:

1. Select a new source clip in your Browser that you want to use as a replacement:

Figure 9.19: Selecting your replacement region from a clip in the Browser

2. Choose **Video Only** from the drop-down menu next to the edit buttons on the left side of the central gray bar:

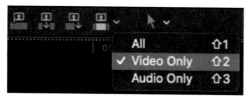

Figure 9.20: The icons will change to show that only video will be added to the timeline

You can replace clips with or without audio, but in this case, we don't want to include audio in the replacement clip. To include audio instead, simply skip this step, or set the menu next to the edit buttons to **All**.

3. Drag the selection directly onto the destination clip in your timeline that you want to replace, and hold the mouse button down:

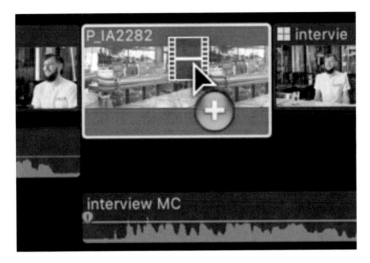

Figure 9.21: This B-roll clip, between two interview clips, can be replaced

At this point, the clip you've dragged onto the timeline will light up, tinted with white. This tells you that a menu is about to appear with replacement options.

4. When the clip highlights in white, release the mouse and select **Replace** from the menu that appears:

Figure 9.22: Choose Replace from the menu, if that's the best option

The original clip will now be replaced with the new clip.

IMPORTANT NOTE

If you'd prefer to use the keyboard (and not wait for that menu to appear), then select both the source (**Browser**) and destination (**Timeline**) clips, and press ⇧R to **Replace** instead.

When you're exchanging one connected B-roll clip with another, this is unlikely to ruffle any feathers. If the new clip is a little longer or shorter, you won't mind, and nothing's going to be pushed out of sync because connected clips are independent. If you're replacing a Primary Storyline clip, connected clips will still be connected, and you never have to delete anything. All good, right? Not quite — there's a gap:

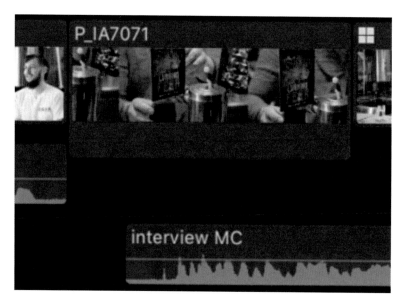

Figure 9.23: After replacing the clip, there's now a silent gap because this new B-roll clip is longer than the old one

Because there's no guarantee that your source and destination clips are the same length, using the **Replace** command could cause your Primary Storyline (or a connected Storyline) to ripple, and potentially change sync relationships further down the timeline. This is especially important if you've added music and synced it to your existing edit; changing the length of any clip could cause sync problems with the music.

Therefore, to make any clip replacements for a nearly finished timeline, you might want to use **Replace from Start** rather than **Replace**. It's almost as simple to use:

1. Select a new source clip in your Browser that you want to use as a replacement.

2. Drag the selection directly onto the shot in your timeline that you want to replace.

   The clip you've dragged onto the timeline will light up once more.

3. Release the mouse and select **Replace from Start** from the menu that appears:

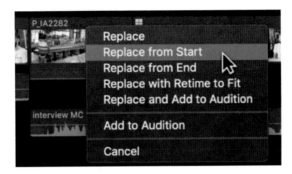

Figure 9.24: Replace from Start, from the same menu as before

The key for this (assuming both clips are selected) is ⌥R, and the outcome is usually closer to what you want. With a regular **Replace**, the In and Out points that were selected in the Browser are both observed, and if the source clip is longer or shorter than the destination clip, the length of that clip changes. But with **Replace from Start**, the timeline clip stays the same length:

Figure 9.25: No silent gap is added as the new clip matches
the duration of the old clip

How? The Out point of the source clip is ignored, and the length of the destination clip in the timeline is used to determine the Out point on the source clip. If there's insufficient media, you'll be given a warning, as any replacement would cause a ripple edit:

Figure 9.26: You'll see this if you replace with media that isn't available

Any time the duration of the timeline clip is more important than the duration of the source clip, I'll use **Replace from Start**. Early in the process, I'm happy to use **Replace**, but once a timeline is close to being completed, I don't want to mess anything up.

There's also a third option, **Replace from End**, which ignores the In point of the source clip and instead starts from the Out point, moving backward until it has enough media to fill in the gap. This is similar to backtiming when connecting or overwriting, and you'd use it when a clip has to finish at a specific point – for example, a smile, a look, or a light activating on a control panel. By default, **Replace from End** has no shortcut key, but you could assign it something like ⌥⇧R if you wanted to add one.

REVIEW — EXCHANGING ONE CLIP WITH ANOTHER

Of all these **Replace**-related options, I usually prefer to use **Replace from Start** because the length of a clip in the timeline is usually the most important. If you frequently use music, you may well feel the same, but if you like to use **Replace** or **Replace from End**, they're totally fine. I do recommend using a keyboard shortcut for these commands because waiting for menus to appear becomes tiresome. Still, I will sometimes connect a clip above and disable it so that I have a backup choice sitting there just in case. Simple operations have their strengths too.

Replacing is a final decision, and though it keeps the timeline neat, it doesn't remember that alternate clip. Wouldn't it be great if there was an easy way to keep both options alive, to offer a client multiple takes while keeping the timeline neat? Turns out there is, and you'll learn about it next.

CREATING AND USING AUDITIONS

Auditions are the happy middle ground between placing a disabled clip above another clip and fully replacing one clip with another. With **Auditions**, any clip can be switched out, at any time, for one of several alternative "picks." You could use them to give a client a choice of several B-roll alternatives, different takes on the Primary Storyline, or even different treatments for titles or effects. The easiest way to use Auditions is pretty similar to replacing:

1. Select a new source clip in your Browser that you want to try as a potential replacement.

2. Drag the selection directly onto the shot in your timeline that you want to replace.

   The clip you've dragged onto the timeline will light up.

3. Release the left mouse button and select **Replace as Audition** from the menu that appears.

The shortcut is ⇧Y if you prefer to use keys for these operations. Either way, after using **Replace as Audition**, the new clip takes the place of the old clip in the timeline. If the length of the new clip is different to the length of the old clip, it will have moved the downstream clips into a Storyline:

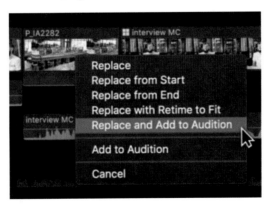

Figure 9.27: Dragging to Replace, but choosing a new option

So far, it's like using **Replace**, but if you look to the clip in the timeline, you'll see a small spotlight icon at the top-left corner. This indicates that the clip is an Audition, and if you click this icon, a popup will show you the other possible options that could be switched in — **picks** within an **Audition**:

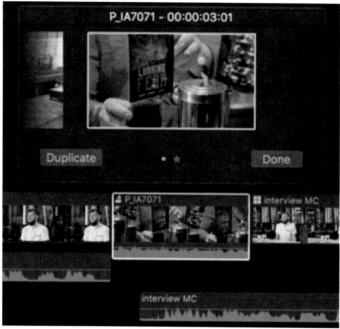

Figure 9.28: As with the standard Replace command, there's now a silent gap because this clip was longer

Indeed, you can repeat this operation, adding as many different picks as you wish to this same Audition clip, and then changing between them. The pop-up **Audition** window uses a star to indicate the currently selected pick and dots to show the others, as well as showing a thumbnail of the currently chosen pick above, with other picks to the left and/or right. Thumbnails can be clicked on so that you can choose a new pick, and you can use shortcuts too:

- ⌃⌥← to switch to the previous pick
- ⌃⌥→ to switch to the next pick

Both the in-timeline pop-up menu and the **Clip** > **Audition** submenu also offer an additional command called **Add to Audition**. This adds a new pick to the list, but doesn't replace the current pick:

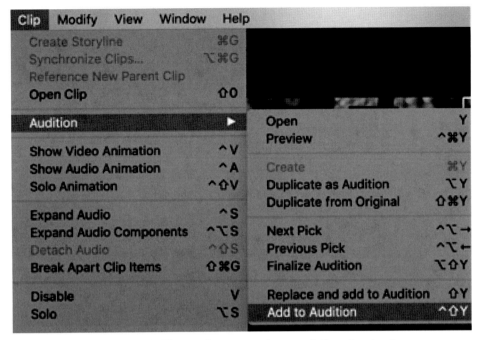

Figure 9.29: The main menu shows all the shortcuts

There's also a **Duplicate** button if you'd like to add another pick based on the currently selected pick. This is useful if you want to present options such as a wider or tighter version of a clip, with two different color correction treatments, or with one clip slipped to show a different part of the same piece of media. Duplicating is handy, and you should return to it once you've learned about color correction, video effects, and audio effects, which you'll do in *Chapter 11, Play with Light: Color Correction and Grading*, *Chapter 12, Refine and Smooth: Video Properties and Effects*, and *Chapter 14, Boost the Signal: Audio Sweetening*. If you're feeling fancy, an alternative command, **Clip > Audition > Duplicate from Original**, duplicates from the first pick in the list. When you're finished, press **Done** to dismiss the **Audition** popup.

There's also one more way to create Auditions — in the Browser rather than the Timeline. If you can't decide which collection of clips is best, then do the following:

1. Click and drag (or use **I** and **O**) to select a "good" region in each of your potential clips in the **Browser**.

2. Hold down the ⌘ key and click on each of the clips you want to include in order to add them to your current selection.

3. Choose **Clip** > **Audition** > **Create** (⌘Y) to create a new Audition clip in the **Browser** window:

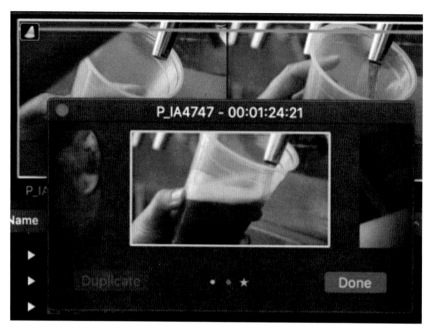

Figure 9.30: In the Browser window, an Audition uses
a floating window rather than a popup

When this Audition clip is added to a timeline, all the different clips are present as picks. If you know that the client will want to see different options, this is a clean way to present them. Still, a few interesting facts about Auditions should be kept in mind if you decide to use them, because they have pros and cons.

Firstly, *the length of each clip within an Audition is remembered*. If you change the length of an Audition pick and then switch to another pick within the Audition, the duration will change to the length of the newly chosen clip. This is good if you want to duplicate an Audition to compare long and short versions of the same clip, but this is something to remember if you don't want your timeline to ripple.

Secondly, *anything connected to an Audition clip on the Primary Storyline is actually connected to the current Audition pick*. This includes any connected clips, and even the durations of those connected clips. If you change to a different pick within the Audition, anything connected to the current pick will disappear and be replaced with whatever's connected to the new pick. This is terrific if you want to quickly switch between different groups of sound effects connected to a clip. Let's look at how to do this:

1. Find a clip you like in the Primary Storyline and connect one or more sound effects to it.

2. Select the clip, then choose **Clip** > **Audition** > **Duplicate as Audition**.

3. Delete any clips connected to the Audition, then connect one or more new sound effects to it.

4. Switch between the different Audition picks to switch all the sound effects connected to them:

Figure 9.31: The "Drink 2" sound effect is attached to the second pick in this Audition

Nice as this is, this feature means you have to be wary when trimming anything that's connected to an Audition clip — your changes may be lost if the Audition pick changes. To be safe, you can use **Clip** > **Audition** > **Finalize Audition** to lock in the current pick and remove the special Audition status.

Thirdly, *there's no command to replace an Audition from the start or end.* Therefore, if you want to add a new clip that's the same length as the old clip, you'll have to:

1. Select the destination clip in your timeline.
2. Press **^D** and note its duration.
3. Select a new source clip in your Browser that you want to try as a potential replacement.
4. Press **^D** and type in the duration you just noted down, followed by **return**.
5. Press **⇧Y** to **Replace and Add to Audition**.

This is obviously a little more work, but it does give you a really nice way to present a client with options that have identical durations.

Auditions can be very powerful, but bring a little complexity due to how they work with the Magnetic Timeline and with connections. If you would like to use Auditions but would prefer to avoid this complexity, consider using Auditions only as connected clips, where pick changes within the Audition won't affect anything else, or remember to **finalize** them when you're sure of your choices. Alternatively, don't use them at all — just toggle clips on and off with **V** instead.

REVIEW — CREATING AND USING AUDITIONS

Auditions aren't essential, but if you're aware of how they work, they can offer a great way to experiment safely, as well as impress your client in a review session. Along with the simpler option of replacing, you should now understand several ways to swap one clip for another in a seamless way, either retaining the original clip or not. Stay aware of the special properties of Auditions, and use them wisely. Impressing clients is great, but confusing yourself in front of a client? Not so much.

SUMMARY

This chapter looked at a variety of high-level ways to swap out one clip for another. With the best planning and careful shooting, you can capture multiple angles at once, and then switch between them on the timeline for a simpler, more flexible editing experience. With or without Multicam, you can present your clients with extra options on the timeline, either through simple visibility toggles, full clip replacement, or the more powerful and more complex Auditions.

If these high-level solutions don't give you enough flexibility, then there are tricks you can use to give you more, and we'll cover these in the next chapter. There, you'll learn how to throw your media into Compound Clips early in the process, grouping parts of a timeline into their own little bubbles and making revisions easier. You'll also discover the lower-level **Relink** feature, see how to navigate in new and useful ways, and make sure that the client review is a simple, error-free process. These are the final editing tricks you'll need, and they're coming right up.

REVIEW QUESTIONS

1. Should you perform Multicam editing in the Angle Editor or a regular Project timeline?

2. Where would you choose how many angles you want to see at once while editing?

3. What modifier key is used to change angles without adding a new edit?

4. In the Angle Editor, which icon indicates the currently selected video angle?

5. What key shows or hides a clip?

6. What operation replaces a clip on the timeline without changing its duration?

7. What features store multiple alternate clips together?

8. If you try to replace a clip but insufficient media is available, what happens?

9. Can you perform a ripple trim edit on a Multicam Clip with the Select tool?

10. What happens when you double-click on the thumbnail of a Multicam Clip in the timeline?

REVIEW ANSWERS

1. In a regular Project timeline.

2. The **Settings** menu at the top-right of **Angle Viewer**.

3. ⌥ (Option) when clicking or typing number key shortcuts.

4. The TV.

5. **V**.

6. **Replace from Start**.

7. Auditions.

8. A warning will appear, and if approved, the replacement clip will be shorter.

9. No, a **Roll** edit will occur. Instead, use the **Trim** tool.

10. It opens in **Angle Editor**.

10 EXPLORE A LITTLE:
COMPOUND CLIPS AND TIMELINE TRICKS

"FCP X has been at the core of my creative life for nine years now, and every year, this tool has surprised me. It's crazy fast, remarkably dependable, and oddly FUN to use.

Since I switched to it, I constantly look forward to my editing work with a new level of inspiration. And after all these years in the trenches, THAT is a remarkable thing to be able to say."

— Bill Davis, 30-year editor, narrator, and producer, Southern California

Feeling confident? With everything you've done so far, you're able to import and organize your shots, create a new Project, add clips to it, remove parts of those clips, connect new ones above, trim, Roll, Slip, and Slide the right parts of clips into the right places, and replace one shot for another in many sneaky ways, and you know about Multicam too. After this chapter, you'll also be able to wrap up parts of your Project for reuse elsewhere, navigate around your timeline, create gaps as you edit, move clips vertically without the mouse, and more — all the weird little things that you'll use now and again, but that you might not use too often. These "good to know" topics include the following:

- Creating and using Compound Clips
- Low-level replacement and relinking
- More tricks with tools
- Adding and navigating with Markers
- Using the Timeline Index

To begin, you'll learn about Compound Clips and other containers.

CREATING AND USING COMPOUND CLIPS

Compound Clips let you group several clips and treat them just like a single clip within a Project. Like Multicam Clips, Compound Clips are containers, and as you'll see soon, containers enable advanced replacement workflows. But a Compound Clip isn't limited to a single angle; it can contain anything a Project can, including any number of simultaneous or sequential clips.

For example, if several icons were positioned at the same time in a Project, all as independent, connected clips, they could be selected and converted into a single Compound Clip, then moved, modified, and trimmed as a single unit. Similarly, you could combine a green-screen clip and its separate background clip into a single Compound Clip. The process is easy:

1. Select one or many clips, either in the Timeline or in the Browser. They can be connected or sequential; any group of clips will do:

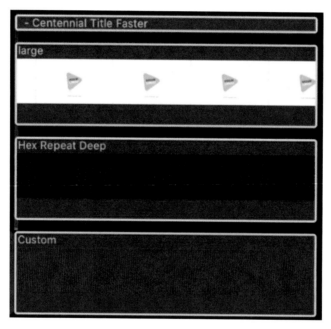

Figure 10.1: Here's a background, then a custom generator above, then a logo, then a title

2. Go to **File > New > Compound Clip** (⌥G) and type a name in the pane that appears:

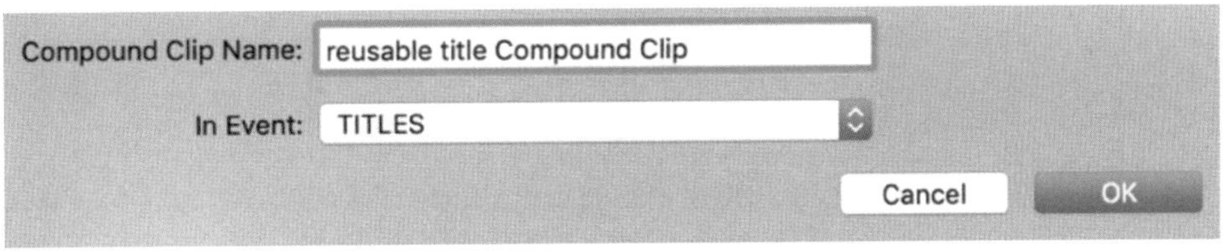

Compound Clip Name:
reusable title Compound Clip
In Event:
TITLES
Cancel
OK

Figure 10.2: Give your new Compound Clip a name

Giving Compound Clips sensible names is something you'll appreciate later:

reusable title Compound Clip

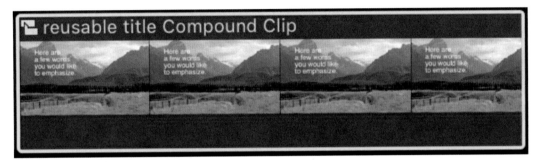

Figure 10.3: Once wrapped up, the display in the timeline becomes much simpler

No matter how the clips are initially selected, you'll create a new Compound Clip in the Browser, and if clips in a Timeline were selected, they will now be replaced by the new Compound Clip. You can open a Compound Clip, from the Browser or the Timeline, by double-clicking on it. Inside, you'll see either the structure you converted from the Timeline or the clips you selected in the Browser in sequence:

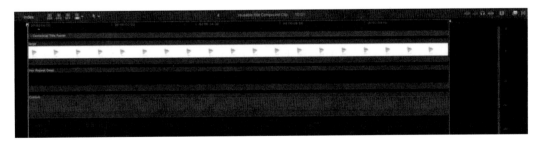

Figure 10.4: The contents of the Compound Clip can be seen with a quick double-click; step back when you're done

You'll see that a Compound Clip is isolated: when you enter one, only its contents are shown. To see the context of its parent timeline, step back by clicking on the arrow to the left of the Compound Clip name in the center of the screen.

If you really need to see the contents of that Compound Clip within its parent timeline, you can break the Compound Clip apart, with **Clip** > **Break Apart Clip Items**. Be aware that the link between the two is lost, and you'll also lose any effects applied to the Compound Clip when you do this. If you want to use a Compound Clip after the **Break Apart** operation, look in the **Browser**, where you'll find a copy of the Compound Clip in the same Event as your current Project:

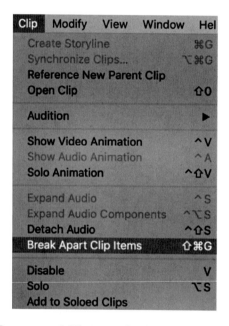

Figure 10.5: Compound Clips can be broken apart, but this isn't usually necessary

The use of Compound Clips is known as "nesting" in other editing applications, and you'd do it for a few reasons:

- To easily reuse complex sequences as a single clip

  This is especially relevant when constructing titles from separate components. For example, if you were to build-up a multi-layer stack of backgrounds, images, and titles to create an animated introduction page for your video, it's a good idea to convert that stack into a Compound Clip. You'll find it far easier to reuse it, and it'll be better protected from accidental editing.

- To apply a single video or audio effect to many clips at once

  Video and audio effects are covered in the next part of the book, but you'll see that you often get different results applying an effect to a Compound Clip than you do when applying the same effect on several individual source elements. One good example: applying the **Broadcast Safe** effect to an entire timeline at once is a good way to make sure the effect applies to every clip, after every other effect.

- To transition between many items at once

  Again, transitions are coming soon, but fading five separate items at once doesn't look quite the same as fading out a Compound Clip containing those five items. It often makes sense to combine several clips into a single Compound Clip, and then add the transition to that single item:

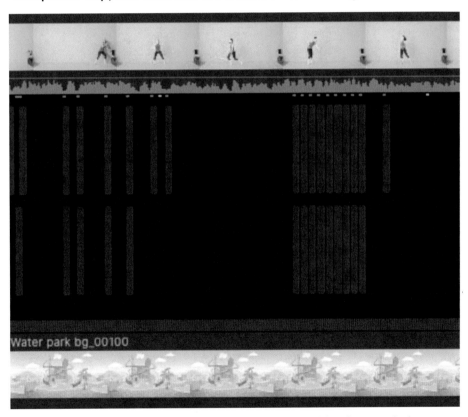

Figure 10.6: Here, a green-screen clip plus several background elements could be combined into a single Compound Clip to simplify and make transitions easier

- To simplify the appearance of a complex timeline

  Sometimes, things are just messy, and hiding complexity makes life easier. Compound Clips can contain any number of clips, while appearing to be a single clip, and take up the vertical space of just a single clip too.

- To edit audio for an entire Project at once

  This will be revisited in *Chapter 14, Boost the Signal: Audio Sweetening*, but the combination of Compound Clips and Roles enables a powerful audio output workflow.

- To convert a sequence of still images into a video

  Have lots of images to run sequentially? Easy. Import an image sequence into FCP, select all the frames at once in the Browser, then press ⌥G to create a Compound Clip, and name it:

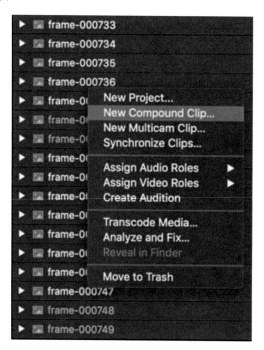

Figure 10.7: These still frames can all be selected and combined into a single Compound Clip

Double-click to edit it, press ⌘A to **Select All**, ^D to change the **Duration**, then **1** and **return** to make every image take exactly one frame:

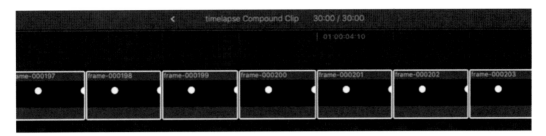

Figure 10.8: Many images, one frame each

Now, you can use that Compound Clip in a regular Project and it'll play just like a video clip — just beware of poor performance. If you've used more than a handful of clips, or the images are large, then the safest option is to share the Compound Clip to a Master File QuickTime Movie, then reimport it and replace the Compound Clip in your Project. There's more on the export process in *Chapter 16, You're Done: Exporting Your Edit and Finishing Up*.

* To treat a clip of variable duration as a fixed duration

Titles are coming up in *Chapter 15, A Few Words: Titles and Generators*, but you'll discover that most titles will span whatever duration you want them to. To fix a title at a certain duration, to allow you to pause, slow down, and speed up a title, you'll need to wrap it up in a Compound Clip first. More on that later:

Figure 10.9: Here's a Compound Clip with Hold Frames added to allow retiming

Here's one more great reason:

* To automatically update a clip wherever it is used

Updating a Compound Clip will update all instances of that Compound Clip, wherever it is used in a Library. This is a great solution when you need to start editing with files that you know are going to change, perhaps the following:

* An early version of a VFX sequence
* An animated logo that's still being worked on
* A watermarked version of an audio or video clip that will be replaced after licensing

While it's entirely possible to simply **replace** those temp clips with real ones down the line, finding and replacing all those clips could be a lot of work. All you'd need to do instead is this:

1. Select a clip in the **Browser**.
2. Go to **File** > **New** > **Compound Clip**.
3. While editing, use that new Compound Clip instead of the original clip:

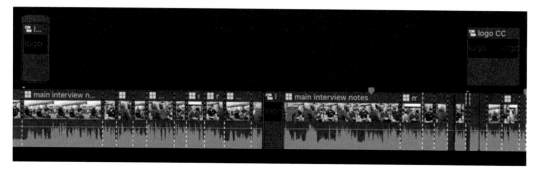

Figure 10.10: In this timeline, "logo CC" has been used three times

If you ever need to change all those Compound Clip instances, you just need to edit the contents of the original Compound Clip. Here are the steps to follow:

1. Open the Compound Clip in a timeline by double-clicking it.
2. Select your new source clip in the **Browser**.
3. Replace the contents of the Compound Clip.
4. Click on the left arrow to the left of the Compound Clip name to step back to your Project.
5. Navigate to an instance of the Compound Clip:

Figure 10.11: All three instances of the logo have changed because the contents of the Compound were replaced

You'll now see that the Compound Clip has been changed to show the new contents, and if the same Compound is used in other Projects, it's been updated there too. But wait: this extends to Multicam containers, which can perform the same trick with some bonus features.

REPLACING MEDIA USING MULTICAM CLIPS

If you know or suspect that a particular clip will be updated, and you need to use it more than once, you could turn it into a Multicam Clip, rather than a Compound Clip, like this:

1. Select that clip alone in the **Browser**.

2. Go to **File > New > Multicam Clip**.

   This will create a new Multicam Clip with just a single angle.

3. Edit using that new Multicam Clip instead of the original clip:

Figure 10.12: The same technique, but with a Multicam Clip instead of a Compound Clip

Just like a Compound Clip, you can double-click on a Multicam Clip, then change its contents — replacing what's inside for something new — and all the instances of that Multicam Clip will be updated instantly. It's similar to the Compound Clip workflow:

1. Open the Multicam Clip from a timeline by double-clicking it.
2. Select your new source clip in the **Browser**.
3. Replace the contents of the first angle.
4. Click on the left arrow to the left of the Multicam Clip name to step back to your Project.
5. Navigate to an instance of the Multicam Clip.

So far, so similar. But why use a Multicam Clip over a Compound Clip? It's all about version control. To compare old and new versions of a clip, you can take advantage of the angles inside a Multicam Clip to keep a previous version of a clip on angle 2 while updating the clip on angle 1. Here's that extended process:

1. Open the Multicam Clip by double-clicking it.
2. From the **Angle** menu on the first angle, choose **Add Angle**:

Figure 10.13: The menu next to an angle's name lets you add an extra angle

3. Hold ⌥ and drag the contents of the first angle to the second angle to duplicate it there. Make sure to use **Snapping** to keep the contents at the same position in time.
4. Select your new source clip in the **Browser**.
5. Replace the contents of the first angle:

Figure 10.14: The clip after replacing the contents of the first
angle and renaming both angles

This is key. The current angle will remain active, even if renamed or reordered, so be sure to replace the existing angle, not the newly created second angle.

6. Click on and rename both angles to match their new content.

7. Return to your Project and navigate to an instance of the Multicam Clip.

8. Switch to **Angle 2** to see the previous version, or return to **Angle 1** to see the new version:

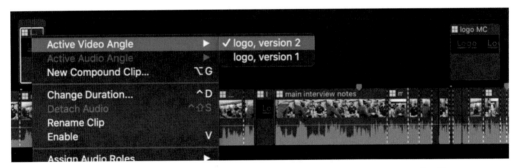

Figure 10.15: All three instances are now updated automatically,
but the older version can be selected too

Both kinds of containers allow you to reuse a clip and make instant changes throughout a timeline, but each has its own strengths and weaknesses:

- Multicam Clips allow extra "version control" flexibility by storing previous options in spare angles, but connected clips aren't allowed within a Multicam angle.

- Compound Clips allow you to connect multiple clips vertically, to store and reuse a more complex timeline, but there's no easy way to compare previous versions.

- For version control with a more complex multi-level timeline, place Compound Clips within Multicam angles.

Using either of these containers enables advanced replacement workflows, but remember a few limitations:

- Compound and Multicam Clips can only be stabilized inside their container, not on the outside.

- Multicam Clips behave slightly differently with regard to Ripple and Roll edits. As discussed previously, the **Select** tool will perform a **Roll** edit by default, while the **Trim** tool can still perform a regular trim edit (a Ripple).

- Containers will not automatically grow to show additional media contained within them, even if the clip at the edge of the container has additional media.

This last point is more obvious with Compound Clips, as they maintain a stricter link to the used part of the clip than Multicam Clips do. When you double-click to enter a Compound, you'll see marked in and out points on the timeline, and since Multicam Clips don't isolate the used part of the clip in the same explicit way, you might find this confusing. Read on to find out how to extend a Compound Clip.

UNDERSTANDING COMPOUND CLIP TRIMMING ISSUES

One limitation of working with Compound Clips is that you can't extend their length to be longer than they started:

Figure 10.16: This Compound Clip is 10 seconds long,
the default still image length, and can't be made longer

Even if the clips inside the Compound have additional media available — and still images can be as long as you want — you can't simply trim a Compound Clip's In point to earlier than its original In point, nor can you move its Out point to later than its original Out point. The fix is as follows:

1. Double-click to enter the Compound Clip.

2. Select the In point of the first clip and move it to the left, or select the Out point of the last clip and move it to the right:

Figure 10.17: The contents of the Compound Clip can
extend beyond its current "out" point

This creates a "handle" beyond the current edges of the clip, shown with darkened crosshatching.

3. Click on the arrow to the left of the Compound Clip name in the center bar to return to the parent Project.

4. Trim the start or end of the clip outward:

Figure 10.18: Back in the Project, you can now extend the Compound
Clip further

Obviously, you can avoid this situation by not turning a clip into a Compound until you're sure you won't need to trim it, or by turning the entire source clip into a Compound and then trimming it within the main timeline.

With the trimming issues covered, you just need to keep a few duplication issues in mind, because duplicating a Project doesn't necessarily create duplicates of containers within that Project.

UNDERSTANDING CONTAINER DUPLICATION ISSUES

If you make heavy use of Compound Clips or Multicam Clips, you'll want to be aware of a difference between the two options for duplicating Projects: **Duplicate Project** and **Snapshot Project**.

If you use **Duplicate Project**, then that's all that happens — the same Compound and Multicam Clips are used in both copies of the Project. Because any changes inside a Compound or Multicam Clip do ripple through all Projects, if you make changes to a Compound Clip used in a later version of a Project, they will flow through to the same Compound Clip used in an earlier version of a Project. Sometimes this won't matter, but if you need to be able to return to exactly the same version of a timeline that you had previously, it's a potential problem:

Figure 10.19: Duplicate as a snapshot to protect Compounds and Multicams

To combat this, if you use **Snapshot Project**, any Compound and Multicam Clips used in that Project are also duplicated. This means that each snapshot is fully self-contained; future changes inside those containers will not affect the earlier timelines, and you can revert safely if you need to. However, these duplicates can also cause your Library to become bloated over time. Is it worth it? That's entirely up to you. I don't personally use snapshots a whole lot, but then again, I don't often need to access pristine versions of my older timelines.

Another way to duplicate a Compound Clip is to select a Compound Clip in a timeline, then choose **Clip > Reference New Parent Clip**. This command duplicates the Compound Clip in the Browser (adding `copy` to the end of the name) and points the timeline copy to that new duplicate.

REVIEW — CREATING AND USING COMPOUND CLIPS

Containers such as Compound Clips (and sometimes Multicams) can be a very useful tool in a complex edit, but they're far more powerful when used early on. If you can predict that you'll need them, they're absolutely worth using. Sometimes, there are a few issues regarding trimming and duplication, but the slightly more complex workflow is worth it.

And yet, despite the best forward planning, stuff happens. The next section is all about getting out of those tricky situations.

LOW-LEVEL RELINKING

Many editors don't like to get down and dirty with the raw media. In fact, the longer you've been in the industry, the more likely you are to have assistant editors to take care of all those details for you. But if you edit videos outside the traditional video and film bubble, you're probably doing it all yourself, and sometimes, circumstances require you to get your hands dirty.

Containers (Multicam and Compound Clips) give you flexibility, but using them requires planning upfront: you have to make the container first, and then edit with it. If you didn't make a container, do you have to manually replace every clip? Not necessarily: you can relink one clip to point at a different source clip if the two files are very similar.

RELINKING TO REPLACE A CLIP

Relinking is a way to replace media behind the scenes, allowing you to point a clip to a different source file. However, this is only assured to work if the new clip and old clip share the same file type, duration, frame rate, frame resolution, and number of audio channels; if the two files are different, the process can fail:

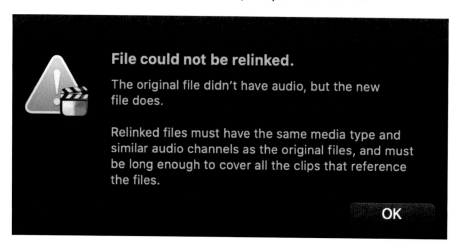

Figure 10.20: You really don't want to see this warning

Since relinking can fail in unlucky circumstances, it shouldn't be your primary update mechanism, but if you need it, here it is.

Let's say you've been provided with a client's animated transparent logo in a short ProRes 4444 file. You've used this clip several times in a number of Projects, and it looks great:

Figure 10.21: Classic: an animated logo above a slow-motion
background shot

You're ready to export, but the client contacts you with great news!

superlogo v1.mov   superlogo v2.mov

Figure 10.22: The new logo has extra sparkle

The logo has just been updated, and you didn't use a container — is that a problem? Maybe not; even without containers, here's a potential quick solution:

1. Select just this one clip in the **Browser**.

2. Choose **File** > **Relink Files** > **Original Media**.

   If you're using a proxy workflow, you'll have to regenerate proxies after this. Alternatively, use the **File** > **Relink Files** > **Proxy Media** command to point directly at a new proxy file too. *This is new in 10.4.9.*

3. Click on **Locate All**, or click on the file and choose **Locate Selected...**:

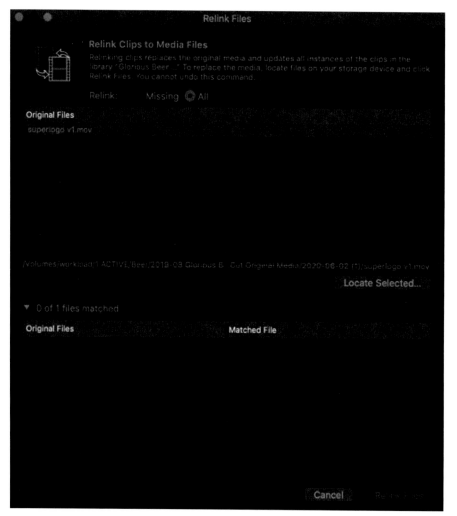

Figure 10.23: Here's the Relink Files dialog, when just a single file is chosen

4. Navigate to the new file, then choose it, and click on **Relink Files**:

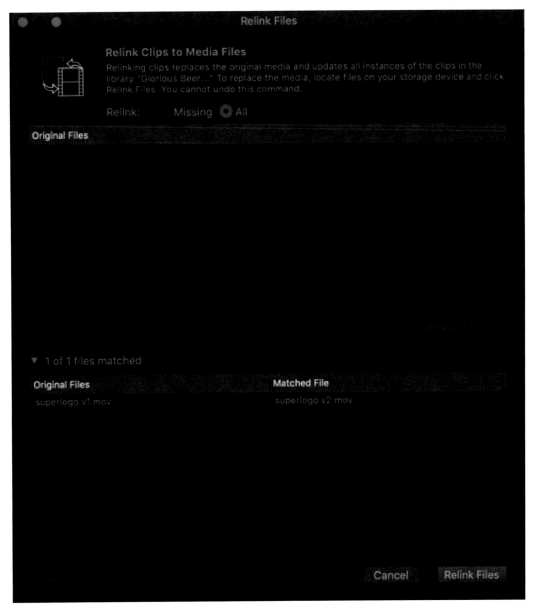

Figure 10.24: The bottom half of this dialog tells the story, listing the original file and the new matched file

This will replace one clip with another throughout every Project in an entire Library in a single hit:

Figure 10.25: Automatically, every instance of the clip will be updated for added sparkle

One thing to be aware of is that clip names are not updated when using **Relink Media**. You may wish to rename the source clip's name from `v1` to `v2` just so you're clear what's happened, but that won't change the names of timeline clips.

If you do use this trick and your media files are managed by FCP (inside your Library, or in an external location) remember to follow it up by consolidating your media. To do that, do the following:

1. Select your **Library** in the **Browser** sidebar.

2. Go to **File > Consolidate Library Media**, then tick the relevant boxes and click on **OK** in the dialog that appears:

Consolidate Library Media

Media Destination: In Library (2020-01 SuperCo Inter... ⌄

Include: ☑ Original Media
☐ Optimized Media
☑ Proxy Media

Original and proxy media will be consolidated to: In Library.
Media stored in external folders will be copied.
The storage location of the library "2020-01 SuperCo Internal Messaging" will remain set to In Library.

Cancel   OK

Figure 10.26: This step copies the new file into the Library

If you don't consolidate, then the relinked file will be pointing at a file outside your Library, and you're opening yourself up to missing media problems down the line. My personal preference is not to relink media unless there's no other option, but if you're working with external media, relinking is something you might have to do more often. Let's take a look at that too.

EXTERNAL MEDIA AND RELINKING

If you work alone and keep all your files inside the Library (as recommended in *Chapter 3, Bring It In: Importing Your Footage*), then relinking is only rarely necessary. But if your media is stored externally, and it's not where FCP expects it to be, you'll have issues. Each icon in the Browser will be the same scary warning symbol in a red box, and nothing will play:

Figure 10.27: You don't want to see this Missing File icon in place of your clips or Projects

The **Relink Files** command lets you redirect all the clips in a Library (or an Event, or a single clip) to the correct location, and if you're lucky, it'll go like this:

1. Click on your Library's top-level icon.

2. Go to **File** > **Relink Files** > **Original Media** or **File** > **Relink Files** > **Proxy Media**.

3. In the dialog that appears, choose **Missing** at the top, then **Locate All...**, then find one of the files on disk:

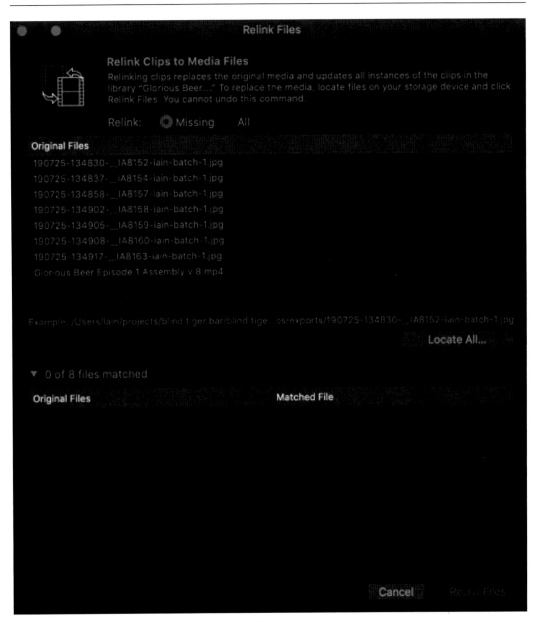

Figure 10.28: Where are these files? Was I careless or just unlucky?

All the files will now be found, angels will sing, and everything will work perfectly forever and ever. Or perhaps you'll have to relink several times, because the media isn't all in one place. Or you have the misfortune to be working with a camera that reuses the same filenames again and again. Or perhaps one file just won't relink at all, for no good reason. From time to time, an error in copying can make a subtle difference in a file, which can cause the relinking process to fail. If that happens, you'll probably have to reimport it and replace it where it was used in your timeline(s), using the techniques discussed in *Chapter 9, Consider Your Options: Multicam, Replacing, and Auditions*. Unpleasant.

Relinking is powerful, but also one of the easiest ways to become unstuck. If you're not rigorous with data management, it's very easy to lose a file (or two, or many more) and not to notice that loss until you recover a job from your archive a year or so later. Always consolidate after relinking to make sure your media stays together. Alternatively, if you don't need to collaborate, just use internal media and you'll never lose a file. Collaboration is discussed in *Chapter 16, You're Done: Exporting Your Edit and Finishing Up*.

REVIEW — LOW-LEVEL RELINKING

Replacing clips works at a high level, but relinking is a decidedly low-level solution. It can fix a problem you hopefully won't encounter and enable you to recover from missing media errors. Good to know, even if you don't need it yet.

Finally, it's time to look at the last secrets of the tool panel.

MORE TRICKS WITH TOOLS

This section looks at a couple of commands to move clips up or down in the timeline, as well as techniques to move around it and change your view, by using tools that haven't been fully explored yet. Although the **Select** and **Trim** tools have had most of the attention, there are other tools that solve some unique problems:

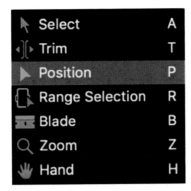

Figure 10.29: There's no tail on the Position tool cursor

Glancing down the **Tools** pop-up menu, you'll see several options. The **Blade** tool has some tricks, the **Zoom** and **Hand** tools have some minor functions, but really, the **Position** tool sees the most use. If you've used the Multicam Angle Editor, you may have already used this tool, and as you'll see, it enables all kinds of sneaky tricks. Let's go there first.

OVERRIDING THE MAGNETIC TIMELINE WITH THE POSITION TOOL

While you should stay with the regular **Select**, **Blade**, **Range Selection**, and **Trim** tools for most purposes, the **Position** tool (**P**) is dangerous but powerful, and it's what you should reach for if you find yourself "fighting" with the Magnetic Timeline. To be clear, if you learn to edit "the FCP way," you're unlikely to feel frustrated.

But if you learned to edit in the classic track paradigm, you may want to put a clip way down the timeline, intending to use it later. You might want to move a clip on the Primary Storyline and not affect the positioning of anything else. You might want to drop a clip somewhere and destroy everything underneath. The **Position** tool does all these things, making FCP 10 feel like FCP 7, and sometimes, this is very handy indeed.

While holding the ` (grave) key or ~ (tilde) key overrides connections and keeps connected clips in their current position, the **Position** tool keeps clips in storylines in their current positions. With the Position tool active, it's impossible to create a ripple edit, so you might choose to use the Position tool if you've got close to the end of the editing process and can't risk moving anything by accident. If you choose the **Position** tool and work on storyline clips, the following things become true:

- When you trim a clip to make it longer, you can't move into another clip, because the Position tool can't cause a ripple edit:

Figure 10.30: The right arrow on the cursor disappears when
it can't move into the clip to the right

- When you trim a clip to make it shorter, a gap is created:

Figure 10.31: When moving the same point left, a gap is created

- When you move a clip into a new position, any clips in that position are overwritten:

Figure 10.32: The clips on the Primary Storyline are about to be deleted

- When you move a clip from a storyline, that space will be replaced with a gap:

Figure 10.33: Trying to reverse the previous operation only leaves a gap

- When you move a clip past the last clip in the timeline, a gap is created to position the clip wherever you drop it:

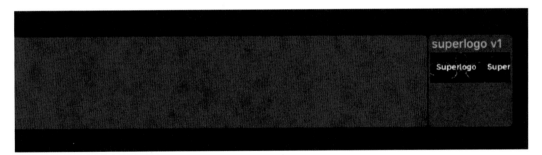

Figure 10.34: "I really want to use that logo later"

Interestingly, the **Position** tool doesn't do anything special with connected clips, but behaves exactly like the **Select** tool. That's because connected clips are already independent, and trimming them doesn't affect anything else.

So, when should you use the **Position** tool? Not too often. If you find yourself reaching for the Position tool all the time, it's likely that you've got some old habits worth breaking. Do you really need to create that huge gap before that last clip, or is it just something you learned long ago? If you don't want to ripple when you edit, the **Roll** operation on the **Trim** tool is a better choice. And of course, simply making use of connected clips is a great way to step outside the ripple-friendly embrace of the Magnetic Timeline.

One occasion where I've found the **Position** tool invaluable for is the creation of gaps, especially in secondary storylines. If you've placed a voiceover in a storyline, removing gaps is easy, but inserting them is hard. Yes, you can add a gap clip with ⌥**W**, but that adds it to the Primary Storyline. But there's a way!

Let's first recap how you might replace unwanted audio with a gap in a storyline:

1. Switch to the **Range Selection** tool (**R**) and select a small region:

Figure 10.35: The yellow selection is around the breath I want to remove

2. Press ⇧**delete** to replace the selection with a gap:

Figure 10.36: After the ⇧delete action, you'll see silence and a pause

This strategy works (as does a longer **Blade**-related method) as long as you have something you want to delete. You can use the regular **Select** tool (**A**) to change the length of that gap.

However, if you've already removed unwanted parts of the recording, you may have split it into separate clips with no gap between, just butting up against one another (and, of course, this happens all the time with video clips too), So, how do you *create gaps* between clips that aren't on the Primary Storyline?

Figure 10.37: Here's a starting position, with two clips
butted up against one another

1. Switch to the **Position** tool (**P**) and trim the edge of one audio clip to make it shorter:

Figure 10.38: Using the Position tool to adjust the edge of a clip
creates a gap

This creates a gap clip that runs for as long as the edit. Nice! And if you didn't actually want to delete that part of that clip, you can use the **Select** tool to get it back, as well as to adjust the gap's length.

2. Switch to the **Select** tool (**A**) and trim the audio clip and/or the gap clip to adjust the duration and position:

Figure 10.39: The Position tool can't adjust a gap clip, but the
Select tool can

This same technique (using the **Position** tool to leave a gap and **Select** to extend that gap) works nicely on the Primary Storyline when you need your subject to pause a little. As long as there's B-roll on top, you won't see the gap, and as long as there's something audible in the background, you won't hear it either. (This is one reason sound engineers record "room tone," the particular flavor of silence that each room offers.):

Figure 10.40: This gap clip on the Primary Storyline is covered visually above and with audio below

The **Position** tool is also vital inside Multicam Clips, where it's the key to moving clips in time to sync them up with clips on other angles. The **Position** tool will be selected by default when you jump inside a Multicam, and it's the one you need.

If you had thought of using the **Position** tool to simplify a timeline vertically, dragging higher clips down to replace parts of the Primary Storyline, instead consider two commands — **Lift from Storyline** and **Overwrite to Primary Storyline** — that live in the **Edit** menu. They can have a similar outcome but offer some clear benefits too.

LIFTING AND OVERWRITING

There's another situation where the **Position** tool might seem like the right choice, and that's if you start with a clip on the Primary Storyline that you'd like to lift up, or with a connected clip that you'd like to move down to the primary. It's common enough to want to "flatten" a timeline out a bit, but the **Position** tool is actually the wrong tool for the job, because dragging a connected clip down to the primary will destroy any audio that's already there:

Figure 10.41: If you wanted both connected clips shown to be on the Primary Storyline, select them first

Instead, use **Edit > Overwrite to Primary Storyline** (⌥⌘↓), which will retain any audio on the primary clip(s) under the connected clip you're moving down:

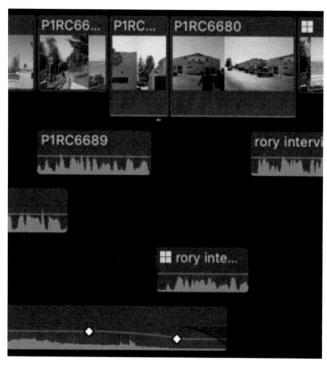

Figure 10.42: Audio will be expanded if needed, and may be detached if its video component is overwritten entirely

It performs this magic trick by expanding the audio on surrounding clips, and even detaching audio from clips where the video is being entirely overwritten. The result looks and sounds the same as it did before, and although the timeline is now simpler, some editing flexibility is lost. Specifically, you'll have to Slide clips on the Primary Storyline, rather than move a connected clip, and detached audio (if present) might be inconvenient.

There's a companion command that does the opposite, **Edit > Lift from Primary Storyline** (⌥⌘↑):

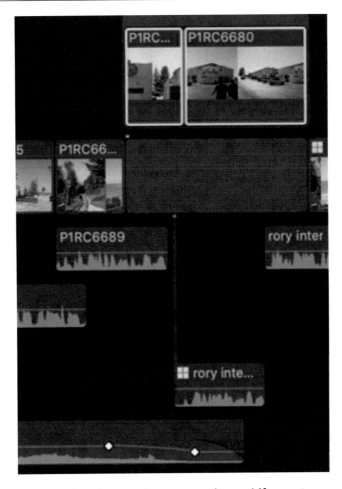

Figure 10.43: Following the previous operation, a Lift creates a connected
storyline, but doesn't restore the lost video component

Similar to dragging a clip up from the primary with the **Position** tool, a Lift leaves a
gap on the Primary Storyline, rather than closing it. This can be useful if you want to
play around with a clip (changing its speed or trimming it) without worrying about
ripples down the timeline. Speed ramping is a popular effect, and it is covered in
Chapter 13, Blend and Warp: Video Transitions and Retiming:

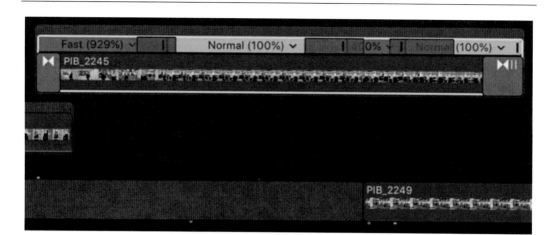

Figure 10.44: This connected clip started out on the Primary Storyline, but speed ramps are easier to manage in connected clips

Together, these two commands relieve most problems you might have had because you wanted a clip to be connected, or because you wanted a clip to be part of the Primary Storyline. They're a nice complement to the Position tool.

BLADING MULTIPLE CLIPS AT ONCE

Now that your timeline is getting a little more complicated, you might wonder how to chop up several clips at the same point. Simple: hold ⇧ as you use the **Blade** tool, and connected clips at that point in time will also be chopped in two:

Figure 10.45: The multi-layer Blade, after a ⇧-click

You'll probably also remember that ⌘**B** blades the clip under the playhead on the Primary Storyline. This command works with connected clips too, but you'll have to select the secondary clip (or its storyline) before pressing ⌘**B**. Finally, to chop up everything at a point in time, press ⇧⌘**B** to blade all the clips under the playhead.

One example of when this can be useful is when you want to end a complex storyline with several connected clips. You can use ⇧⌘**B** at the point where you want it all to stop, then select everything past that point and simply press **delete**.

ZOOMING AND SCROLLING WITH TOOLS

Although you learned other ways to zoom and pan the timeline earlier, it's worth mentioning that there are dedicated tools for these functions. At any point, you can press **Z** to switch to the **Zoom** tool, and then do one of the following:

- **Click** to zoom in.
- **⌥-click** to zoom out.
- **Drag** over a region to zoom to that region.

These functions aren't life-changing, and if you prefer to use the keyboard's plus and minus keys instead, you're not alone. Still, if you've ever pressed **Z** (the **Zoom** tool) instead of ⇧**Z** (**Fit View**) and wondered what happened, now you know:

Figure 10.46: Click to zoom in or ⌥-click to zoom out, just like ⌘plus and ⌘minus

Similarly, pressing **H** switches to the **Hand** tool, which lets you click and drag to scroll in any direction:

Figure 10.47: Use the Hand tool to grab the timeline and scroll in any direction — if you like

If you have a Magic Mouse or Magic Trackpad, you could already swipe sideways to move along the timeline, so this isn't a hugely important tool. While some third-party mice include a sideways scroll wheel, if you're using a regular mouse without one, you can hold ⇧ as you use the scroll wheel to move sideways. I think we can safely list the **Hand** tool as the least essential tool. If you see the hand, you probably pressed **H** by accident.

REVIEW — MORE TRICKS WITH TOOLS

Unexciting as the **Zoom** and **Hand** tools might be, at least now you know what they all do. The **Position** tool has definite strengths (even if using it feels risky): blading multiple layers at once is useful for multi-layered compositions, and lifting and overwriting to or from the Primary Storyline is surprisingly handy from time to time.

Time to dive back into Markers: stepping stones you can scatter across not just your clips but also your timelines.

ADDING AND NAVIGATING WITH MARKERS

Way back in *Chapter 5, Choose Your Favorites: Selecting, Rating, and Searching*, we added Markers to clips in the **Browser**. They're great in the **Browser**, but even more useful when added to clips in the **Timeline**, where **Markers** can help you to navigate, to track your progress through a review, and even to provide user navigation in some kinds of exports. In every case, the Marker will be attached to a clip and not a timecode, meaning Markers ripple up and down the timeline as changes are made, and you'll see why that's important in a moment.

Let's recap how to add a Marker:

1. Skim to or click on a clip in the timeline.

2. Press **⌥M** to create a Marker and edit its name. (If paused, you could alternatively press **MM**.)

3. Type a name for the new Marker in the text field that appears:

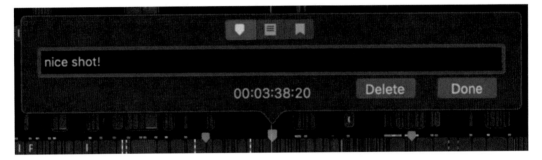

Figure 10.48: Markers can be used for all kinds of things, even simple praise

In this context, you can use Markers to note places where you need to add a scene, where you know you're going to need a title, where sound effects should go, or where the music needs to be replaced. The standard blue Marker is fine for all these tasks, but there are extra options available. The pop-up text field that lets you name a Marker also includes a switch at the top with three options:

- Press the first icon to switch a Marker to a **Standard Marker** (blue).

- Press the second icon to switch a Marker to a **To Do Marker** (red).

- Press the third icon to switch a Marker to a **Chapter Marker** (orange).

The To Do Marker gives you a list of things you haven't done yet, and satisfyingly, a **Completed** checkbox in the bottom-left corner:

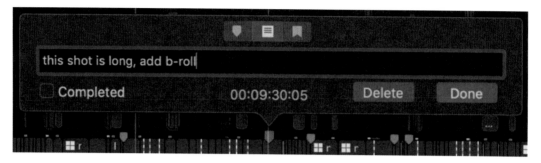

Figure 10.49: The red To Do Marker is hard to miss, and can be ticked off when done

Checking this box not only brings satisfaction from a job well done but also turns the Marker green:

Figure 10.50: A green Completed To Do Marker is a happy Marker

Use these Markers for every change list you're ever given, and you'll be able to show your client exactly where and how you've fulfilled their every request.

> IMPORTANT NOTE
>
> If you want to add a Marker but don't want to give it a name, simply press **M**. Double-click the Marker to edit the name if you change your mind. The **Command Editor** allows you to define a shortcut to **Add ToDo Marker**, but none is assigned by default, and there's no command for *Add and Edit ToDo Marker*.

To Do Markers can also solve one of the biggest problems with the old-school list of time-stamped changes: having to make changes in reverse order. To see why, imagine you're presented with this list of three changes to a 10-minute piece:

- 01:30 — trim 5 seconds off the tail of this shot.
- 4:45 — start this shot 2 seconds in.
- 7:03 — remove this shot.

Tackling those changes from start to finish would mean that the timecodes for the second and third changes now point you to the wrong clips, and you could make a critical mistake. So yes, you could work backward through the list, but why not really impress your client and turn those requests into To Do Markers instead? Because Markers are attached to the top clip under the playhead, they'll be attached to the clip that needs to be edited, and will move backward and forward as earlier edits are made.

Another client-impressing feature is that you can jump directly between Markers with a couple of shortcuts:

- **^semicolon (^;)** to jump to the previous Marker
- **^apostrophe (^')** to jump to the next Marker

Now all you need to do is figure out how to get your clients to use one of those fancy online review sites, rather than sending you a list of timecodes in an email, and you'll be set!

Figure 10.51: Client feedback should be converted into To Do Markers where possible to allow ripple edits to be made

There are many sites that allow online review, with varying levels of integration to FCP, but check out Frame.io, Vimeo, and/or Postlab if you're keen to improve your client feedback loop.

The last type of Marker, the **Chapter Marker**, is useful only in limited contexts. If you export longer movies to DVD, Blu-ray, or a QuickTime movie that you'll be playing directly on an Apple device, Chapter Markers will be automatically listed in a table of contents that the viewer can jump directly to. But that's it. If you're delivering shorter videos, you won't need these, and if you're delivering to online video sharing sites such as Vimeo or YouTube, they (sadly) don't understand how to read them:

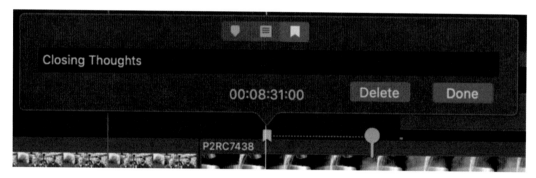

Figure 10.52: A Chapter Marker with an offset thumbnail

In some contexts, the **Chapter Marker** will be shown with a thumbnail, and this thumbnail can be generated from a different time than the Marker's actual position. Clicking on the orange Marker and moving the orange circle around is all you'll need to do:

Figure 10.53: Here in QuickTime Player, the Chapter Markers can be displayed from a pop-up menu

If you put a Marker in the wrong position, while it can't be moved by dragging, you can right-click on a Marker to cut it, and then skim elsewhere and paste it into the right spot. Right-clicking also lets you change a Marker's type:

Figure 10.54: Right-click a Marker to access this menu

Time for a quick recap.

REVIEW — ADDING AND NAVIGATING WITH MARKERS

So far, so good. You know how to add Markers, how to change their names, how to switch between the different types, and how to tick off a To Do Marker as completed. But right now, you're probably just using shortcuts to jump between them, or searching for them in the Browser. Isn't there a better way? I'm glad you've asked, because there is.

USING THE TIMELINE INDEX

The **Timeline Index** allows you to view, search, and instantly navigate to everything in your timeline, including Markers, Keywords, clips, Roles, and much more. You can open the **Timeline Index** by pressing the **Index** button to the left of the central bar, and you'll then see it pop up to the left of the timeline:

Figure 10.55: The Timeline Index, showing clips in the current timeline

At the top of this pane, you'll see a **Search** field, but before you type anything there, it's best to focus on the three words just below it: **Clips**, **Tags**, and **Roles**:

- **Clips** includes all the items in the timeline, including video, audio, auditions, Multicam, Compound, and gap clips, as well as transitions.

- **Tags** includes Markers and Keywords of all kinds that are applied to the clips in the timeline.

- **Roles** shows all the Roles applied to any of the clips in the current timeline, and lets you control visibility and display the order of clips based on their Roles.

One of these can be active at any one time. With Markers fresh in your mind, you should now click on **Tags** so that you can see them all together, and you'll see a list of all the Keywords and Markers used in your current timeline. Next, glance to the bottom of the pane and click **All** to make sure you're seeing all the Markers and Keywords.

The options to the right of **All** allow you to limit the display to just one of the following:

- Standard Markers
- Keywords
- Automatically generated Keywords, such as **Group Shot** and **Close Up**
- To Do Markers (that haven't been marked as **Completed**)
- Completed To Do Markers
- Chapter Markers

Your client review process just became much simpler. With your To Do Markers all together in a simple list, you can click on one of them and the playhead will jump to it:

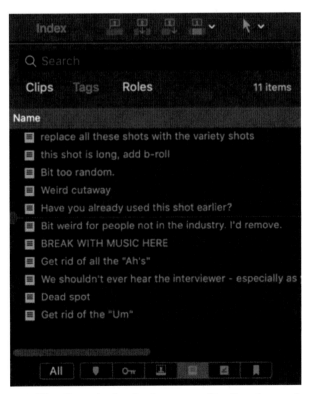

Figure 10.56: The first draft of a longer edit often has a few issues

Make the change required, and then click on the To Do Marker's icon to complete it. If you're only viewing To Do Markers, that To Do will now disappear from the list, but if you're viewing **All** tags, you'll see the icon change (if you click on a To Do in error, you'll see it in the **Completed** To Do list, and you can click it again to "uncomplete" it):

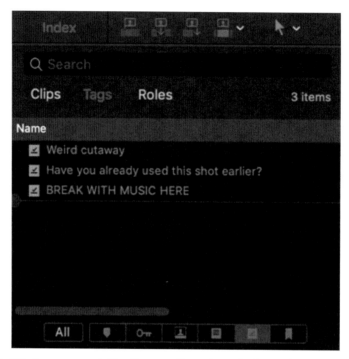

Figure 10.57: As you mark To-Dos as Completed, they show up in the next section along

For larger, more challenging Projects, a client might ask you to fix a specific issue first, and you can search for anything by typing in the **Search** field. As mentioned, as Markers are attached to clips, it doesn't matter what order you attack your to do list in. Timecodes can date and become incorrect quickly, but Markers won't.

Searching is probably most useful when referencing your media, so click on **Clips** to see a list of all the shots you've used, in the order you used them. If you know the name of a particular shot, audio sample, or music piece, you can find every instance of it by typing its name, and jump to it in the timeline by clicking on it in the list that appears— great if you need to replace clips that you didn't place in containers. You can also search for any notes you've attached to an entire clip:

Figure 10.58: This classical music has "Variatio" in the name, so I can find it all very quickly

This is where planning in the organizational stages comes in very handy; if you know you're going to need to find a needle in a haystack later, why not paint that needle bright pink upfront by changing the clip's name or adding a note?

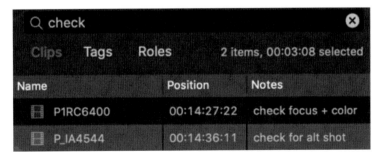

Figure 10.59: A search for "check" could be a good last-minute verification step

A few things you can set up early to search for later are:

- `Important shot`
- `Check Copyright`
- `Check status`
- `Check for alternative`
- `Director's Pick`
- `USE THIS`
- `Watermarked`
- `Replace if possible`
- `Temp shot`
- `Royalty payable`

Depending on the kind of production you're working on, you might be using archival media, where you edit with low-resolution watermarked footage and then purchase only what you need for the final product. You might work with footage that's yet to be cleared; you might have to include certain shots or replace certain other shots. The **Timeline Index** is a great place to find and track all of that, and you just need to add some info in the **Notes** field or as part of the clip name. But do it early — adding notes to a Browser clip after you've added it to the Timeline won't flow through to that Timeline copy.

> IMPORTANT NOTE
> If you need to keep track of a lot of this information, look at applications such as Producer's Best Friend and CommandPost, both of which allow you to export spreadsheet files based on the contents of your timeline.

Crucially, you can select clips in the **Timeline Index** to select them in the timeline, and vice versa. Selecting multiple clips at once works as you'd expect:

- **Click** to select a clip.
- **⇧-click** to extend a selection, including all clips from the previous clip selected.
- **⌘-click** to select or deselect additional individual clips:

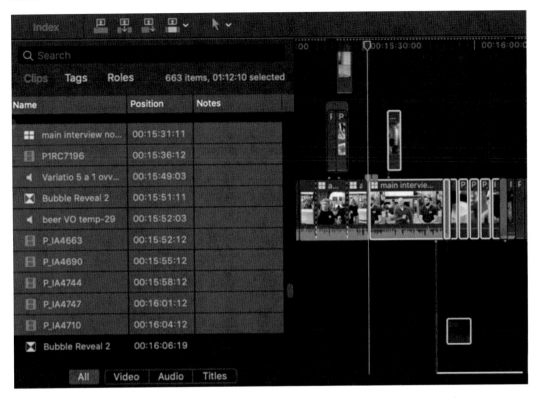

Figure 10.60: Select in the Timeline Index to also select in the timeline — or vice versa

Selecting clips like this can be a massive timesaver because it means you're relying far less on your eyes and your mouse to select clips. It's also a big help when toggling visibility with **V**, changing duration with **^D**, and nudging clips around with the **comma** and **period** keys.

The last major trick that the **Timeline Index** enables is the **Roles** area — click on that now to check it out. Whatever Roles are in use in your timeline are now shown in a list, and a checkbox to the left of each Role lets you disable or enable it:

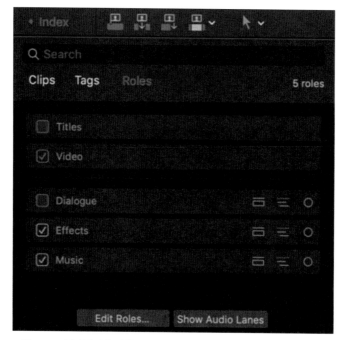

Figure 10.61: No Titles, no Dialogue — no problem

If you want to hear what your timeline sounds like without music, that's simple — just turn the **Music** Role off. If you've added titles already (coming up in *Chapter 15, A Few Words: Titles and Generators*), you can disable them easily by turning off the **Titles** Role.

Audio Roles display three additional buttons on the right-hand side. These buttons allow you to enable or disable the following:

- **Audio Lanes** for this Role, meaning that all clips tagged with this Role are gathered together in a named horizontal lane in the timeline.

- **Subroles** for this Role, allowing you to selectively hear only some of the available Subroles (for example, different speakers could be given Subroles within a Dialogue Role).

- **Focus** on this Role, minimizing all the other Roles to thin lines to allow you to concentrate on only part of the edit:

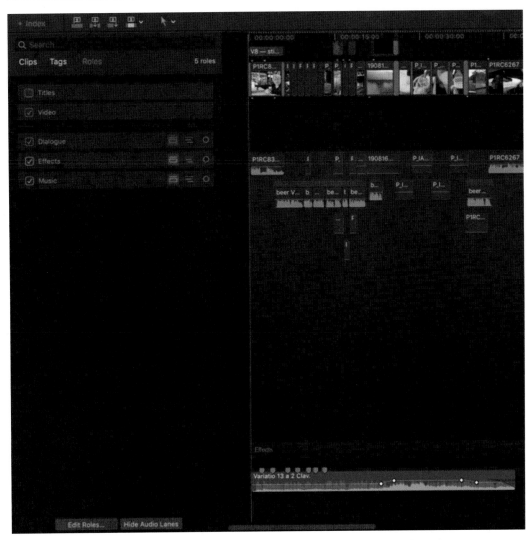

Figure 10.62: Audio Lanes isolates each type of audio visually to
make it easier to see what's happening

The **Audio Lanes** function is important enough that you can enable lanes for all Roles
at once with a dedicated button at the bottom of the pane: **Show Audio Lanes**. This
feature allows you to visually reorder all the audio clips by dragging the order of the
audio Roles in the Timeline Index. For example, you could bring music to the top and
place dialogue just below, without having to manually drag dozens of clips. Audio
sounds the same no matter where it's stacked, so put these clips wherever you wish:

Figure 10.63: Here, the Music Role has been given focus and reordered to the top

Lastly, there's another button for **Edit Roles**, but that's also available by right-clicking on a clip in the **Browser**, and with **Modify > Edit Roles**. Roles are best set up early in the edit process, but better late than never. And, of course, they can be used to add a bit of color to your timeline, even if they don't mean much. Go crazy!

The ability to expose Roles and use them to organize and view your entire timeline selectively is a magic feature here. If you need to export different versions of your timeline, such as a "music and effects" mix (without dialogue or titles, for overseas dubbing), then you'll find it simple. There are more details about that coming up in *Chapter 16, You're Done: Exporting Your Edit and Finishing Up*, but if you want to hide part of your edit while you work, the Timeline Index is the way to do it.

REVIEW — USING THE TIMELINE INDEX

The Timeline Index has many uses, and though you're unlikely to use them all on any one job, it's still great. Searching for names or notes by typing is great, clicking to navigate is great, seeing your to-do list in an actual list is great — it's all great. But you'll really love it when you use **Audio Lanes** while editing audio. Something to look forward to.

SUMMARY

Containers for easy replacement, relinking, tool secrets, and the Timeline Index — wowsers! Planning for change by using containers is a smart idea, but if it's too late, there are still ways to rescue yourself. When a client is over your shoulder and a clip's just not landing where you want it to, the Position tool will get you out of trouble, and the Timeline Index can help you to track down all the copyright-laden clips you know are there but can't find by skimming. These are the controls that avoid disasters, and if you're working with clients for money, you should make them part of your future.

This is the end of *Part 2*, so now you must know how to edit by now. Right? Maybe, maybe not. Editing is far more of an art than a science, and this book's focus is on learning Final Cut Pro, not editing. There are many books and online tutorials that can help you grow as an editor, and there are many different ways you could specialize (reality TV, features, vlogs, social media, and so on).

While it's true that most of the editing content of the book is now done, the job of an editor has changed over the years, and many clients will now expect you to have at least a passing interest in color correction, the VFX skills to blur out someone's face, a sense of how to transition with style, a loose understanding of audio, familiarity with the current titling trends for social media, to know whether slow-motion is still cool, and of course, to know what codecs are hot this year.

All that is coming up in *Part 3*, in the super-sized *Chapters 11* through *16*, and it's going to be fun. But it's not really about editing, as such. Trimming just a couple of frames off one clip, nudging a bit here and there — you've got it already. Experience will guide you as to where your deft touch is needed. Next up, though: color! And it's not nearly as difficult as you've heard.

REVIEW QUESTIONS

1. What's the shortcut to create a Compound Clip?
2. If the contents of a Compound Clip are changed, what happens to instances of that Compound Clip within Projects?
3. Why might you consider using Multicam Clips instead of Compound Clips?
4. What command duplicates Compound Clips within a Project?
5. What's a common reason for relinking failing?
6. If you relink a file then give your Library to another editor and they see a **Missing File** icon in its place, what didn't you do?

7. If you select the **Position** tool, then drag a Primary Storyline clip on top of another Primary Storyline clip, what happens?

8. If you make a clip shorter with the **Position** tool, what is created?

9. What feature shows all the clips in the current timeline in a vertical list?

10. What color is a completed To Do Marker?

REVIEW ANSWERS

1. ⌥G (**Option-G**).

2. The instances are updated to show the new content.

3. To offer a client a choice between two versions of a clip on a single timeline.

4. **Snapshot Project**.

5. If the new file has different properties to the old one.

6. Consolidate media.

7. A gap is left where the clip was dragged from, and any media in the area where the clip is dropped will be deleted.

8. A gap.

9. The **Timeline Index**.

10. Green.

SECTION 3: FINISHING AND EXPORTING

In this section, you will learn how to correct color, how to work with effects, transitions, titles and generators, how to fix audio, and how to export and archive.

This section comprises the following chapters:

- Chapter 11, Play with Light: Color Correction and Grading
- Chapter 12, Refine and Smooth: Video Properties and Effects
- Chapter 13, Blend and Warp: Video Transitions and Retiming
- Chapter 14, Boost the Signal: Audio Sweetening
- Chapter 15, A Few Words: Titles and Generators
- Chapter 16, You're Done: Exporting Your Edit and Finishing Up

11 PLAY WITH LIGHT:
COLOR CORRECTION AND GRADING

"Has Final Cut Pro X made me a better editor? Undoubtedly. I have the freedom to experiment with just a few clicks, move things around and everything stays in sync, go through all the 'could we just...', the 'what happens if we...' and the 'what would be really nice is... And those are the processes that turn an average production into a great production."

— *Peter Wiggins, experienced broadcast editor, motion graphics artist, and editor of FCP.co*

At this point, if you've been working along with the book, you should have your edit mostly complete. This third part of the book will show you how to add all the finishing touches: changes to color, to video effects, transitions, audio effects, and then titles and captions. While it's entirely possible to fix color or sound earlier in the process, or indeed to make final editing changes very late in the process, you'll find the suggested order here quite helpful in most jobs.

This detailed chapter explores the color workflow from top to bottom. You'll learn all about Video Scopes, comparison tools, the variety of automatic corrections available, and how to perform your own primary corrections to white balance, exposure, and saturation. Once you've mastered primary corrections, you'll learn all about different methods for controlling contrast and ways to control color selectively, drawing attention to parts of the image and adding the final touches that the cinematographer (or you) couldn't achieve in camera. Finally, a selection of more advanced techniques is discussed, including obvious and hidden ways to duplicate color corrections, and how to install and use Adjustment Layers. This is a monster, but don't skip it. Specifically, you'll find out all about the following topics:

- Understanding the color workflow
- Correcting white balance, exposure, and saturation
- Finessing contrast and more
- Selective corrections
- Advanced color techniques

Many editors don't know enough about color correction, and that's a real shame. As jobs broaden in their scope, every editor should know at least a little about color because it's really not hard, and no shot is perfect straight out of the camera. Even if you're on a large production with a dedicated colorist involved, there's no harm in doing at least part of the job yourself, and FCP does provide a suite of professional-grade tools. The best place to start is with an overview of the workflow.

UNDERSTANDING THE COLOR WORKFLOW

Though there are many ways to approach color correction, the goal is always the same: to make the image look better. At the very least, you'll want all your shots to match, to look like they belong together. Your subjects shouldn't bounce around between light and dark, or between yellow and orange; it's distracting and unappealing:

Figure 11.1: Ideally, the Leaning Tower of Pisa shouldn't look dark in one shot, then bright in the next

Getting the basics of exposure, saturation, and white balance sorted is usually called **primary color correction**. To make those first basic fixes, you might start out with an automatic adjustment like **Balance Color** or **Match Color**, before adding several manual adjustments such as the **Color Board** and/or **Color Wheels**.

To take it further, **secondary color correction** is all about being selective, making changes to just parts of the image. You might brighten up someone's face, finesse contrast in a more subtle way, boost the saturation of an object, or darken down the corners of the frame. These selective adjustments can be made with a built-in feature called **masks**, but the **Color Curves** and **Hue/Saturation Curves** tools can also be used selectively.

> IMPORTANT NOTE
>
> The terms *color grading* and *color correction* are sometimes used interchangeably, but most often, mechanical changes to make an image look natural are considered "correction," while aesthetic or atmospheric changes are considered "grading." Many secondary color corrections and some primary color corrections could be seen as color grading, but the line between correction and grading can be hard to put your finger on. Don't worry about where that line falls, but do try to make your image look natural before you make it more emotive.

Before diving any deeper, let's make sure we're working in the right way, with the right parts of the user interface on show.

PREPARING FOR COLOR CORRECTION

Several new interface panes will be important during a color correction pass, and they can all be toggled on or off with dedicated shortcut keys. Here are just two for now:

- **Video Scopes** (⌘7, also in the **View** menu in the Viewer)
- **Inspector** (⌘4)

Most interface panes can be found in the **Window** > **Show in Workspace** menu, and you can show or hide any of them independently:

✓ Sidebar	⌘`
✓ Browser	^⌘1
Event Viewer	^⌘3
Comparison Viewer	^⌘6
✓ Inspector	⌘4
✓ Timeline	^⌘2
✓ Timeline Index	⇧⌘2
Audio Meters	⇧⌘8
✓ Effects	⌘5
Transitions	^⌘5

Figure 11.2: Find this submenu in Window > Show in Workspace; checked means visible

An option there, the **Event Viewer** (^⌘3), brings up an additional Viewer window that's dedicated to source clips from the Browser, leaving the regular Viewer for the Timeline. If you're new to editing, you probably don't need this, but if you've gotten used to a dual-Viewer workflow from other applications, feel free to use it while editing — though we won't need it right now.

That's because if you've been following this book's recommended workflow, you probably won't be adding many new clips at this point, and so you don't need to see the Browser (^⌘1) any more. Handily, you can quickly switch to a new **Workspace** that sets up everything you need, like this:

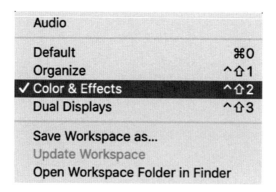

Figure 11.3: Find this submenu in Window > Workspaces; the Audio Workspace will be created in the next chapter

There are a few useful defaults here, and you can switch between them any time you're switching between editing tasks. They are:

- **Default (⌘0)** — including the Browser, Timeline, and Inspector for general-purpose tasks
- **Organize (⌃⇧1)** — hiding the Timeline when you don't need it
- **Color & Effects (⌃⇧2)** — hiding the Browser, showing the four-up Video Scopes and Effects
- **Dual Displays (⌃⇧3)** — like **Default**, but with the Browser moved to a second screen

When you've checked out a few of these, reset the interface for color work:

- Choose **Window** > **Workspaces** > **Color & Effects** or press ⌃⇧2, to show this:

Figure 11.4: Four Video Scopes in the top left, Inspector on the right, Timeline below, and Effects to the right of that

With the **Video Scopes** active, you're now ready to look around.

UNDERSTANDING VIDEO SCOPES

The displays here each show a different representation of the image, to allow you to make objective judgments about it:

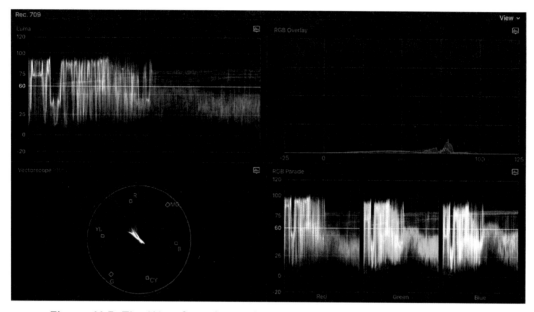

Figure 11.5: The Waveform (top left and bottom right by default) is most informative here

A quick glance at a scope can tell you if an image is too bright or too dark, if visible skin tones are close to accurate, and if a shot is roughly balanced. No matter how your screen is calibrated or what's in your immediate environment, the scopes don't lie and should be trusted.

To quickly get a handle on how scopes work, activate **Skimming (S)** if it's not active already, then hover along your Timeline while watching the scopes. The **traces** are the colored lines and dots that update as you move, and they represent the image's **Luma** (how bright it is) or another aspect of the image. The Color Workspace defaults to showing four different Video Scopes, as follows:

- **Histogram**, currently shown in the top-right quadrant with the **RGB Overlay** mode
- **Vectorscope**, currently shown in the bottom-left quadrant
- **Waveform**, currently shown twice, in the top left with **Luma** (brightness) and in the bottom right as an **RGB Parade**

Each individual scope has a drop-down menu indicated by an icon in its top-right corner. This menu lets you choose which scope is active in that section and which channels it currently shows, as you can see:

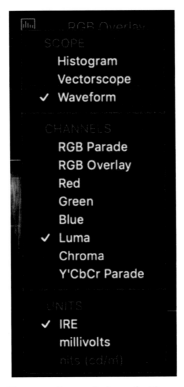

Figure 11.6: Look for the small graph icon in the corner of each scope; this is Waveform's menu

Each type of scope has different options, with the **Waveform** giving the most flexibility and with **Vectorscope** offering the least.

In the very top corner of the Video Scopes pane there is a **View** menu that allows you to change how many scopes are shown, from one to four, in a variety of layouts:

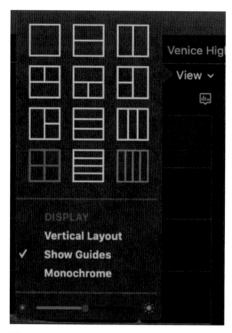

Figure 11.7: This View menu, at the top right of this pane, governs all the scopes

This same menu also allows you to change the brightness of the traces, and to move between a horizontal layout (with Video Scopes to the left of the Viewer) and a vertical layout (with Video Scopes below the Viewer). For now, we'll stay with the default four-up view and explore each scope type. In the following screenshot, you can see an example of the **Histogram**:

Figure 11.8: This Histogram shows a fairly even spread of data, with a large amount of brightish blue

The Histogram will be familiar to photographers. It's an area graph that shows how much of an image sits at each value along a horizontal scale, often representing Luma (brightness). That scale shows one or more channels, one of Luma, Red, Green, or Blue, or a combination of the last three drawn together (RGB Overlay) or separately (RGB Parade). The scale defaults to **IRE** (from Institute of Radio Engineers), and you can think of it like a percentage scale. For Luma, 0 IRE means black and 100 IRE means white.

With the Luma or RGB Overlay displays, if a graph is higher on the left than the right, there are more dark areas. If there's a peak near 50 IRE, a chunk of the image sits around the midtones, the medium-toned areas. And with the RGB Overlay and RGB Parade displays, if part of an image should be neutral gray, then the traces should be at the same spots in the R, G, and B channels.

However, the Histogram is purely about the values; it doesn't tell you physically where in the image the data sits. In contrast, the **Waveform** *does*, as you can see:

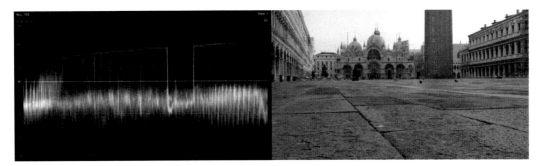

Figure 11.9: This Waveform tells you that the blacks aren't 0%; the sky gets brighter to the right, and the flagstones aren't quite gray

For most uses, the Waveform is superior because it tells you where that image data is in the image. The Waveform corresponds directly to the image in the Viewer from left to right, and shows the image brightness (or another channel) vertically. While the Histogram might tell you that "most of the image is dark," the Waveform can show you exactly which parts of the image are light or dark, or the midtones of skin, or the brighter blues of sky. There's a wider choice of channels available here than with the Histogram: **RGB Overlay**, **RGB Parade**, **Red**, **Green**, **Blue**, **Luma**, **Chroma**, and the odd **Y'CbCr Parade** that looks like this:

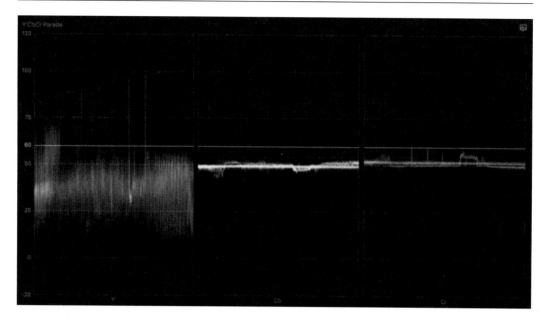

Figure 11.10: The same image as the last as a Y'Cb'Cr Parade; notice the spike in Cr around the red tower

For most purposes, the Luma or RGB Overlay options are easiest to read, but technicians might find the Y'CbCr Parade informative. Most often, though, those concerned with color and saturation prefer to view that data in a circle rather than a vertical graph.

The following screenshot shows an example of the **Vectorscope**:

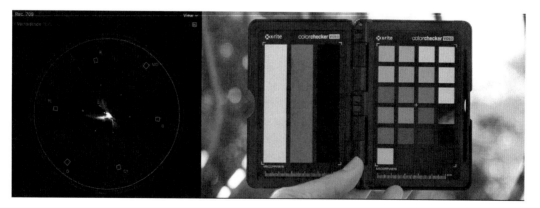

Figure 11.11: The Vectorscope only shows color and saturation — handy with a color chart

The circular Vectorscope is used for judging color, but it doesn't show brightness. The traces reach out from the center of the graph toward a color, indicated by the circle's outline and by six boxes indicating (clockwise from top) Red, Magenta, Blue, Cyan, Green, and Yellow. The further the traces are from the center, the greater their saturation, or vividness. Shoot an image of a color chart as shown, and you can correct it until you see spikes moving exactly toward each named box.

As with the Histogram, the image traces display only the amount of data at a particular value and not their position in the image, so sometimes you'll have to guess which spike corresponds to someone's face and which spike corresponds to that orange wall behind them. A low-saturation image will have small traces, and any areas of neutral gray should be dead-center in the graph. Here's another example:

Figure 11.12: The scope from a shot of the author (who needs a haircut) wearing a blue shirt against a yellow-green-blue background

The gray line between yellow and red is the **Skin Tone Indicator**, and all human skin tones sit on or near this line. Options here are more limited; you can increase the scale to `133%` to make the traces a little larger, hide the Skin Tone Indicator if you don't need it, and rotate the graph to another phase, but that's it.

The purpose of all these scopes is to inform you while you make color adjustments. If you want a "normal" image, you'll want to put the blacks near 0 IRE and the whites near 100 IRE on the default Luma scale; make sure grays are gray to neutralize any color shifting; put skin tones on or near the Skin Tone Indicator; and make any other creative decisions. If you push the image data too far, below `0` or above `100`, then part of the image will be clipped off and lost. While you might indeed choose to do that for creative reasons, it should never happen by accident. Always watch the Video Scopes as you adjust color or brightness, and make sure you don't push things too far.

> IMPORTANT NOTE
>
> For the best color correction experience, you'll need to be working with a high-quality monitor, in a controlled environment, and with a dedicated external monitor — but any Mac's built-in screen will probably do. Higher-end targets will have higher-end requirements, but if you're delivering online, most of your audience will be watching on a phone. Preview the final output on your own iPhone, and you'll have seen what many of them will.

Remember: the Video Scopes are always right, even if a screen is a bit bright, a bit dark, or a bit too contrasty. Each display your work will be shown on may be a little different, but what you see here in FCP should be very similar to what you see in **QuickTime Player**, and on an iPad or iPhone. Don't worry too much if things appear very slightly different after uploading to an online video service — some variation is unavoidable. Your Apple hardware is color-managed, but not everything else is.

UNDERSTANDING WIDE GAMUT AND HDR

The vast majority of Projects today (and this book!) will use the same standard color space, called **Rec. 709**, which gives you a range of legal Luma values between 0 and 100 IRE. However, it's possible to use a wider color space, **Rec. 2020**, which allows you to extend your image across a wider range of brightness values and colors. This can look better on newer, more capable TVs and monitors, but older devices won't be able to display the extra color and brightness information, and (depending on delivery requirements) you may need to deliver different versions of your Projects for Rec. 709 and Rec. 2020 standards.

While we will use the standard Rec. 709 color space for examples here, if you want to try the newer Rec. 2020 space, do the following:

1. Select your **Library** in the **Browser**.
2. Press the **Modify** button in the **Inspector**.
3. Switch to **Wide Gamut HDR** and click on **Change**:

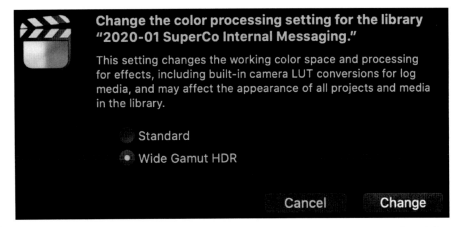

Figure 11.13: To try HDR, switch the Library first, then the Project(s)

4. Select a **Project** that you want to switch to Rec. 2020.

5. Click the **Modify** button in the **Inspector**.

6. In the **Color Space** menu, choose **Wide Gamut HDR – Rec. 2020 PQ** and click **OK**.

Of the color space options, all the **Wide Gamut** options include a wider range of colors, and **HDR (High Dynamic Range)** also enables a wider range of brightness values.

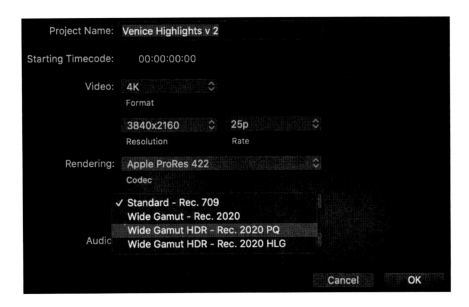

Figure 11.14: If you want to use HDR, this is a decent place to start

HDR standards include many ways to represent an increased brightness range, and two are supported here. **PQ (Perceptual Quantizer)** and **HLG (Hybrid Log Gamma)** are available, and while PQ is more widely used right now, Dolby Vision on modern iPhones is a flavor of HLG. Either way, if you decide to use **Wide Gamut HDR**, you'll find that brightness is no longer capped at 100 IRE but can go much higher, depending on the standard you choose to work with. The color correction tools covered here will work slightly differently too.

> IMPORTANT NOTE
>
> In a video context, HDR means extending the brightest possible value to one that goes beyond normal values. It shouldn't be confused with photograph-style HDR, in which multiple photographs are combined to compress a wide range of brightness values into a smaller space.

Wide Gamut and HDR are going to become more important, but right now, they are largely used by more expensive productions. Standards here are still shifting, and if you need to deliver to a service that requests HDR data, make sure you understand exactly what they need before you begin. Having to correct everything twice is a serious downside of some Wide Gamut HDR workflows, and *for your first few Projects at least, you should stay with Rec. 709*. If you switched your Project and/or Library to Wide Gamut + HDR, switch it back to Rec. 709 to follow along.

It's also worth noting that the iPhone 12 can record in Dolby Vision. If you want to work with this footage in a standard Rec. 709 timeline, you'll have to add an instance of the HDR Tools video effect and choose its *HLG to Rec. 709 SDR* mode.

Before we jump into corrections, let's quickly recap on a few important aspects of selections in the timeline.

UNDERSTANDING TIMELINE SELECTION SUBTLETIES

While the Skimmer is amazing for quickly inspecting clips, there are a couple of subtle points you should be aware of to avoid confusion:

Figure 11.15: Clip Skimming is on by default, but can be disabled

First, know that there's an option called **Clip Skimming** in the **View** menu, on by default, which affects what you see as you skim. When on, it shows the exact clip the cursor is over rather than the clip at the top of the stack in the timeline. This is usually fine, but if you prefer to always see the final composite image, turn this off. Note that you can always skim above the clips in the timeline to see the final composite image anyway.

Second, the Skimmer is great for viewing, but not so good for making adjustments. As it disappears when the cursor leaves the Timeline, you'll have to click to place the Playhead if you want to make any adjustments in the Inspector:

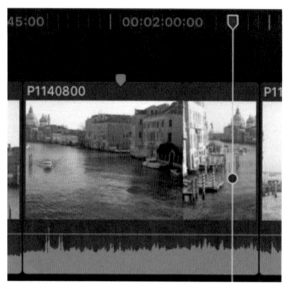

Figure 11.16: If there's no selection, a white dot indicates the clip that will be affected

Third, selections are really important. If you don't select a clip at all, you'll see a small white dot on the highest clip underneath the Playhead, and that's the clip you'll be adjusting in the Inspector. In a simple timeline this is fine, but as timelines grow into multilayered monsters, you'll want to select a clip explicitly, to define which clip you're adjusting. But don't just click on a clip to select it! Instead, my strong recommendation is:

- *Always ⌥-click on the clip you want to adjust in the Inspector.*

Why is this so important? Because if you select a clip simply by clicking on it, the Playhead stays where it is, meaning that you could be looking at a different clip while you adjust the selected clip in the Inspector! Here's an illustration:

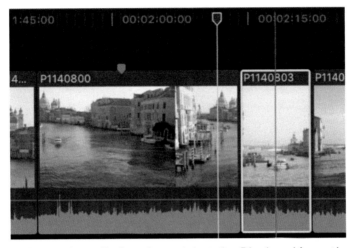

Figure 11.17: The yellow clip is selected, but the Playhead is on the previous clip, and the Playhead controls what you see in the Viewer while working in the Inspector

It's rare that you'd want to work on a clip that you're not looking at, so remember the following:

- To move the Playhead and select the clip, always **⌥-click** the clip, for this result:

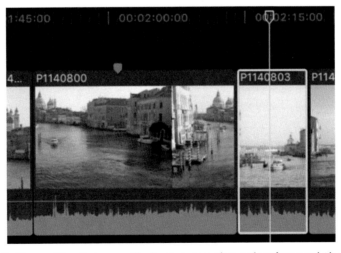

Figure 11.18: If you ⌥-click, you'll always see the selection and the Playhead in the same place

If you're a big keyboard fan, there are a couple of shortcut keys that will help:

- **C** usually selects the Primary Storyline clip under the Playhead or Skimmer (however, if the Skimmer is absent and no clip is selected, a connected clip under the Playhead may be selected).
- ⌘↑ selects the clip above the current clip.
- ⌘↓ selects the clip below the current clip.
- ⌘← selects the previous clip in the same role.
- ⌘→ selects the previous clip in the same role.

With these keys, it's possible to jump swiftly between different clips without the mouse. Also, if you'd like to correct B-roll and A-roll clips independently, you could have an easier time of it by assigning a special Role to B-roll clips, and then jumping through all the clips you've used in a timeline.

REVIEW — UNDERSTANDING THE COLOR WORKFLOW

You've got this! With the Video Scopes up in a dedicated Workspace, an understanding of what they all mean, and a firm grip of how to select things, you're ready. From this point onward, and for the next four chapters, you'll need to **⌥-click** frequently, to specify the clip you want to adjust in the Inspector. Let's do it, starting with the basics.

CORRECTING WHITE BALANCE, EXPOSURE, AND SATURATION

Before you can get creative you have to normalize, and that's what this section is all about. Fixing any issues with white balance, exposure, and saturation is the first step in basic correction, and you've got options. There are several ways to approach this, and there's no right or wrong way. But here's a rough guide to your options, for each clip in your timeline:

- **Balance Color** to automatically correct brightness and white balance. This sometimes works well, but the fully automatic option often fails, either going too far or being fooled by the image content. There is a manual override, but no way to turn it down; this is on, or off.
- **Match Color** to make one clip look like another. This can work well when two shots have very similar content, but otherwise it's not very useful.

- **Color Board** to adjust the exposure, saturation, and color of different parts of the image, adjusting the shadows, midtones, highlights, or the whole image. There's a lot of control here and it's pretty quick, but it's a manual process.

- **Color Wheels** to adjust the exposure, saturation, and color of different parts of the image, as well as the overall color temperature, tint, and hue. This is more compact than the Color Board, and though it has a few other differences, it does essentially the same job.

All of these corrections are best used with the Video Scopes active so you can see what's happening. First, the automatic options.

USING BALANCE COLOR AND MATCH COLOR

These automatic options are found in the second menu of three to the lower left of the Viewer/Video Scopes area:

Figure 11.19: The second "magic" menu is what you want here

It's called the **Enhancements** menu, and its icon is a small magic wand. To apply **Balance Color**:

1. **⌥-click** on a clip to select it and move the Playhead to that point.

2. Choose **Balance Color** or press **⌥⌘B**. Here's a before/after illustration:

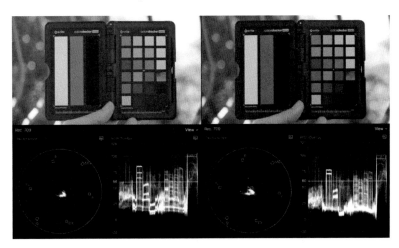

Figure 11.20: Before on the left (shot with incorrect white balance) and after on the right, on Automatic

You'll see the clip change color, but the degree of change will vary from clip to clip. Essentially, it tries to make the image look "normal", so a shot with a variety of content in different colors and some grays and blacks will look much the same or a bit better. If there are large areas of color in shot, the colors could be shifted wrongly:

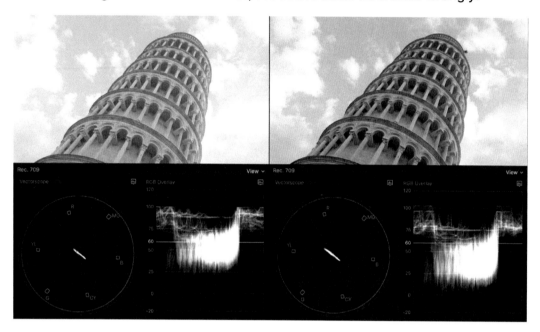

Figure 11.21: This overexposed shot with limited colors has exposure improved, but colors tinted yellow

It's not just colors that shift; it's contrast too. Balance Color tries to make sure that the shadows are at 0 IRE and the highlights are at 100 IRE. The auto-exposure features in many cameras will do this anyway, but shots that are especially bright or dark might change quite drastically.

To override a Balance Color that's gone wrong, you'll need something in your shot that's gray. Any gray will do, but overexposed white or underexposed black won't work. The process:

1. In the **Inspector**, select the first tab, **Video**.

   Almost all the color correction tools use the second tab, **Color**, but these first automatic adjustments are only found in the **Video** tab.

2. Change **Method** from **Automatic** to **White Balance**.

   You'll see that a small blue eyedropper icon becomes active in the Inspector, and that an onscreen instruction and a cursor-based eyedropper appear in the Viewer.

3. In the **Viewer**, click (or click and drag) over part of the image that is gray, or nearly white.

The area you click or drag on will be shifted to neutral gray, and if the image had a tint toward orange, or green, or yellow, it should now be gone:

To set the white balance, click or drag over an area that should be pure white.

Figure 11.22: Dragging over white or gray areas will define a new gray

Clicking designates a single pixel, while dragging to create a small circle uses the average color of the area within the circle. The result:

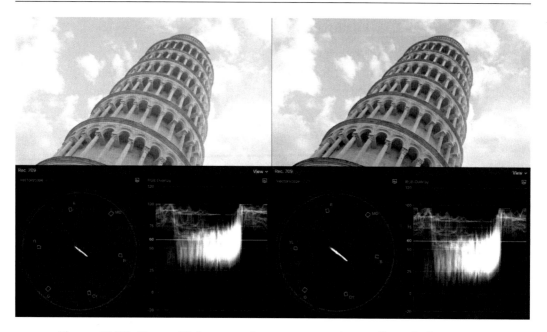

Figure 11.23: Now with improved exposure and no yellow tinting — but not perfect

You can click or drag as many times as you want to get a slightly different result, but you'll need a neutral area in frame. This is just one reason why it can be useful to record a brief shot of a gray card or color chart — it's a guaranteed neutral source. Later in this chapter, you'll learn how to copy a Balance Color correction from one clip and paste it onto others, so you don't need to film a color chart in every shot.

The eyedropper and its onscreen instruction will stay active as long as the eyedropper icon to the right of the Method menu is toggled on (in blue) and the Balance Color effect is selected. Any video or color effects with onscreen controls can only show those controls while the effect is selected, and this is indicated by a yellow outline around the effect in the Inspector:

Figure 11.24: Uncheck the eyedropper if you don't want to use it; uncheck the effect to turn it off

As mentioned earlier, there's no way to turn the Balance Color correction down, but if you want to turn it (or any effect) off, just click on the blue checkbox to the left of its name, or even uncheck the box next to Effects. Unchecked effects are disabled and can be re-enabled with another click. If you don't like an effect and want to remove it entirely, select the effect in the Inspector by clicking on it, then press **delete**.

It's also worth trying **Match Color**, as follows:

1. **⌥-click** on a clip to select it and move the Playhead to that point.

2. Choose **Match Color** or press **⌥⌘M**.

3. Click on a frame within a different clip in the timeline, one that has colors you want to imitate.

   This clip should have similar content to the clip you want to change, unless you're trying to create a strong tinted effect. Here's what you'll see:

Figure 11.25: Matching the second clip to the first will produce very strong results

4. Click again, on another frame within the same clip, or another clip entirely.

   Note that Browser clips can be used as a color source, but not while the Browser is hidden.

5. To approve the change, click the **Apply Match** button in the bottom-right corner of the **Viewer**, or press **Cancel** if you don't like the results.

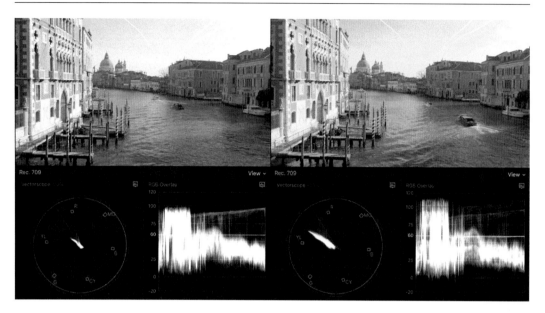

Figure 11.26: Before on the left and after on the right — this wasn't
the most successful Match Color

To revisit this effect in the future, you can press the **Choose** button in the Inspector to try again, turn it off, or delete it. Personally, I haven't had much luck with this feature, but I've found that Balance Color can get to a good starting point quite quickly. Most of the time, I'll try Balance Color, and if it looks good, I'll leave it on. Either way, I'll nearly always make some changes with the Color Board.

ADJUSTING EXPOSURE WITH THE COLOR BOARD

Even though most cameras perform some kind of automatic correction to keep the image within "normal" bounds, you'll often want to make an image at least a little brighter or darker. To get started, first make sure that the Color Board is your default, as follows:

1. Choose **Final Cut Pro** > **Preferences**, then **General**.

2. From the **Color Correction** menu, choose **Color Board**:

Figure 11.27: Choose the Color Board for now, and maybe switch to Color Wheels later

It's likely that you'll prefer the Color Board or Color Wheels for your default correction, so let's start simply. You'll perform these steps every time you want to add a correction to a clip:

1. **⌥-click** on a clip to select it and move the Playhead to that point.
2. Press **⌘6** to add the default color correction to this clip.

The Inspector now opens to the **Color** tab. Technically, a Color Board instance isn't added to the clip until you change one of the controls here. So, what are you looking at?

There are three tabs (**Color**, **Saturation**, **Exposure**) along the top of the interface, and you'll usually attack them in reverse order, from right to left. Click on **Exposure** to begin. The four pucks here can be moved up and down to make part of the image brighter or darker, and the four areas are:

- **Master** — the whole image
- **Shadows** — adjust the darkest areas of the image and lock the highlights
- **Midtones** — adjust the middle areas of the image while locking the highlights and shadows
- **Highlights** — adjust the lightest areas of the image while locking the shadows

As well as the pucks, if your screen is tall enough, you'll see the same information in number form below those pucks:

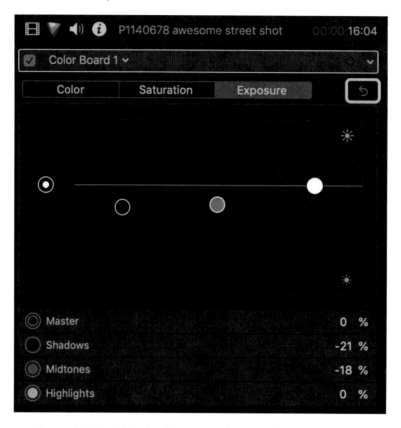

Figure 11.28: With the Exposure board slightly tweaked

You can drag directly on the numbers (up and down, or left and right) to change them if you'd prefer, and if you do drag on the numbers, you can hold ⇧ to change more quickly or ⌥ to change more slowly. There's also a **hooked arrow** at the top right (highlighted in the image) that will reset all settings if pressed. Press it if you mess up.

Each of these controls affects a wide part of the image; it's not like with photo-editing software, where "highlights" means only the brightest parts. Pushing the highlights puck adjusts the highlights more than the shadows, but the whole image will shift to some degree. In the following screenshot, you can see that the highlights are already at 100, and increasing highlights would discard that highlight detail:

Figure 11.29: Here's a fresh image without correction — highlights are already clipped, but shadows aren't at 0

The kind of adjustment you'll make depends on what's wrong with the image, and you're probably going for "normal", at least at first. Here's one workflow, watching the **Luma Waveform** in the top left:

1. Push **Master** or **Shadows** (not both) up or down until the darkest part of the traces touches 0 IRE.

2. Push **Highlights** up or down until the brightest part of the traces touches 100 IRE.

3. Push **Midtones** up or down until it looks right.

4. Adjust **Highlights** and **Midtones** repeatedly until the image is balanced, with the brightest traces touching or near 100 IRE.

Choosing to push Master or Shadows in that first step will give you different results, and you'll want to try it both ways.

Figure 11.30: Moving Shadows and Midtones (not the already blown Highlights) gives a better image

The goal with these steps is to create a balanced image that covers the full tonal range from black to white. However, not every image contains the full dynamic range available, so these steps won't work with every image, and you'll have to use your judgment.

You'll also find that if your camera was on automatic settings, you'll already have shadows near 0 IRE and highlights near 100 IRE. In that case, you'll skip *Step 1*, and that's OK. But don't try to do everything here. The Color Board and/or Color Wheels are a useful initial adjustment, but they're not the best way to create contrast.

Figure 11.31: This image has been pushed too far beyond the
0–100 IRE range

If you push the shadows lower than 0 IRE, that's called "crushing the blacks", and while it does increase contrast, it also destroys shadow detail. Lifting the highlights (past 100 IRE) similarly loses highlight detail. At this stage, try not to do either; just watch the Waveform scope to make sure your images use the full dynamic range, and move on to the next step.

ADJUSTING SATURATION WITH THE COLOR BOARD

After Exposure, you might need to tweak **Saturation**:

1. Click on the **Saturation** tab at the top of the **Color Board**.
2. Move the **Midtones** slider up (or perhaps down) until it looks good.
3. Optionally, move the **Shadows** slider up (or perhaps down) until it looks good.

If a shot starts out life underexposed or overexposed, it's likely to be undersaturated. Some footage is also slightly undersaturated by nature, but if the image looks very flat then it might have been shot in "log" mode, and you'll find out how to deal with that later in this chapter.

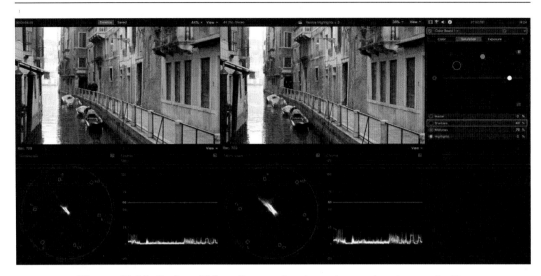

Figure 11.32: Before/After Saturation boosts are best seen in the Vectorscope, or in Waveform set to Chroma

For now, if any parts of the image look unexciting and dull, boost Saturation. Midtones is most likely to need work (as it's the puck you probably changed the most under Exposure), but Shadows can look good boosted too. Boosting Highlights usually looks a little unnatural, and you might want to reduce highlight saturation slightly. While you can watch Saturation change in the Vectorscope, there's no hard and fast rule here — stop when it looks good. Subtle changes to Saturation are important in some looks, but other tools will give you more control. If you need to, you can revisit Saturation after the next section: changing white balance with the **Color** area.

ADJUSTING WHITE BALANCE WITH THE COLOR BOARD

With Exposure fixed and Saturation slightly tweaked, you'll want to fix any remaining white balance issues. No matter how careful the camera operator is, you'll almost certainly have to fix a yellow, green, blue, or orange tint at some point. Most footage can be adjusted at least a little, but high-quality recording formats allow for more extreme adjustments. Fixing color is slightly trickier than the other adjustments, because you have more freedom. To start:

1. Click on the **Color** tab at the top of the **Color Board**.

You'll see four pucks, which can be moved horizontally to choose a color, and vertically to define the strength of the movement. Colors have opposites, and moving the puck toward red is exactly the same as moving it away from cyan. You can ignore the lower half of the board for now if you like.

2. Move the **Highlights** puck up and along to move the image toward a particular color, or down and along to move the image away from that color, like this:

Figure 11.33: The original shot was clearly too cool, and now that the RGB Parade traces look more similar around the midtones, it's more neutral

What's the goal? If there's a white or gray area that looks like it has a color cast, watch the Waveform's RGB Parade (or RGB Overlay) as you move the pucks around. The traces should line up at the same height in any true grays or near-whites, and in general, correcting for white balance will nearly always make an image look right. Judge that with the Video Scopes, not your eyes — line up the R, G, and B traces by moving that Highlights puck around.

Watching a Vectorscope can also be useful here. If there's a person in shot, you can try to line up the traces representing their skin near the skin-tone line.

Figure 11.34: Skin tone too warm, versus skin tone about right — just check the Vectorscope

Push that Highlights puck around, keeping an eye on the Vectorscope for skin tone while keeping the Waveform's R/G/B traces in line for white or gray areas. It's a balance, and you'll get better with practice.

Sometimes, if the recorded image has a stronger color cast, you'll also have to move the Midtones, which will affect skin tone more strongly than white balance.

3. Optionally, also move the **Midtones** puck up to move the image toward a particular color, or down to move the image away from that color.

Most cameras always record neutral blacks, and the Vectorscope can confirm this by showing traces in the center of its graph. Therefore, moving the Master or Shadows pucks here is more likely to create problems rather than solve them. Still, if the shot has a strong color cast (and Balance Color can't help), you might have to drag the Master color puck (or all of them!) to re-center the data in the Vectorscope. As you can see, it can get messy:

Figure 11.35: Correcting this white balance error manually requires complex puck movements to line up the traces on the left-side white/gray/black bars

Adjust **Exposure**, then **Saturation**, then **Color**. When balancing most shots, that's all you need to do, but if you've had to move the color pucks more than a little, take another look at the Exposure tab and see if you've lost any significant data. There's no problem bouncing between the tabs to push things a little one way or the other.

Down the track, if you decide to push a look a little further, you might push Shadows in one direction and Highlights in the opposite direction, to create an extreme "color contrast" effect. More on that fun stuff later, though. Time to explore **Color Wheels**, which you can use as an alternative to the Color Board.

USING COLOR WHEELS

You can use the Color Wheels instead of the Color Board, or use both together. All the same principles and approaches from the Color Board apply to Color Wheels, but there are a few additional controls that are important, and some subtle differences too. Let's begin with some familiar steps:

1. **⌥-click** on a clip (with no corrections applied) to select it and move the Playhead to that point.

2. Press **⌘6** to add the default color correction to this clip.

   For now, that's going to show the Color Board, but we can change that. At the top of the Color Board, you'll see it says **No Corrections**, and if you were to make any adjustment now, it would show **Color Board 1** instead. We'll switch it for something else:

3. Click on **No Corrections** and choose **+Color Wheels** from the menu, as shown:

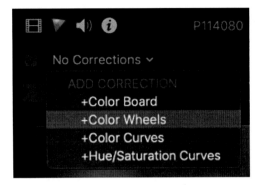

Figure 11.36: Add a new color wheel

At any point, no matter if a correction has been added to a clip or not, you can add a new correction on top of any existing ones by choosing an option from this menu starting with **+**. You can also access existing corrections on this clip from the top half of the same menu.

Let's take a look at Color Wheels in more detail:

- **Master**, **Shadows**, **Midtones**, and **Highlights** wheels correspond to the four pucks found in the three tabs of the Color Board.

- Each wheel incorporates an **Exposure** slider on the right, a **Saturation** slider on the left, and a **Color** puck in the center. Each wheel also incorporates a hooked arrow reset button to its lower right.

- These controls are duplicated in slider and numeric form in named sections near the bottom of the panel. Press **Show** to expand each one, and **Hide** to contract it.

- Below the wheels, **Temperature** and **Tint** sliders offer another way to adjust white balance.

- A **Hue** wheel enables more drastic color shifts by transforming colors around the spectrum, rather than pushing all colors toward a single target.

- At the very bottom, a **Mix** control allows all controls to be gradually turned off.

This is what it looks like:

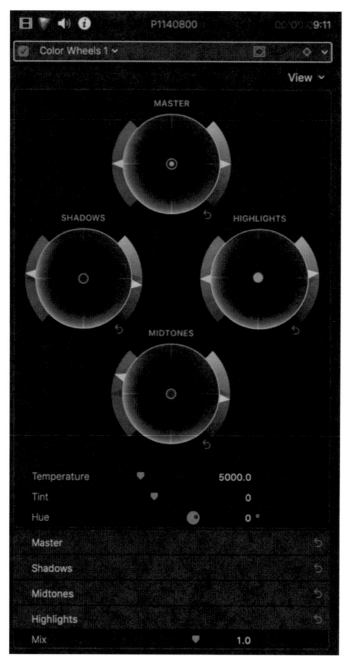

Figure 11.37: The Color Wheels correction with a few tweaks applied

If you decide to use Color Wheels rather than the Color Board, you'll find that you won't spend as much time switching the interface around, but you may miss the precision of the more prominent numbers. Personally, I prefer using the Color Board for minor white balance fixes because I find it more predictable and consistent, but others will enjoy using the wheels instead. Any choice here is fine.

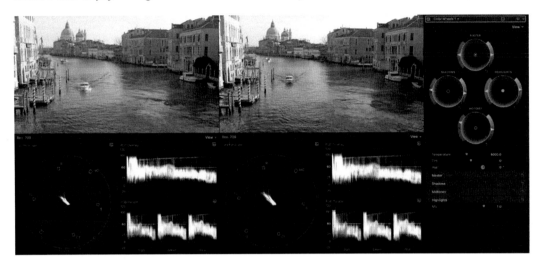

Figure 11.38: The before/after difference of that last correction, now a bit punchier

The additional **Temperature** and **Tint** sliders are common in a photography workflow, and if you've transitioned to editing from that field (or your client uses terms such as "warm" and "cool"), then you might like to use them here. You can see them just below the wheels here:

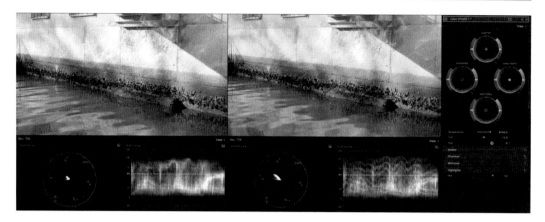

Figure 11.39: The Temperature and Tint sliders are enough to strongly warm up this image

If you're unfamiliar with them, Temperature is essentially a cyan-yellow (cool to warm) slider, while Tint is a green-magenta slider. If you've worked with the **Lab** color space, **Temperature** is a and **Tint** is b.

Hue is a different beast. You can see where the colors sit in each of the color wheels, and the Hue wheel moves everything around in a circle, clockwise all the way to 360°. It's easy to make something strange like this:

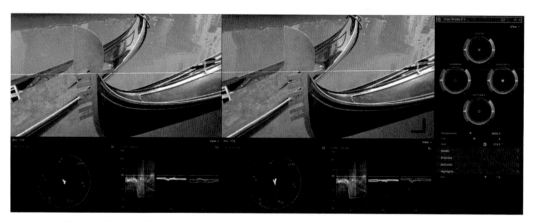

Figure 11.40: The Hue wheel recolors everything, easily seen in the Y'Cb'Cr Parade

Hue is a drastic change best reserved for shots recorded on entirely the wrong settings, or crazy color grades. Be aware that Hue is likely to create visible artifacts with compressed footage, especially with higher saturation values.

At this point, take a few minutes to work through your timeline, correcting each clip in turn to ensure that it's balanced and that the exposure looks about right. Try out the Color Board and Color Wheels, pick a favorite, and then choose it as your default color correction in the first page of **Preferences**.

Either way, you should always color-correct with the Video Scopes active, and make sure that the changes you're making aren't pushing image data beyond the 0–100 IRE range. When you're comfortable with how to use all these controls on a single clip, it's time to expand your view to nearby clips.

USING THE COMPARISON VIEWER

So far, you've been looking at just a single clip at a time, but context is incredibly important. We get used to things quickly, and while a viewer might not even notice that an entire Project is a little bright, or dark or yellow, they'll instantly notice a single shot that's brighter than the last. The **Comparison Viewer** will help you spot these issues quickly, and it's easy to find:

- Choose **Window > Show in Workspace > Comparison Viewer**, or press ⌃⌘6:

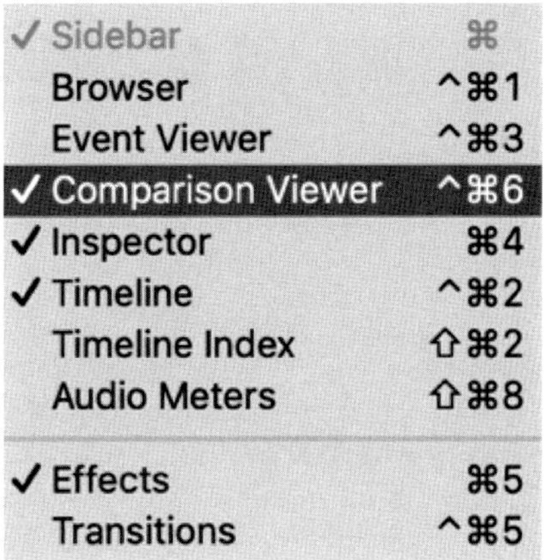

Figure 11.41: Under Window > Show in Workspace

When active, the Comparison Viewer sits to the left of the Viewer and/or Video Scopes. In fact, the Comparison Viewer has its own View menu, and from that menu you can bring up an additional set of Video Scopes (horizontal or vertical) if you wish, as shown:

Figure 11.42: All the recent two-up screenshots have used the Comparison Viewer; vertical Video Scopes (below the image) are best for this

At the top of the Comparison Viewer, you'll see a two-switch tab, **Timeline** or **Saved**. With **Timeline**, an option at the bottom of the pane lets you choose between the **Previous Edit** and the **Next Edit**. This is ideal for comparing one shot with a neighbor, but not for anything fancier.

To present any frame at all for comparison, proceed as follows:

1. At the top of the **Comparison Viewer**, click **Saved** at the top, to see this:

Figure 11.43: In Saved mode, you'll have access to the Frame Browser in the bottom left, and Save Frame in the bottom right

2. Scrub anywhere in any timeline, and click to place the Playhead on a relevant frame.

   The Comparison Viewer won't change yet, but the main Viewer will.

3. At the bottom right of the **Comparison Viewer**, click **Save Frame**.

   The last frame saved is now shown in the Comparison Viewer.

4. At the bottom left of the **Comparison Viewer**, click **Frame Browser** to bring up this window:

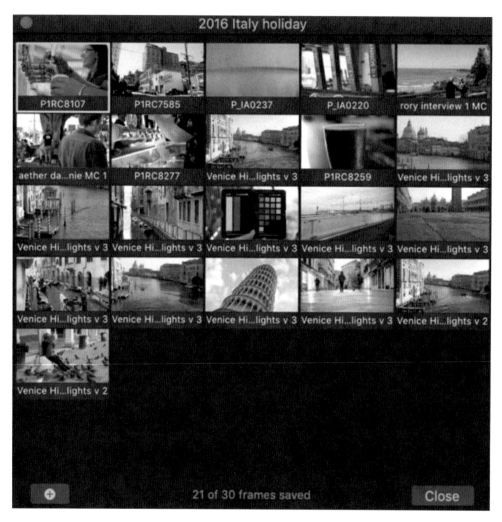

Figure 11.44: A Frame Browser full of images

This displays an additional floating window that lets you choose from up to 30 previously saved frames. Although you can fill the Frame Browser with frames from any open Library, this particular collection of frames belongs to the parent Library for the current Project.

Clicking any frame here shows that frame in the Comparison Viewer, and additional frames (from source clips or timelines), can be added with the **plus** button in the bottom left. When you're done, you can close it. There's no more convenient way to make sure all your shots match.

REVIEW — CORRECTING WHITE BALANCE, EXPOSURE, AND SATURATION

This monster section in this monster chapter covered a lot of ground, and you've learned many techniques to balance out a series of clips. **Balance Color** is a great way to start, **Match Color** is handy sometimes, and manual controls are always important. **Exposure**, **Saturation**, and **Color** can be pushed with the **Color Board** or with **Color Wheels**, while **Temperature**, **Tint**, and **Hue** are only found in **Color Wheels**. The **Comparison Viewer** is essential when matching shot to shot, and it works with everything else, including **Video Scopes**.

All these controls are the right choice for initial color adjustments, but they're not always the only tools you'll use. For finer, more subtle control, read on to the next section.

FINESSING CONTRAST AND MORE

With the image looking roughly balanced, it's now time to move a little more toward the aesthetic world of color grading, by dialing in just the right amount of contrast. The best way to add contrast to a shot without losing shadow or highlight detail is to use **Color Curves**, which can also be used for powerful creative color adjustments. Here, we'll look at both, and also find out what the eyedropper does.

USING COLOR CURVES TO CHANGE CONTRAST

There's no better way to understand this than to do it yourself:

1. ⌥**-click** on a clip (with no corrections applied) to select it and move the Playhead to that point.

2. Press ⌘**6** to add the default color correction to this clip.

3. Click on **No Corrections** and choose **+Color Curves** from the menu:

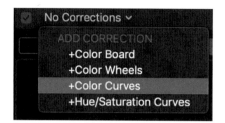

Figure 11.45: Add a new Color Curves adjustment to get started

The image won't change yet, because (as with any correction) it starts out blank.

1. Click on the white line to create a new point, then drag it up and watch the image get brighter, as shown:

Figure 11.46: Before and after a quick "lighten" curve — no clipped highlights

2. Click on the point you just made and drag it down, watching the image get darker:

Figure 11.47: Before and after a quick "lighten" curve — no clipped shadows

3. Click elsewhere on the line to create a second point, then move them both up, down, left, and right to see what happens.

If you're familiar with curves from the world of photography then you'll understand what's going on here, but let's have a quick chat about this graph:

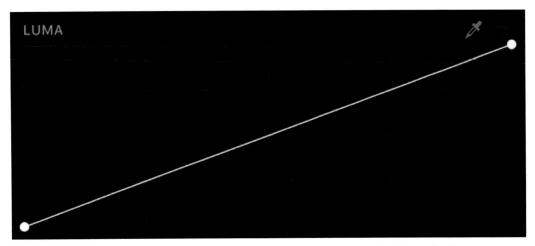

Figure 11.48: The unedited "straight" Luma curve graph doesn't change anything yet

Imagine that the image data enters the graph along the bottom edge (along the *x* axis) from black on the left to white on the right. The data moves upward, and where it hits the line, it moves out to the left-hand side (the *y* axis), where black is at the bottom and white is at the top. The graph is a rectangle rather than a traditional square, but the input along the bottom edge exactly correlates to the output along the left edge, as seen here:

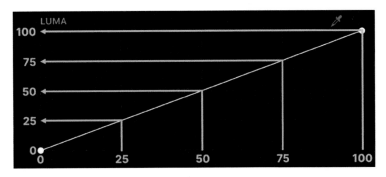

Figure 11.49: Illustrating the movement from the bottom edge to the left edge

When first applied, the default straight line results in no change to the image: 25 in gives 25 out. However, the line can be moved by adding additional points to it, then moving those points. A curve that moves upward around the center will push the image brighter around the midtones but will affect the shadows and highlights less:

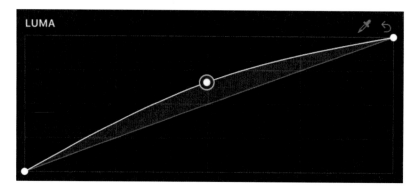

Figure 11.50: A "lighten" curve

And again, with an illustration of the change in the raw image numbers:

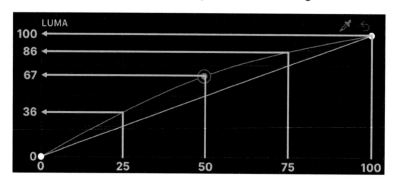

Figure 11.51: That same lighten curve with an illustration of
how it changes the image data

You can see that while the 0 and 100 points don't move at all, the change is most pronounced in the midtones.

The opposite curve would darken the image, again affecting the highlights and shadows far less than the midtones:

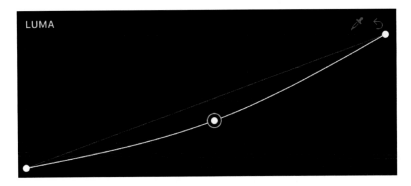

Figure 11.52: A "darken" curve

Still, the best curve to increase contrast is an S-curve, like this:

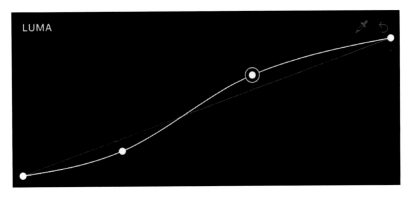

Figure 11.53: A contrast-boosting "S-curve" pushes midtones
toward the extremes, without clipping

You can clearly see what's happening in the **Waveform**, as image data is pushed from the middle (midtones) to the top (highlights) and bottom (shadows) of the graph. The image is more moody now that the light is stronger, and a viewer's attention will be more clearly focused toward the brighter areas:

Figure 11.54: This S-curve is a bit too strong for this image,
but doesn't clip the shadows or highlights

You can make as many additional points as you wish on the curve, but the fewer points you have, the easier it is to keep the line smooth. Excess points can be removed by simply clicking them and tapping the **delete** key.

With this knowledge, you can achieve far more subtle results than are possible with the earlier tools. For example, you could boost only highlights while leaving shadows where they are, like this:

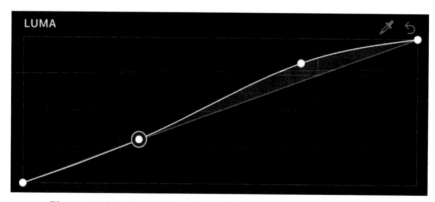

Figure 11.55: Boost only highlights; don't move shadows

Or, you could boost shadows while lowering highlights slightly, like this:

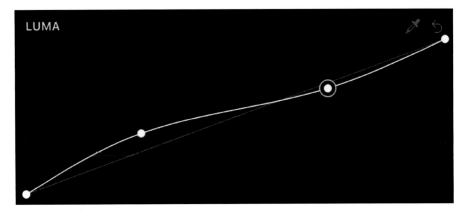

Figure 11.56: Boost the shadows; dip the highlights slightly

Or, if you want to get really fancy, reduce the contrast slightly around the midtones, while leaving highlights and shadows alone, with this curve:

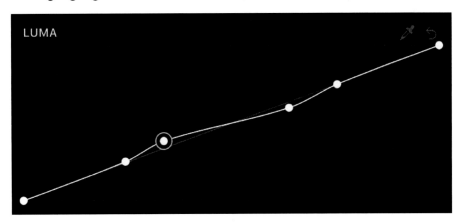

Figure 11.57: Reduce contrast, but only around the midtones

Quick changes in the curve's direction are likely to produce unwanted sharp or noisy artifacts in the image. Keep the curve's direction consistent from bottom left to top right, too. A curve that goes up and then down will produce strange results indeed:

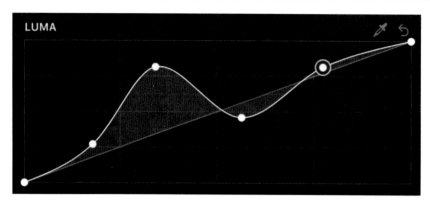

Figure 11.58: Wacky backwards curves — a bad idea

Crucially, with all these curves, the extreme shadows near 0 IRE and highlights near 100 IRE don't move at all. As a result, no shadow or highlight detail is lost outside those boundaries; the data moves within them instead.

> IMPORTANT NOTE
> Curve adjustments can behave quite differently in a Wide Gamut HDR Library. If you're experiencing more dramatic changes than illustrated here, be sure that you're working within a standard (Rec. 709) Library.

However, if you were to move the points at either end of the curve, bad things will happen: moving the edges horizontally could cause clipping, while vertical movement would reduce the dynamic range of the image. Don't do this:

Figure 11.59: Moving the left curve point up lifted the shadows above 0;
moving the right curve point left clipped the highlights

For safety, make only a few points along the curve, keep the curves gentle, watch the scopes, and *don't move the ends*.

USING THE EYEDROPPER TO SAMPLE THE IMAGE

Sometimes, it's quite useful to mark a point on the curve that matches a point within the image. You might do this to note a part of the image that should stay at its current brightness, or a part that should change. Here's the process:

1. In the **Inspector**, *click the eyedropper* to the top right of the Luma curve to toggle it on (blue).

2. In the **Viewer**, *click on part of the image with the eyedropper,* like this:

Figure 11.60: Click with the eyedropper to make a point on the curve

That's it: a new point on the curve will be created at the Luma value you clicked on, and you can click more than once if you wish. For completeness:

3. In the **Inspector**, *click the eyedropper* to the top right of the Luma curve to toggle it off (white).

If you now move the new point up, it'll get brighter; moving it down makes it darker. Don't move it to the left or right, because the point will then refer to a different source brightness.

If you don't want that part of the image to change, then leave the point exactly where it is. Instead, create new points a little way along the curve, and then move those points up or down. Done. If you mess anything up, there's always **Undo (⌘Z)** and a hooked arrow reset button in the top-right corner.

With the contrast sorted, and the Luma curve eyedropper used to lock in certain values, you're ready to get creative by playing with individual channels.

USING THE COLOR CHANNEL CURVES

If you want to fix a big problem, or introduce a strong "look" to the image, the **Red**, **Green**, or **Blue** curves are a good way to do it. These function similarly to the **Luma** curve, but only adjust a part of the image.

Instead of *making the image brighter*, on Green you'd be *making the image greener*. Instead of *increasing contrast with an S-curve*, on Blue you'd be *making the highlights bluer and the shadows more yellow*. That's called color contrast, and an S-curve on the Red channel will give you an instant "trendy vintage" look suitable for social media. Check this out:

Figure 11.61: Darkening the highlights in Luma with an S-curve on
Red for style

While the channel curves here are really good for creative color contrast adjustment, the Color Board and Color Wheels are probably better suited for basic balancing tasks.

Probably the most fascinating thing about these channel curves is that they don't have to stay set to Red, Green, or Blue. The eyedroppers next to these channels are quite different from the Luma eyedropper, so follow these steps:

1. In the **Inspector**, click the eyedropper to the top right of the **Red** curve to toggle it on (blue).

2. In the **Viewer**, click on a part of the image that's not red, to see something like this:

Figure 11.62: One eyedropper click can turn Red into Sea Foam

The Red curve now changes to reflect the color you just clicked on: **Orange**, **Pink**, **Aqua**, or even **Sea Foam**. For completeness, once more:

1. In the **Inspector**, click the eyedropper to the top right of that curve to toggle it off (white).

   If you want to fine-tune the color:

2. Click on the new name of the curve to bring up a tiny circular color menu, and then turn it to select a new color.

Indeed, you can use this color menu from the start (instead of the eyedropper) if you wish:

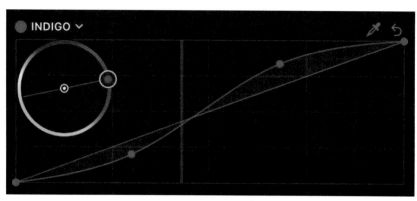

Figure 11.63: Click the name of the color to access this circular color picker

You're now free to affect just that one color within the image, reducing its strength by dragging down, increasing its strength by dragging up, or increasing color contrast around that color. This doesn't let you "make all orange things dark", but instead "makes things less orange" — a stranger concept than you might think. This is something worth experimenting with, though it's very easy to move into "grading" rather than "correction" at this point.

REVIEW — FINESSING CONTRAST AND MORE

The **Color Curves** adjustment is one of the most powerful adjustments in your color arsenal, but it shouldn't be your first. After using the Color Board or Color Wheels, it's the ideal way to increase contrast or to fix something specific that the blunter instruments couldn't. Master the S-curve and you're 90% of the way there. If you want to get further into creative aesthetic looks, then using curves with individual channels is a really easy way to get into it. Two quick drags and you're ready for social media.

With the image looking crisper, it's time to look at correcting just part of the image.

SELECTIVE CORRECTIONS

Selective (or secondary) corrections allow you to correct just part of the image. You'll first need to decide which part of the image you want to change — a color, or a specific area of the frame. To change a color or a range of colors, a good place to start is the **Hue/Saturation Curves**. It's also possible to do the job with masks, which can limit the effect of any color correction module by their color, or by a specific shape. With one or both strategies here, you'll learn how to tweak any individual part of the image just the way you want to.

USING HUE/SATURATION CURVES TO CHANGE COLOR

The Hue/Saturation Curves do quite a different job to Color Curves, and their main use is to change the hue or saturation of one specific part of the image. Let's play:

1. **⌥-click** on a clip (with no corrections applied) to select it and move the Playhead to that point.

2. Press **⌘6** to add the default color correction to this clip.

3. Click on **No Corrections** and choose **+Hue/Saturation Curves** from the menu, as illustrated in the following screenshot:

Figure 11.64: Add new Hue/Saturation Curves

The eyedroppers on each curve are usually the best way to quickly select a particular area:

1. In the **Inspector**, click the eyedropper to the top right of the **Hue vs Hue** curve to toggle it on (blue).

2. In the **Viewer**, click (or click and drag) on a part of the image that's a different color to the rest of it, like this:

Figure 11.65: Three points are created when you click and drag

Clicking creates three points in the **Hue vs Hue** graph, while dragging selects a wider range of colors, with three points that are further away from one another. Note that if you click on a reddish color then you may see two points at one side and a third at the other, but they are all connected.

Wherever the three points are on the line, if you want to change the color you clicked on, you don't need move the outer two points at all. Instead, proceed as follows.

3. Drag the middle point up or down to change the color of that area, as shown:

Figure 11.66: Only the water changes to green

The further you drag, the more the hue shifts, and the more you try to change that area, the more likely the image is to break up. (Higher-quality recording formats such as ProRes can be pushed further than compressed formats.)

4. Drag the outer two points outward to extend the range of colors affected, or inward to condense the range of colors affected:

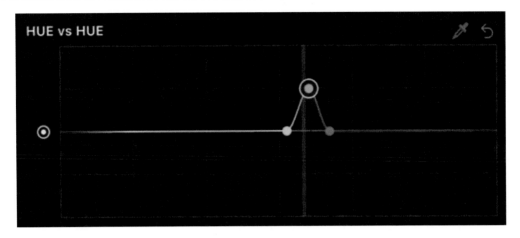

Figure 11.67: This tighter range of colors won't affect green areas

Avoid dragging these outer points up or down, as that will affect the color for the entire image:

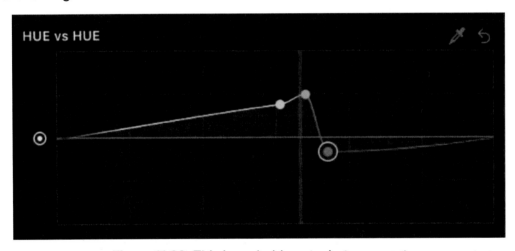

Figure 11.68: This is probably not what you want

So far, so amazing, and you can play this video to see how the correction works as it plays. Hue vs Hue is powerful, but it's just one of many features. There are several different curves available within this correction, and each one allows you to select a specific area (by its hue, saturation, or luma) and then change it in one way. The options can each be summarized as *A vs B*, where you *select with A*, then *change B*. They are listed as follows:

- **Hue vs Hue** — Select a **Hue** range and modify its **Hue**, to make a beige building pink, or a yellow shirt blue:

Figure 11.69: Hue vs Hue has changed the color of the buildings, but nothing else; note the three reddish points are shown at two ends of the line

- **Hue vs Sat** — Select a **Hue** range and modify its **Saturation**, to make a beige building gray, or a yellow shirt white:

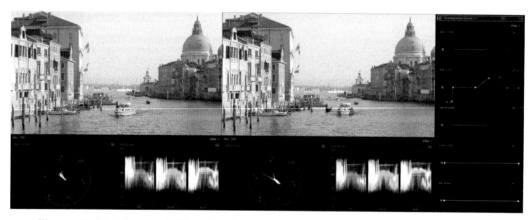

Figure 11.70: Some additional points here have made the buildings gray and the water and sky more vivid

- **Hue vs Luma** — Select a **Hue** range and modify its **Luma**, to make a beige building brown, or a yellow shirt brighter:

Figure 11.71: This Hue vs Luma adjustment is a little noisy; it's more likely to break up compressed footage

- **Luma vs Sat** — Select a **Luma** range and modify its **Saturation**, to modify saturation in a more surgical way than the Saturation controls in the Color Board or Color Wheels:

Figure 11.72: This Luma vs Sat boosted saturation a little on shadows, a lot on midtones, and turned it down on highlights — a vintage postcard

- **Sat vs Sat** — Select a **Saturation** range and precisely modify its **Saturation** based on the existing values:

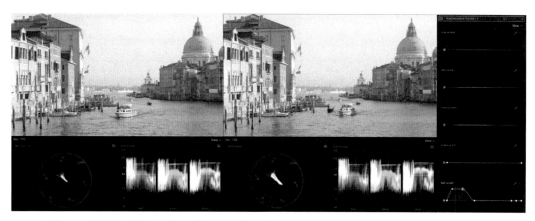

Figure 11.73: This subtle Sat vs Sat boosted saturation on areas that had low saturation (the water), and didn't boost those that already had it

- **Orange vs Sat** — Select a **specific color** (not just Orange), then modify its **Saturation** according to its brightness:

Figure 11.74: Orange vs Sat to (mostly) boost only skin tone midtones

This lets you modify the Saturation for specific brightness levels within a specific color (or more accurately, a range of colors near a specific color). The Orange is just a starting point and can be set to any color, but it's close to skin tone by default. As the *x* axis here represents Luma, dragging one point up in the middle would boost Saturation only for orange midtones. Very specific indeed, and a little tricky in practice — but there's an alternative.

Terrific as these controls are, it's not always possible to select the part of the frame you want to adjust based solely on one of its Hue, Saturation, or Luma values. Using a **Color Mask**, you can apply any correction to a specific color, and make that color selection with a combination of Hue, Saturation, and Luma.

USING A COLOR MASK TO RESTRICT A CORRECTION

Masks can be added to any kind of color correction, and indeed to any kind of video effect at all. Hover your cursor around the middle of the title bar to see this:

Figure 11.75: The "oval in a box" icon is where you find the mask controls

Here, we'll limit the effect of a simple Color Board instance, but you could use the same technique to limit the effect of a blur, or a glitch effect, or added noise:

1. **⌥-click** on a clip to select it and move the Playhead to that point.

2. Press **⌘6** to add the default color correction to this clip.

3. Make a simple but obvious change, pushing the entire image toward orange with the Master color puck.

   This could be any adjustment at all — just make it easy to see.

4. At the top of the **Color** pane, hover over the title bar of the color correction, then click the small mask icon (a circle inside a rectangle) and choose **Add Color Mask**, as illustrated in the following screenshot:

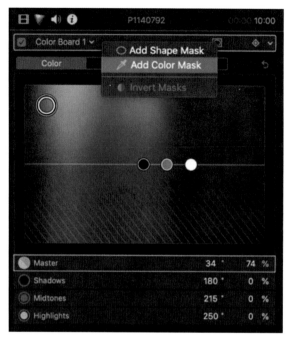

Figure 11.76: You'll only see the mask icon when you hover over the title near "Color Board 1"

An eyedropper now becomes active when the cursor moves over the Viewer.

5. Click and drag in the image to define a range of colors to be selected:

Figure 11.77: Click or click and drag to turn the gray into color and select it

When you start dragging, the whole image desaturates to light gray, but as you drag, more of the image will return to normal, to indicate that the colors have been selected and that those selected colors have been added to the color mask. When you release the mouse, the "desaturation" disappears, and you'll see the effects of your earlier adjustment within any selected areas. Any parts of your image that have a similar color to those you dragged over will now be pushed toward orange.

Still, it's unlikely that the color mask is perfect. To change the range of colors in the color mask:

- **⇧-drag** in the image to include more colors in the color mask
- **⌥-drag** in the image to remove those colors from the color mask
- **Drag** (with no keys held) to restart the color selection process

It can be tricky to get exactly the right part of the image selected using only the eyedropper, because dragging the circle over a light area can easily select all the light areas in your frame:

Figure 11.78: With a partial mask in place, only part of the sky is orange;
now, ⇧-click to expand the mask area

For finesse, there are additional controls in a new pane at the bottom of the **Color Board**. A color mask can be one of the following two types:

- **3D**, which selects "similar" colors, and which can be softened:

Figure 11.79: The Softness slider can fix some selections, but not all

- **HSL**, which allows you to combine any or all or **Hue**, **Saturation**, and **Luma**, selecting any range within each of those properties, each with a controllable selection edge:

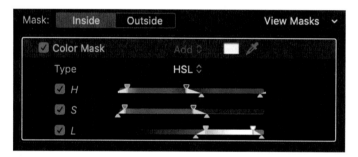

Figure 11.80: All three criteria now have to be satisfied to be inside the mask area

The HSL type is more powerful, and allows you to select quite specific areas of the image. Dragging the top two triangle controls on each range controls which parts of the Hue, Saturation, or Luma are included, while dragging the bottom two controls governs the transition, from included to not included. Therefore, you should drag the top controls until it's nearly right, then move the bottom controls to soften the edges. Even with all these controls, if you're trying to change something substantially (such as making it very orange!) you may not be able to get to a perfect result. Lies are easier to pull off if they're close to the truth.

The last masking technique can be used to finesse a color mask further, or independently. After all, you'll often want to brighten up a person in the middle of a shot, or darken the corners. Since those tasks have nothing to do with the colors in those parts of the image, for those tasks you want a shape mask.

USING A SHAPE MASK TO RESTRICT A CORRECTION

Starting again on a new clip is the best way to learn this:

1. **⌥-click** on a clip to select it and move the Playhead to that point.

2. Press **⌘6** to add the default color correction to this clip.

3. Make a simple but obvious change, pushing the entire image darker with the **Master** exposure puck.

   You'll see the whole image go darker.

4. At the top of the **Color** pane, click the small mask icon (a circle inside a rectangle) and choose **Add Shape Mask**:

Figure 11.81: Adding a shape mask to a darkening color board

You'll now see two circles in the center of the screen. Inside the inner circle, the image is darker, and the effect reduces toward the outer circle. Beyond the outer circle, the image is unaffected:

Figure 11.82: The default shape mask on the image, with darkening now only in the center

You can control the shape mask in many ways:

- Drag the central marker or a blank area within the mask to move it around
- Drag the edge of the inner circle to change the size of the mask
- Drag the edge of the outer circle to increase the softness of the mask
- Drag the green dots to change the shape and size of the circle (to an oval)
- **Hold** ⇧ as you drag the green dots to keep the current aspect ratio
- **Hold** ⌥ as you drag the green dots to change just one side of the mask
- Drag the white dot to transform the circle into a square, or a rounded rectangle
- Drag the handle connected to the center of the mask to rotate the mask

Great — you can make the mask any size you like, and any simple shape. Soft edges mean that a viewer won't see the edge of your corrections:

Figure 11.83: The Shape Mask is now darkening an area at the
edge of screen

But what if you want to change the area outside the mask rather than the inside? There are two ways to do that. The quick way is to invert the mask, so that the effect applies outside it rather than inside it:

- In the **Masks** menu at the top of the **Color Board**, choose **Invert Masks**:

Figure 11.84: In the Masks menu, this third option flips things around

That's great if you just want to darken down the area outside the mask. However, there's a more complex option if you want to apply a different correction to both the inside and the outside areas of the mask:

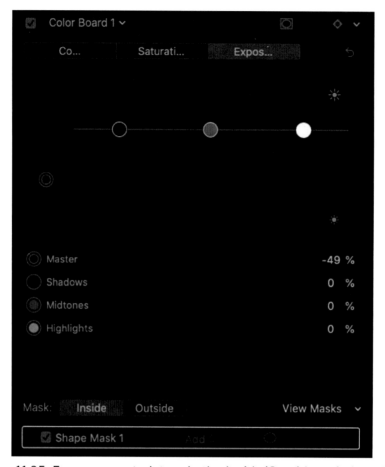

Figure 11.85: For more control, toggle the Inside/Outside switch and use different corrections for each

At the bottom of the Color Board, you'll see a switch: **Inside/Outside**. With **Inside** selected, as it is now, you're adjusting one side of the mask. Clicking **Outside** allows you to apply an entirely different correction there, starting from scratch. (As you've already inverted the mask, that's probably a little confusing because Inside and Outside are flipped, but it's handy if you want to take this further next time.)

Darkening the corners of a shot adds a *vignette*, and if you make it large enough and subtle enough, it's a great effect:

Figure 11.86: A vignette is one of the easiest ways to make an image
look appealing

If you keep an eye out for them, you'll notice that vignettes are pretty common, and they're often created in post-production scenarios. But a single oval or rectangle, or a single color selection, can only go so far. That's OK — you can use multiple masks at the same time.

COMBINING MULTIPLE MASKS TOGETHER

Multiple shape masks and color masks can be combined in a number of ways to create a more complex selection than is possible with a single mask. It will be easiest to explore this last feature of masks if you have a shot of a person, ideally a seated interview-style shot. Throw it onto a timeline and we'll begin, as follows:

1. **⌥-click** on the clip to select it and move the Playhead to that point.

2. Press **⌘6** to add the default color correction to this clip.

3. Make a tiny change, pushing any puck just a tiny amount, to create a new correction.

4. At the top of the **Color** pane, click the small mask icon (a circle inside a rectangle) and choose **Add Shape Mask**.

5. At the bottom of the **Color** pane, click **Outside** to switch to the other side of the mask.

6. Make a more obvious change, dragging the **Master** exposure puck down to darken down the outside of the circle.

7. Reposition and resize the mask so that it is positioned over the person's face, as a reasonably soft oval.

8. At the top of the **Color** pane, click the small mask icon (a circle inside a rectangle) and choose **Add Shape Mask** to add a second shape to the mask.

   The two masks will now add together.

9. Reposition and resize the mask so that it is positioned over the person's shoulders as a soft, wide oval, like this:

Figure 11.87: With two shape masks added together, you'll see something like this (note that the shoulder mask has been enhanced here)

The two masks now should combine to roughly select the person.

10. Adjust the edges of both masks to soften the edges appropriately.

    It's OK if the edges of the face and shoulders are not fully covered.

11. Adjust the **Exposure** of all parts of the image to darken the area behind the subject.

12. Reduce the **Saturation** of all parts of the image to subtly de-emphasize the area behind the subject further.

13. At the bottom of the **Color** pane, click **Inside** to switch to the other side of the mask.

14. Increase the **Exposure** of the subject slightly to make them more prominent.

15. Hide the edges of the masks by clicking on the oval icon to the right of **Shape Mask 1** or **Shape Mask 2**, whichever one is currently blue.

    Clicking the blue mask icon turns it white and hides it. To show it, click it once more. The result:

Figure 11.88: This is the effect you're aiming for, to emphasize the subject and de-emphasize the background

Lighting is a critical part of drawing attention to the right part of a frame, and if the camera operator couldn't get it right on the day, you can fix it now. Don't be afraid to add light where you want people to look and to darken down areas where they shouldn't. You can make this effect strong or subtle, depending on the job.

As well as multiple shape masks, it's also possible to combine shape masks with color masks; so, if you can't isolate an area with just one mask, just add another.

Figure 11.89: Sky Boost: Shape Mask to select top half, Shape Mask to subtract buildings, Color Mask to only match the correct Saturation and Luma ranges

Each additional mask can be set to **Add**, **Subtract**, or **Intersect** with the other masks, so you can make it as complex as you like. Lastly, if you want to animate your masks to track people as they move around a shot — yes, you can, and you'll find out how in the next chapter.

REVIEW — SELECTIVE CORRECTIONS

Primary correction comes first, but secondary correction is often important too. Is an object the wrong color? Hue/Saturation Curves to the rescue. Is a person too dull? That'll need a shape mask. Something more complex? Use color masks, finesse the edges, add shape masks, and get fussy with your curves: throw everything at it. There's a ton of power here.

Though not every shot requires selective correction, it's worth spending a little time making your hero shots look their very best. While it's best to avoid problems on set if you can, don't be afraid to fix it in post-production if you have to.

Before this chapter closes out, here are a few techniques that'll save you a lot of time.

ADVANCED COLOR TECHNIQUES

Correction isn't hard, but you don't want to correct every clip from scratch. In this section, you'll learn how to copy a correction from one clip to another in a few ways, how to get a head start on correction with effects presets, and how to correct entire scenes with a single adjustment. These tricks are serious time savers, and some of them are far from obvious, so don't skip this.

COPYING AND PASTING COLOR ADJUSTMENTS

If multiple clips were shot in the same location at the same time, they'd probably need the same treatment, and there are a few ways to make that happen. The first and most obvious is copy and paste, and it works pretty well:

1. Apply several kinds of color correction to a clip.

2. Select that clip, then **Edit > Copy (⌘C)**.

   This step copies the clip and its video properties, including effects and color corrections.

3. Select a similar clip or clips, then choose **Edit > Paste Effects (⌥⌘V)** to instantly paste the color correction to these clips.

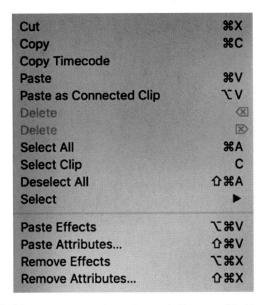

Figure 11.90: Many copy and paste variations, with their shortcuts

The downside of **Paste Effects** is that it just pastes *everything* onto the target clip(s), and you don't always want the volume changes, scale changes, and every type of color correction at once. Another option is this:

4. Select a different clip or clips, then choose **Edit > Paste Attributes** (⇧⌘V) to bring up a dialog that lets you choose exactly which properties to paste:

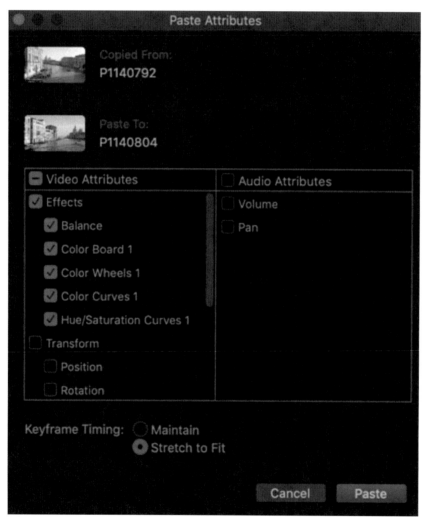

Figure 11.91: You can now choose which attributes you want to paste

This takes a little longer, but it's far more powerful. You don't have to choose to paste everything, but you can uncheck items you don't want. A quick way to uncheck everything is to **⌥-click** on any checkbox, and everything else will be deselected. This works separately in the **Video** or **Audio** columns, so a couple of clicks may be required.

Pasting is fine, but there's still an issue, because if the target clip(s) had any kind of color correction applied already then these new corrections will be applied in addition to the existing corrections. That may be what you want, or it may not.

The first way to deal with that is to clear out existing attributes before you paste, using one of these commands from the **Edit** menu:

- **Remove Effects** (**⌥⌘X**), to remove all existing properties without asking
- **Remove Attributes** (**⇧⌘X**), to bring up a dialog that lets you selectively remove existing properties

This way, you could **Copy** from one clip, then **Remove Effects** and **Paste Effects** on the target. Since these commands work not just for color, but for video properties and effects and audio properties and effects, you will get to know them pretty well. The hidden trick is that color correction is a special case, and there are three hidden commands that are far easier than copying and pasting.

APPLYING COLOR CORRECTIONS FROM NEARBY CLIPS

While performing a color correction pass on your edited timeline, you'll want to reuse the same corrections on subsequent clips. To do this in the absolute best way possible, you'll need to enable some hidden commands, as follows:

1. Open **Final Cut Pro** > **Commands** > **Customize**.

2. In the top-right corner, search for `color`:

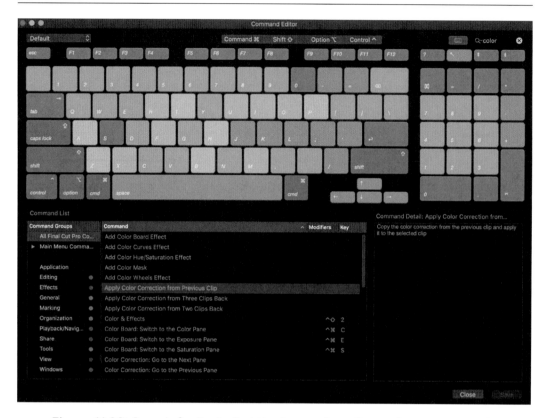

Figure 11.92: Search for "color" at the top and you'll see three commands starting with "Apply" down below

In the lower central area, you'll see three commands that have no shortcuts and that don't appear in any menu:

- **Apply Color Correction from Previous Clip**
- **Apply Color Correction from Three Clips Back**
- **Apply Color Correction from Two Clips Back**

The alphabetical sort has put these commands out of order (one, three, and two clips back), but they perform magic. These hidden commands *copy all corrections* from a prior clip in the timeline, and then use those corrections to *replace* any color corrections on the selected clip. They don't apply on top of existing corrections, so there's no need to clear out existing corrections, and they don't affect any other video or audio properties or effects. Even nicer, "color corrections" in this context means everything we've looked at so far, including a Balance Color, Match Color, or any manual correction from the Color tab. All you need to do is:

3. Assign these three commands to three unused sequential keys on your keyboard. You can do this in the same way we did it earlier in the book:

- Choose the modifier keys you want to use (if any) at the top, and then drag the commands to unused keys.

- Choose the command you want to assign, and then use your physical keyboard to press the shortcut combination you want to use.

If you have an extended keyboard, I use these enough to assign them to **F17/F18/F19**, and I like **⇧7/⇧8/⇧9** on a laptop. Both options are shown here:

Apply Color Correction from Previous Clip		F19
Apply Color Correction from Previous Clip	⇧	9
Apply Color Correction from Three Clips Back		F17
Apply Color Correction from Three Clips Back	⇧	7
Apply Color Correction from Two Clips Back		F18
Apply Color Correction from Two Clips Back	⇧	8

Figure 11.93: Pick your own keys if you like, and single-key commands are easiest to hit

4. **Save** and **Close** when you're done.

These commands are faster than any other technique I've used for basic color correction. Correct one clip, and then use that correction as a starting point for the next. The third clip can use either of the two previous clips as its starting point, and if you're bouncing between two or three shots, you'll nearly always have a good color source nearby.

If you revise an earlier clip's corrections, it's now trivial to update all the corrections on another similar clip that's two or three clips down the timeline. You can even select many clips at once, and then use these keys to copy the correction from a clip just prior to the leftmost clip.

One thing to be aware of is that only clips in Storylines can have "prior clips," and so you'll have to fall back on copy and paste techniques with connected clips. But that's no big deal. These commands work really well with anything in a connected Storyline and in the Primary Storyline, and that's enough to save a lot of time.

IMPORTANT NOTE

If you've shot with a camera system that can record in ProRes RAW, you can find some controls in the **Settings** metadata view in the **Info** tab in the Inspector (*new in 10.4.9*). If you'd prefer to adjust the ISO there (and possibly also **Exposure Offset** and **Temperature**, if supported by your camera) before using the standard color adjustments, go ahead. Similarly, if you've shot on RED, you may wish to use the RED plugin's custom floating window to make adjustments.

Lastly, if you've shot in **Log** format, you can make that "flat" camera footage look "normal" by setting the **Camera LUT** setting also found in the **Settings** metadata view. Note that metadata-based adjustments apply at the clip level, before all other adjustments, and can sometimes be quite strong. You may prefer to turn this off and correct it manually.

For more control over how a Color **LUT** (or **Look-Up Table**) is applied to a clip, and to work with pre-packaged "look LUTs," use the **Custom LUT** effect. This is covered in *Chapter 12, Refine and Smooth: Video Properties and Effects*.

While we're on the topic of saving time, fancy shortcuts aren't the only tool you have. Adjustment Layers aren't official, but they are real, and amazing.

USING ADJUSTMENT LAYERS

The **Adjustment Layer** exists in FCP almost by accident, and though it's easy to make one with Apple's companion program Motion, there isn't one installed by default. Just search online for `free fcp adjustment layer`, and you'll find free installers from a number of plugin makers. Once you've downloaded one of these and installed it, you'll find it easy to use, but in an unexpected place. Here are the steps:

1. Reset to the **Default** Workspace by pressing **⌘0**.

2. Look in the **Titles** browser (yes, titles!) in the top left of the interface, then search for `adjust` to find the **Adjustment Layer** you installed:

Figure 11.94: Search for "adjust" in the top-right corner, and you'll find it —
probably with this default thumbnail

3. Drag the **Adjustment Layer** to your timeline, and change its duration to span
a few clips:

Figure 11.95: The Adjustment Layer is purple because it's a Title, and the
color for that Role is purple

4. **⌥-click** on the **Adjustment Layer** to select it and move the Playhead to that point.

5. Press **⌘6** to add the default color correction to the **Adjustment Layer**.

6. Make an obvious change, pushing any puck or slider in any direction.

Skimming up and down the timeline, you'll see that the Adjustment Layer affects
everything underneath it. An entire scene now needs only a single adjustment, and
that's revolutionary; there's no need to repeat the same correction on each clip in
your timeline. My color correction workflow usually looks like this:

1. Perform basic color correction and shot-to-shot matching on all clips, using
the Apply Color Correction commands to duplicate corrections as needed.

2. Perform secondary color corrections where necessary, again, on each clip.

3. Add creative or aesthetic color corrections to Adjustment Layers, one per
scene. It might look something like this:

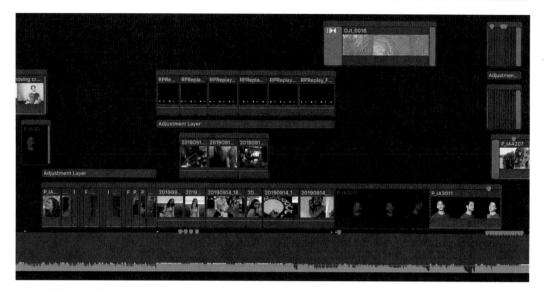

Figure 11.96: Part of a real timeline ("Gravitate" by "Ky.") with Adjustment Layers used to give different looks to a few separate "scenes"

This works because individual clips need individual attention, but looks are best applied broadly, to several clips at once. You can even duplicate an Adjustment Layer as an Audition to instantly offer a client different looks for an entire scene, or even an entire timeline. Used wisely, Adjustment Layers are probably the single biggest time saver in color grading.

They do have one issue, however. As soon as an Adjustment Layer ends, the color change ends, and unfortunately, it's not simple to fade or otherwise transition an Adjustment Layer. While it is possible to keyframe a color effect (as you'll discover in the next chapter), that's more work.

REVIEW — ADVANCED COLOR TECHNIQUES

Once you've mastered the basics of color correction, make sure you master how to apply those corrections to many clips quickly. Copy and paste is OK for connected clips, but the three hidden commands to apply color from previous clips are more powerful and will speed up your work hugely.

Adjustment Layers are a revolution to the color grading workflow, and though simple Projects won't need to bother with them, I've used them on a variety of more complex Projects to greatly simplify the production and review process. Vital stuff.

SUMMARY

This is the largest chapter so far, and that's OK, because using what you've learned here will make a massive difference to the quality of your work. While it's true that becoming good at color correction won't necessarily make you a better editor, it's a part of the overall package that many clients expect. Start out with the simple auto options, then move into manual corrections, and if you have the time and inclination, enhance contrast and specific areas of the image with the more advanced "grading" techniques. Even the simpler corrections can benefit from the advanced ways to copy, paste, move, and re-apply corrections, though; don't overlook these time savers.

In the next chapter, you'll find out a whole lot more about video effects but also a little more about color, because some of the video effects are color-related. You'll learn how to save any number of color corrections as a color preset (stored as an effect), and also how to use Color LUTs to apply an instant color correction. Oh, and also everything to do with blurs, retiming, positioning, scaling, cropping, stabilization, animation, transitions, and just a few other things. Practice as much as you can, and see you on the next page.

REVIEW QUESTIONS

1. What are the three main panes of the Color Board?
2. What's the best way to objectively assess image data?
3. Which term is used to describe brightness values that go beyond traditional limits?
4. Which modifier key should you hold down to make sure you are looking at the right clip in the Inspector?
5. How do you manually choose a white or gray point in Balance Color?
6. If an image is slightly underexposed, how would you fix it with the Color Board or Color Wheels?
7. Which Luma curve increases contrast?
8. What are two ways you could change the color of only the blue areas in your image?
9. Which command allows you to paste only some clip attributes onto another?
10. Which free third-party title allows you correct color for many clips at once?

REVIEW ANSWERS

1. Color, Saturation, Exposure.

2. Video Scopes.

3. HDR.

4. ⌥ (Option).

5. Change Method to White Balance, and then click on the Viewer with the eyedropper.

6. Usually, push the midtone exposure control upward.

7. An S-curve.

8. Any color correction with a color mask, or with the Hue vs Hue curve in Hue/Saturation Curves.

9. Paste Attributes (not Paste Effects).

10. An Adjustment Layer.

12 REFINE AND SMOOTH: VIDEO PROPERTIES AND EFFECTS

"FCP X has allowed me the creative freedom to shoot with multiple cameras, mix various types of footage in different resolutions from an iPhone to 8K RED and still get a seamless output. I really have built my entire career and business using Final Cut and it's only been getting better as the time goes on."

— Justine Ezarik (iJustine), YouTube Tech personality, host, and actress with over 1 billion views on YouTube (www.youtube.com/iJustine)

With the color of your sequence under control, you'll want to take a look at some of the other visual changes that you can apply to your clips. That includes different ways to resize clips, remove shakiness through stabilization, and much more through the wide world of video effects. There's no need for effects to be static; you'll also learn how to animate effects, transforms, and even color corrections over time, and how to use color and shape masks to limit them. It's another big one, but in bullet form, this chapter covers:

- Adjusting video properties
- Animating with keyframes
- Applying and using video effects

It's entirely possible to finish your edit and fix color before applying any effects, but don't feel constrained. If you prefer to add effects or transforms while you're still trimming and adding cutaways, that's OK and up to you. Certainly, some of the basic transform operations are simple enough to handle on-the-fly during an edit, and that's where we'll start.

ADJUSTING VIDEO PROPERTIES

In this section, you'll find out how to control how a clip is presented, by adjusting its blend mode, position, scale, cropping, and corner positions. You'll discover various ways to change these video properties in the Video tab of the Inspector, and in the Viewer directly. Video properties will allow you to zoom in or crop to a particular part of the frame, to shrink a clip down for a picture-in-picture effect, or to let one clip visually interact with the clips below it:

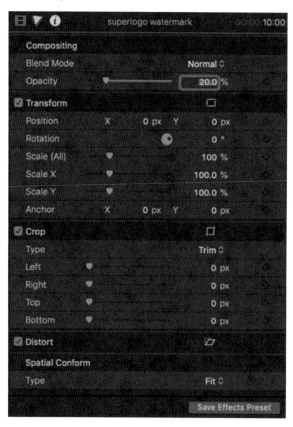

Figure 12.1: The Video tab in the Inspector has many options

There are many reasons to tweak how a clip looks in this way, and you'll find these controls straightforward.

After the previous chapter, *Chapter 11, Play with Light: Color Correction and Grading*, you're probably used to ⌥**-clicking**, and the same rules apply here:

- To make sure you're viewing the clip you're editing, **always ⌥-click the clip first**.

The other golden rule here is:

- Always adjust values in the Inspector by *dragging on the numbers*.

While most of the properties here have sliders (or other controls) next to the numbers, sliders have a fixed range, and the numbers can often go beyond those ranges. Here's how you can use these numbers:

- Click and drag (left and right, or up and down) directly on the numbers to change them.
- While dragging, hold ⇧ to change values more quickly, for large adjustments.
- While dragging, hold ⌥ to change values more slowly, for finer control.

If you simply click rather than dragging, you can:

- Type a new value directly, pressing **return** to finalize your input.
- Adjust the existing value with the ↑ and ↓ keys.

The three most important sections here also have on-screen controls, which are often (but not always) helpful. Here, we'll work from top to bottom, so make sure you have a timeline with a collection of clips to play with and at least some connected clips on top.

COMPOSITING

This section allows you to control how visible a clip is and exactly how a clip is shown to you. The **Opacity** slider is easiest to understand and straightforward to adjust:

1. ⌥**-click** on a connected clip (above other clips) to select it and move the playhead to that point.
2. Drag on the **Opacity** value to change it.

As the value goes lower, you'll see the top clip fade away, revealing the clip(s) underneath it. While this produces an arty effect with regular video, it's far more useful with a small logo when used as a watermark:

Figure 12.2: Opacity is easy to change and most useful with a watermark

However, the menu just above Opacity, the **Blend Mode**, is both weirder and more useful. Different blend modes change the formula that governs how a clip above is mixed with a clip below, and it's worth moving to a different connected clip to try it out. The different blend modes are:

- **Normal** — Just display the clip as usual. If Opacity is 100% then you won't see through the clip.

- **Subtract/Darken/Multiply/Color Burn/Linear Burn** — These use the top clip to darken any clips. **Multiply** is especially handy as a "natural-looking" darkening mode, and all of these remove lighter areas from a clip:

Figure 12.3: The top clip on the left set to Multiply for a natural darken

- **Add/Lighten/Screen/Color Dodge/Linear Dodge** — These are lightening modes, all the opposite of the darkening modes just mentioned. **Screen** gives a "natural-looking" brightness boost, and these will all remove darker areas from a clip:

Figure 12.4: The modern "camcorder" effect: cover your iPhone's camera, press record, then record the iPhone screen; take that screen recording, as seen in the top-left, apply the Screen blend mode, and connect it above another clip

- **Overlay/Soft Light/Hard Light/Vivid Light/Linear Light/Pin Light/Hard Mix** — These modes all combine the previous two categories, but you'll need to experiment with different clips. **Overlay** is the easiest to understand, as it's a combination of **Screen** on the highlights and **Multiply** on the shadows:

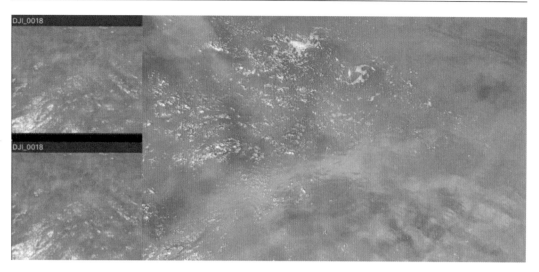

Figure 12.5: Two duplicate clips one above the other, with the top clip set to Overlay — a quick contrast boost

- **Difference/Exclusion** — These are two kinds of "opposite" modes that try to remove similarly colored areas. They are more useful for technical operations than for general editing:

Figure 12.6: Two copies of the same clip, with the top clip slipped and set to Difference

- **Stencil Alpha/Stencil Luma/Silhouette Alpha/Silhouette Luma/Behind** — These very useful **masking** effects are for revealing (**Stencil**) or hiding (**Silhouette**) part of a clip below, based on the brightness (**Luma**) or transparency (**Alpha**) information of the clip on top. **Behind** is very sneaky indeed: it virtually shuffles this top clip to the background. This enables some special techniques that we'll look at soon:

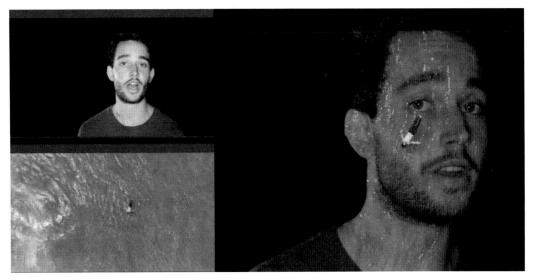

Figure 12.7: The top clip is set to Stencil Luma, showing the clip below where there's light

- **Alpha Add/Premultiplied Mix** — These are for tweaking transparency (alpha) information. You probably won't need these unless you're doing something pretty fancy with masking or keying.

For most editors, Normal will be the most commonly used blend mode by far; it's the default. For ditching light or dark areas, Screen and Multiply are most handy, and while Overlay is useful, if you're adding contrast, then an S-curve in Color Curves gives far more control.

Stencil Alpha is probably the most useful mode if you'd like to replace a logo with video. Alpha means "transparency," so if your top clip is a transparent PNG or another clip with a truly transparent background, you can use Stencil Alpha to play video inside the logo. (To play video outside the logo, Normal works just fine, though if you wanted to hide the non-transparent areas for some reason, Silhouette Alpha will do that.)

If there's no transparency, use Stencil Luma to show lower clips in the lighter areas or Silhouette Luma to show lower clips in the darker areas:

Figure 12.8: Silhouette Luma on the top clip deals with this logo on a white background

But these blend modes punch through all layers, not just the one immediately below. So, how do you show video inside a logo above another clip? To isolate the effect of a Stencil or Silhouette blend mode, do the following:

1. Select the top clip set to **Stencil Alpha** (or Luma) and any other clips you want to affect.

   Do not select any background clips.

2. Create a new Compound Clip with **File** > **New** > **Compound Clip** (⌥G) and give it a name.

The Stencil mode is now contained, limited inside the compound clip. The blank area around the logo will now show any clips underneath it in the timeline:

Figure 12.9: The previous Silhouette Luma example wrapped in a Compound Clip, then a separate clip underneath

Compounds provide a solution to complex blending problems, but for simple problems like the one shown here, there is an alternative strategy with the Behind blend mode. Instead, with the same three clips from the previous Stencil Luma example, we can do this:

1. Switch to the **Position** tool (**P**).
2. Move the background clip to the very top.
3. Switch this top clip to the **Behind** blend mode:

Figure 12.10: The middle clip is Stencil Luma, while the top clip is Behind and sits underneath? Witchcraft!

That's it! Oddly, you can indeed put the background at the top of the stack.

TRANSFORM

This important section in the Inspector lets you change the size, position, and rotation of any clip — simple but useful stuff. It's straightforward when the aspect ratio of both your source clips and project is identical. As you'll discover soon, the situation is a little different when the two aspect ratios aren't the same, so stick with 16:9 widescreen for the moment.

The Transform controls allow you to:

- **Make a picture-in-picture** — shrink and reposition a connected clip.
- **Correct a tilted horizon** — rotate and enlarge any clip.
- **Reframe a shot** — scale up and move around to change the framing. (Note that Crop also provides a way to do this.)
- **Punch in for emphasis or disguise a jump cut** — increase scale after a jump cut edit.

To make these changes, you can use on-screen controls in the Viewer, or adjust the sliders, wheels, or (best of all) values in the Inspector. If you can't see the Inspector settings, hover to the right of Transform to reveal the word **Show**, and then click it:

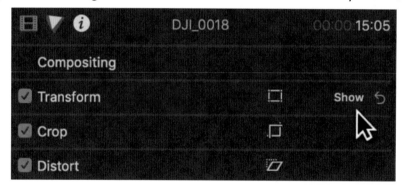

Figure 12.11: If Transform is not visible in the Inspector, be sure to Show it first

Those Inspector properties are as follows:

- **Position X** (horizontal) and **Y** (vertical) — These change where the clip's image sits within the Viewer, in pixels. If an image starts out covering the screen exactly, then changing just this setting will push some part of it off-screen and reveal any clips below:

Figure 12.12: Moving the top image around is easy enough with X and Y

- **Rotation** — This tilts the image, in degrees. Always increase the Scale to cover the full frame, or you'll see blank areas at the corners:

Figure 12.13: Compensate for a wonky horizon with Rotation and the Show Horizon option in the Viewer's View menu

- **Scale (All)** — This changes the frame size, to punch in, or to hide edges after for repositioning or rotation with the previous controls. Scaling up can create a new shot, like shooting with a zoom lens, but don't push too far. If you shoot 1080p and deliver 1080p, then pushing past 120% can produce noticeable softening, as the missing pixels must be created through interpolation. This is a big reason why shooting 4K for 1080p delivery is popular; you can zoom in up to 200% before you run out of real pixels. *Don't use* **Scale X or Scale Y** *unless you want to distort the image*:

Figure 12.14: The original oversized shot has been duplicated and scaled

- **Anchor (X and Y)** — These change the point around which rotation occurs; useful for some animation purposes but not widely used otherwise.

The on-screen Transform controls can be enabled by pressing a white icon found in two places:

- To the right of the word **Transform** in the **Inspector**.

- In the leftmost corner below the **Viewer**, next to a menu that lets you access on-screen controls for **Transform**, **Crop**, and **Distort**. If the **Transform** icon is on top here, you can click the icon to activate its on-screen controls, but if it's not, you'll have to choose **Transform** from the menu next to it:

Figure 12.15: The blue on-screen controls for Transform are found in two places — click either icon to toggle it

When on-screen controls are active, the clip's Position can be changed by dragging anywhere within the frame in the Viewer or on the center point. Dragging the small handle attached to the center point adjusts Rotation, and dragging any of the corner handles adjusts Scale. (The edge handles adjust only X or Y, so mostly avoid those.)

> IMPORTANT NOTE
>
> *New in the 10.4.9 release*, it's now possible to see what's happening outside the visible image area in the Viewer, with **Transform Overscan**. A small icon to the left of the **Reset** button toggles this display and allows you to see which parts of a selected clip are off-screen and invisible. This is easiest to see if you zoom out slightly with the menu above the Viewer.

The on-screen controls are convenient, but the numbers in the Inspector are more precise, so don't be afraid to use both systems. To move a clip horizontally or vertically, dragging on a Position value in the Inspector is a safer choice because you'll automatically limit movement to a single dimension.

For similar reasons, the on-screen scale controls seem like a good idea, but as soon as a clip is made larger, the handles quickly vanish beyond the edges of the Viewer. It's also easy to accidentally resize the Viewer when trying to adjust the scale handles, so I usually end up adjusting the Inspector values instead. (If you do want to use on-screen controls for scale, you may find that you need to reduce the View percentage to 50% or 25% rather than using the default "Fit" setting.) As an alternative, you may find it easier to use the Crop options discussed in the next section:

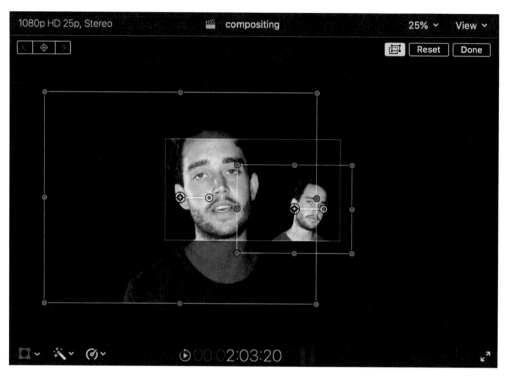

Figure 12.16: Reduce View percentage to see all of the on-screen controls; both clips are selected at once here

Lastly, the Rotation handle works well enough if you drag it a long way from the center point (for accuracy) but the values in the Inspector offer finer control. If you do use the on-screen controls, always remember to press **Done** in the top-left corner of the Viewer or by clicking on the (now blue) on-screen controls icon once again. While on-screen controls are active, Skimming doesn't work, so it's important to turn them off when you're done.

While on-screen controls are active, a **Reset** button sits next to **Done** if you want to start from scratch. For finer control, hover over the far-right side of any property in the Transform panel to see a hooked arrow Reset button appear; clicking it resets that property alone. Hover to the far right of the word Transform to see a hooked arrow that resets all options at once.

Just below Transform, you'll find the next important section.

CROP

Unlike the Transform controls, the on-screen controls here are quite important. While you can switch between the options using the Inspector, the best way to start is to press the **Crop** on-screen control icon and look at the Viewer. The bottom of this display shows the three Crop options:

- **Trim** — This removes parts of the edge of the frame and is useful to turn a rectangle into a square for picture-in-picture purposes or to reveal part of a clip underneath.

- **Crop** — An alternative to Scale, this is another, more direct way to punch in, which lets you choose exactly which part of the image to show.

- **Ken Burns** — This is an animated way to automatically pan or zoom across a frame.

To look at these in more detail, we'll use the on-screen controls.

Trim gives you simple controls to remove pixels from the left, right, top, or bottom edges, and that's about it. Personally, I don't use this often; I find that effects, generators, or titles can give better results more quickly, but it's easy to understand:

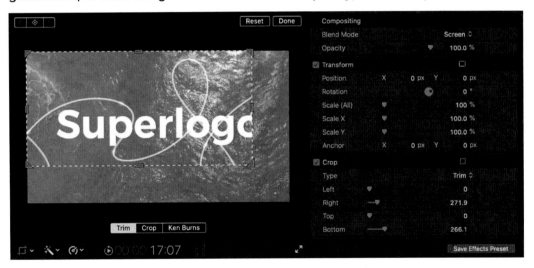

Figure 12.17: Drag on these edge controls to trim off the edges of a clip

Crop is great for punching in. While scaling up and moving over with the Transform controls is a perfectly good option, you've seen that the on-screen scale controls are difficult to use for this purpose. The Crop mode here lets you see the whole image while you choose which part of it to show, dragging the frame to reposition and dragging the edges or corners to rescale:

Figure 12.18: With the on-screen controls, the aspect ratio always matches the project

Click **Done** when you've finished. The aspect ratio here will stay locked to the aspect ratio of the canvas, which makes it easy to find the best frame for any shot, even for odd vertical or square social media deliverables:

Figure 12.19: After confirming the Crop operation, the on-screen controls disappear to reveal a punch-in

> IMPORTANT NOTE
>
> For the simplest delivery to multiple aspect ratios, you'll want to shoot wider than normal, preferably in a higher resolution and with the normal amount of space between your subject's head at the top of the frame — the "common top" strategy discussed in *Chapter 2, Before the Edit: Production Tips*. When you crop or scale to reframe for different aspect ratios, place the top of the clip at the top of the frame to maintain the common distance, and be more flexible with the sides and bottom edges. Also, note that **Spatial Conform** (at the bottom of the Inspector) will affect Scale or Crop settings, so choose one or the other. Spatial Conform is a good first step.

Ken Burns, named for the documentary filmmaker's signature effect, performs an automatic animation between two defined Start and End crop boxes. Click on either box to control its size and position, and try a few configurations:

- One box inside the other produces a zoom.
- One box above the other produces a tilt.
- One box beside the other produces a pan.
- These can be combined, as in a smaller box to the lower right of a larger box.

It's easy to swap the current Start and End boxes around with the button to the top left, and just to the right is a button that previews the current effect:

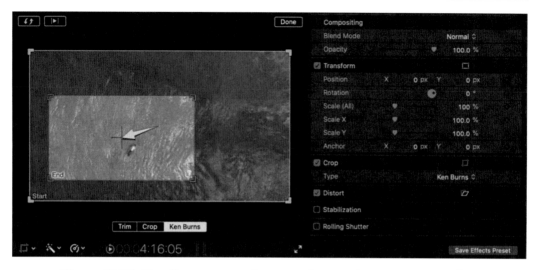

Figure 12.20: Ken Burns moves from one box to the next — try a few
different configurations

While the technique was invented to give life to still photos from the American Civil
War, it works with video too and can be quite effective.

> IMPORTANT NOTE
>
> **Ken Burns** is a great effect, but it will always start at the very
> beginning of a clip and finish at the very end. If you need more
> flexibility than this, such as a late start or an early finish, search
> for and install the free effect **Alex4D Grow/Shrink**.

Click **Done** when you're finished, and try this out on a series of back-to-back stills
to see how it looks. You'll find that the effect varies a little along the timeline, and
that a quick crossfade applied to all clips (⌘T) really helps. There will be more on
transitions soon.

DISTORT

This last set of properties let you control the corner positions of a clip, and the on-screen controls are probably the easiest way to perform this "corner-pinning" task. If you need to perform a screen replacement (and the screen isn't moving), then this works well. After you activate the on-screen controls, do the following:

Move the corner handles to adjust a single corner point.

1. *Move the side handles* to adjust two corner points together.

2. When finished, click **Done**:

Figure 12.21: Screen replacement, easy when it's not moving

For finer control, you may find you need to zoom in, which you can do with ⌘**plus** or with the zoom-level menu at the top of the Viewer. When zoomed in, you'll see a small widget to the right of the Viewer, which uses a red box to indicate which part of the frame you're looking at. Drag that red box to reposition, and press ⇧**Z** to return to the **Fit** view when done. Here's an illustration:

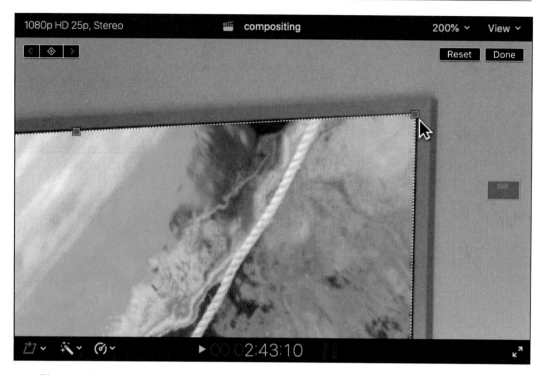

Figure 12.22: When zoomed in to 200%, it's easier to get the corners exactly right; move the red box to scroll about

Not everyone needs to replace screens, though. If you find that you don't use this very much, hover over the word **Distort**, then click **Hide** to the right.

For our next trick, we will make hand-held shots more stable.

STABILIZATION

If your shot is shaky due to unsteady hands or filming while moving, you may be able to fix the problem by activating **Stabilization**. Turn it on, wait for the clip to be analyzed, and then play the clip through to see how it looks.

One of two methods will be selected, depending on the kind of shake detected:

- **InertiaCam** is the preferred option but only works with lower amounts of shake. If needed, **Smoothing** can be turned up or down, and there's also a **Tripod Mode** checkbox that eliminates all movement.

- **SmoothCam** will be automatically selected if the movement was too strong for **InertiaCam**, but it can also be manually chosen if needed. The power of this option is that separate **Translation Smooth**, **Rotation Smooth**, and **Scale Smooth** sliders can be adjusted, but there's no Tripod Mode here:

Figure 12.23: InertiaCam on the left and SmoothCam on the right

If you can't get a good result after playing with all of the options here, then you'll have to replace the shot. Next time, use a gimbal for a moving shot or a tripod for a static shot.

ROLLING SHUTTER

By their nature, the sensors inside most cameras don't record the entire frame in one instant, but scan from top to bottom. This means that if a camera or its subject is moving quickly, the image may be at an angle:

Figure 12.24: When you move cameras too quickly, vertical utility poles lean sideways

Rolling Shutter tries to fix this and allows for several levels of correction, but the problem can be tricky to fix, especially when objects move quickly. Try to pan more slowly if your camera suffers from this.

SPATIAL CONFORM

If your footage is a different aspect ratio to your timeline, for example, if you're delivering to square for social media, then you'll want to choose how your footage is shown:

- **Fit** — Show the entire frame, but leave black areas blank around the clip.
- **Fill** — Zoom the clip up to fill the entire frame, cropping the edges of the clip.
- **None** — Don't change the size at all:

Figure 12.25: These three modes are great as a starting point or for further Scale and Position tweaking

You can use the Crop and Transform properties with any of these options, but **Spatial Conform** is designed to be used as a first step. If you change Scale and then change Spatial Transform to Fill, it'll zoom in more than you might expect.

A new alternative to Spatial Conform is **Smart Conform**, *added in the 10.4.9 release*. Select one or more clips, then choose **Modify** > **Smart Conform** to intelligently scale and reposition your images according to their actual content. Because this is especially useful for delivering to multiple aspect ratios, we will use this in *Chapter 16, You're Done: Exporting Your Edit and Finishing Up*.

RATE CONFORM

This frame rate control is only present if the frame rate of your clip doesn't match the frame rate of your timeline. The options here govern which frames are shown, but if you have a slight mismatch, it's likely that none of the basic options here (**Floor**, **Nearest Neighbor**, or **Frame Blending**) will look terrific. If you encounter this problem, address it with one of these options:

- Use **Retime** > **Automatic Speed** (discussed in *Chapter 13, Blend and Warp: Video Transitions and Retiming*) to change the clip speed to match the timeline frame rate.

- Use the **Optical Flow** method to intelligently create new frames as needed:

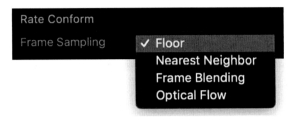

Figure 12.26: Optical flow effectively morphs between neighboring frames, like most TVs do with the dreaded "motion smoothing"

With any luck, you've shot your footage at the right frame rate, and this won't be an issue.

REVIEW — ADJUSTING VIDEO PROPERTIES

You've learned a lot about video properties, but it's all consistent and easy to navigate. Use the on-screen controls if you wish or drag on values in the Inspector for precision. If you **⌥-click** every time you select a clip, you'll avoid all confusion.

Moving a duplicate timeline to a new aspect ratio is simple these days and made even easier if you've framed the original shots with reframing in mind. If you're not the cinematographer, ask them (nicely) to shoot wider, with a common top line in mind, and you'll get great results.

Even for a single aspect ratio delivery, don't be afraid to punch in a little (or a lot) to give yourself new framing options in the edit. You'll be able to use this technique far more effectively if you can oversample, recording in a larger resolution than you need to deliver, and you've learned multiple ways to do that with crop and scale.

But what about moving shots? So far, all of these controls (except Ken Burns) have been static, but they absolutely can change over time. In the next section, you'll learn how to animate them.

ANIMATING WITH KEYFRAMES

Animation doesn't necessarily mean movement — it means changing the value of a property over time. You could:

- *Fade a clip in or out* by animating **Opacity**.
- *Grow or shrink a clip* over time by animating **Scale (All)**.
- *Reveal a clip* by animating **Crop (Trim)**.
- *Brighten a clip* over time by animating a color correction:

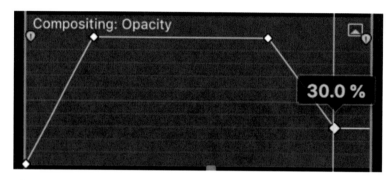

Figure 12.27: This Opacity starts at 0%, grows to 100%, stays there, then fades out to 30%

Keyframing is a universal solution that can be applied to almost any property in the Inspector — those are just a starting point. Here, we will start with the Inspector-focused controls, move across to the Timeline's controls, and then pop back to the Viewer too. If keyframes are too hard, there are alternatives, and you'll find out about those as well.

ANIMATING IN THE INSPECTOR

The keyframing system in the Inspector is bare-bones, but it still provides a simple, clean way to understand and control any property. For this exercise, you'll need two different clips placed above one another in the timeline, and you'll be working on the previous connected clip. However, now that you'll be changing an effect over time, you'll need to consider not just *what* the properties are, but *when* a property's values need to change. Keyframes are indicated by diamonds, and each one stores a value (*what*) at a point in time (*when*).

In the **Inspector**, you'll see arrows that jump between keyframes on the left, then a blank space if there's no keyframe or a yellow diamond if there is one:

Figure 12.28: No keyframe is shown on the left, but you can see a yellow keyframe on the right

But hover the mouse over the spot where a keyframe lives and you'll see what will happen if you click: the **+** and **–** only appear while you hover. A black outlined diamond with a plus indicates there is no keyframe, though you can click to add one. Hovering over a keyframe shows a minus, and you can click to delete that keyframe:

Figure 12.29: If you see a plus you're going to add a keyframe; a minus means you're going to delete one

We'll take this step by step, with examples of how you might choose to animate several sections in the Inspector.

ANIMATING THE CROP PROPERTY

Crop is a good place to start — it's obvious, it can look quite good, and it's easy to understand. Here, you'll animate the Left Crop edge in, from a large value down to zero. If you've already adjusted Crop on this clip, reset it before you begin, and make sure you're on the default **Trim** setting:

1. **⌥-click** on the connected clip, two seconds from its start point, to select it and move the playhead to that point in time.

    To animate a clip on to the screen, start with a keyframe at the *end* of that animation, locking in the "normal" property first — it's far easier.

2. In the **Inspector**, to the right of the **Left** property in the **Crop** section, press the diamond with a **+** to create a new keyframe:

Figure 12.30: When you're at the correct time, press the + diamond

A keyframe remembers a value at a point in time, and you've just locked in "normal" for this clip. The keyframe is now shown as a yellow diamond, and if you move the mouse away, you'll see it. Don't click the same button again, as it now shows a – inside the diamond as you hover over it, and clicking that would remove the keyframe.

3. Press ↑ to move the playhead back to the start of the current clip.

Once a keyframe has been created on a particular property, changing that value at a different point in time will automatically create a new keyframe.

4. Drag on the value for **Left** (initially **0**) until the clip entirely disappears:

Figure 12.31: Changing the value while at a new point in time (the start) creates a second keyframe

You'll have to drag this value out to at least the width of this clip. Note that the slider probably won't go far enough — always drag on the numbers directly.

5. Play through this clip to see the **Crop Left** property animate.

Importantly, if you were to change any other Crop property, no animation would be created because each property has independent keyframes. You only need to click the **+** *inside the diamond* once on each property, but that first keyframe is important.

The exception to this is that sometimes, you'll want to lock in the same value twice. For example, you might start a value at 0%, increase it to 50%, stay at 50% for five seconds, and then fade back down to 0% again. For that, you'd lock in two identical keyframes in a row in the middle of the clip, and you would use the **+** inside the diamond to add that second keyframe. To help you visualize that, here's a graph of what you would be aiming for with **Opacity**:

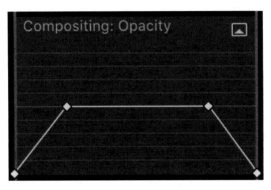

Figure 12.32: From 0 to 50, to 50, to 0, as shown in a Video Animation graph, coming soon

One final note is that if you ever need a keyframe on the final frame in a clip, you can't just press ↓ because that jumps to the start of the next clip. Instead, you need to press ↓, then ← to jump back one frame.

ANIMATING A COLOR CORRECTION

Color corrections can be animated too. If the light changes while recording a shot, then you can compensate for that change by locking in two different exposure settings — darkening the lighter part of the shot and lightening the darker part of the shot. To learn the technique, any shot will do:

1. **⌥-click** on a clip to select it and move the playhead to that point.
2. Press **⌘6** to add the default color correction to this clip.
3. Use the keyboard controls (JKL and arrow keys) to **move to an early point** in the clip.

Using the keyboard here means that you can't accidentally deselect the clip. If you want to use the mouse instead, drag in the ruler bar at the top of the timeline to avoid losing your selection.

4. Correct the Color/Saturation/Exposure as you wish at this point in the clip.

5. Hover in the title bar for this correction, and click the **+** inside the diamond to create a new keyframe:

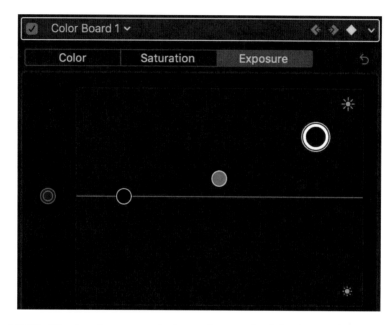

Figure 12.33: The keyframe controls at the top lock in the entire panel below at a specific time

The color correction is now locked in at this point in time. Changing the exposure settings at another point in time will lock in a second exposure setting and then a third.

6. Use the keyboard controls to **move along the clip** a couple of seconds.

7. Correct the Color/Saturation/Exposure as you wish, making an obvious change.

8. **Play through this clip** to see the color correction animate.

In a real-world situation, this technique works if you can add a keyframe on the exact frame where the exposure starts to shift and another on the exact frame where it finishes that shift. Of course, you can always hide this transition with a cutaway on top instead.

If you mess everything up, click on the hooked **Reset** arrow (or choose **Reset Parameter** from the small menu to the right of the keyframe controls) and you can start from scratch.

ANIMATING A MASK

You'll probably be able to figure out this process by now, but yes, you can animate masks too — ideal for tracking a person or object as they move around a shot. If you want to try this out, follow these steps:

1. **⌥-click** on a clip to select it and move the playhead to that point.

2. Press **⌘6** to add the default color correction to this clip, and make an obvious change, such as darkening the clip.

3. From the **Mask** icon at the top of the correction, add a **Shape Mask**.

4. Change the shape and size of the mask to roughly match the position of an object in the frame.

   You can invert the mask if you would prefer the correction to sit outside the mask shape.

5. Move to a point in time where the object starts to move.

6. At the lower part of the Inspector, next to **Shape Mask 1**, click the **+** inside the diamond to create a keyframe:

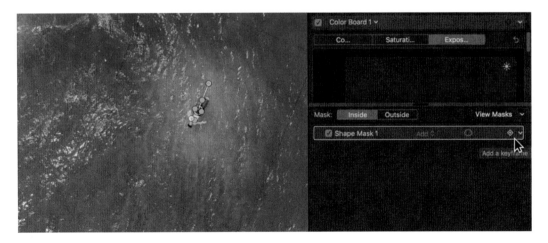

Figure 12.34: Make sure to use the keyframe controls in the mask section

You've now locked in the position, shape, and size of this mask.

7. Use the keyboard controls to move along the clip, ideally to a point where that object stops moving.

8. Move the mask to where that object is positioned.

9. Skim backward and forward to make sure that the mask follows the object throughout the clip.

10. At any point in time, move the mask to more closely match the object position to lock in another keyframe.

You could place a new keyframe every few seconds or at every point when the direction or speed changes, but try to keep this effect smooth. Use as few keyframes as you can get away with — too many can appear jerky:

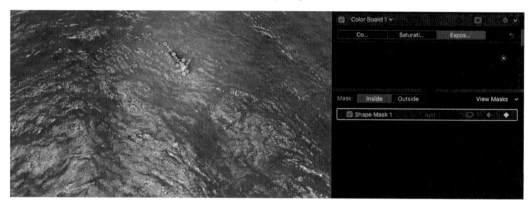

Figure 12.35: This person floating in the waves is now tracked across the clip, with a soft outline

When a mask requires extreme precision, you may be tempted to put a keyframe on every single frame for accuracy, but know that it's very hard to get this right by hand. If this is the kind of task you'll be performing often, consider purchasing a third-party tracking plugin. You can also try using a shape mask with a soft edge, to make any minor mistakes less noticeable.

Mistakes can also be fixed by re-editing existing keyframes, and that's easy.

EDITING KEYFRAMES IN THE INSPECTOR

Once keyframes have been added to a property, it's common to want to jump back to those existing keyframes. This allows you to change the setting recorded at a keyframe and to delete a keyframe outright. To move to existing keyframes, look to the left of a property's keyframe diamond to see two additional arrows:

- To move to the previous keyframe, press the *Previous Keyframe left arrow*.
- To move to the next keyframe, press the *Next Keyframe left arrow*:

Figure 12.36: Previous and Next are the two buttons to the left of the keyframe icon here

And to recap the keyframe diamond, we can do the following:

- While on a keyframe, press the **–** in the diamond (hover to see the minus sign) to delete it.
- While not on a keyframe, press the **+** in the diamond to create a new keyframe and record the current value.

While these controls are fine for simple tasks with just a few keyframes, it's possible to manipulate keyframes on the timeline too; read on.

ANIMATING ON THE TIMELINE WITH VIDEO ANIMATION

Video Animation provides a better way to see exactly when a keyframe has been recorded, though it doesn't usually provide a full traditional keyframe graph. To see this in action, you'll need a clip with keyframes applied to video properties in the Inspector — any of the previous clips will do:

1. **⌥-click** on a clip to select it and move the playhead to that point.
2. Press **⌃V** to display **Video Animation** for this clip in the Timeline.

The new **Video Animation** section displays small diamonds to indicate when a keyframe has been placed on any and all video-related properties for this clip:

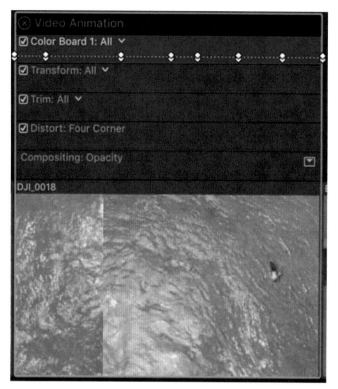

Figure 12.37: Now you can see all the keyframes for the previous Shape Mask movement at once

However, remember that each color correction and each area in the Inspector has several properties you can keyframe. As they may have been animated independently, you should choose which one to focus on, because viewing **All** properties for an area doesn't differentiate between the different types of keyframes.

For example, if you have a Color Board with a Shape Mask, you could view **All**, **Inside Correction**, **Outside Correction**, or **Shape Mask 1**. Switching to any individual property allows those keyframes to be repositioned in time or deleted, while other areas are shown in black and are protected from editing:

Figure 12.38: With Shape Mask 1 selected, Inside and Outside Correction keyframes can't be moved

As well as moving in time and deleting, it's also possible to create a new keyframe for any property by ⌥-clicking on its keyframe line. (This is also a workflow that can be used for controlling audio volume keyframes, but more on that in the next chapter.) However, most properties here offer only a single dimension. You can see *when* a keyframe is positioned, but *not the value stored* at that point in time. For that, you'll need to glance up to the Inspector, and the two areas do work pretty well together.

However, there is one property here that can be expanded to a two-dimensional graph — Opacity. Pushing the small icon to the right of the Opacity line causes this section to grow vertically, to show both time and Opacity for this clip:

Figure 12.39: When you push the icon to the right, you'll expand the graph

To vary Opacity over time with this graph:

1. In **Video Animation**, click the small icon to the right of the Opacity line to display the Opacity graph.

2. ⌥-click twice on the Opacity line to create two new keyframes:

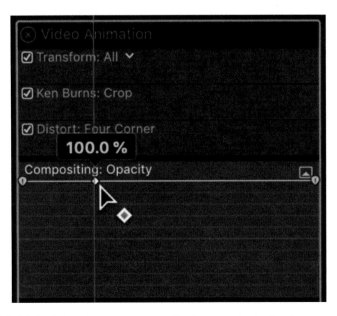

Figure 12.40: Hold ⌥ and the cursor will change, to indicate a new keyframe will be created

3. Drag one keyframe up or down to change the value at that point in time:

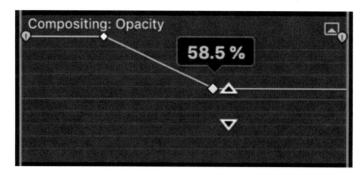

Figure 12.41: Dragging that second keyframe creates animation between the two keyframes

The animation between two keyframes is usually **Linear**, meaning that the change happens at a continuous speed:

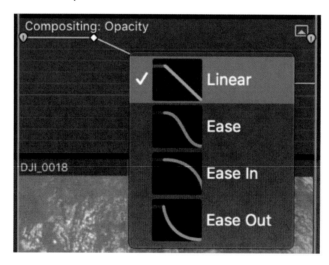

Figure 12.42: The four different types of graphs affect how the change is made between two keyframes

For a more natural result, you can right-click on the line between two keyframes, then choose a new curve type:

- **Linear** — continuous speed, the default (no acceleration)
- **Ease** — the change starts slow, speeds up in the middle, and slows down at the end (accelerating, then decelerating)

- **Ease In** — the change starts slow, speeding up toward the end (accelerating)
- **Ease Out** — the change starts fast, slowing down toward the end (decelerating)

Notably, of the standard video properties, only Opacity offers this graph, and therefore most properties can only be animated in a Linear way. You'll see soon that some other properties will show a graph, but only if they exist in a range of 0–100, like a percentage.

Incidentally, right-clicking on audio fade handles offers a similar set of curve options, though the default **+3dB** option is often the best. There will be more on that in *Chapter 14, Boost the Signal: Audio Sweetening*.

The keyframe graph does offer one additional trick, which is that you can fade any clip in or out with built-in fade handles. These work in a very similar way to the audio fade handles that were discussed in *Chapter 8, Neaten the Edges: Trimming Techniques*, and which will be revisited *Chapter 14, Boost the Signal: Audio Sweetening*:

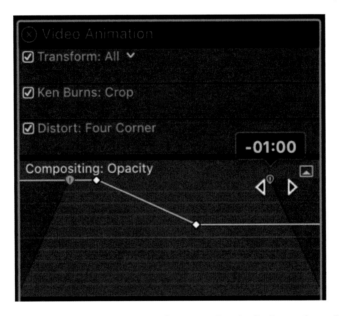

Figure 12.43: Fade handles for Opacity, built-in and useful

Look to the left and right edges of the Opacity graph to see the familiar teardrop shape, then drag that teardrop inward to create a fade in or out. These fades always occur at the start or end of the clip (even after trimming) while keyframes remain fixed in time.

In *Chapter 13, Blend and Warp: Transitions and Retiming*, you'll learn about transitions, which are usually the easiest way to fade a clip in or out, but from time to time this technique can be a useful alternative.

When you're done with Video Animation, you can hide it to simplify your timeline:

- Press **^V** to hide **Video Animation**.

Now that you know how to work with the Inspector and the Video Animation pane, it's time to head back to the Viewer.

ANIMATING IN THE VIEWER

While the Viewer only allows you to work with the Transform, Crop, and Distort properties, it does let you control some parameters in uniquely powerful ways. Firstly, the Viewer displays buttons in its top-left corner to allow you to:

- Jump to the previous keyframe.
- Add or delete a keyframe at the current frame.
- Jump to the next keyframe.

With these controls, it's possible to use the on-screen controls in the Viewer for basic keyframe management and navigation:

Figure 12.44: Additional, conveniently placed keyframe buttons in the top left of the Viewer

You'll still need Video Animation if you want to *move* a keyframe in time, but the duplication is convenient. The best reason to use these controls is for the most traditional kind of animation: creating movement by animating **Position**. To explore this, you'll need one clip above another as before, but this time we'll create and animate a fly-on picture-in-picture effect:

1. **⌥-click** on the connected clip above to select it and move the playhead to that point.

2. In the Viewer, activate the **Transform** on-screen controls with the menu in the bottom-left corner.

3. Shrink the clip down to about 25% by adjusting its blue corner handles or by using the **Scale (All)** parameter in the Inspector.

4. Click on the clip and move it to near the top-left corner.

5. Use the keyboard controls (or drag in the timeline ruler) to move to a point in time about a second in from the start of the clip.

6. In the top-left corner of the Viewer, click the **Add Keyframe** button to lock in the position at that point.

   This will add keyframes to all of the Transform properties:

Figure 12.45: All of those diamonds mean that a lot of properties have been locked in here

If you only change Position from this point, that won't cause any problems, but the on-screen controls will keyframe every Transform property together.

7. Zoom the **Viewer** out by pressing ⌘**minus** twice.

   Most of the time, you'll stay with the default **Fit** view (⇧**Z**), but for this task, you'll need to see the area outside the canvas. Make sure you've toggled the **Transform Overscan** button to the left of the **Reset** button on so that you can see everything you need.

8. Press ↑ to move to the first frame of this clip.

9. Move the top clip to the left, outside the canvas.

You'll see a red line joining the current Position (where the blue handles surround the clip outline) and the first keyframe you created:

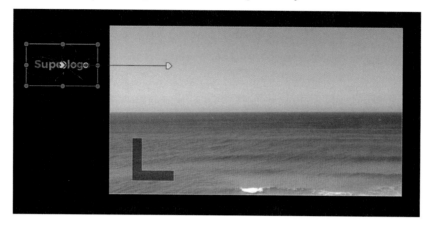

Figure 12.46: A full motion path is shown if you want to do this sort of thing

Every Position keyframe will be shown in the Viewer, from the first point (an arrow, indented on both sides) through intermediate keyframes (diamonds) to the last point (an arrow, indented on one side only).

10. Click **Done**, then Skim through this area of the clip to see the animation.

You may notice that there's some acceleration on these movements, and that's because position keyframes default to **Smooth**, similar to the Ease discussed with Opacity. Unless you choose otherwise, the transition between two keyframes will accelerate in and decelerate out. It's usually fine, but if you want to remove the speed changes:

• Right-click on any Position keyframe and choose **Linear** instead of the current **Smooth**:

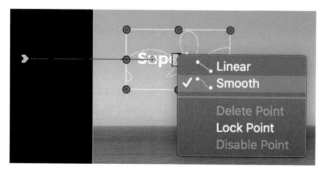

Figure 12.47: To choose Linear versus Smooth, right-click on a point

This change can be applied to any position keyframe, but Smooth is probably a good option for a movement like this, helping the picture-in-picture to come to a slightly more gentle halt. Note that you can change any Crop setting here, and because they haven't had any keyframes applied, no Crop animation will be added.

If you mess anything up, Undo or Reset and give it another shot. If you're attempting a complex animation and becoming frustrated, perhaps consider another way forward.

ALTERNATIVE ANIMATION METHODS

These animation controls work well for simpler jobs, but for finer control, you'll have to approach the problem in a different way. If you need full manual control over keyframes, with custom easing handles, consider using Apple's companion product, **Motion**. This excellent (and inexpensive) program allows not just manual keyframing, but also an alternative animation strategy — behaviors:

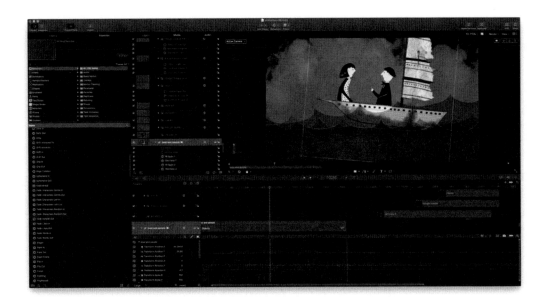

Figure 12.48: Motion is a spectacular program for motion graphics and works amazingly well with FCP

While you can use Motion to create a one-off animation piece, the recommended approach is to use Motion to create a template: a generator, a title, an effect, or a transition that can be used directly back in FCP. This strategy allows far more complex and sophisticated animations to be pre-built, either by you or as part of a third-party animation toolkit. The free "Alex4D Grow/Shrink" effect mentioned earlier uses behaviors to create a scaling animation, and there are far more complex options available too. You'll learn more about effects and transitions very soon, so stay tuned.

REVIEW — ANIMATING WITH KEYFRAMES

Mastering the art of keyframes will expand what you can do as an editor because you'll be able to quickly make your clients happy. If you need to fake a zoom with animation, you'll need to know how to keyframe **Scale (All)**; if you want to add a pan or tilt, you can scale up, then keyframe two **Positions**. Add that keyframe in the Inspector if you wish, by **⌥-clicking** in **Video Animation**, or even in the Viewer: the principle is the same.

When planning an animation, try to keep it simple; two keyframes are a good place to start. And if you're using two keyframes to animate a clip in, always lock in the later keyframe first to record the clip's normal properties. With the later keyframe recording normality at the end of the animation, you can add your earlier keyframe and go crazy with spins, fades, or movements. But if it's too hard? Motion, and third-party plugins made with Motion, will give you plenty of other options.

Speaking of options, it's time to widen your horizons with a look at video effects.

APPLYING AND USING VIDEO EFFECTS

This topic is huge, but if you want to blur, glitch, focus, sharpen, warp, distort, or otherwise stylize your clips visually, video effects are the way to get that done. Found in the **Effects Browser** to the lower-right of the interface, there are over a hundred effects included by default, and that's enough to get started with. When you need some more, you can install hundreds of additional third-party effects (free and paid) or even make your own with Motion. As you'll see, some effects have only a few controls in the Inspector, while others include many customizable options with draggable on-screen controls:

Figure 12.49: On-screen controls come in all shapes and sizes, such as this double-ring control on Droplet

But — surprise! — you've actually used effects already. The color corrections you added in the previous chapter are video effects, from the Color category of the Effects pane. While color correction instances are edited in the Color area of the Inspector, they can all be activated, re-ordered, and deactivated under Video, in the same way as all other video effects. In this chapter, you'll learn how to apply effects, how to animate them, which are the most useful effects, and how to use masks to restrict effects.

ADDING VIDEO EFFECTS

To get started, you'll need to see the **Effects Browser**:

- Show the **Effects Browser** by pressing ⌘**5** or clicking the icon second from the right in the central gray bar:

Figure 12.50: On the central gray bar, look to the right for the second last icon to bring up Effects

The **Effects Browser** has a sidebar to the left and actual effects to the right:

Figure 12.51: The Effects Browser sits in the lower right of the interface; here, the Distortion category is selected

In the sidebar, you'll see **Video Effects** on top and **Audio Effects** below. (We will return to Audio Effects in the next chapter.) At the top of the menu, you'll see **All Video** and **Audio**, and below that, **Video** then **All**:

- Click **All**, just under **Video**, to see all of the video effects in the pane to the right.
- Click **any category name** to see only the video effects in that category.

Video effects can be previewed before being applied to a selected clip:

- Hover (skim) over an effect to see that effect applied to the selected clip:

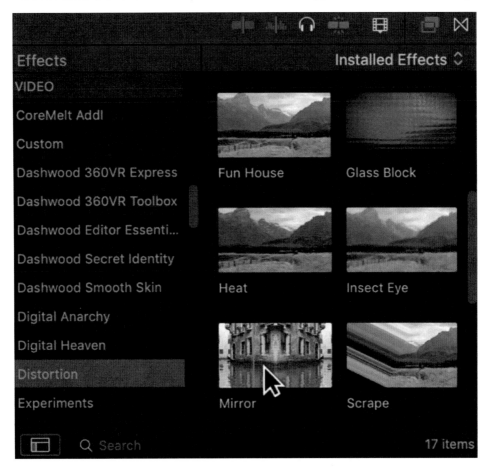

Figure 12.52: Hovering is a good way to preview the effect on the current clip

However, as effects can often be extensively customized, remember that you're only seeing a preview of the default setting of an effect here. You can get a slightly more informative preview, though:

- Hold ⌥ as you hover over an effect to change the primary control within that effect.

Normally this "primary control" is the strength of the effect, and it's a useful way to see how an effect will appear with slightly different settings. You can release ⌥ and skim over the clip to see the new setting applied to the rest of the clip.

To apply a video effect to a clip, there are two methods:

* Select one or more clips in the timeline, then *double-click an effect* to apply it.
* *Drag an effect* to a clip in the timeline.

Either of these works fine, and you'll be able to see that the clip has changed by skimming over it or playing the video.

If you find yourself using a specific effect regularly, you can assign it as the default by right-clicking and choosing **Make Default Video Effect**. That default effect can be added to a clip with ⌥**E**.

Most effects work in real time on most Macs, but some complex effects (especially noise reduction) can be very slow. If your Mac isn't fast enough to play back video effects in real time, you can try the following:

* Switching to **Better Performance** (not **Better Quality**) from the **View** menu in the **Viewer**:

Figure 12.53: Look to the Viewer for this one

* In **Final Cut Pro > Preferences (⌘comma)** under **Playback**, enable **Background Rendering**:

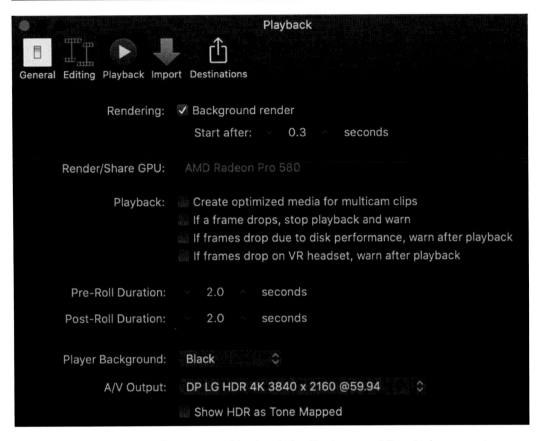

Figure 12.54: Preferences > Playback for Background Rendering — not needed on a fast Mac

With **Background Rendering** active, you'll need to wait for a few seconds for your newly applied effect to be calculated, and you'll see small dots in the timeline's ruler bar disappearing as this calculation happens:

Figure 12.55: The dots above the ruler are shown before rendering and disappear after

Rendering is the process of creating the final version of your edited video, and once rendered, everything will always play smoothly. Rendering does take time and requires hard drive space to store, so if your Mac is fast enough, you may not need to render in the background at all.

If you do leave Background Rendering turned off, you can still render selected parts of the timeline on request:

1. Make a selection, with the **Select** tool or the **Range Selection** tool.
2. Press ^R to render the selection.

You may wish to turn an effect on and off to see whether it's working, and that's easy:

- Click the checkbox next to an effect's name to turn it on or off.

If you decide an effect is not right, you can remove it:

- Select the effect by clicking on its title bar, then press **delete**.

For bulk operations, you can't beat these:

- To instantly remove all effects from a clip, press ⌥⌘X to **Remove Effects**.
- To selectively remove effects from a clip, press ⇧⌘X to **Remove Attributes**, then check all effects to be removed and approve the dialog.

> **IMPORTANT NOTE**
> Remember **Adjustment Layers** from the previous chapter? You
> can apply effects not just to individual clips, but to Adjustment
> Layers too. With an Adjustment Layer above all or some of your
> timeline, it's easy to apply as many effects as you wish to as many
> clips as you wish. If you haven't installed a free Adjustment Layer
> yet, search one out and install it.

Awesome, you've got the effect applied and you can see that it worked. It's time to
tweak!

ADJUSTING VIDEO EFFECTS

It's always wise to *change an effect's settings from the defaults* to make sure that
you're not applying exactly the same effect as 90% of other editors. The vast majority
of effects and titles are applied unchanged, and if you want to stand out from the
crowd, make sure your work is unique — adjust a slider!

To change settings, you need to look in the **Video** tab of the Inspector. There, you'll
see that the effect has been added to the clip, and that's where you can control
exactly how it works. Let's move through a simple example with a common filter, the
Gaussian Blur:

1. **⌥-click** on a clip to select it and move the playhead to that point.

2. In the **Effects** pane, click on the **Blur** category.

3. Hover over the **Gaussian** effect and see the preview effect applied to the clip.

4. Hold ⌥ as you hover over the **Gaussian** effect to see what Gaussian looks like
   at different strengths.

5. Double-click the **Gaussian** effect to apply it. (Alternatively, drag the effect to
   the clip.)

6. In the Inspector, move the **Amount** slider up and down to see how different
   strengths look in the Viewer, and reduce the effect overall:

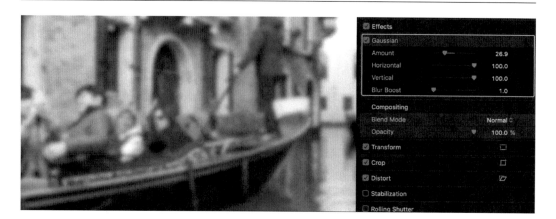

Figure 12.56: Blurry, but not too blurry

This should look much the same as it did earlier when you held ⌥.

7. Change the other settings in the Inspector (**Horizontal**, **Vertical**, **Blur Boost**) to try for a different look.

While you might not want to blur out a regular shot, a blur can be a useful way to de-emphasize a background clip behind a title. It can also be a useful effect to animate over time, turning down a blur to bring a shot back into focus. (More on this soon.)

Some more complex effects include on-screen controls to allow direct manipulation of the effect in the Viewer. Here's how to use one:

1. **⌥-click** on the same clip to select it and move the playhead to that point.

2. In the **Effects** pane, click on the **Tiling** category.

3. Hover over the **Kaleidoscope** effect and see the preview effect applied to the clip. (Holding ⌥ doesn't do anything here.)

4. Double-click the **Kaleidoscope** effect to apply it. (Alternatively, drag the effect to the clip.)

5. In the Viewer, *move the center control and the two connected handles* to adjust the positioning of the effect and the two angles by which the Kaleidoscope is generated:

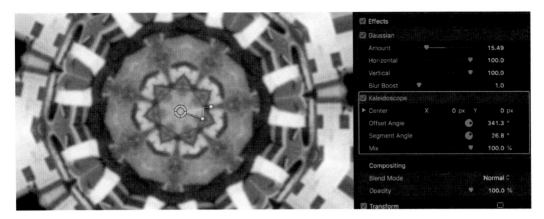

Figure 12.57: This effect is terrific, but it's tough to convince corporate clients to use it

With the on-screen controls in the Viewer, the Inspector is less important, though it can still be helpful. For consistency across multiple clips, the Inspector allows you to repeat specific values or adjust position in only one dimension while dragging an on-screen control is less precise. And with more complex effects, not every property is exposed through an on-screen display; indeed, the **Mix** control on this effect is only visible in the Inspector.

With two effects applied to the same clip, you'll find that order is often important: effects are applied from the top down. This order can be changed, by dragging any effect up or down in the stacking order. It's subtle here, but if you drag Gaussian to second in the list, it will remove some of the Kaleidoscope's finer details.

Finally, note that you'll only see the on-screen controls if the effect is selected (with a yellow outline) in the Inspector. This is always the case when an effect has just been applied, but if you've added a few effects to a single clip, only one set of on-screen controls can be active.

Now while the Kaleidoscope effect is very cool, it's hardly something you'd use every day. Abstract art can be wonderful in the right place, but most corporate videos are not that place. So, what are the most useful effects that you should know about? I'm glad you asked.

THE MOST USEFUL VIDEO EFFECTS

In this quick section, I'll move through the built-in categories, pointing out some of the most useful individual effects. There are many effects not listed here that are still great, though.

BASICS

This is a handy collection of common effects that didn't find a home elsewhere:

- **Noise Reduction** is an effective way to clean up noisy shots, but (like all noise reduction) it can be a little slow.

- **Negative** is a quick way to invert black and white in your image.

- **Threshold** reduces the number of colors in your image, but there are dedicated comic effects elsewhere if that's your goal.

- **Timecode** is a vital tool for a more complex post-production pipeline, displaying the timecode of the source clip or the Project on the clip itself:

Figure 12.58: Timecode for a source clip or Project — you'll know if you need this

Several other effects in this category adjust color and contrast, but you may prefer to use the color correction tools (such as Color Curves) for more control.

BLUR

These are tools to make things softer or (oddly) sharper:

- **Defocus** is a blur that resembles real-world camera blur, but it's slower than the simpler **Gaussian** option:

Figure 12.59: Defocus looks a little nicer than Gaussian, but is it worth the time? Your call

- **Focus** blurs the edges of the frame while a center area remains in focus. Tweak the settings!

- **Directional**, **Radial**, and **Zoom** are all different kinds of blur that suggest movement.

- **Prism** offsets the color channels for a nice color distortion effect:

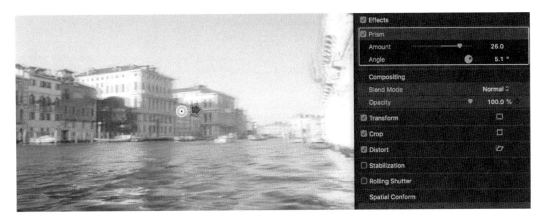

Figure 12.60: The trendy, trendy prism effect

- **Sharpen** lets you improve the clarity of a clip, but be careful not to overdo it. It's OK on defaults, but this is one case where dragging on the numbers doesn't give as much control as the slider. Note that an alternative strategy for sharpening, the Unsharp Mask, is in Motion and is available as a free third-party FCP effect (search online for "unsharp mask fcp free").

COLOR

Several effects here are either the actual color corrections available in the **Color** tab or perform similar functions. The other effects in this category include:

- **Black & White**, **Colorize**, **Sepia**, and **Tint** give slightly different ways to remove color, optionally tinting the result.

- **Broadcast Safe** can limit the range of colors to broadcast-approved values. Adding this to an Adjustment Layer that covers your entire timeline is a quick way to make sure all your video levels are within valid ranges.

- **Custom LUT** allows you to add a pre-made color transform, a **Look-Up Table**, to your clip. This could be an aesthetic combination of very specific color and contrast changes, a mechanical conversion from Log-style shooting to a more normal range, or something else. LUTs are widely available for free and for purchase, and this effect lets you apply them. As you add LUTs with **Choose Custom LUT** from the menu, they'll be remembered in the menu for future application, and source and target color spaces can be adjusted here too:

Figure 12.61: Custom LUTs give a specific look to your footage — add in your entire collection

> IMPORTANT NOTE
>
> A quick sidestep on LUTs here to address a minor issue. While you can use the Custom LUT effect to apply either a mechanical or an aesthetic LUT, there's another way to apply a Log conversion, and footage from some cameras will have this conversion applied automatically. To find it, look in the **Info** tab in the Inspector, under the Settings metadata view, and find Camera LUT. This affects a clip throughout a Library, is applied before any other corrections, and sometimes, can cause clipping in highlights or shadows. Turn Camera LUT to off if it's causing problems, and you can still correct Log footage using the normal color correction workflow shown in *Chapter 11, Play with Light: Color Correction and Grading*.

- **HDR Tools** lets you convert HDR footage into Rec. 709 color space and vice versa. If you've been given footage that seems brighter than you expected, it could be HLG, and this effect can rescue it.

COMIC LOOKS

All of these effects are awesome if you want to make your footage look like a comic, but not very useful if you don't. As ever, tweak the settings:

Figure 12.62: If you do go for this effect, use the matching titles and transitions

DISTORTION

While most of these effects are terrific for special occasions, they're very noticeable and not in the least subtle. There are some standouts, though:

- **Crop and Feather** is great when you want to trim a clip but apply soft edges or round corners.
- **Flipped** lets you horizontally (flip) or vertically (flop) reflect your shot because sometimes you just want things going the other way. Beware of words and cars.
- **Trails** adds echoes in time and works really well with fast-moving objects.
- **Underwater** gives you the classic wavy look.
- **Water Pane** really does make a clip look like it's behind glass in the rain:

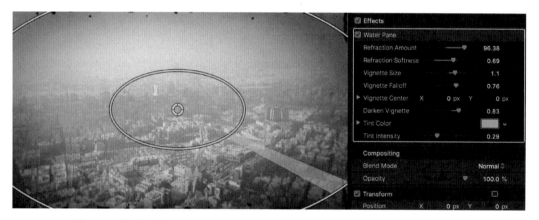

Figure 12.63: From a dry day to singing, just singing in the rain...

KEYING

Keyer removes a color from the shot (usually green, but sometimes blue) and it's a critical part of the workflow for many kinds of productions. If you want to shoot against a green screen, get it right in production (light both subject and screen, and be sure to separate them to avoid green spill on your subject) and this effect will work well. Once you've applied a Keyer to a clip, you'll see through (where the green was) to other clips behind, and it's a good idea to have the final background clip in position underneath this clip before you tweak the settings much further:

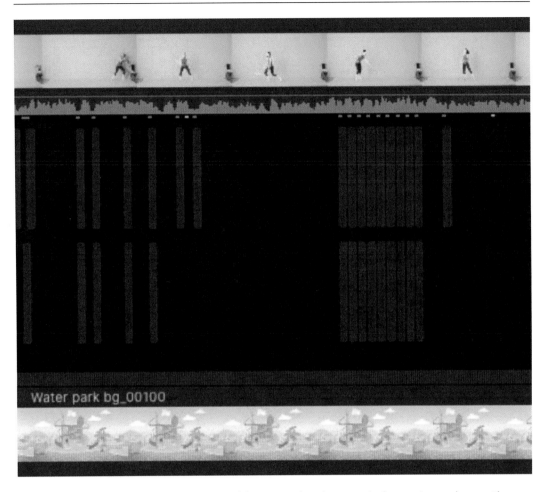

Figure 12.64: You'll need to position your background elements underneath the green screen clip (Credit: Smart Pointe)

There are many, many settings to tweak to isolate a subject from a green background, but every shot will need its own adjustments. Move from top to bottom, selecting the **Sample Color**, finessing the **Edges**, then trying the other main settings (**Fill Holes, Edge Distance, Spill Level**) before finessing the color selection, matte, spill suppression, and light wrap in their dedicated sections. With a clean shot, hopefully, you won't need to do much:

Figure 12.65: So many settings — it'll take a while to understand them all
(Credit: Smart Pointe)

Luma Keyer is simpler because it removes part of the image based on its brightness and has fewer controls. However, it's exactly the right tool to remove the lighter or darker part of an image. If you can shoot an object against a pure white background, this lets you remove that background pretty easily:

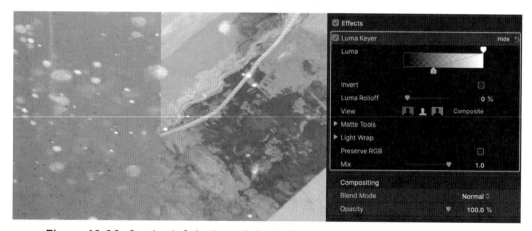

Figure 12.66: On the left is the original clip; on the right, the darker areas
have been removed with Luma Keyer

With either of these keyer operations, the effect is best used to separate the subject from its background, and you might not be able to clean up the very edges of the frame while keeping the subject well isolated. For that, use a **Draw Mask** effect (to be discussed soon) to exclude the edges.

Lastly, if you need to adjust both the subject and the background together, you'll need to combine them into a compound clip or use an Adjustment Layer above both clips.

LIGHT

Sparkly things always grab attention:

- **Aura**, **Bloom**, **Dazzle**, and **Glow** all add a shiny glow to the image.
- **Streaks** adds blockbuster-style anamorphic blue highlights to the image. It's not subtle, but you can turn it down:

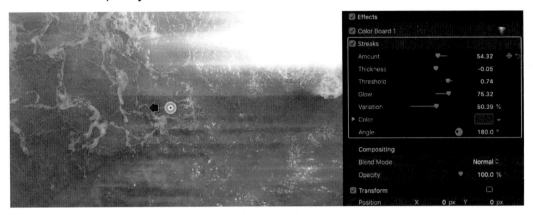

Figure 12.67: Streaks — can you hear the BWAAA?

Most of the other effects here largely add moving highlights or shadows to imitate various environments or add strong flashes.

LOOKS

Many of these effects are like strong color LUTs, a look that evokes a particular feel. Some also include a blur (**Dream** and **Romantic**) or imitate a well-known movie look (**Combat** and **Teal & Orange**) or even light rays (**Glory**):

Figure 12.68: This is clearly a cerebral period drama... with modern boats?

- **Night Vision** adds a traditional "binocular" mask, with alternative shapes and optional overlays too.

MASKS

This important category lets you control which part of a clip is visible, allowing you to blend one clip with another based on a shape or a gradient, rather than the content of that clip like the Keying category does. These control *clip visibility* and shouldn't be confused with the regular Shape Masks or Color Masks that control *color or effect visibility*:

- **Draw Mask** lets you click to create polygonal lines, or click and drag to create curved lines, to create any kind of shape. The shape can become quite complex, as you can double-click on the edge to create new points then move them around. Selected points can be deleted, and handles can be set to Linear or Smooth, then dragged to affect the curve using industry-standard bézier shape controls. You can use this to cut around a simple outline, or in combination with keying effects as a *garbage matte*, to clean up the edges of a green screenshot. To use a complex mask to control a color correction or other effect, duplicate a clip above itself, then apply the color correction or effect to the top clip and add a Draw Mask to it:

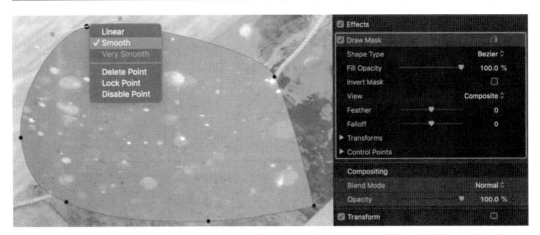

Figure 12.69: Any clip can be made into any shape you wish with Draw Mask

- **Graduated Mask** fades out the top or bottom of a shot. Potentially useful for sky enhancement, if used to hide part of the existing sky in a shot.

- **Image Mask** allows you to hide a shot based on the Alpha, Luma, Red, Green, or Blue of a second clip, similar to the Stencil and Silhouette Blend Modes.

- **Shape Mask** offers the same controls as those available to color correction — circles, ovals, squares, rectangles, and anything in between, with optional soft edges. If you start here and want to make the mask a little more complex, click the **Convert to Points** button to convert it into a **Draw Mask** effect.

- **Vignette Mask** is much like a large soft oval Shape Mask locked to the aspect ratio of the source clip.

NOSTALGIA

To look back on the past with rose-tinted glasses, try these:

- **Newsprint** adds a scalable dot pattern with contrast and noise.

- **Security** roughs up the image with noise, scan lines, image pixellation, and overlays:

Figure 12.70: The camera tells the story

STYLIZE

This grab-bag category includes a wide variety of aesthetic and utility effects and is worth a longer look:

- **Add Noise** and **Film Grain** both add noise to the image for aesthetic reasons or to protect the image against certain artifacts. In **Add Noise**, look to the **Type** menu to change its function, and use **Blue Noise** there to reduce banding in a flat background or gradient.

- **Aged Film** and **Aged Paper** give a tea-stained look.

- **Bad TV**, **Camcorder**, **Frame**, **Projector**, **Raster**, and **Super 8mm** add the look of devices from the past:

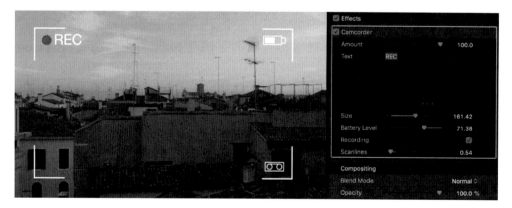

Figure 12.71: Ah, camcorders, or what we imagine they might have looked like

- **Cartoon** is a simpler version of the Comic category of effects.
- **Censor** allows you to blur, pixellate or black out a circle or oval or to black out a rectangle. Keyframing the center value allows you to track a person in shot, and we'll do this soon.
- **Cross Hatch**, **Graphic**, and **Halftone** all imitate printing artifacts.
- **Drop Shadow** adds a customizable shadow behind any clip. This is most useful for logos or on clips where the size has been reduced by cropping or scaling.
- **Handheld** adds fake camera shake to a static shot. This can be useful when you need to perform camera trickery that's easier with a locked-off tripod shot and then add fake camera movement afterward.
- **Letterbox** adds black bars on the top and bottom of the image to function as a crop. While a better alternative is to use Custom dimensions for your Project instead, this effect can be used on an Adjustment Layer across an entire timeline:

Figure 12.72: Black bars aren't necessary unless a client requests them

- **Photo Recall** turns a clip into a wider photo or an instant photo. Keyframing the Amount slider creates an effective animation.
- **Pixellate** reduces resolution to big squares and can be used with a Shape Mask to censor part of an image like the Censor tool.
- **Rain** adds some weather, while **Raindrops** flips the image and reflects it in a puddle. To use both together, add **Rain** second.
- **Sketch** and **Textures** add an animated real-media touch.
- **Vignette** adds both a darken and a blur to the corners of the frame, with a handy on-screen control. For extra finesse, create your own with Shape Masks instead.

TILING

When one clip isn't enough, make more! These effects can make use of a whole clip or just part of one:

- **Kaleidoscope** is one of the easiest ways to make art from your clips. It's rewarding to explore and heaps of fun, but I wish I could use it more often.

- **Tile** repeats a clip in a grid, while **Kaleidotile** adds reflection to produce a funhouse mirror, and **Perspective Tile** lets you extend the effect into 3D:

Figure 12.73: Perspective Tile has a handy on-screen control and is good for backgrounds

- **Visual Echo** is a little like **Trails** in that it overlays previous frames from the clip to create a dreamy "timey-wimey" effect.

THIRD-PARTY EFFECTS

There are thousands more effects to explore, both free and paid, from many third-party effects providers. Some of these can enable entirely new workflows by providing object tracking or advanced keying, but they go beyond the scope of this book.

It's time to get moving, with a few examples of how to animate effect properties.

ANIMATING VIDEO EFFECTS

The keyframing system works just as well on Effects as it does on any other property accessible in the Inspector, and here, you'll see a couple of examples of how to use it well. A quick way to find out whether an effect will look good when animated is to move one of its sliders up and down, then see whether you like the effect. The process should feel familiar:

1. ⌥-click on a clip, two seconds from its start point, to select it and move the playhead to that point in time.

2. Choose the **Blur** category, then drag **Gaussian** to the clip (or double-click **Gaussian**).

3. Set **Amount** to zero, to deactivate the effect.

   As before, we will lock in the second keyframe first, at the *end* of the animation.

4. In the Inspector, to the right of the **Amount** property in the **Gaussian** section, press the + inside the diamond to create a new keyframe.

5. Press ↑ to move the playhead back to the start of the current clip.

6. Increase **Amount** to a large value, 50 or more.

7. Play through this clip to see the image come into focus:

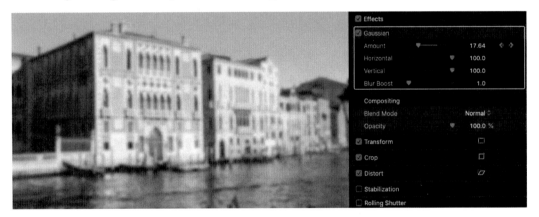

Figure 12.74: Playing through the clip, the animation will reduce the blur
from a high value to 0

Note that if the image remains somewhat blurry while Amount is set to zero, you may need to choose **Higher Quality** from the **View** menu in the Viewer. **Better Performance** reduces resolution to optimize performance, and this looks like a blur.

This isn't a real "focus pull" because the image all comes into focus at the same time and because a Gaussian Blur doesn't try to emulate a real camera. The **Defocus** effect tries harder but is much slower, and you'll need to Render before playing it back. If Background Rendering is enabled, just wait a few seconds for the render to happen, but if not, press ⌃**R** to render just this clip.

Another good example is **Censor**, which you can use to pixellate someone's face as they move around:

1. **⌥-click** on a clip of a person to select it and move the playhead to that point in time.

2. Choose the **Stylize** category, then drag **Censor** to the clip (or double-click **Censor**).

This time, we'll keyframe all the way along, from the start.

3. Press ↑ to move the playhead back to the start of the current clip.

4. Change the **Amount**, **Radius**, and **Center** to position the circle over a person's face:

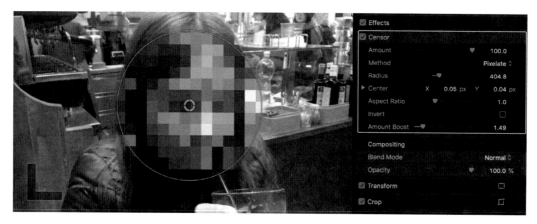

Figure 12.75: Disguise that person, on frame 1

5. In the **Inspector**, to the right of the **Center** property in the **Censor** section, press the **+** inside the diamond to create a new keyframe.

6. Press ⇧→ to move 10 frames down the timeline.

7. Use the on-screen controls to move the effect's Center to remain on the person's face. If they haven't moved far, still make a tiny nudge to place a new keyframe.

8. **Repeat** until keyframes have been placed along the full length of the clip:

Figure 12.76: Different positions all of the way down the timeline should look like this in Video Animation

If you find that there's very little movement, you can move a greater distance between keyframes to save time. When protecting identity like this, play through to make sure that you have obscured a face completely and add new keyframes to cover sudden movements.

Here are a few ideas for further animation:

- **Stylize** > **Photo Recall**, animate **Amount** from 0 to 100 to turn a clip into a photo.

- **Distortion** > **Wave**, animate **Amount** and **Offset** to produce a classic sci-fi teleporter effect.

- **Blur** > **Prism**, animate **Amount** up and then down, in time with the beat, for a quick distortion punch.

- **Light** > **Dazzle**, animate **Brightness** or **Threshold** to create subtle or strong flashing light effects.

To finesse keyframes over time, you can use the keyframe jumping and creation controls in the Inspector, as well as the positioning controls in Video Animation. There, you'll see a new line for each effect on a clip, and a keyframe graph (as seen in Opacity) can be activated for any property that has a range from 0 to 100. The graph can be shown by choosing the appropriate effect property and then clicking the icon to the right of the property. Common examples include **Opacity**, **Amount**, and **Mix**, all good ways to animate an effect on or off:

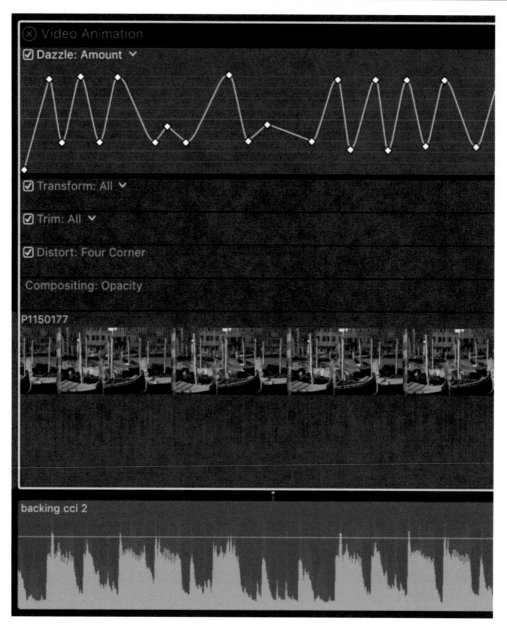

Figure 12.77: These complex curves pulse the Dazzle in time with the beat

Adding animation to a video effect lets you vary it over time, but you can do more. With masking, you can vary them in space too, and that's next.

MASKING VIDEO EFFECTS

The process of masking a video effect is almost exactly the same as masking a color correction, with a similar outcome: an effect is limited to only part of the frame. A shape mask limits the effect to a particular part of the frame, while a color mask would limit the effect to particular colors or brightness values.

> ## IMPORTANT NOTE
>
> Masking applied to a video effect is not the same as the category of video effects called **Masks**. Those effects (**Draw Mask**, **Graduated Mask**, and so on) govern visibility for an entire clip. Masking applied to an effect just changes which parts of a clip are changed by an effect.

Here's an abbreviated series of steps:

1. Apply an effect to a clip as usual.

2. Hover over the effect's title bar, then click the Mask icon and choose **Add Shape Mask**.

3. **Reposition**, **reshape**, **resize**, and **rotate** the mask as needed:

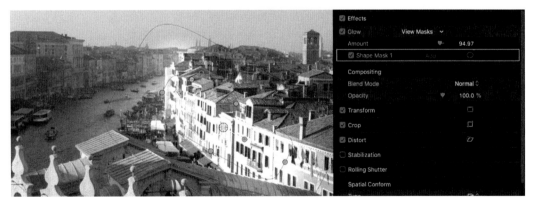

Figure 12.78: Here's a shape mask applied to a Glow effect

While the effect will now be limited to the inside of the mask, the menu allows you to Invert the mask to affect the outside instead. Masks are shown immediately underneath the effect to which they are applied, and a menu to the right of the mask's name allows you to Reset or Delete the mask.

Here are a few examples of when masking can be useful:

- **Sharpen** to focus attention on the subject
- **Blur** to de-emphasize the background
- **Comic Looks** to turn only part of the image into a cartoon
- **A color correction vignette** to darken the extreme corners of the frame
- **Underwater** or **Wave**, limited to water, to add ripples to it:

Figure 12.79: Some extra-wavy water, by applying Underwater to the green parts of the frame

Depending on what you're trying to do, the shots you're working with, and the effects you're trying to apply, this can work well or fail badly. There's always more than one way to get the job done, so if it doesn't work the first way, try another.

CREATE AND USE EFFECTS PRESETS

Effects Presets combine one or more effects or color corrections into a single, reusable effect, like a pre-copied set of effects ready to be pasted to as many clips as you like — and a few are pre-installed. If you look in the **Basics** category of effects, you'll see several **Vintage** effects that make your image look old and fashionable. These are actually Effects Presets, which combine an **Add Noise** effect with a couple of color corrections:

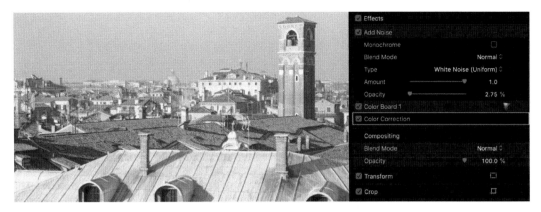

Figure 12.80: When Vintage – Soft Green is applied, multiple effects are added

To extend this example, if you're a fan of a particular color look, you might want to reuse it in different projects, and an Effects Preset would be a great way to maintain consistency. Effects Presets are most likely to be useful for corrections that create something distinctive, such as a vignette or a complex vintage look, and are straightforward to use. Here's an example using a single color correction (though you could combine more):

1. **⌥-click** on a clip to select it and move the playhead to that point.
2. Press **⌘6** to add the default color correction to this clip.
3. Darken the exposure quite strongly.
4. At the top of the **Color** pane, use the **Masks** menu to create a new Shape Mask.
5. Resize the mask into a large oval with a soft edge.
6. Invert the mask and resize so that only the corners are darkened.
7. At the bottom of the Inspector, click on **Save Effects Preset**.

   In the dialog that appears, you can choose to save any effect(s) applied to the clip as a new preset that can be applied in a single action.

8. If there's anything that shouldn't be part of the preset, uncheck any properties or effects that you don't want to include:

Figure 12.81: Here, only the Color Board effect is checked

For example, if this clip has a Crop or Scale applied that's only meant to be used on this clip, uncheck it.

9. In the field at the top, type a new name for this effect such as *Darken Vignette 1*.

10. From the **Category** menu, choose **Color Presets** if it's present. (If it's not there, choose **New Category** from the end of the list and create it.)

When you're done, you'll find your new **Effects Preset** in the **Effects** pane, in the category you saved it in, ready to preview with a hover. Feel free to experiment further by combining a few video effects together into a single **Effects Preset**, perhaps:

- **Raindrops** plus **Rain**, to really add the weather
- **Film Noir**, **Projector**, and **Letterbox**, for an extreme "film" look
- Several color corrections that you want to use together
- Any effect with customizable settings, tuned to your preferences

After applying an Effects Preset, all controls are fully accessible, just as if you'd performed a Paste Effects after a Copy. This is great for flexibility, but you won't be able to turn multiple effects down together.

Phew. It's time for a quick look back.

REVIEW — APPLYING AND USING VIDEO EFFECTS

Video effects fall into two categories: those you notice and those you don't. While you're learning, it's easiest to work with the more obvious effects, to experiment with the settings, masking, and animation in a really obvious way. In this section, you've learned how to do all of that, and there are so many effects that it's worth spending time getting to know your options. But once you've got a handle on how to use everything here, try applying effects in more subtle ways, to enhance shots rather than changing them utterly. Anyone can add a LUT, but only an expert knows how to make that effect (with added noise and vignette) on their own.

SUMMARY

This has been another monster chapter, but there was a lot of ground to cover.

It's your job to make the edit look good as it's not always possible to get everything right on set. If the cinematographer is a farmer who provides the ingredients, you're the chef who assembles them into a meal. Video properties are how you cut and present those ingredients, showing only the best parts, and turning imperfect shots into perfect ones. Video effects are your salt, pepper, and spices, helping each shot to shine, while animation... actually, the metaphor breaks down a little here.

Animation can let you add life where the shots couldn't, and it injects not just movement, but interest.

To return to the metaphor: get cooking, and make the best of what you have. In the next chapter, you'll find out how to move between clips with transitions and how to manipulate time with speed changes.

REVIEW QUESTIONS

1. What modifier key should you hold while dragging on a property value if you want to have more control?
2. What happens if you apply the Multiply blend mode to a connected clip above another clip?
3. What property moves a clip up or down?
4. Which Crop mode includes animation?
5. Where can you find an animation graph for Opacity?
6. Which effect adds a natural-looking Blur?
7. Where can settings for an effect be adjusted?
8. What effect removes a green-screen from a shot?
9. How could you save a blur and vignette effect together?
10. What effect can disguise someone visually?

REVIEW ANSWERS

1. ⌥ (Option) for more control.
2. The connected clip darkens the lower clip.
3. Position Y.
4. Ken Burns.
5. Video Animation.
6. Gaussian.
7. In the Viewer, if the effect has on-screen controls, and in the Inspector.
8. Keyer.
9. Save an Effects Preset.
10. Censor.

13 BLEND AND WARP: VIDEO TRANSITIONS AND RETIMING

"You know something is designed well when all you need to use it is a single head-switch. The power-to-accessibility ratio of FCP helped me find my passion for creativity."

— *Christopher Hills, CEO at HandsOptional*

Now that you've added and animated all of the special additions you want to make to clips, it's time to adjust the way that one clip moves to another and how fast those clips move. Here, you'll learn techniques for working with transitions, including some sneaky tricks and recommended options. Fade, dissolves, pushes, and crazy timeline pins on a bulletin board are all here.

After that, you'll learn retiming: how to speed up, slow down, and pause your clips with finesse. While these techniques work best with high-speed footage (and your iPhone does a great job of it), you can apply these tricks to any footage.

This chapter covers:

- Applying and editing transitions
- Retiming basics
- Speed ramping and more

To begin, let's see how shots can transform into other shots. Though you might not use these all the time, you've got many, many options.

APPLYING AND EDITING TRANSITIONS

Transitions change one shot into another, in a simple or complex way. Here, you'll find out which are the best ones to use for various purposes and how to adjust their settings, duration, and positioning, as well as why they might not always work.

There's an old film school joke where the teacher asks their class what the best transition is. The answer is "a cut." While there's some truth to this, in that a story can be told without fancy transitions or noticeable effects, the world of video encompasses many more types of content than a short or long film for "serious" audiences. If you're creating something for social media, sports, kids, or you have to inject life into a dull corporate piece, then a good transition, well used, is exactly what you want:

Figure 13.1: A timeline with plenty of fancy transitions that isn't a disaster

However, like a slide-based Keynote presentation, you shouldn't go completely crazy. Every novice user of a page layout program uses every font they can, every child learning slide transitions uses all of them, and it's never good. Think of a fancy transition in a video as a fancy slide transition in a presentation — it grabs attention, but it shouldn't overstay its welcome, nor should it be repeated over and over. Don't use ten different types of transitions in the one video.

Even something as simple as a dissolve can be overdone. If you start adding transitions on every cut, the remaining straight cuts will feel harsh, and every edit will feel too prominent. Transitions should be used sparingly, to help the story along, for a scene break, to indicate the passage of time, or to hide a jump cut edit honestly, in plain sight.

There are exceptions, of course: if your job is to present a company's best photos in a video to be shown at their yearly Christmas party, go nuts! Transition between each and every photo, with slightly different versions of the fanciest transition that works.

ADDING TRANSITIONS

Much like effects, you'll start by opening the **Transitions Browser**, and you'll find its icon right next to the Effects Browser icon:

1. Show the **Transitions Browser** by pressing ^⌘5 or clicking the icon to the far right in the central gray bar:

Figure 13.2: The bowtie, all the way to the right of the gray bar

2. Click **All** at the top, to see all of the transitions in the pane to the right.

3. Click any category name to see only the transitions in that category:

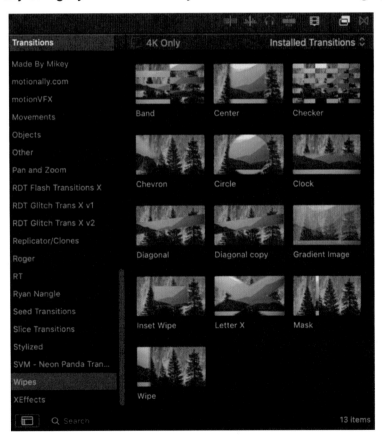

Figure 13.3: Ah, the Wipes category, perfect for a sci-fi homage
and much more

4. Hover (skim) over an effect to see a preview of this transition.

A transition may have additional options, but you can only preview the defaults, and with two fixed images, a red tree scene transitioning to blue mountains. To see a transition with your own media, you'll need to apply it.

To apply a video transition to a clip from the **Transitions Browser**, there are a few options:

- Select an edit in the timeline, then double-click a transition to apply it to that edit.
- Select a clip in the timeline, then double-click a transition to apply to both sides of the clip.
- Select multiple clips or edits in the timeline, then double-click a transition to apply it to all selected clips or edits.
- Drag a transition from the **Transitions Browser** to an edit in the timeline:

Figure 13.4: Dragging a transition into place makes sense visually, and previews its duration

That last "drag" option shows a preview of the transition in place before you drop it, which is convenient. Dragging also allows for *moving* a transition from one edit to another and for *replacing* a transition, by dragging onto an existing transition.

Duplication works too. If you've already added a transition, you can use it again:

- Copy one transition, then select another edit and paste.
- ⌥**-drag** one transition to another edit to duplicate it.

Lastly, if you're keeping it simple, there's another option. Select an edit or clip, then:

- Add the default transition, a simple **Cross Dissolve**, with ⌘T.

In everyday edits, I use the **Cross Dissolve** transition pretty frequently, though I like to keep it short. The duration of this default transition can be defined in **Final Cut Pro > Preferences**, under **Editing**, and I recommend **0.4** seconds or so:

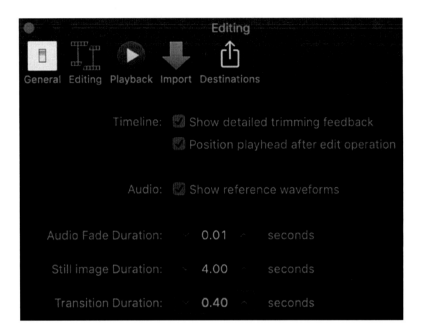

Figure 13.5: Preferences > Editing for transition and fade durations

Shorter is better for simple transitions; it gets out of the way quickly. More complex transitions need more time, perhaps even a few seconds, but not every edit can support a transition — the source clips must have additional extra media beyond the edits, called **handles**.

If you're not sure how much media is available, the **Precision Editor** mode (double-click on an edit, **Escape** to leave) will let you see. You'll need extra media on the end of the outgoing clip and at the start of the incoming clip, enough to cover the transition on both sides. After all, you can expect to see at least part of both underlying clips as a transition plays, so there has to be something to show:

Figure 13.6: The Precision Editor tells the story — there's no more media on the outgoing clip

Generally, you'll find out something's wrong when you try to add a transition and an error pops up to tell you that there's not enough media:

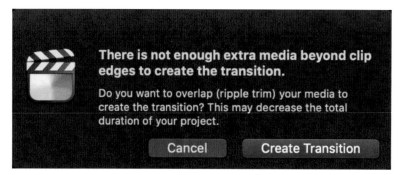

Figure 13.7: Oh no — not enough media!

If you approve the alert, one or both clips will be shortened to gather the extra media that the transition needs. If that shortening would ruin the edit, cancel, then tweak the edit to make more room. Usually, a quick roll edit is enough, but you might have to slip.

Note that if you drag and drop a transition to an edit where there isn't enough media, it won't display a preview of the transition in place, but will still pop up the error and allow the transition to be added.

After adding a transition, you'll see it as a new gray box covering the edit, and depending on the zoom level of your timeline, you could see one of three different displays. When zoomed all the way out, you'll see a simple gray box:

Figure 13.8: Zoomed all the way out, a gray box with no visible controls

When you zoom in a little more, the gray box has a **bow tie icon** (this indicates an In and an Out point together, but it really does look like a bow tie):

Figure 13.9: Zoomed in a little, to see the bow tie

When you zoom in even further, the gray box has the bow tie and a double-line handle on each side of it:

Figure 13.10: And zoomed in further, to see the bow tie and handles on both sides

To find out more about what your options are, read on.

ADJUSTING A TRANSITION

The three things you can change about every transition are any custom settings it provides, its duration, and its position around the edit. Not all transitions offer customizable settings, but some do, including the **Dissolve**:

1. **⌥-click** a **Cross Dissolve** transition in the timeline to select the transition and move the playhead to that point.

   Note that you might need to move the playhead (with ← and →) to reach the middle of the transition.

2. In the Inspector, experiment with different options in the **Look** menu, reviewing the results with **?** (⇧/) after choosing each one.

These options govern how the **Cross Dissolve** appears, and it's worth looking at the **Film**, **Additive**, and **Subtractive** options to examine the differences. There's also an **Ease** control and **Ease Amount**, though these won't be too noticeable in a quick transition:

Figure 13.11: The Cross Dissolve options are more extensive than you'd think

Every transition also includes a built-in **Audio Crossfade**, and in fact, if you expand audio on the clips around the transition, you'll see an indication of the default audio fade. Therefore, there's no need to apply a separate Crossfade to the audio. The menu in the Inspector allows the usual choice of curves to fade with, and further manual control is possible too. If you move the audio edges (even by a frame) the default fade will disappear, and you can define your own audio transition with the audio fade handles instead:

Figure 13.12: Audio fades are applied automatically, but can be overridden by dragging the fade handles

To change the duration of the transition, drag on its left or right edges — the change is symmetrical, affecting both sides at once. You'll see the standard trim cursor when you're in the right place, but there's no filmstrip on the icon because this isn't a ripple operation:

Figure 13.13: Duration is easy to change, drag the gray edges — lower down if you've zoomed in though

Zooming in to reveal the bow tie icon lets you drag on the transition to move its position. A **Roll icon** will appear to indicate that yes, you're performing a Roll operation, but there's no need to switch to the **Trim** tool; it happens automatically:

Figure 13.14: Drag on the bow tie to roll the edit back and forward

This lets you trade one clip off against another, and you might make a different decision now that you've added a transition.

You can drag as far as media allows, though even a very fancy transition is unlikely to play for much more than a second or two. Experimentation will lead to experience here, and if you want consistency, you can always use the keyboard:

- Select a transition and press **^D** followed by a timecode and **return** to set its Duration.

As before, **^D2.** means two seconds, and **^D15** means 15 frames.

Zooming in one more time to show the handles on either side reveals all of the controls at once. With visible handles, you can still drag the transition's edges to change duration, but you'll now need to drag on the lower-left or lower-right sides of the transition. The upper handles let you perform ripple edits to one clip at a time:

Figure 13.15: Dragging the upper edges with the handles visible lets you adjust In and Out points on these clips

Dragging on the upper-left side performs a ripple edit on the incoming clip on the right while dragging on the upper-right performs a ripple edit on the outgoing clip on the left:

Figure 13.16: The Transition Editor (double-click an edit) shows how much media you'll need after adding a transition

That might seem contradictory, but the two clips do overlap — as the **Precision Editor** shows. The right handle is indicating the true out point of that outgoing clip.

Now that you know how to apply and manipulate transitions, what types of transitions are you going to add?

THE MOST USEFUL TRANSITIONS

Cross Dissolve is useful and, as you'll probably use it a lot, leave it as the default with ⌘T. There are many other transitions here but, as a lot of them come with plenty of character, you might struggle to fit them into most edits. Here are some of the most practical options:

BLURS

Softening between clips often looks slick, and it's a safe option for many jobs:

- **Gaussian** is an easy transition to use, with a blur out and then a blur in to the next clip.
- **Directional**, **Zoom**, and **Zoom & Pan** provide blurs with a little more movement.

DISSOLVES

The vital **Cross Dissolve** lives here, but this section has two other important transitions as well:

- **Fade To Color** is a fade to black by default, and it won't offend anyone. This is probably the second most useful transition after Cross Dissolve, and if you want to fade to some other color, just change the color in the Inspector:

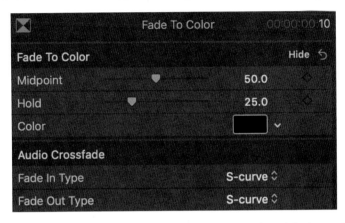

Figure 13.17: You can fade to any color with the color chip here, but black is most useful

- **Flow** provides a morph that will sometimes smooth over a jump cut. When you apply this transition, the surrounding clips are analyzed, but if the positions of the subject in the two neighboring frames are close enough, you can disguise the cut completely. What works? A tripod shot of an interview, with similar mouth and head positions on Out and In frames:

Figure 13.18: This frame isn't real — the Flow transition created it to cover a jump cut

LIGHTS

Changing shots with a sudden light change is an old trick:

- **Flash** quickly flicks to white and then back down to the next clip.

- **Light Noise** doesn't have any options, but it flashes some gentle white lights up on the edge, to the full screen, and then down. This one works well over a slightly longer duration, and you'll find many third-party *light leak* transitions like it:

Figure 13.19: A pleasant way to move between shots, but don't overdo it

- **Static** is a classic analog "channel changing" effect, but since TVs haven't done this for a while now, it's becoming less recognizable.

MOVEMENTS

This is a collection of kinetic transitions, and while most of these are for special occasions only, there are a few generally useful ones too:

- **Push** can work in one of the four cardinal directions and is a simple, widely used transition that moves one clip out while the other moves in.

- **Slide** is similar, but the outgoing clip doesn't move at all, and the incoming clip has a blur:

Figure 13.20: The new clip moves over the old one, with an
on-screen control

OBJECTS

Moving things in front of shots and using shapes to move between them can add
some style, but can be quite attention-grabbing:

- **Arrows** is pretty slick, and there's flexibility about the ends of the arrows.
- **Curtains** is good to start a video of a stage production:

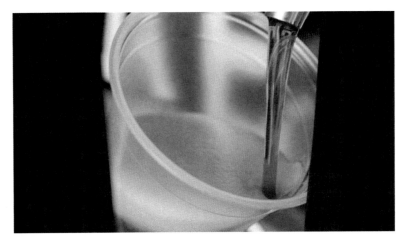

Figure 13.21: Perfect in the right circumstances, a little odd in others

- **Leaves** throws some leaves down to cover the change in clips.
- **Veil** throws down some white fabric and should be useful for weddings.

STYLIZED

There's some really interesting stuff here in the **Bulletin Board**, **Comic Book**, **Film Strip**, **Photo Album**, and **Scrapbook** categories, and you'll need a long transition duration (at least a few seconds) to get the most out of them:

Figure 13.22: The Comic Book transitions work well with the Comic effects

All of these transitions start from the outgoing clip, zoom out to reveal that you're looking at a single frame of many, pan and move around to show other clips, and then zoom in to one photo as the transition ends and the clip restarts:

Figure 13.23: Images shown in the transition are chosen with Timeline Pins on the Primary Storyline

Each clip that's visible here is actually a still frame from the Primary Storyline on the current Project, and while the transition is selected, you can drag the numbered **Timeline Pins** around to position them anywhere you want in the Project. This means that you can give advanced warning of a shot that's coming up or recall a shot that's already passed, and that's unique.

WIPES

Some of these are pretty good, but be careful — if you use the **Clock Wipe** or **Wipe** with a soft edge and a slow duration, you could recall a famous sci-fi film. Some other options:

- **Chevron** is a quick wipe-based transition that implies a little movement, so it's great for moving clips:

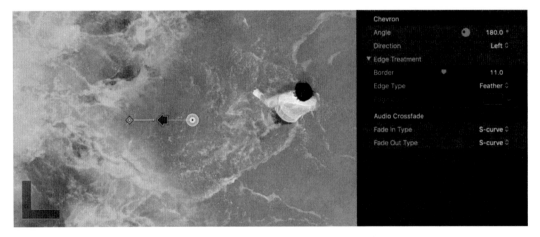

Figure 13.24: A little nudge in the right direction

- **Diagonal** and **Mask** are simple and effective ways to quickly transition between clips.

THIRD-PARTY TRANSITIONS

As with effects, there are thousands of third-party transitions out there. You can make your own with Motion or enjoy what others have already made. Some of the most interesting ones add glitches or light leaks, and you'll find both paid and free options.

RECAP — APPLYING AND EDITING TRANSITIONS

Transitions are not the devil; sometimes, they bring just the right amount of life to a dull edit or spice to a lively edit. When you add an appropriate transition, get the settings and duration right, and tweak the position a little, you can get great results. You'll still be **⌥-clicking** to see what you're doing, changing values in the Inspector, and reviewing until you're happy.

RETIMING BASICS

In this section, you'll learn how to play clips faster or slower than normal, for special effects, for slow motion, or even to deal with footage at the wrong frame rate. After a quick look at the different kinds of footage you might need to deal with, you'll discover how to apply an overall speed change to a clip.

All of the important retiming commands are in the same menu — the third icon (a speedometer) at the lower left of the Viewer. To get started, you'll need a few clips in a timeline and ideally some high-speed clips for slow-motion. If you have an iPhone, switch it into **Slo-Mo** mode now and record something moving. For great results, blow a raspberry to the camera, create a water splash somehow, or dance.

If you have used your iPhone, don't Airdrop it to your Mac because that will lock in a pre-defined slow-motion effect. Plug the iPhone into your Mac and import it to FCP directly to get the full original clip.

From other cameras, just import as usual. If some of your clips are high-speed clips, that's great, but they don't need to be. Let's move onward:

1. **⌥-click** on a clip to select it and move the playhead to that point.
2. From the **Retiming** menu, choose **Slow** > **50%**, and play the footage back.

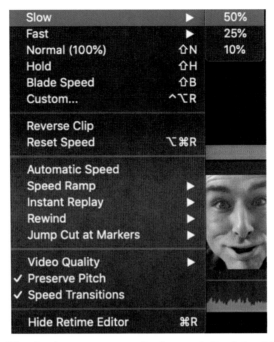

Figure 13.25: The Retime menu, at the lower-left of the Viewer (pay no attention to the silliness behind)

This clip will now run for twice as long, using the same part of the clip that it did before. You'll also see a new colored bar above this clip, the Retime Editor, showing the new speed of this clip, and a drop-down menu that offers the most important options from the main Retime menu:

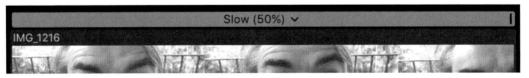

Figure 13.26: The Retime Editor is a simple and effective way to govern speed; Orange means slow

The **Retime Editor** can be shown or hidden with **⌘R**, and will currently be Orange to indicate that the footage has been slowed down. Orange indicates a slow down, while Green indicates normal speed, and Blue indicates a speed up.

3. Drag the single-line handle to the left until the line becomes Blue, and play the footage back:

Figure 13.27: Blue means fast, the same video over less time

The handle controls the speed at which the clip plays back. Dragging it to the left means the clip speeds up, taking less time to play. While it's possible to drag the handle to whatever speed you wish, you can achieve slightly smoother slow-down results with the menu's options: 10/25/50%. Another alternative is to use **Custom** speed.

4. Choose **Custom** from the **Retime** menu, the **Retime Editor** menu on the clip, or by pressing ⌃⌥R:

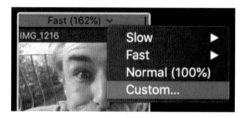

Figure 13.28: Custom speed has a few neat tricks

The Custom dialog offers some unique features, allowing you to express the clip's speed by defining a new speed as a percentage or a duration and to reverse the clip.

5. Set **Rate** to 20% in the dialog and press **return** to apply.

Don't overlook an important checkbox here: **Ripple**. If you change a primary timeline clip's speed by dragging the handle or using a pre-defined speed option, it will change the clip length and cause a ripple down the timeline. If this isn't what you want, you could Lift that clip up to be a connected clip, but sometimes that's not an option either:

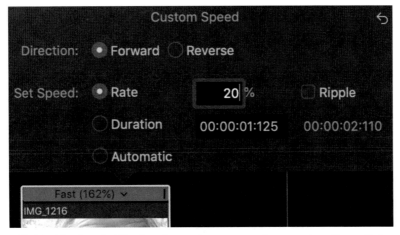

Figure 13.29: Uncheck Ripple, then change a primary storyline clip's speed
to avoid length changes

With the Ripple option disabled, the timeline clip length remains constant, no matter whether it's connected or in a Storyline. The speed change, therefore, controls how much of the clip you see — if you set the speed to 200%, you'll see twice as much of the clip as you did before, playing twice as fast. When this happens, the In point is locked, but the Out point (of the source clip) will change. It's a little like a Slip, but by changing the speed of the source clip, and indeed, you can switch to the **Trim** tool (**T**) and Slip the resulting video if you're not seeing the best part of the clip.

6. Choose **Retime** > **Reverse Clip** to play the clip backward.

   Reverse is indicated in the **Retime Editor** with arrows pointing to the left, and with a negative speed percentage:

Figure 13.30: Reverse is shown by arrows on top of whatever speed change
is already applied

It's most useful with a tracking shot over a mostly static subject, such as a drone shot over a mountain, but it's more fun with footage of people eating.

There's one more way to change a clip's speed, and it involves no dialogs. If you mark the In and Out point of a source clip, then drag it onto a timeline clip that you'd like to replace, you can choose **Replace with Retime to Fit** from the pop-up menu that appears:

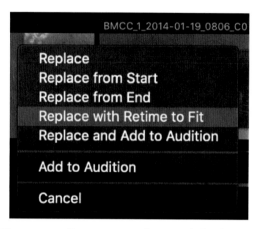

Figure 13.31: Drag one clip onto another, wait for it to go white, then Replace with Retime to Fit from the menu

A speed change will then be automatically added to fit the chosen clip in the duration available.

So far, so good — these are the basics of changing the speed of a whole clip to be faster, slower, or backward. Before looking at speed ramping, let's take a quick look at how to get the smoothest possible output.

UNDERSTANDING SLOW MOTION AND AUTOMATIC SPEED

To get the best results from slow motion, you'll need to know exactly what's happening, and that's what this section is about. You'll find out how slowing down footage works and how to use **Automatic Speed**.

When you speed up footage, as in a time-lapse video, frames will be skipped. The speed-up factor can get very, very large; if you record an hour of continuous footage and want to present it as a timelapse over a few seconds, you might use a speed of **20,000%** or more:

Figure 13.32: If your camera can't record time-lapse, record regular video
for a long time, then speed it up

Big speed changes are generally fine, but a small difference, such as 30fps footage playing at 25fps, will be more noticeable and is likely to stutter. Remember — *if you're not shooting for slow motion, record at the frame rate you want to deliver*.

To slow down footage, you'll get the best results if you've recorded at a higher frame rate because no new frames will need to be invented. With regular speed footage (say, 24fps footage in a 24fps Project), one of three modes will be used after a speed reduction:

- **Normal** — Frames are repeated, usually with a visible stutter.
- **Frame Blending** — Nearby frames are blended together, often overly smooth and unconvincing:

Figure 13.33: Overlapped frames don't look great in a still frame,
nor in motion

- **Optical Flow** — New frames are created by morphing nearby frames, which takes time to process, and can be good with some kinds of movement but bad with others:

Figure 13.34: The same frame with Optical Flow is much better on the central bird, but it can fail in odd ways

These options can be chosen from **Retime > Video Quality**. But with planning and the right camera, and if the source footage was recorded at a higher speed, real frames can be used instead, and nothing needs to be invented. Surprisingly, your phone is likely to do a better job of this than most professional cameras, and it will present its footage a little differently.

High-speed iPhone footage plays back in "real time" by default, skipping a lot of frames — for example, shooting 240fps and then playing back just one in ten of those frames at 24fps:

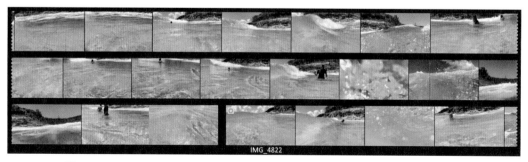

Figure 13.35: Modern iPhones are great for capturing slow motion underwater — look for the high speed icon

Slowing the footage down displays more of those frames, and it's going to look pretty good. But for the smoothest, slowest natural results, use **Retime** > **Automatic Speed**, to play every frame that was recorded at the speed of the timeline:

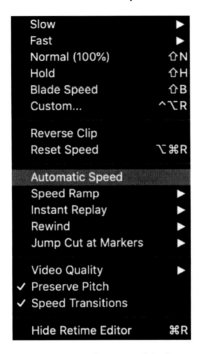

Figure 13.36: Show every frame with Automatic Speed

Automatic Speed is especially helpful with B-roll clips that are slightly off the correct frame rate. If your timeline is at 24fps or 25fps, but you've been given footage at 30fps, just apply Automatic Speed and they'll play just slightly slower than normal, using every frame available and giving a slightly slower, quite appealing look. Note that this will affect audio speed too, though the on-by-default **Retime** > **Preserve Pitch** option will prevent chipmunk noises.

However, you won't always need to choose Automatic Speed because many cameras perform a slow-motion conversion for you, at least with the highest frame rates. For example, a GH5 set to record 180fps will actually perform an "automatic speed conform" by recording all of those frames to a file with a "regular" frame rate, anything from 24fps to 60fps:

Figure 13.37: The Panasonic GH5, in "VFR" mode, converts a higher frame rate into a lower one in-camera

The file will claim to be that slower frame rate and will play for a much longer time than you recorded. Therefore, it's been pre-conformed and you don't need to slow it down (though you might choose to speed it up).

Outside of special high frame rate modes, most cameras will accurately tag a clip's frame rate up to 60fps, and you'll need to choose Automatic Speed to slow down these clips yourself. You'll be able to find out what your camera does without too much trouble, but in general, frame rates up to 50fps or 60fps are treated as normal while frame rates higher than that are likely to be slowed down in camera.

A good strategy for footage that you *might* want to slow down is to record at double your normal frame rate: 50fps rather than the usual 25fps or 60fps instead of 30fps. That gives you the option to easily slow any part of it down to 50% though you may have to compromise on shutter speed.

> IMPORTANT NOTE
>
> To satisfy the 180° shutter angle rule, a shutter speed of 1/(double the frame rate) gives the appropriate amount of blur. Shooting at 1/50 for 25fps, 1/60 for 30fps, 1/100 for 50fps, and 1/120 for 60fps would be ideal. So, if you shoot at 50fps but then use the footage at 25fps, the footage will appear slightly choppier than usual, with less motion blur. You can see this in real-world productions too — if it's a little choppy, expect a speed ramp at any moment. But don't worry too much about this rule at higher speeds; there's little blur to be had.

The bottom line: for the best quality slow motion, record more frames than your timeline requires.

REVIEW — RETIMING

Just a few years ago, high-speed recording was only possible at the high end of town. And while many cameras still struggle to record at high speeds, phones have come to the rescue. In many cases, you'll trade some image quality to achieve those higher speeds, but even 50fps or 60fps footage can be used effectively to create beautiful B-roll. With only regular-speed footage, Optical Flow can help, but there's no substitute for real frames. Start out with high-speed footage and simply set it to Automatic Speed if you want to use every frame you've shot.

But what if you don't? If you've got enough frames, you can go "full manual" to create a fast-slow-fast attention-grabbing piece. And that's up next.

SPEED RAMPING AND MORE

In this section, you'll find out all about speed ramping, in which a clip's speed changes over time. You'll also find out about freeze and hold frames, when to use a few trick-shot techniques, and the extra settings that can make all the difference for a tricky speed change.

So far, we've adjusted the speed for an entire clip, but a speed ramp involves a change in speed: slow to fast or fast to slow. There are two main ways to create a speed ramp:

- Select a region of a clip (with the **Range Selection** tool or **I** and **O**) and then choose a new speed for that region from the Retime menu:

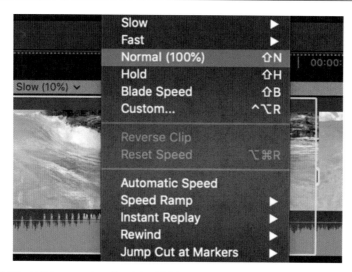

Figure 13.38: With a region in this 10% speed clip selected, I can return that section to 100%

- Hover above a selected clip then break it up into speed regions with **Retime** > **Blade Speed** (⇧B, not the regular **Blade** tool). Choose a new speed for each region from the **Retime** menu or the **Retime Editor** pop-up menu:

Figure 13.39: Create new speed regions, then change the speed in each

With both these techniques, the clip will be split into two or more speed regions. Each region has its own speed, and the speed ramp is created by an automatic transition, a gray box that bridges the two regions in the **Retime Editor**.

Each region's speed can be adjusted by using the pop-up menu in the **Retime Editor** or by the single-line handle on the right-hand side.

The transition duration, and therefore the length of the speed ramp, can be adjusted by dragging on either side of the gray transition zone:

Figure 13.40: Drag the gray transition edges to govern how long the speed change takes

To use this effectively, you'll ideally want a fresh clip where something exciting happens in slow motion. The clip should start out at normal speed, playing right up until just before the key moment — a bike flying off a ramp, an indie musician jumping, or a drink being spilled on someone — the moment of amusing disaster. Find that moment, and then:

- If you prefer to use the **Range Selection** method, select from the key moment forwards, then choose **Retime > Slow > 10%** to get started.

- If you prefer **Blade Speed**, hover just before the key moment, press ⇧B, and then use the Retime Editor pop-up menu on the second part to choose **Slow > 10%.**

Either way, you'll then want to finesse the length of the speed transition to make it longer or shorter. In general, a shorter transition period works best. Next, to enjoy the aftermath at normal speed, do one of these:

- If you prefer to use the **Range Selection** method, select from where the key moment has ended, then choose **Retime > Normal 100%**.

- If you prefer **Blade Speed**, hover just after the key moment ends, press ⇧B, and then use the **Retime Editor** pop-up menu on the second part to choose **Normal 100%**:

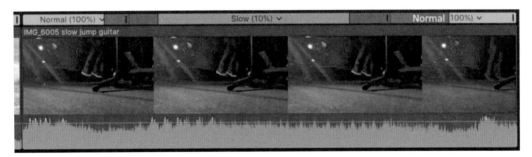

Figure 13.41: When you're done, this is what your clip should look like

You'll see three speed regions set to **100%**, **10%**, and **100%** and you can finesse the duration of that second speed transition as needed.

If something's not quite right, it's possible to use the Range Selection tool again, selecting parts of existing speed regions, and then choosing a new speed, even 100%. However, if you have placed the speed regions at the wrong points in the clip, a little too early or late, it's not obvious how to fix it. Dragging the single-line handle at the end of the Retime Editor changes speed but not the part of the clip that's been selected. To effectively roll the transition point between two speed regions, follow these steps:

1. Double-click the single-line retime handle between two speed regions on the **Retime Editor**:

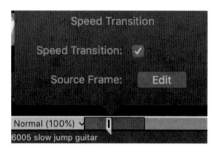

Figure 13.42: This popup will appear

2. In the small popup that appears, click **Edit** next to **Source Frame**.

   A small control appears, in the shape of a piece of film, just under the Retime Editor.

3. Drag the frame control left and right along the top of the clip's thumbnail to move the point where the speed change happens:

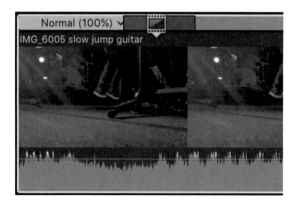

Figure 13.43: Dragging this icon performs a roll between different speed regions

4. Double-click the frame control to return to the retime handle.

This is extremely well hidden but very useful. Picking the right point to begin a speed ramp is as important as getting an edit in just the right place, and you'll master it with time.

As well as the **Edit** button, the small popup you saw in that process also allows you to remove a speed transition completely. Speed transitions can also be removed in the main Retime menu.

If you've made a big mess and want to start from scratch, do the following:

- Choose **Retime** > **Reset Speed** (⌥⌘R) to remove all speed changes from the clip.

It's often easier to **Reset Speed** than to fight with several regions.

USING SPECIAL SPEED MODES

While I normally prefer to create speed ramps by hand, there are some "trick shot" modes that perform complex tasks. They're available in the **Retime** menu and are:

- **Speed Ramp**, **to 0%** or **from 0%** — This creates several blended regions that slow down a clip to a standstill or speed up from a standstill. I find I rarely want to come to a complete stop, so I don't use this often.

- **Instant Replay** (various speeds) — Play the clip at normal speed, then play it again at normal speed or slowed down, with an "Instant Replay" title. The title can, of course, be replaced or deleted, but usually, I'd prefer to duplicate the clip with an ⌥-drag, then slow down the second clip.

- **Rewind** (various speeds) — Play the clip at normal speed, then play backward at normal speed or faster (4x) is good, then play the clip again. This can be fun:

Figure 13.44: The Rewind mode is good when you just want to see something again

- **Jump Cut at Markers** — When you apply this to a clip with markers, it skips a chosen number of frames at each marker point with speed changes while keeping the clip continuous. It's for special occasions.

HOLD FRAMES AND FREEZE FRAMES

In educational and other videos, it's common to pause a clip midway, to be able to draw attention to some aspect of it, before playing the rest of the clip. There are two ways to pause a clip, and the method you choose will depend on how you prefer to manage your timeline. If you want to keep a clip whole and use speed changes, do the following:

- Hover where you want to add a pause, then press ⇧**H** to add a **Hold Frame**:

Figure 13.45: This clip pauses with the Hold Frame integrated into the clip

A **Hold Frame** is a speed region with 0% speed, shown in Red. The duration of a Hold Frame can be changed by dragging the standard single-line handle in the Retime Editor.

If you would prefer that the still frame become an entirely separate clip, do the following:

- Hover where you want to add a pause, then press ⌥**F** to add a **Freeze Frame**:

Figure 13.46: This clip also pauses but via a separate Freeze Frame clip

A **Freeze Frame** functions much the same as a **Hold Frame**, but it creates three separate clips. These are the first and second parts of the video, and a new still image in between, which can simply be trimmed to change its duration. A downside is that any effects or color corrections will now need to be managed independently. However, this can be a good strategy on longer clips, if managing multiple speed ramps on a single clip is becoming unwieldy.

Either of these techniques can be used with titles, for example, to pause between subsequent bullets, but you'll have to turn the title into a Compound Clip first. There'll be more on that in *Chapter 15, A Few Words: Titles and Generators*.

RECAP — RETIMING AND SPEED RAMPING

Speed changes are a great excuse to dust off that old action camera and get moving or at least to blow a raspberry to a slow motion camera. It's always hilarious. Start simple, then build up complexity when the situation demands it. Timing is everything.

SUMMARY

If you're not editing a feature film or serious short, straight cuts are not always enough. Transitions can help you to smooth the relationship between two shots, sure, but they can also grab attention on their own. Maybe the shots around a transition need breathing room, a creative connection, or a way to keep them separate or you're disguising a cut you had to have. Or maybe the content is boring, and you need to inject some life to keep the audience awake. Even my least favorite transition, Page Peel, can justify itself in the right context.

Retiming brings a whole new dimension to clips that a video effect can't — playing with time. Newer cameras have given us the power to record footage at higher frame rates than ever before, and with or without all of those extra frames, you now have a way to bring attention to specific moments.

Transitions and retiming can be used for great things, but they can also contribute to wildly over-the-top edits. So, yes, you could shoot everything in slow motion and use every transition possible, but most edits can't justify that. They really are fun, but... *just because you can doesn't mean you should*.

When you're ready, head back here to learn how to fix your audio.

REVIEW QUESTIONS

1. What shortcut key displays the **Transition Browser**?
2. Where on a transition should you drag if you want to change its duration?
3. How do you quickly duplicate a transition to another edit?
4. What transition creates new frames to seamlessly blend out a jump cut?

5. What feature incorporates frames from elsewhere on the primary storyline into a transition?

6. What color does the **Retime Editor** use to indicate a speed up?

7. If you want to change the speed of a clip but not change its duration, what should you do?

8. What does **Automatic Speed** do?

9. What **Video Quality** setting creates new frames rather than blending or repeating other frames?

10. What's the shortcut for **Blade Speed,** to create a new speed region?

REVIEW ANSWERS

1. ^⌘5 (**Control-Command-5**).

2. On its edges — but only on its lower edges if handles are visible at the top edges.

3. ⌥-drag it.

4. Flow.

5. Timeline pins.

6. Blue.

7. Choose **Custom speed**, then uncheck the **Ripple** checkbox before changing the speed.

8. Plays every frame of the source clip at the timeline's frame rate.

9. **Optical Flow.**

10. ⇧B (**Shift-B**).

14 BOOST THE SIGNAL: AUDIO SWEETENING

"To me, "driving" Final Cut Pro feels the same as taking control of an Autodesk Flame or Smoke — you truly feel like an artist and a musician, where the tools can keep up with your mental thought process."
— Chris Hocking, LateNiteFilms, co-developer of CommandPost,
latenitefilms.com

With the picture looking good, this chapter shows how audio can be improved, or *sweetened*. To make sure you have some appropriate content to work with, we'll begin by recording an original voiceover. With those fresh voiceover clips in hand, we'll move on to audio adjustments. Starting with simple controls over volume, you'll discover more complex ways to animate (or automate) volume over time. Few recordings are perfect, so you'll find out how to remove problematic parts of the audio such as background hiss and hum, how to massage levels in subtle ways, and how to apply more complex audio effects for compression, advanced **equalization (EQ)**, and special effects. Lastly, you'll discover the special tricks that Roles can perform when combined with Compound Clips. In bullet form, the following topics will be covered:

- Recording and editing a voiceover
- Adjusting volume levels
- Audio enhancements
- Applying and using audio effects
- Using Roles with audio

> **IMPORTANT NOTE**
>
> While you can often figure out a lot of visual techniques yourself, it takes more effort to become really good at audio. It's also true that something that sounds good to you might not sound so good to an audio engineer — they're hearing things wrong with your audio that you hadn't even considered. Some of that is down to their higher-quality speakers or headphones, and some of it is simply their better-trained ears. If you're new to audio, you've got more to learn than you thought.

This chapter's goals are modest: to teach you how to make your audio sound better. Audio is a complex field that's not easy to explain in a static medium like a book, and while you might not finish this chapter as an expert, you'll hopefully leave it better informed.

Different types of productions will use very different kinds of audio, but a common addition to many productions is a voiceover narration, and it's also a good way to recap how split edits and fades can help. To get started, let's get your voice on a timeline, and then trim and fade it to fit.

RECORDING AND EDITING A VOICEOVER

Here, you'll use the built-in **Record Voiceover** tool to capture and edit a voiceover, using whichever microphone you have available. Though we're adding a narration to an edit already in place, workflows can vary widely — you might get a voiceover early or late in the process. However, postponing the official voiceover recording until the edit is near-final allows for late script changes, or limited availability of voice talent. Stay flexible.

> **IMPORTANT NOTE**
>
> To obtain a recording suitable for final output, a high-quality microphone will need to be set up in a good environment for audio recording, and connected to a high-quality audio interface. For temporary recordings, you can use the built-in microphone in your Mac, but for professional work, you might need to invest in some extra gear, such as a high-end USB microphone or an XLR microphone with an external interface device. Some audio recorders (including many made by Zoom) can also function as external interfaces.

As it's much easier to judge timing with a voiceover than without, a good workflow is to record a temporary *scratch* audio track yourself, based on the first draft of the script. You can edit the video to match that draft voiceover, and even suggest changes where the script doesn't quite match the video captured:

Figure 14.1: Scratch audio (the disabled clips highlighted here) helps you edit to a script before the final audio is ready

After the final script has been delivered to a voiceover artist, they can provide you with final audio files, and you can replace your draft voiceover in the edit. For other Projects, you might actually provide the final voiceover yourself, perhaps adding it quite late in the process as we are here. Whatever works for you is fine, and to get started, choose **Window > Record Voiceover** (or ⌥⌘8):

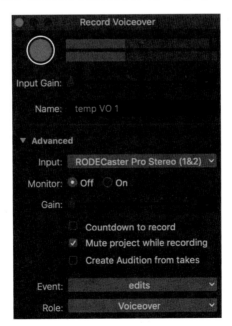

Figure 14.2: Recording a voiceover straight into a Project while tagging it with a new Subrole

Clicking the big red button will add a new recording to the timeline at the current Playhead or Skimmer position, and it'll stop when you click it again. The options here are mostly self-explanatory:

- **Name**: The name that will be given to the newly recorded voiceover clip.

- **Input**: The recording device and channel(s) being used. Note that the "Stereo" option pictured is actually from a mono microphone, and this is common.

- **Monitor**: When **On**, you can hear the recording through your current output device. To avoid feedback, this should only be used when you're wearing headphones.

- **Gain**: A virtual volume knob that some devices offer — the interface referenced in the preceding illustration has hardware volume controls instead of virtual ones.

- **Countdown to record**: If active, a visual and audible countdown plays before the official recording begins.

- **Mute Project while recording**: If active, the current timeline is silenced while recording. Essential if not using headphones.

- **Create Audition from takes**: Combines multiple recordings at the same timeline position into a single Audition clip. Very useful if you are going to be recording multiple takes, as the different takes will end up as separate Audition picks in a single clip.

- **Event**: The Event in the **Library** where the recording files will be stored.

- **Role**: The Audio Role that will be assigned to the recordings. Use **Dialogue**, or create a special Role or Subrole especially for voiceovers if you'd like to treat them differently.

To begin, you'll want to assemble a few clips in the timeline that could have a voiceover added. A more complex timeline with connected clips is fine; anything that would benefit from a narrator. With that ready, here are the simple steps:

1. Open **Record Voiceover**, and choose either your built-in microphone or another connected microphone from the **Input** menu.

2. Make sure that when you speak, the level meters are moving, and that they aren't too loud (peaking in the red on the right) or too quiet (barely moving in the green on the left).

    Higher quality audio devices will record lower levels of noise. Recordings made with better devices can therefore be made much louder without also amplifying background hiss, so it's worth investing in good equipment and preparing your environment if you plan to use these recordings in your final delivery.

3. Click on a spot in the timeline where a single sentence could be added.

4. Click the red button (a circle) and then speak a few good words into your built-in microphone, leave a pause that's slightly too long, and then say a few more good words.

5. Press the red button (now a square) to stop recording.

You'll see that your recording has been added to the timeline as a connected clip:

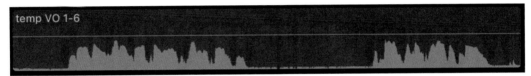

Figure 14.3: A voiceover recording with a pause in the middle

If you were now to use the **Range Selection** tool to select and then delete the unwanted section of the clip, you'd be left with two independent clips, and the second would be in the wrong spot:

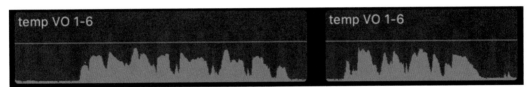

Figure 14.4: Deleting a part you don't want would create two
independent clips

Instead, while the voiceover is still selected, wrap it up first:

1. Press **⌘G** to wrap the voiceover clip inside a Storyline.

2. Press **R** to switch to the **Range Selection** tool, select the unwanted pause, and then press **delete**.

Now, you'll see that the gap between the two good parts is closed as you delete the unwanted pause:

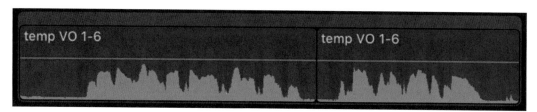

Figure 14.5: Deleting part of a clip inside a Storyline removes the gap too

If there's any kind of audible glitch around the edit, perform the following steps:

1. Select the two clips and press ⌥T to add a **Crossfade**.

2. Double-click the waveform to expand one or both sides of the edit.

3. If needed, drag the fade handles to fade the ends of the two clips where they meet.

4. If needed, change the type of fade by right-clicking each fade handle.

5. If needed, trim the video component on either or both sides to overlap the two audio waveforms:

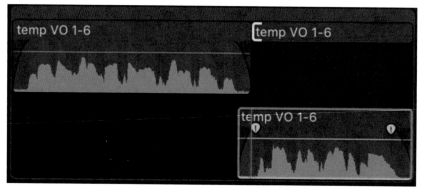

Figure 14.6: Pauses can be removed entirely with fade handles and trimming

While a short recording like this could simply be deleted in full and re-recorded, Storylines are a great way to clean up any longer recordings. One of my favorite techniques when reading an entire script is to **cough loudly** whenever I make a mistake, and then repeat the problematic phrase before continuing. This makes it easy to spot the mistakes visually in the finished waveform, and I can select the bad parts with **Range Selection** and hit **delete** without even listening back to them:

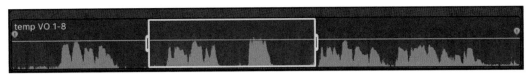

Figure 14.7: The mistake and the cough are selected for easy deletion

Professionals make mistakes too, and scripts are sometimes revised after voiceover recording is complete. It's therefore sometimes necessary to chop apart professional voiceovers in order to steal a fragment of audio (a word, a syllable, a few seconds of room tone) from one spot and re-insert it somewhere else. The rough workflow is as you'd expect:

1. Select and copy what you need from the source clip.

2. Skim to where you want it and paste.

3. If you need to remove part of the original recording, **Blade** the destination to make an insertion point, and then drag the new audio fragment to that spot.

4. **Crossfade** with ⌥T, then trim, expand the audio, and adjust the fades to get the job done.

If you only need to add content, the new clip can be independently connected, but a Storyline (connected or Primary) is a big help if you'd prefer to close gaps as you work.

Locations have their own sound, so don't forget to re-introduce room tone if you take out a few words and need to add a pause:

Figure 14.8: The not-quite-silent room tone clip below fills in the gap
created by the edit above

Split edits and fades within a Storyline are a great way to make audio edits sound seamless, and there a few more techniques related to the **Position** tool back in *Chapter 10, Explore a Little: Compound Clips and Timeline Tricks.*

By now, you'll be familiar with the editing part — chopping up clips should be second nature. You've also probably dragged audio volume levels up and down a little as part of the editing process. Next, you'll find out how to take those adjustments further.

ADJUSTING VOLUME LEVELS

A clip's volume, or audio level, is one of its most obvious properties. You can hear it, and you can see it (in a few forms) in the Browser, Inspector, and Timeline. Audio levels have been discussed in passing throughout the book so far, so while this shouldn't be unfamiliar, there's definitely more to learn.

The unit used to describe audio volume is decibels, or **dB**, and it's used in both absolute and relative ways. However loud a clip is recorded, on a timeline it starts out at a neutral **0 dB**. Adjustments made to that clip are relative, going from a louder **+12 dB** all the way down to the silence of **-∞**:

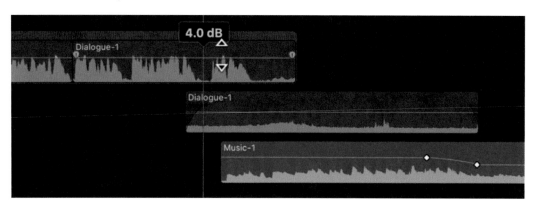

Figure 14.9: Audio volume levels on a few clips

When you play back a timeline, it's quite different. All sound playing at a particular moment is summed together, creating an absolute value, also measured in dB, and visible in the **Audio Meters (⇧⌘8)**. These dancing meters show the total audio at any point in time, with the previous peak recorded by thin lines on the meters and by numbers at the top of each channel:

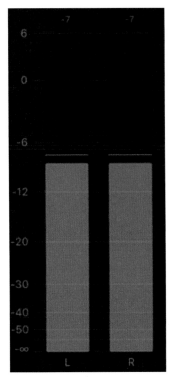

Figure 14.10: The full-size audio meters sit in the lower-right corner

The output value should always remain negative, and its level should vary depending on your target output. The old rules for TV delivery stated that you should average around **-12 dB**, with the loudest sounds (peaks) at **-6 dB**. While that largely carried across to online delivery, there's no widely used standard, and some videos peak louder than this, around **-3 dB**. The only agreed standard is that you should never hit (or go past) **0 dB** because that will cause distortion.

> IMPORTANT NOTE
> If you have to deliver to a platform with more stringent requirements, such as a streaming service, cinema ad system, or TV station, you'll have to follow their specifications closely. Standards vary internationally, but are likely to involve a more complex measurement of loudness over time. Many higher-end workflows perform final processing with a third-party application or plug-in (and leave the scope of this book), but it's possible to do it from FCP, too.

To get started, you should first make a Workspace that makes audio easier to work with, and then we'll tackle the basic controls, before moving on to more complex animated controls.

CREATING A CUSTOM AUDIO WORKSPACE

Way back in *Chapter 1, Quick Start: An Introduction to FCP*, you learned about Workspaces, which let you instantly show or hide any combination of panes at whatever sizes you choose. As there's no pre-defined Audio Workspace, making one now is a good way to understand Workspaces better:

1. Press ⌘0 to start with the **Default** Workspace.

2. Choose **Window > Show in Workspace > Audio Meters** or press ⇧⌘8.

3. Make the **Audio Meters** wider or narrower (as you wish) by dragging on the left edge.

4. ⌥-**click** the green window control in the top-left corner of the interface to make sure the main window takes the maximum space possible.

5. Double-click the title bar of the **Inspector** to expand that pane to the full height of the window.

6. Click the word **Index** to the left of the central gray bar, or press ⇧⌘2, to open the **Timeline Index**.

7. In **Timeline Index**, click **Roles**.

8. Save the workspace by choosing **Window > Workspaces > Save Workspace as**.

9. Name your workspace `Audio`.

All done, and you should see your new custom Workspace in the **Window > Workspaces** window. If you also want to increase the height of clip waveforms, use the settings in the **Clip Appearance** popup just to the left of the **Effects** icon to focus on audio waveforms while hiding or shrinking video thumbnails:

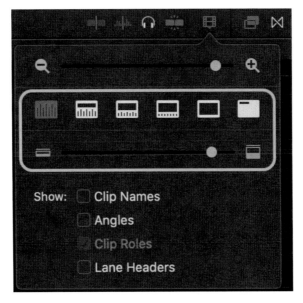

Figure 14.11: Use the highlighted options together to control how big the audio waveform is

You can also try adjusting clip height with ⇧⌘**plus** and ⇧⌘**minus**. (Finally, you might also choose to add **Effects** to this workspace later.) Here it is:

Figure 14.12: A usable Audio Workspace with a full-length Project

While you continue with the rest of the chapter, leave your volume set at a consistent level so you can judge your changes as you go. If you have high-quality speakers, do use them, but remember that you should always preview your work on a variety of output devices, including built-in computer speakers, headphones, and mobile devices too.

Though audio devices vary widely in their quality, you can always use an objective visual measure to judge volume: waveforms. More on those now.

UNDERSTANDING WAVEFORMS

The basics of audio levels were mentioned in *Chapter 7*, *Cover It Up: Connections, Cutaways, and Storylines*, and audio fade handles were covered in *Chapter 8*, *Neaten the Edges: Trimming Techniques*. We'll take volume a little further here, and to understand everything, you should prepare a timeline with a person talking and some music behind it. If you've already edited a piece, that's fine, but just a plain single-camera shot and any audio track behind is fine too.

Each clip that includes audio will show a waveform, just below its visual thumbnail (if any). As you'll remember, the **Clip Appearance** popup menu in **Timeline** can control how large the audio waveform is, and you might want to bump up the size of the audio waveforms now. The keyboard shortcuts ⇧⌘**plus** and ⇧⌘**minus** can help with this:

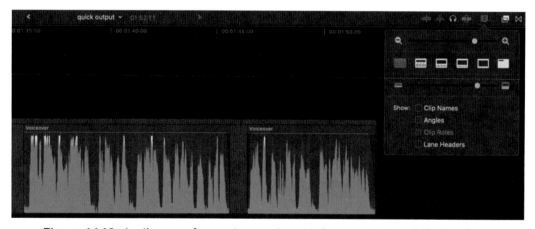

Figure 14.13: Audio waveforms, larger than before and potentially too loud

The height of these waveforms tells you how loud a particular piece of audio is. Gaps between sentences are clearly seen by a valley between peaks. Low-level noise is shown by the valleys never hitting the true floor. Peaks that turn yellow are getting loud, and peaks that turn red are probably too loud. Adjusting the volume levels will change the height of the waveforms and therefore their color. How do you make the peaks the right height? Let's cover this in the next section.

CHANGING VOLUME LEVELS

On top of the audio waveform, you'll see a line, and this line controls the volume. To adjust the line directly on the clip, you have a couple of options:

- **Drag the line up or down** to move it quickly.
- **⌘-drag the line up or down**, moving it slowly (gearing down) for greater precision.

You can also use keyboard shortcuts to adjust one or more clips. Select them, and then press one of these:

- **^plus** to increase volume (+1 dB)
- **^minus** to decrease volume (-1 dB)

Those two commands live in the **Modify > Adjust Volume** sub-menu, alongside:

- **Silence (-∞)**
- **Reset (0 dB)**
- **Absolute (^⌥L)**
- **Relative (^⌘L)**

The **Absolute** and **Relative** commands allow you to define a new value from scratch (Absolute) or expressed as a change from the existing value (Relative). Each command uses the timecode display below the Viewer to show the change that's going to occur, and like typing a timecode, you can type a positive or negative value, followed by **return**:

Figure 14.14: Absolute and Relative volume adjustments appear just below the Viewer

Finally, if you prefer to use the **Inspector**, you'll find **Volume** right at the top of the **Audio** tab, with a slider, a number that can be dragged or typed into, and even the familiar keyframe controls. However, you'll probably ignore these and use the visual **Timeline** display instead:

Figure 14.15: Volume controls and keyframing in the Inspector

Setting the overall level of a clip is an important first step, and if a single clip is to be the dominant sound at any one time, the waveforms should probably be peaking in yellow, but not moving to red. This color indication can vary between mono and stereo clips, so check the final output to be sure:

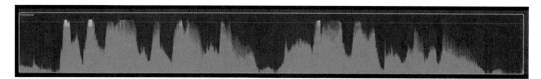

Figure 14.16: This clip is getting a little loud in parts

If you're hearing lots of audio (sound effects, music) at once, you can't judge the overall audio by an individual clip's waveform, and you'll have to watch **Audio Meter** to see the timeline's total audio level. It uses similar color markings, but the numbers are more important.

No matter how you adjust the volume, you'll almost certainly find a clip that is loud in some parts and quiet in others, and that's where you might need to set different volume levels over time.

CHANGING VOLUME LEVELS OVER TIME

To change audio levels in different regions, it's easiest to use the timeline. Volume changes, often called automation, are keyframe-based, and you can use the same keyframe techniques:

1. **⌥-click** on the volume line to create a keyframe at a point in time.

2. **⌥-click** elsewhere on the volume line to create a keyframe at a different point in time.

3. Move either keyframe up or down to change the volume at that point.

4. Move either keyframe left or right to change its position in time.

Excess keyframes can be deleted with a right-click and choosing **Delete Keyframe**:

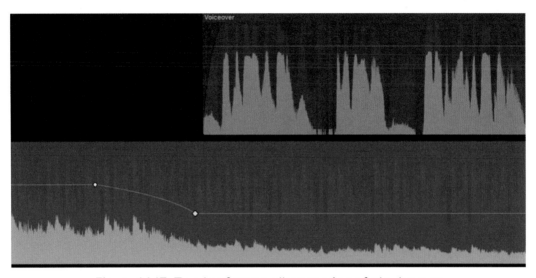

Figure 14.17: Two keyframes allow music to fade down to
a lower level and stay there

That technique works when you only want to make two keyframes, such as music that starts at full volume, and then fades down to background levels to make room for someone speaking. However, when you want to dip or raise the audio level temporarily, you'd have to make four keyframes. Let's take the example of music that dips underneath someone speaking (called **ducking**) and consider where the keyframes would be placed:

- At the start of the change, to mark the start of the fade down
- A second or two along, to mark the end of the fade down
- Further along, at the start of the fade up, at the same level as the previous keyframe
- A second or two along, at the end of the fade up, at the same level as the first keyframe

With four keyframes added, you would see this:

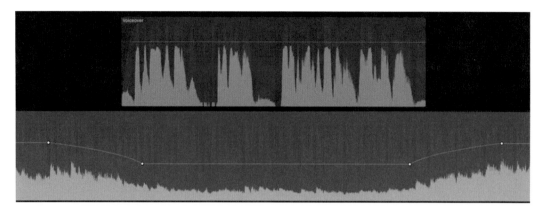

Figure 14.18: Four keyframes to control the music underneath a
person speaking

If you were to do this by manually placing keyframes, you'd have to ⌥-**click** four
times. While the keyframes are the outcome you want, there's a much easier way to
do the same thing with **Range Selection**:

1. Choose the **Range Selection** tool (**R**).
2. Click and drag to select an area of a clip:

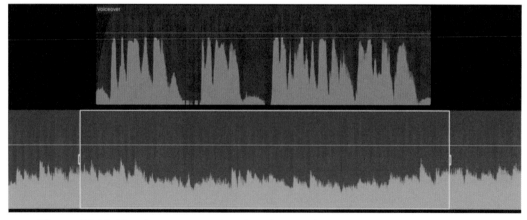

Figure 14.19: Here's a range selection, just before dragging the volume line

Alternatively, use **I** and **O** to select a Primary Storyline clip.

3. Drag the volume line in that region (or use any of the previously discussed techniques):

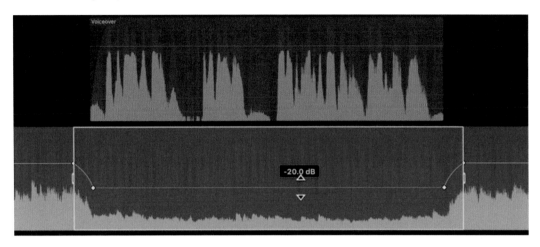

Figure 14.20: Four keyframes, created in one step

This technique is faster and easier, and creates four keyframes that can be moved as needed. Move the outer keyframes outward to make the fade less abrupt, and move the line between the two central keyframes to adjust the lowered volume. Two keyframes can be selected and moved at once by moving the line connecting them.

Do note that if you use the shortcuts (**^plus** or **^minus**) to change volume by **1 dB**, existing keyframes are retained, and moved up or down. To remove all keyframes and start again, use **Modify > Audio > Absolute** or **Modify > Audio > Reset**.

IMPORTANT NOTE

Before you go crazy adjusting the volume a little bit here and a little bit there, in order to try to equalize a clip's volume across its entire length, know that some effects can do this (to some degree) for you, and we'll be looking at them soon. By all means use volume controls for manually ducking audio, but don't proceed with minor tweaks until you've applied some common audio effects.

Finally, you'll remember from *Chapter 8, Neaten the Edges: Trimming Techniques*, how to fade volume at the ends of a clip using audio fade handles. These provide a better way to start or end a clip softly because they move with the clip edges as a clip is trimmed. Keyframes don't move unless you move them yourself:

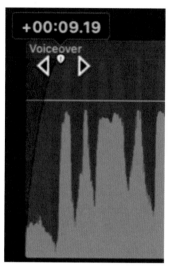

Figure 14.21: Hover over the edges of a clip's waveform to see the audio fade handles, and then drag them inward

Now that you have a handle on volume, you'll need to understand what's happening in a more complex workflow. The good news is that most simpler cameras will just record two channels, and they are likely to be detected correctly in most situations. However, if your devices record multiple channels in each clip, you'll want to pay attention to **Audio Configuration** before tackling the full audio workflow.

UNDERSTANDING AUDIO CONFIGURATION

At the bottom of the **Audio** tab in the **Inspector**, you'll see a section called **Audio Configuration**, and you may need to drag a small separator up to expose it. This section will help you make sure you use the right part of your recordings, which may have been a stereo recording, a mono recording, or something fancier. You can adjust panning (audio position in space, in **Stereo** or **Surround**) later on, but you'll need to make sure that your clips are tagged correctly first:

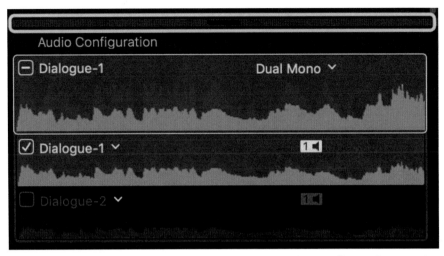

Figure 14.22: Here's a Dual Mono clip in the Audio Configuration section, with the separator line highlighted above

With a clip selected, you'll see whether the clip is one of the following:

- **Mono** (one channel)
- **Dual Mono** (two channels)
- **Stereo** (two channels, left and right)
- **Reverse Stereo** (two channels, right and left)
- **Multitrack** (multiple channels, such as in a Multicam clip or from a multitrack recorder)

One type of source can be switched to another if it is incorrectly interpreted, and individual channels can be disabled if they aren't needed. For example, some devices record the same mono microphone input to two tracks at two different recording levels, one channel at a normal level, and the second channel at a lower level. If the recorded sound becomes too loud in the first channel, you can fall back to the second channel instead to avoid distortion. Audio such as this should be interpreted as **Dual Mono**, and the loudest clean channel should be used. So, if it was incorrectly tagged as **Stereo**, manually interpret it as **Dual Mono**, and then turn off the channel you don't need with the appropriate checkbox as shown:

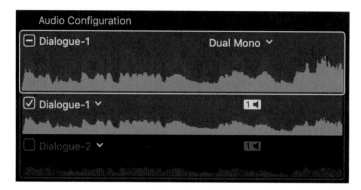

Figure 14.23: The first track was fine, so we don't need the second

If this clip had been interpreted as **Stereo** and no components deleted, all the audio will be slightly panned to the left, as the first channel was louder. This is a surprisingly common problem online, so make sure that you check your final output on a stereo speaker. And if your audio is Stereo but the mics are transposed (each in the wrong channel), you can choose **Reverse Stereo** now to fix it.

With a single speaker, things will be pretty simple. However, more complex Multicam audio situations can require a little extra work, and here's how you can manage the process.

ADJUSTING MULTIPLE AUDIO CHANNELS

In most Multicam or multi-track recordings, you'll probably use just a single channel of audio — whatever sounds best. But if the chosen microphone has an issue at some point, how do you switch to a backup? And how do you actively incorporate audio from multiple microphones at the same time, as in a multi-person audio recording? There are a few extra tricks for dealing with audio components in the timeline.

You'll remember that double-clicking on an audio waveform expands audio, moving it below the video and allowing for split edits. When there's more than one channel, here's an extra trick:

- **⌥-double-click** an audio waveform to expand audio components.

Now you can see all the audio components at the same time. To control each channel separately, you can use the volume controls already discussed, adding keyframes and so on, or explore an additional neat trick. With a multi-component clip on the timeline, and audio components visible and active, perform the following steps:

1. Switch to the **Range Selection** tool (**R**).

2. Select part of one of the audio waveforms that you want to enable or disable.

3. Press **V** to turn that section off:

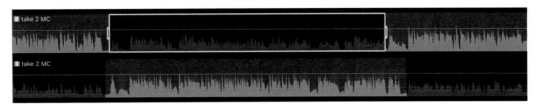

Figure 14.24: With some sections enabled and others disabled

The section of audio goes dark, just as it would if the entire track was disabled. Pressing **V** again will bring it back if you change your mind. But let's soften those transitions first.

4. At the edge of the disabled audio section, hover near the volume line until you see the teardrop-shaped audio fade indicator.

   That's right — the audio fades that appear at the edges of clips work here too.

5. Drag the teardrop audio fade indicator sideways, toward the enabled section, to add an audio fade:

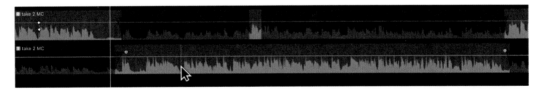

Figure 14.25: With fades applied, and some overlapping areas

If the edges of any of these regions are in the wrong place, they can be rolled, and you'll see the roll cursor pop up as you hover over the edges:

Figure 14.26: Edges in the wrong place? Just roll them to where
you want them

This technique allows you to jump between active microphones or use both at once. This way, you can record two or more subjects independently, and then use as many or as few channels as you wish in the final edit. There's no need to blade, no need to detach audio, and it's a softer approach than simply switching audio along with video in a Multicam clip.

One minor gotcha, though. As you work with multiple channels at once, remember that if you hover over a single channel and then tap the **spacebar**, you'll only hear the channel that the red Skimmer is currently visible on. To hear everything, first hover in the timeline bar or in empty space nearby to let the Skimmer cover all channels:

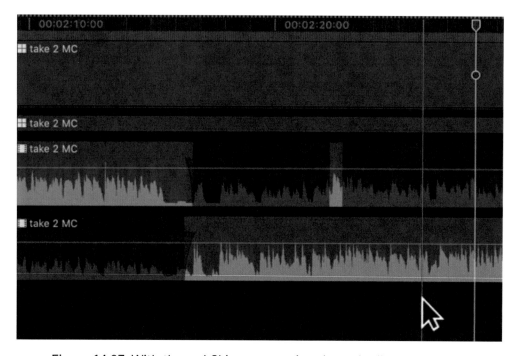

Figure 14.27: With the red Skimmer passing through all channels, it's all audible

For a more complex edit, with multiple subjects visible and audible at once, you may also wish to position them within a stereo soundfield. That means controlling *panning* as well as volume, and here's how.

ADJUSTING PANNING

Most Projects use **Stereo** sound, and so this is simply the positioning of each audio source in a left-right one-dimensional space. The most common workflow is to ignore this entirely: mono microphones sit in the middle, and stereo background music means that there's a little liveliness in the stereo soundfield. But you can do more, by positioning mono microphones in stereo space. Some cameras will record stereo audio, which is good for environmental sound (atmosphere), but most dedicated microphones are mono, and end up dead center by default.

If you want to position your subject in space more flexibly, look for a **Pan** control below **Audio** enhancements in the **Inspector**. Show it if necessary, and then follow these steps:

1. Choose the appropriate channel setup in **Audio Configuration**, setting **Mono** for one channel or **Dual Mono** for two.

2. For **Dual Mono** only, in the individual channels below, select the channel you wish to adjust by clicking on it.

3. Under **Pan**, choose **Stereo Left/Right**, and then an **Amount** underneath.

Zero is center, negative values pan left, and positive values pan right; each channel can be set to a separate position in space to roughly approximate a sound source's position. This isn't strictly necessary in most productions, but it's a nice touch. Panning can also be keyframed, using the standard controls, to accommodate movement within a frame:

Figure 14.28: This clip is now positioned a little to the right

Now, if you want to get really fancy, and your delivery platform can handle it, consider delivering to a surround setup. Your Project can be set to *5.1 surround* in its settings, and then you can position any clip in not just 1D space, but 2D space, all around the viewer:

Figure 14.29: Switch your Project to Surround with the Inspector's Modify button here — fun to use, but harder to deliver

At a simple level, you can switch panning to **Basic Surround** and then drag the puck to wherever you'd like it to come from. If you don't have time, use some quick fixes:

- **Dialogue**: Positioned mostly toward front center
- **Ambience**: Positioned more toward the surround (rear) speakers
- **Music**: Positioned evenly across the surround space:

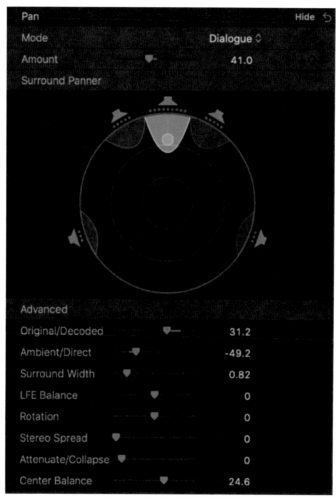

Figure 14.30: The Dialogue surround panning mode emphasizes the front speaker

And if you're animating a pan, pay more attention to what the **Amount** control does. Choosing one of these options might not appear to do anything, but the Amount slider behaves very differently in each of the options here:

- **Basic Surround**: A left/right pan within surround space
- **Create Space**: More of a central/front bias; uses more of the surround field at 100
- **Dialogue**: 0 means no effect, 100 is all the way to front center
- **Music**: Evenly spread around, uses more of the surround field at 100
- **Ambience**: 100 pushes the audio to surround only, and 0 returns it to the middle of the space
- **Circle**: Audio comes from a specific area in 360° space
- **Rotate**: Any existing audio position is rotated in 360° space
- **Back to Front**: Moves from the back to the front of the surround space
- **Left Surround to Right Front**: Like a bullet shot, from behind on the left flying past you to ahead of you on the right
- **Right Surround to Left Front**: Like a bullet shot, from behind on the right flying past you to ahead of you on the left

These options are pretty cool, but as you can't currently deliver surround sound to popular video sharing sites, most people won't hear it. Until more delivery methods become available, these techniques are only important for fancier deliverables. Support is improving, so don't be surprised if surround becomes more popular over time:

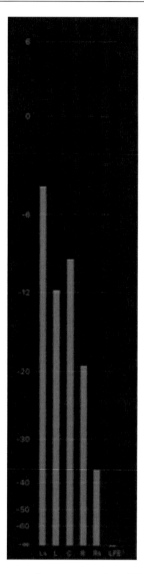

Figure 14.31: These meters tell you exactly which speakers the audio is being sent to

REVIEW — ADJUSTING VOLUME LEVELS

The audio volume controls were a great place to start, and keyframes let you take it a lot further. Add in fade handles, stereo, and surround panning, and you should now be able to make everything sound as loud as you need it to, and make it come from the right places — even in a complex, multi-channel audio situation.

Now that volume and panning are pretty close to sorted, it's time to find out how to change the way audio sounds, starting with the built-in Audio Enhancements.

AUDIO ENHANCEMENTS

This section explores how to make audio sound better in a few simple ways, making use of a dedicated section in the **Inspector** called **Audio Enhancements**. By the end of this section, you'll understand what can be done here, as well as what can be done better elsewhere. Note that if an audio clip has multiple components, you may need to select a single component (by clicking on it) before you can adjust the options shown here.

At the top of the list is **Equalization**, often known as EQ, and that's followed by **Audio Analysis** and its **Loudness**, **Noise Removal**, and **Hum Removal** subsections. These are by no means the only ways to make these changes to clips, but they are simple, and built in:

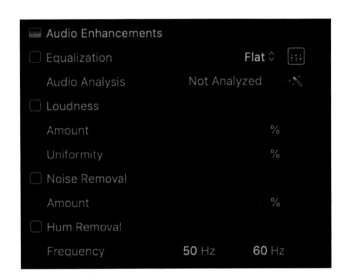

Figure 14.32: The Audio Enhancements section of the Inspector

In fact, if you check **Analyze and fix audio problems** on import, some of these options may already be active, and if that's the case, turn them all off so that you're starting fresh:

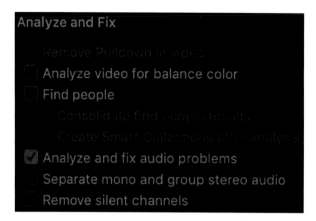

Figure 14.33: Auto analysis on import? I'd leave this off

Bear in mind that these are always the first things applied to a clip, before any other audio effects, and, as you'll find out, that can sometimes be a limitation. Now it's time to dip into EQ.

EQUALIZATION

Every sound is made up of waves traveling at specific frequencies. A low frequency (bass) sound is deep, like a bass drum or a tuba, while a high frequency (treble) sound is a sharp, piercing noise like a violin or a child's scream. While many headphones advertise a frequency range of something like 20–20,000 Hz, most humans can't hear that full range, and most speakers can't reproduce it anyway. But that's OK, there's plenty to work with.

Equalization lets you increase the volume of certain frequencies while decreasing others, enhancing some kinds of sounds while making others less audible. You can use EQ to make one clip sound a little more like another, to emphasize or de-emphasize an aspect of a sound, or to do something special. One neat trick is to edit the EQ for a piece of music, turning down the frequencies that speech uses. That makes speech placed over that music sound clearer, and means that any volume change (ducking) doesn't need to be as obvious:

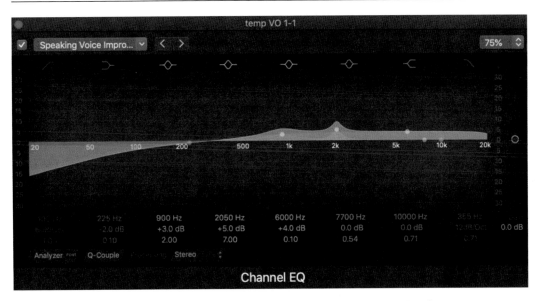

Figure 14.34: The Speaking Voice Improve preset in the fancy
Channel EQ effect

While the Equalization section of Audio Enhancements does allow for a range of presets as well as full manual controls, there are more advanced EQ options in Audio Effects, and we'll get to those soon. We're just getting started.

MANUAL EQ

To begin, you'll want to hear what a clip sounds like, before you add any EQ. And if anything is playing at the same time, it's a good idea to focus on just the one clip. To hear the clip on its own, without background music:

1. Select a clip in the timeline.

2. Press the **Solo** icon, the headphones between **Audio Skimming** and **Snapping**, or press ⌥S.

   Now, only that clip can be heard, and all other audio is grayed out and disabled. You can click the **Solo** button once again to bring it back.

3. Activate looping by choosing **View** > **Playback Loop Playback** (⌘L) and making sure the menu option is checked.

   When looping is active, you can also see a ring around the **playback** button below the Viewer.

4. Play just the selected clip by pressing **/** (slash).

   This is the **Play Selection** command. Listen to the clip once or twice to make sure you know what it sounds like. If the clip is too long, you can use the **Range Selection** (**R**) tool to select just a range, and then press **/** once again.

   Now it's time to experiment. Currently, the EQ is *Flat*, or deactivated.

5. As the region plays, try several different options from the **Equalization** menu, and listen for the differences.

   You should be able to clearly hear the difference between opposing settings, such as **Treble Boost** and **Treble Reduce**, but it's easiest to see them visually, and there's an interface for that.

6. Push the small button next to the **Equalization** menu.

   This activates the advanced equalization window, which looks like this:

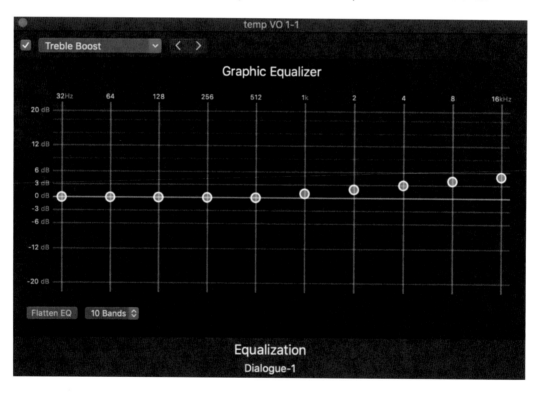

Figure 14.35: Treble Boost pushes up the higher-end frequencies

At the top left of this window, you can see a menu from which you can choose the same presets as before. In the body of the window, you can adjust pucks corresponding to any of these frequencies independently. It's also possible to drag a selection across multiple bands and then adjust selected pucks together, but be careful: to select multiple bands this way, you have to start your drag on one of the lines, not one of the pucks, and not the empty space between the lines. Instead, it's easier to **right-click and drag across all the pucks at once** to set new values instantly.

To the bottom right of the window, the **Flatten EQ** button resets the panel, and the pop-up menu allows you to switch between *10 bands* as shown previously, and a more precise *31 bands* option shown next. This lets you be more selective about which frequencies are adjusted, but now that you have more sliders to play with, it can take more effort to get the job done:

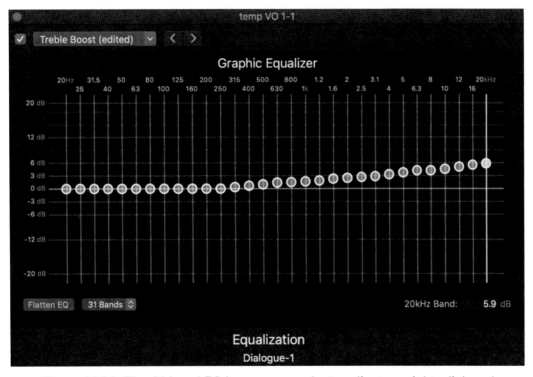

Figure 14.36: The 31 band EQ has many pucks to adjust, so right-click and drag to set them all at once

What's the goal? Trying to remove unwanted sounds, and enhancing the good ones. If there's a rustle, or a hum, or mic handling noise, you can try reducing sliders where you think the frequencies are, and moving to other frequencies until you isolate the problem. It's not always possible to invisibly remove a sound unless it's very localized to a particular frequency, but sometimes it works wonders.

This window is a good place to start with EQ, but for more powerful adjustments, including a visual display of the frequencies being used in a particular clip, you'll want to use specific advanced audio effects instead. We'll look at them soon, but there's a unique trick to the built-in EQ feature, called **Match EQ,** that's worth a quick look.

MATCH EQ

The Match EQ feature provides a very quick way to make two clips sound more similar by applying a custom EQ. Like the **Match Color** feature, it can't be turned down, though it can be turned off. You'll need two audio clips: a target clip, and a source clip. For good results, the two recordings should share some similarities but not all; they could feature the same person in two different environments, or the same person through two different recording devices. With those two clips on a timeline:

1. Select the target clip you want to change.

2. Choose **Match** from the EQ menu or **Match Audio** from the **Audio Enhancements** menu (the magic wand icon at the lower left of the **Viewer**).

3. Click on the source clip.

4. Click **Apply Match** to apply the effect:

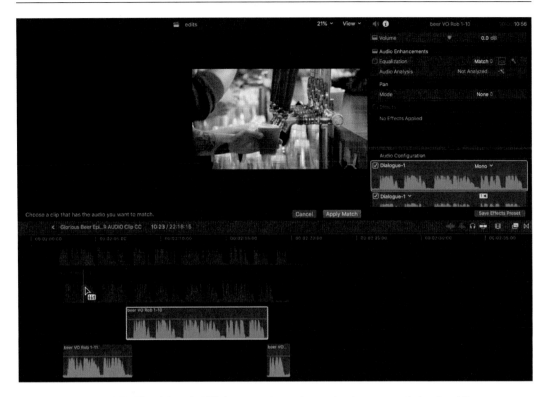

Figure 14.37: The Match EQ in progress doesn't show much in the Viewer,
but follow the instructions below it

5. Play the selected clip with **/**.

With any luck, you'll be able to hear the difference, and also hear that the selected clip now sounds more similar to the source clip. To try again, you can repeat the same steps, or press the new **microphone icon** that has appeared to the far right of the Match menu to pick a new source clip.

Pressing the button immediately to the right of the Match menu brings up a new window, where the Match EQ effect is shown, and you'll see that this is a more complex adjustment than a simple band-based EQ:

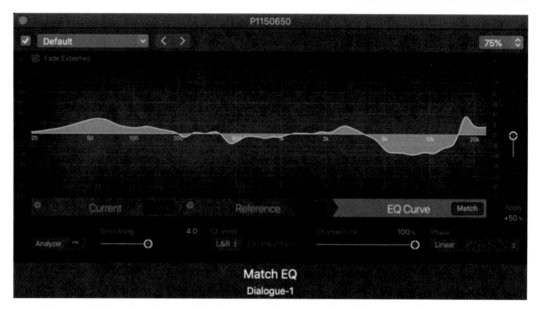

Figure 14.38: The Match EQ dialog, with two quite different clips as source

I find that this feature does do a decent job quite quickly and, if nothing else, it's useful as a starting point for further work. To apply a Match EQ from one clip to another, you can copy it and then select **Edit > Paste Effects** or **Paste Attributes**, just as with video effects.

After EQ, the other Audio Enhancements are worth a look, even if you don't use them often, and we'll look at them in top-down order.

AUDIO ANALYSIS

The next three sections (*Loudness*, *Noise Removal*, and *Hum Removal*) can be activated automatically, if analysis deems it necessary. Personally, I prefer to leave this off and apply these fixes manually as required, but if you want to try the fully automatic experience, click the **Magic Wand** button next to **Audio Analysis**. That button analyzes the clip and turns the next few sections on if needed, and in fact, you can do this analysis during the import process if you're in a hurry:

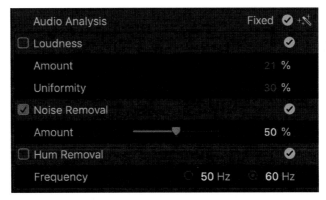

Figure 14.39: Was the noise problem here magically fixed? Doubtful

If a problem is detected but you decide to turn the correction off, you'll now see a yellow or red warning symbol next to that area. Easy to use, convenient... so why don't I like to use this? Read on to find out more about these adjustments.

LOUDNESS

This is actually more of a complex effect than you might think; it doesn't just turn up the volume, but applies *compression*, turning up quiet parts of the audio to make the audio level more consistent. This reduces the dynamic range of the clip, and it's a key part of the audio processing workflow. However, if there's any noise in your recording, you should remove that noise before applying this effect, and unfortunately, **Loudness** is applied early, straight after EQ. Therefore, if there's any noise or hiss in your recording, this feature can amplify it, and make it harder to remove — a limitation of its early processing position. For more advanced workflows, you'll want to use Audio Effects instead.

NOISE REMOVAL

Noise and hiss are incredibly common, and include both self-noise (from cheaper microphones) and background noises (air conditioning, traffic, and so on). While this feature does remove noise, it can reduce the quality of what's left, leaving audible artifacts, like a robot talking underwater:

Figure 14.40: At 27%, this shouldn't sound too robotic, but you might still hear some noise

By default, this will be set to 50%, and I find that it can cause problems at more than 30%. Personally, I use a third-party noise reduction plugin later in the process because this feature is good, but not great.

HUM REMOVAL

With good production practices, you won't need this. From time to time, electrical interference (often near cables) can cause an audible hum at the frequency of the electrical system in your country (50 Hz for PAL territories, 60 Hz for NTSC territories). If this happens to you, choosing the correct frequency will remove it nicely. Note that there's an EQ option that does a similar job:

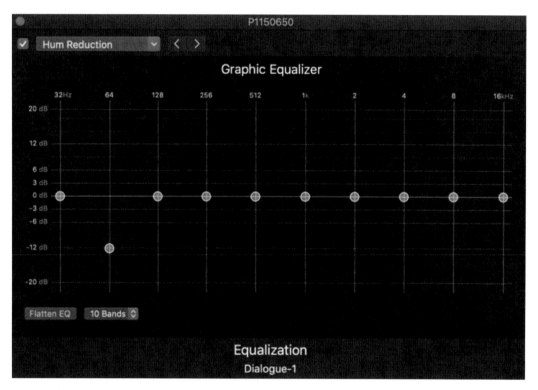

Figure 14.41: The Hum Reduction EQ option if you want more control

However, the EQ option, at 64 Hz, is a little less specific than the dedicated **Hum Removal** option, which targets 50 Hz or 60 Hz.

REVIEW — AUDIO ENHANCEMENTS

As a quick fix, these options are appreciated, but if you've got more time, their limitations become obvious. Match EQ is useful for a rogue recording or two, and the other EQ options are useful for simple tasks. Still, just as I don't trust a camera's automatic white balance, I'd be very wary of trusting my final output to fully automatic audio analysis. Loudness, Noise Removal, and Hum Removal are important, but you might not find all the controls you need here.

To take things further, you may wish to control the order in which operations are performed. For this, along with far more subtle controls, audio effects are the way to go. Many are built in, and they are easy to use.

APPLYING AND USING AUDIO EFFECTS

To make audio sound clearer, or make voice more robotic, or to compress dynamic range, or distort it in all kinds of crazy ways, you need audio effects, and you'll learn about many of them here. As you might expect, audio effects function much like video effects, and are found at the bottom of the same **Effects Browser** interface pane. There's a wild variety of included effects (including many from Apple's Logic Pro) and third-party effects are also supported, so you'll be able to cover most tasks.

> IMPORTANT NOTE
> Audio effects can be added to individual clips, to components of clips, or to many clips at once. While we'll approach this simply at first, applying effects to entire clips, you'll find out how to deal with more complex workflows in the following section, *Using Roles with audio*.

In this section, you'll discover the basics of audio effect editing, find out how to access some of the more adventurous interfaces, find out what your goals should be when sweetening audio, and use some built-in effects as a starting point to process voice. We'll start with the basics, and it should feel familiar after the last chapter.

ADDING AUDIO EFFECTS

To get started, you'll need to see the Effects Browser:

- Show the **Effects Browser** by pressing ⌘5 or by clicking the icon second from the right in the central gray bar.

As you'll remember, in the sidebar you'll see **Video** effects on top and **Audio** effects beneath:

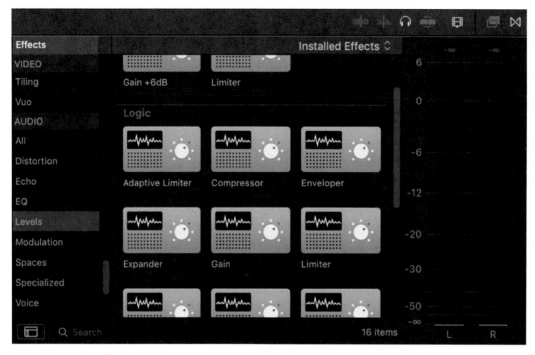

Figure 14.42: The Levels effects within the Effects pane

It's simple to look only at audio effects, or to look at a specific category:

- Click **All**, just under **Audio**, to see all the audio effects in the pane to the right.
- Click any category name to see only the audio effects in that category.

Audio effects can, of course, be previewed before being applied, but you'll need to activate **Audio Skimming** first:

1. If it's not already active, press ⇧**S** to activate **Audio Skimming**.
   The Audio Skimming icon will light up blue when it's turned on.
2. Hover (skim) over an effect to hear that effect applied to the selected clip.
   As with video effects, this is only a preview of the default setting of an effect. To apply an audio effect to a clip, one of these will work:

- Select one or more clips in the timeline and then double-click an effect to apply it.
- Drag an effect to a clip in the timeline.

As usual, verify that the effect has been applied by skimming over it (if Audio Skimming is still active) or just playing it.

For a quick demo, we'll apply some fun effects and play with the settings. Using a voice clip you recorded earlier would be perfectly appropriate.

3. **⌥-click** on a clip to select it and move the Playhead to that point.

4. In the **Effects** pane, click on the **Echo** category.

   Within this category, you'll find headings separating three types of effects: **Final Cut**, **Logic**, and **macOS**. While it doesn't matter where an effect came from, the Logic-based effects tend to be more sophisticated, and with more extravagantly diverse interfaces. Let's throw on something crazy first.

5. Drag the **Delay Designer** effect to your clip.

   This is one of the **Logic** effects, and you'll be able to clearly hear what it does.

6. Play the clip back by pressing **/**.

7. In the **Inspector**, without stopping playback, choose one of the other options from the extensive **Preset** menu:

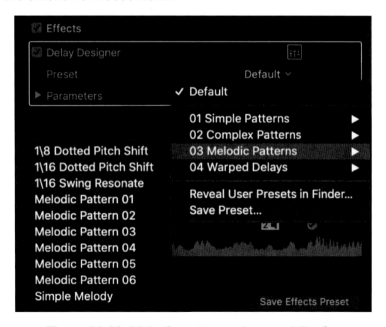

Figure 14.43: Melodic patterns do sound like fun

There are sufficient options here to keep you busy for a few minutes, and some of these options sound awesome.

8. When you're done, click the small controller icon to the right of **Delay Designer**.

A new window will appear with many dials, graphs, and controls:

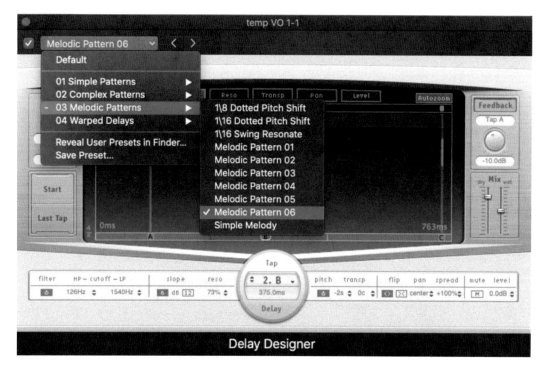

Figure 14.44: This is one of the tamer skeuomorphic interfaces in audio effects

Every Logic-based effect is a little different, but you'll find it easiest to get started by choosing new presets from the menu in the top left and seeing what changes.

9. Explore the dialog, switching tabs at the top, clicking and dragging, and figuring out what some of the settings do.

Everything can be tweaked, but to explore even this one effect in depth would take some time; there's a lot going on. Be careful, as some settings (such as the **Feedback** option to the right) can produce deafening results. If you do find settings that you'd like to use again, you can save them.

10. From the **Preset** menu in the top-left corner, choose **Save Preset...**:

Figure 14.45: The presets are at the effect-level for Logic and macOS effects

11. Type a name and then press **Save**.

Not all effects work in the same way. While the **Logic** and **macOS** effects include their own presets in their menus, the **Final Cut** audio effects don't. This is because they are a little like native FCP **Effects Presets**; each one combines one or more individual audio effects to create a pre-determined outcome. The individual components can be tweaked, but you're stuck with the built-in preset options. In some cases, the preset choices will actually change the underlying effects.

If you'd like to explore these effects, perform the following steps:

1. **⌥-click** on another clip to select it and move the Playhead to that point.

2. In the **Effects** pane, click on the **Echo** category.

3. Drag the **Echo Delay** effect to your clip.

4. Play the clip back by pressing **/**:

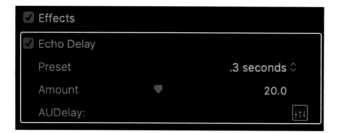

Figure 14.46: A default Echo Delay in the Inspector, using the AUDelay effect

In the Inspector, you'll see that the controller icon is next to the AUDelay line rather than the effect name. AUDelay is actually one of the other effects in this category, down in the macOS section.

5. In the **Inspector**, change to **Metallic PA Echo** in the **Preset** menu while it's playing:

Figure 14.47: Echo Delay after switching to a different preset, with a different underlying effect

You'll now hear something quite different, and see that the underlying effect changes to **AUDistortion**.

6. In the **Inspector**, change back to **.3 seconds** in the **Preset** menu while it's playing.

7. Click the small icon to the right of **AUDelay**.

8. In the window that appears, click and drag in the graph vertically (to change feedback) and horizontally (to change the delay):

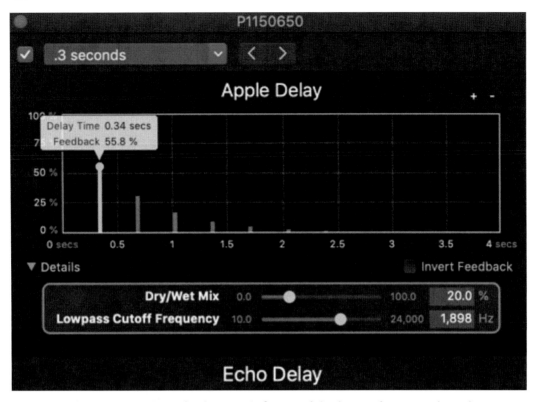

Figure 14.48: Drag in the graph for a quick change in strength and delay time

Other controls are available in the sliders below, and this is obviously a much simpler interface than **Delay Designer**. While it's less powerful, you'll find it much easier to understand and to tweak. The top-left corner of this effect gives you access to the same **Preset** menu that the Inspector offers, but can lead to big changes:

9. In the floating window, change to **Metallic PA Echo** in the **Preset** menu:

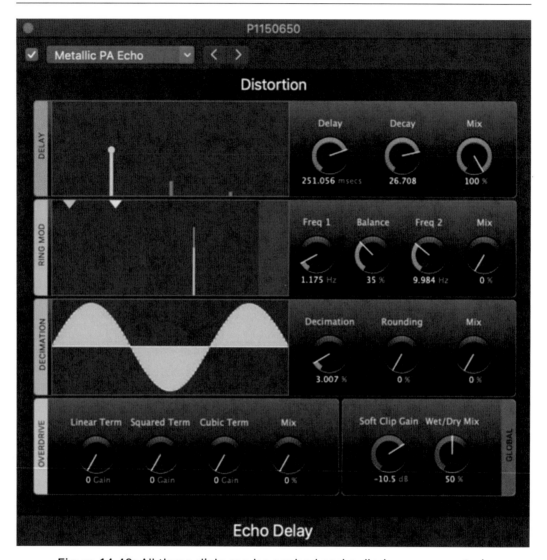

Figure 14.49: All these dials can be pushed and pulled — more control,
but more to learn

You'll see that the underlying effect (and the visual display) changes from **AUDelay** to **Distortion**, an effect from a different category that nevertheless can produce an echo. There are many dials to play with here, and it's worth experimenting with them. When you're done, close the window.

While most effects do include a **User Presets** system, the **Final Cut** group of audio effects do not. To access presets for the individual effects inside one of these (such as AUDelay or AUDistortion inside Echo Delay), you'll have to find those original effects in the **Logic** or **macOS** sections instead.

You can tweak an effect's manual settings no matter how you applied it, and you can create your own combinations of multiple effects, too.

To re-use the current clip's effects, including all current parameters, you should click the **Save Effects Preset** button at the bottom of the Inspector, as you did for video effects in the previous chapter:

Figure 14.50: Saving an Audio Effects Preset for a collection of audio effects

When you save a preset, be sure to only include the sections you want to re-use. **Volume**, for example, may be keyframed, may need to change in any case, and should usually be unchecked here.

What effects should you be using in those presets? I'm glad you asked!

THE BEST AUDIO EFFECTS

In this section, I'll take you through some of the most useful standalone effects and effect combinations. If you'd like to add these to one or more of your clips, go ahead, but just remember the standard effect rules:

- Click the checkbox next to an effect's name to turn it on or off.
- To delete an effect, select it by clicking on its title bar and then press **delete**.
- To instantly remove all effects from a clip, press ⌥⌘X to **Remove Effects**.
- To selectively remove effects from a clip, press ⇧⌘X to **Remove Attributes**, and then check all effects to be removed and approve the dialog.

Along the way, we'll explore some of the goals you should keep in mind when sweetening audio.

DISTORTION

Honestly, all these options are fun, but none of them make your audio sound *better*. Instead, they all make the audio sound much worse, but in very interesting and configurable ways:

Figure 14.51: Ringshifter is a fun, crazy way to make things sound strange

The **Final Cut** effects here imitate outdated tech such as radios and walkie-talkies, while if you're looking for a fun **Logic** interface, **Ringshifter** is your friend.

ECHO

Echo Delay (as you've seen) is a simple option that works well, and **Delay Designer** has the craziest interface:

Figure 14.52: Many Logic effects have a modern, clean interface, like Stereo Delay

The other **Logic** effects here use simple dials and sliders, and should be straightforward to decipher.

EQ

This is where it gets pretty interesting, as the **Channel EQ** effect at the top and **Linear Phase EQ** under **Logic** provide a much more interactive way to look at your audio. There are many useful presets, but choose **05 Voice** > **Voice-Over EQ** for a quick voiceover fix. During playback, you can click the **Analyzer** button in the lower-left corner to see the active frequencies in a live graph (pre- or post-effect):

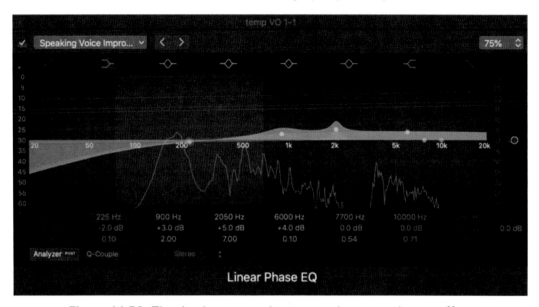

Figure 14.53: The Analyzer can show a graph pre- and post-effect
to see whether you're changing the right things

Each adjustment point on the graph can be pushed up or down manually, or by dragging the numbers under each one. For a simpler, more traditional take, try **Fat EQ**:

Figure 14.54: Fat EQ has an older look, and it's a little simpler too

The **Final Cut** effects here provide useful presets to remove high or low frequencies, making use of the **macOS** or **Logic** effects. Technical tasks such as high-pass and low-pass are well catered for here.

LEVELS

First to the basics. As the built-in volume controls can only increase volume by **+12 dB**, you'll need an effect to make a clip louder than that. The **Gain** filter can add another **+24 dB** (as well as phase inversion and stereo swapping), but it's not the only effect that includes a gain feature. The **Fat EQ**, **Linear Phase EQ**, **Limiter**, and **AUDynamicsProcessor** can do the same job, so consider them instead:

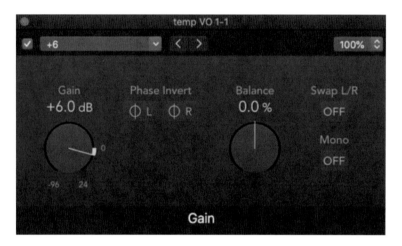

Figure 14.55: Gain is very simple, but you can get the same controls elsewhere

Next, the more advanced options, including the various limiters and compressors, are geared toward reducing the dynamic range between the quietest and loudest parts of a recording. **Limiter** and **Adaptive Limiter** are simple enough to understand: push up the input by some amount on the **Gain** dial, then turn down **Output** to the maximum level you want to hear, and the gaps between the quietest and loudest sounds are reduced, so everything comes out more even:

Figure 14.56: Push everything up, and then push the loudest parts down again

Logic's **Compressor** is more subtle, using **Threshold** and **Ratio** controls to govern the volume changes, and with a built-in **Limiter** at the end of the chain. This is a powerful effect that takes time to understand (read the built-in help!) and you'll need to tune the settings to suit:

Figure 14.57: Sounds above the Threshold are reduced according to the Ratio, Knee, and more

AUDynamicsProcessor is a lower-level tool with a graphical curves-based interface that shows you when audio is being shaped, and over which volume levels that shaping occurs:

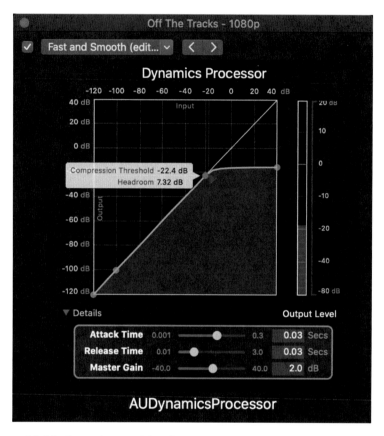

Figure 14.58: Sounds reaching into the red are reduced as the graph indicates, and Master Gain is applied at the end

Expander is the opposite of a **Compressor**, expanding the dynamic range to make your clip sound more lively.

IMPORTANT NOTE
Understanding the order of operations is important, and these levels-based controls are often applied as the final step in processing. Remember as you experiment here that you may wish to apply effects not just to individual clips, but to entire Roles at a single stroke.

Another effect to know about is **Noise Gate**, which silences quiet sounds below a certain threshold. This can be used as a simple form of noise reduction, but be careful that it doesn't sound too noticeable:

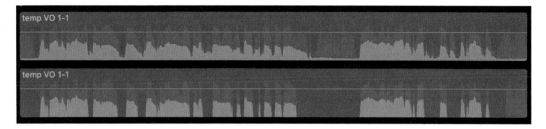

Figure 14.59: The Noise Gate on the lower clip is too strong — silencing not just quieter regions, but good audio too

Levels controls are valuable, and we'll return to them in just a moment when we look at the **Voice** controls.

MODULATION

These can best be described as *fun distortion*. **Phaser**, **Phlanger**, and **Scanner Vibrato** live here:

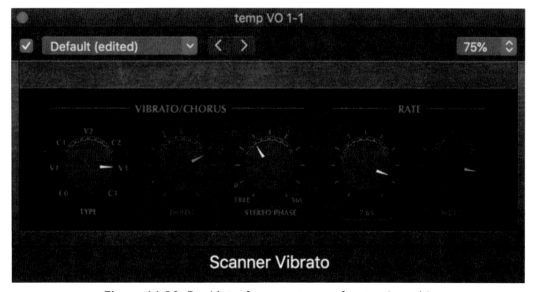

Figure 14.60: Real interfaces are more fun to play with

Not something you'll do every day, but if you want your voice to sound like a chorus of similar voices, this is a good starting point.

SPACES

This collection of reverberation and echo effects can make a recording sound like it was taken in a much larger room, even in a specific, real-world hall or cathedral:

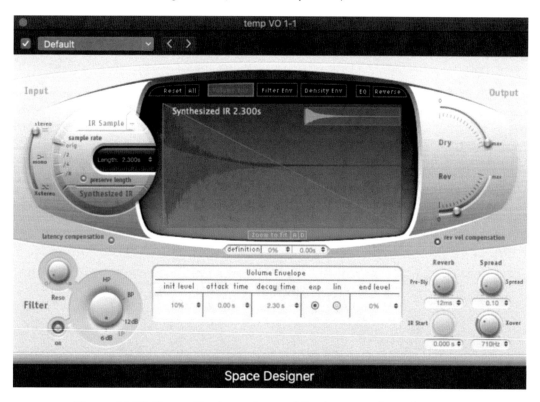

Figure 14.61: Space Designer has a ridiculous number of presets
to imitate the sound of real-world spaces

This is useful when trying to make a clip sound more like it was recorded in an entirely different space. For example, you might record replacement audio in a studio, but need that clip to sound as if it's in a large hall.

SPECIALIZED

This group of effects can be safely ignored unless you know you need them:

Figure 14.62: The Multimeter, if you want a deeper analysis

Test Oscillator turns your clip into a 12 dB test tone or a sine-based sweep; **Exciter** tries to add a little life; **Stereo Spread** tries to distribute mono sounds across both left and right channels. **Multimeter** provides some advanced monitoring tools, but not an auto-fix for broadcast deliverable audio levels.

VOICE

While most of these effects are for pitch-shifting or vocal silliness (Monster, Robot, Helium, Disguised), there's one standout worth further attention. **Voice Over Enhancement** provides an all-in-one fix for voice, combining a **Compressor** to equalize volume levels, a **DeEsser** to reduce sibilance, and a **Channel EQ** to enhance specific vocal frequencies:

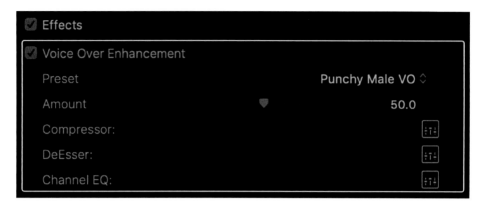

Figure 14.63: Tempting as an all-in-one starting point, but tweak to suit

The presets here provide different Channel EQ settings to enhance male and female voices for smooth or punchy results. This effect can be a great starting point for further tweaking to suit particular voices, and if you work with a voiceover artist regularly, consider saving a preset specifically for their voice.

THIRD-PARTY EFFECTS

Below all the built-in effects, you'll find any other effects that you've purchased from third parties. Not every audio effect designed for Logic Pro will work in Final Cut Pro, so check for compatibility (or test out a trial) before purchasing. Though there are many third-party effects available, if you only buy one, make it a good noise reduction plugin.

REVIEW — APPLYING AND USING AUDIO EFFECTS

Now you know: audio effects are a lot like video effects. Many effects are original, while others function like Effects Presets, and while it's easy to find something silly, the most useful effects are the most subtle ones. You know how to apply effects and make presets, so explore and get comfortable with your options. The categories have a fair bit of crossover, but you'll quickly find your favorites and learn how to tweak the settings to your liking.

If you work with voice, like many videographers do, focus your efforts there. Voice Over Enhancement is an effect that could well see a lot of use, and once you grow more confident, you'll be messing with EQ, compressors, and limiters to make the fussiest clients happy. But wait! Before you apply effects to every individual clip, consider an alternative workflow. Read on to find out how to use **Roles** for audio processing.

USING ROLES WITH AUDIO

Roles make audio processing simpler by allowing adjustments and effects to be applied to an entire class of audio, such as Dialogue or Music. In addition, Roles can make it easy to hand over isolated audio stems to another application for more specialized processing, and all without tracks. In this section, you'll learn about how the audio signal flow works, and how to use Compound Clips to control audio at the Role level. By the end, you'll know how to maintain the Roles you defined for your media (way back at import time) all the way through the production process.

UNDERSTANDING SIGNAL FLOW

The path that an audio clip follows from camera to export doesn't have to be complex, but you'll need to know what's happening to avoid a few issues. Applying an effect at the wrong point in the chain, or to a certain kind of container clip, can cause Audio Roles to be combined, and potentially cause some confusion.

> IMPORTANT NOTE
> This topic can be complicated, and since many readers won't need to worry about the finer details, I'll keep it brief here. For all the fine print, search for an online White Paper from Apple called *Audio Roles in Final Cut Pro* [currently available at https://www.apple.com/final-cut-pro/docs/Audio_Roles.pdf].

Each clip in a timeline can have multiple components, and while usually they would have the same Role (often **Dialogue**), that's not always the case. More complex clips, such as a Compound Clip, may combine different **Audio Roles**, such as **Music**, **Effects**, and **Dialogue**. It's also possible that a single clip might contain audio from multiple microphones that are assigned to separate Subroles:

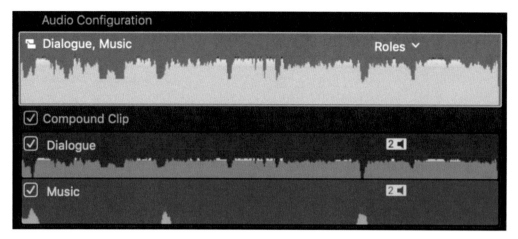

Figure 14.64: Dialogue and Music are present in this longer Compound Clip

In each of these cases, the separate Roles or Subroles are safely separated when viewing the timeline with **Audio Lanes**, and can also be exported independently. However, applying an effect to a clip that shares Roles or Subroles will cause the distinctions between these Roles to be lost, because the separate audio components are mixed together before any effects are applied. Instead, such clips are given a new *Mixed Audio* Role, which is less than ideal.

One solution is simply not to apply any effects at all, and let a dedicated audio specialist handle the job. That's certainly an option, but you don't have to go that far. Instead, if a clip has mixed Roles, apply effects to *audio components* rather than to entire clips. How is this done?

At the bottom of the **Audio** tab in the **Inspector**, you'll find the audio components section. In a simple clip, this will probably show as **Mono** or **Stereo** with a single component underneath, but if you've chosen **Dual Mono**, there will be two channels underneath, and in a Multicam clip, you'll see a channel for each angle's audio. Each can be selected independently, and when a single audio component is selected, any effects you add will be applied to just that component:

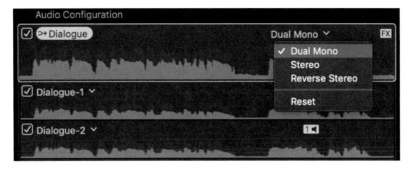

Figure 14.65: Choosing Dual Mono shows two individual channels underneath

The following points are important:

- If the first item underneath **Audio Configuration** is selected (as it is by default), then an effect listed above applies to the whole clip.

- If a component or channel is selected, effects shown above will only apply to that component. Those effects can only be seen when that component is selected, so be careful — effectively, *you can apply an effect to only one component of a clip*, and you won't be able to see that when selecting the whole clip.

The situation is a little different for Compound Clips. Instead of channels, the audio components section shows the Roles contained inside this clip. A drop-down menu to the right lets you choose whether you want to show **Roles** or **Subroles** as components below, and choosing Roles effectively mixes any Subroles together. You would choose Subroles if, for example, you had applied different Subroles to different character's microphones, and wanted to apply different effects to each one:

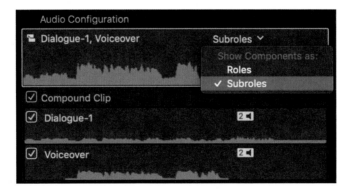

Figure 14.66: This Compound Clip has dialog from camera and a voiceover too

Multicam Clips will output their Role components based on the angle currently chosen. Due to the nature of Multicam Clips, those angles are likely to share the same parent Role, though each angle could use different Subroles.

Synchronized Clips will show separate Role components for their Storyline (the original camera audio, usually disabled) and the secondary audio (a separate track, usually enabled).

The outcome of all this? If Roles are important in your output, don't apply effects to clips with more than one Role, and if Subroles are important, don't apply effects to clips to multiple Subroles. Instead, do one of the following:

- Select a Role or Subrole at the clip level, and apply effects to a single component.
- Double-click a Compound Clip to open it, and apply effects to individual clips inside the Compound Clip.

These strategies are especially important when used with the **Timeline Index** to mix an entire timeline at once.

USING COMPOUND CLIPS FOR AUDIO MIXING

If applying effects to hundreds of individual clips seems daunting — don't. Instead, it's possible to apply effects to entire Roles at once, by turning your entire Project into a Compound Clip, and then viewing individual Roles or Subroles using the **Timeline Index**. It's going to be useful when exporting (in *Chapter 16*, *You're Done: Exporting Your Edit and Finishing Up*), but it's also useful for the audio mixing stage right now.

> IMPORTANT NOTE
>
> Before we continue, it's worth remembering that you don't necessarily have to follow these steps in this order, or even at all. Fairly simple jobs might use just a few audio clips, easy enough to deal with separately. On other jobs, you might be provided with fully processed audio that needs no work at all. And of course, you can tackle the audio processing in multiple stages in whatever order you wish. You might apply some effects to a few problematic clips, finish the visual side of the edit by adding titles, and then return for the final audio mix. Alternatively, you might do the final audio mix first in a Compound Clip, and then dip inside that Compound Clip to add the titles. Either approach is fine; don't feel constrained to strictly follow the order of every chapter in this book.

The first step before beginning an overall audio mix is to duplicate your Project, in case something goes badly wrong. For this exercise, you'll need a near-complete Project with several different Audio Roles, and Subroles if you'll be using them too. So, grab that TV pilot you've been working on (or a test Project with multiple Audio Roles) and follow these steps to get started:

1. In **Browser**, click to select your Project, and then press ⌘**D** to duplicate the Project.

2. Rename the new duplicate to add "audio mix" to the name.

3. Double-click the new duplicate Project to edit it.

4. Click in the **Timeline** pane, and then press ⌘**A** to select all its clips:

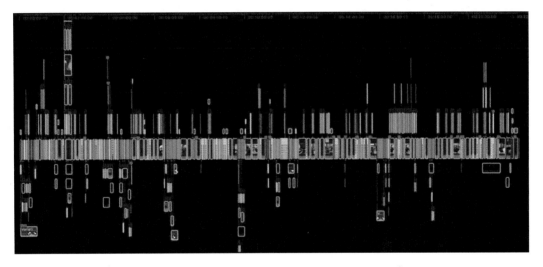

Figure 14.67: In a complex timeline, this might take a few seconds

5. Press ⌥**G** to convert the entire timeline to a new Compound Clip, and name it in the sheet that appears:

Figure 14.68: All combined into a single Compound Clip

6. If it's not already visible, show the **Timeline Index** by clicking **Index** at the left of the central gray bar or by pressing ⇧⌘**2**.

   You'll remember the Timeline Index from *Chapter 10, Explore a Little: Compound Clips and Timeline tricks*.

7. If it's not already selected, click **Roles** at the top of this pane.

8. Click **Show Audio Lanes** at the bottom of this pane.

9. In the **Clip Appearance** menu to the right of the central gray bar, check **Clip Roles** and then uncheck **Clip Names**:

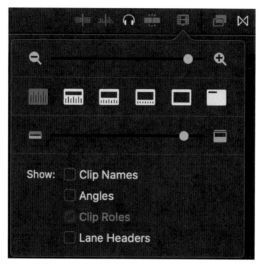

Figure 14.69: Showing Clip Roles instead of Clip Names to keep things simple

At this point, each Role within the Compound Clip is shown as a clip-length item in its own lane, with a small icon indicating that a mixdown has occurred:

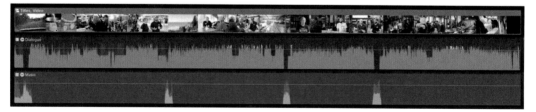

Figure 14.70: The audio in each Role can have effects applied or volume adjusted (this needs work!)

Each component can be adjusted just as easily as if it were a single clip, including volume adjustments, audio enhancements, panning, and effects. Selecting a component in the timeline selects the appropriate Role component in the **Inspector**, and everything works just as it does on individual clips.

If you've tagged your clips with appropriate Roles and Subroles, you can use this technique to do the following:

- Apply the same Voice Over Enhancement effect to every voiceover
- Apply different Voice Over Enhancement effects to male and female voiceovers
- Apply different audio effects to each character speaking
- Apply different compression or EQ effects to music, effects, and dialog
- Apply different volumes to music, effects, and dialog
- Apply different surround panning treatments to music, effects, and dialog
- Duck (reduce) the volume of all music and effects elements while a person is speaking

While overall adjustments are useful and powerful, you can still adjust the clips inside the Compound Clip, so don't be afraid to double-click your way inside. If a particular clip needs special treatment, go ahead and add that effect or change those levels. A Compound Clip doesn't need to be a locked-off silo, but usually the overall audio mix is a step you'd perform last, or near the end of the process.

REVIEW — USING ROLES WITH AUDIO

Roles are a unique feature for Final Cut Pro, and one which saves a lot of time. And even if you don't use Compound Clips to perform Role-level adjustments or add effects, you might want to use them to control how your work is exported — stay tuned to the final chapter for more on that. And finally, even if you're just exporting a simple video yourself, and don't need Roles for their mastering or export controls, you can use them simply to add color to your timeline. It's nice to be able to see what a clip does at a quick glance, and Roles do that too. Let's wrap this up.

SUMMARY

Audio is a critically important part of a video. Even though it's often treated as less important by an editor who's more aligned with the video side of things, bad audio will ruin a good video every time. The standard approach, to buy good equipment and use it properly, will work most of the time, but however careful you are, you'll need to be able to turn down that uncontrollable air conditioner or bird, level out that person who spoke at an inconsistent volume, and find a way to deal with the microphone that's rubbing on that jacket or suffering electronic interference.

Now that you know how to add a voiceover, control its volume, add effects, and manage Roles, those tasks are much easier. Because you also understand how Roles can be applied, more complex tasks should be easier too. With the audio taken care of, at least for now, it's time to look at the world of titling and captioning.

REVIEW QUESTIONS

1. Why would you record scratch audio?
2. If you make a mistake during a voice recording, what should you do?
3. How loud can the volume level be set?
4. What command increases volume by 1 dB?
5. If you reduce music volume underneath someone speaking, what is this called?
6. Where can you control which audio channels are audible?
7. Where could you position audio to come out of rear speakers?
8. What feature makes one clip sound more like another clip?
9. What effects can affect the difference between the volume of loud and quiet parts of audio without keyframes?
10. What feature describes the type of audio that an audio clip contains?

REVIEW ANSWERS

1. To give you something to edit with before the final audio is available.
2. Cough loudly during recording, and then look for the cough in the waveform.
3. +12 dB with the volume control, though audio effects can go beyond this.
4. **^plus** (Control-plus).
5. Ducking.
6. **Audio Configuration**, at the bottom of the **Audio** tab in the Inspector.
7. In the **Surround Panner**.
8. Match EQ.
9. Many effects, including **Compressor**, **Limiter**, and **AUDynamicsProcessor**.
10. Roles.

15 A FEW WORDS:
TITLES AND GENERATORS

"FCP X not only changed the lives of editors who use it in post production, it also changed that way those editors interact with directors/story-producers like me. I use it every day."

— Cirina Catania: filmmaker, host of OWC RADiO, a partner in Lumberjack System and most known for co-founding the Sundance Film Festival cirinacatania.com

Words are an important part of many videos, especially today. As more of us consume more video online, we're doing so in more places, often without audio, and augmenting the audio with words is a great way to compensate. Titles can be purely informational or can bring extra emphasis to important points, while captions allow anyone who can't hear your audio to understand what's being said. Generators fill in the gaps that your videos and photos can't, and give your work some extra flair.

In this chapter, you'll learn all about the process of choosing, adding, and manipulating titles, including an extra look at the most flexible general-purpose option, the **Custom** title. Generators are important too; they can provide not only backgrounds for titles but also ways for an editor to build complex composites, with built-in and third-party options available. You'll also learn about captioning, which is important for accessibility, searchability, and more.

In bullet-point form, you'll discover more about the following topics:

- Adding and editing titles
- Advanced title techniques
- Adding and editing Generators
- Captioning and subtitles

Titling is a key task, and the strong integration between Motion and Final Cut Pro (FCP) makes amazing titles easy. In other non-linear editing systems (NLEs), it's common to outsource production of titles to a separate motion graphics artist, or use extremely simple static titles that simply fade in and out. Here, you can do it all yourself, and you can go as crazy as the job allows, or create something with elegant, subtle movement that can enhance the most restrained timeline.

Usually, titles are used to add words, but you can enter emojis to include color symbols as well. It's also possible to use dingbat fonts such as Zapf Dingbats, Google's Material Icons, or FontAwesome to add custom symbols, arrows, and other shapes. If you're happy with single-color titles, these fonts (unlike emoji fonts) also work in 3D and are an excellent idea if you want to label a shot without words, or just point at something. An example can be seen in the following screenshot:

Figure 15.1: Yes – this 3D arrow is a title

The titling workflow in FCP is really excellent: fast, flexible, and powerful. If you want to go beyond what the built-in templates allow, you can build your own or modify any existing templates, with Apple's companion product Motion. But it all begins with a basic title, so let's get started there.

ADDING AND EDITING TITLES

In this section, you'll find out how to add one of the many built-in title templates to add a full-screen title, a lower third, or anything else you wish. You'll find out how to edit text parameters on every title, learn how to change any parameters that a particular title template has exposed for editing, and understand **Find and Replace Title Text**.

The very first titles we'll add are static, simple, and boring, but don't worry — we'll animate them soon enough!

To start, you'll need a timeline with some clips in it, and ideally, you'll also include a shot of a person who needs an onscreen title:

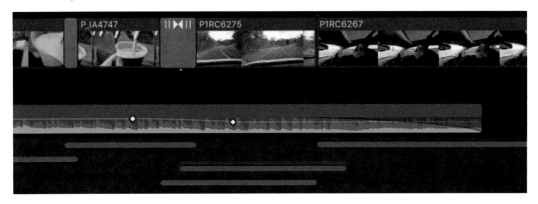

Figure 15.2: A timeline with a person needing a lower third title in the clip to the top right

Any resolution and frame rate will do, and when you've got it ready, follow these steps:

1. Click on the **Titles and Generator** icon at the top of the **Browser**, as shown here in blue:

Figure 15.3: The third icon along is the one you're looking for

2. In the **Browser**, click the small disclosure triangle next to the word **Titles**, to expose the categories within.

3. Click on the **Bumper/Opener** category.

All these titles can be previewed by hovering over them, though obviously you'll only see their default state this way:

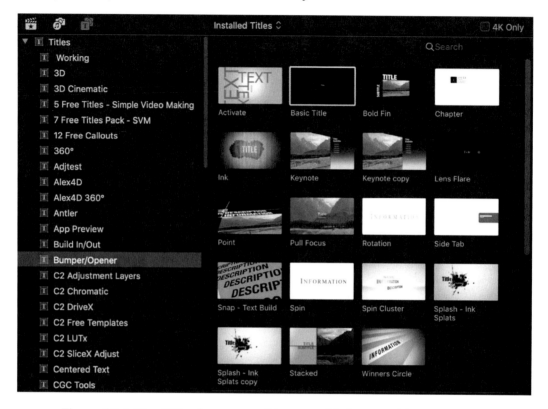

Figure 15.4: The Titles browser, with many third-party titles and some Motion-based experimentation too

4. Drag the **Basic Title** to a spot in the Primary Storyline.

Though each title defines its own standard duration, you can change its length by trimming, as you would with any other clip. Skimming over this particular title in the timeline will simply show the word **Title** in a default font, but each title is different. It'll look like this:

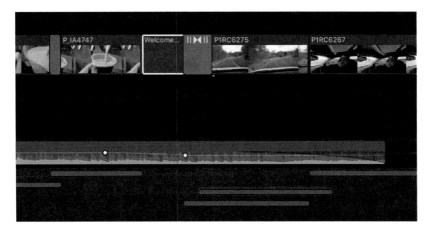

Figure 15.5: A title placed on the primary storyline takes up a full clip height

5. In the **Viewer**, double-click on the word **Title** to edit it, then overtype with your own title.

There's plenty of flexibility in how the text appears, and we'll look at that soon.

6. Click on the **Lower Thirds** title category, and drag **Basic Lower Third** to connect above another clip.

This time, the title includes two text elements and takes up much less height in the timeline, displaying no thumbnail filmstrip:

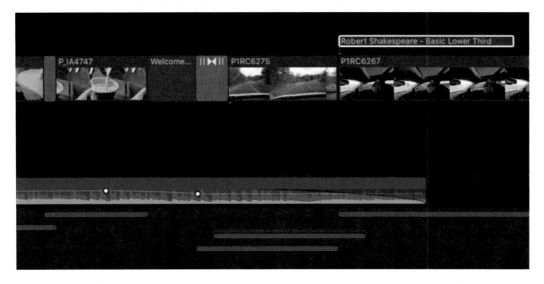

Figure 15.6: A connected title is more compact than a regular clip

The default positions and sizes are appropriate for giving a name and position to a person on the screen, so it's ideal for use as a connected title. Each of the two elements can be edited and repositioned independently, using these controls:

- Double-click a text element in the **Viewer** to select it.
- Overtype the selected text to edit it.
- Drag the text element's crosshair to reposition it.
- Press **Escape** to stop editing a text element.
- Use the **Text Layer** arrows at the very bottom of the **Inspector** to switch to other text elements within the same title. Multiple text elements will appear like this:

Figure 15.7: Double-click on a text element to edit it; Escape to stop

Most of the time, you'll need to reposition the text with regard to the content of the frame, the size of the text, and overall composition, but there are subtleties, as you'll discover next.

POSITIONING TEXT ELEMENTS

While most text elements in the built-in titles feature a crosshair, some text elements are designed to accept an entire paragraph of text, with resize handles at the corners and sides. These boxes will automatically wrap text at their edges and are more convenient for larger amounts of text. Line breaks can be added manually to either type of text, though.

When you move text elements around the Viewer, consider how the video will be viewed. Text at the bottom of the screen is often obscured by a playback bar, at least for the first few seconds of playback, so avoid that zone early on. It's also a good idea to choose **Show Title/Action Safe Zones** from the Viewer's **View** drop-down menu:

Figure 15.8: Use the Title/Action Safe Zones when positioning your text elements

Two yellow boxes will appear on the screen: the **Action Safe** (90%) box outside, and the **Title Safe** (80%) box inside, indicating where the edges of the screen might be cropped off entirely or distorted on an older TV set.

It's now possible (*new in 10.4.9*) to use a **Custom Overlay** in a similar way to the safe zones. This overlay file can be any image, though using a mostly transparent PNG file that matches your project's aspect ratio and resolution is recommended. Your image could include custom safe zone areas, a reference example of previous text or image positioning, a screenshot to remind you where playback controls are often shown, or simply a grid. The process is straightforward:

1. Create or download your graphic.
2. From the Viewer's **View** menu, select **Choose Custom Overlay** > **Add Custom Overlay**.
3. Locate your graphic.

4. Change the opacity of the overlay (to 25%/50%/75%/100%) with the submenu underneath **View** > **Show Custom Overlay**.

5. Hide or show the overlay by selecting the **Show Custom Overlay** option directly, rather than an opacity in the submenu:

Figure 15.9: This custom grid includes safe zones, extra markings, and a reminder that the bottom part of the screen is often obscured

A custom overlay can help you to make sure that you position your text in exactly the same spot every time, and when used with the safe areas, can help you make sure that your text is always seen.

While images are cropped less often on modern devices than on CRT televisions, the edges of a video can still be cropped off in some circumstances, so avoid putting text at the very edges of the screen. Some modern TV guidelines call for text to sit within the 90% outer boundary, so if you position the text within the outer Action Safe box, you should be safe on most devices. However, a wide phone set to fill its screen might crop into that zone on the top and bottom, so consider using the height of the original Title Safe box for critical elements. Also, remember that the text will be unreadable if it's too small.

EDITING BASIC TEXT PROPERTIES

You're not stuck with the default font or size, but you'll need the **Inspector** to edit most text properties. As you might expect, **⌥-clicking** on a title is a good way to make sure that you're working (in the **Inspector**) on the same thing you're looking at (in the **Viewer**). With titles, there's another option, because *double-clicking on a title* selects the title and moves the Playhead to its center.

There are two tabs in the Inspector that are important to understand when working with titles. The *first icon* (a **T** in a box) is the **Title Inspector**, and it's different for every title. We'll come back to that soon, but here, the second icon is highlighted in blue:

Figure 15.10: The Text Inspector (second icon along) is selected here

The *second icon* (a few lines of text) is the **Text Inspector**, and it offers the same controls for every text element in every title. No matter which title you're using, the **Text** controls will be reliable and predictable, selected automatically after you double-click on a text element. Importantly, if pasted text includes styles (font, size, and color information) then those styles will be *maintained if you paste into the Viewer, but discarded if you paste into the Inspector*. Because I usually want to style the text myself, I nearly always select the text in the Inspector before pasting.

> IMPORTANT NOTE
>
> Choosing a good font is important, doubly so because many editors never do. Many years ago, in the *Classic Final Cut Pro* days, I remember watching a famous awards presentation in which 9 of the 10 nominees for best short and long documentary had used the same default font (**Lucida Grande**) for their titles. I've since seen people in the real world using titles that I've designed, using (you guessed it!) the default font that I chose in the first place. Whichever font you end up with, make sure it's not the default, because your work will look like everyone else's if you do.

To start editing the text properties, find the **Basic Lower Third** title you've already added, and then follow these steps:

1. Double-click the title to select it and move the Playhead to that point.

Double-clicking also selects all the text within the first **Name** element in this title. If you want to replace the text with new words that's fine, but be sure to reselect the text with ⌘**A** if you do so.

2. In the **Inspector**, experiment with the settings in the **Basic** section, including **Font** and **Size**, **Alignment**, **Line Spacing** (leading), and **Tracking**.

   A client will often provide a style guide to define how their titles should appear. Here, we'll use the principles of **Contrast**, **Repetition**, **Alignment**, and **Proximity** from *The Non-Designer's Design Book* by Robin Williams.

3. Set **Font** to **Avenir Next Bold** and **Size** to 70.

   This is big and bold, but not so big that longer names would be hard to accommodate.

4. Double-click on the smaller **Description** text element, and then set **Font** to **Avenir Next Regular**, **Size** to 40, **All Caps** on, and **All Caps Size** to 100.0:

Figure 15.11: Contrast between the two lines of text draws the eye to the most important information first

This is a good combination with the bolder name style, allowing **Contrast** to draw the eye to the name first, and their title second. With the two styles working well together, we can reuse these easily in future titles. This **Repetition** principle ensures consistency and makes your job easier. To save these text settings for future use:

1. Double-click again on the larger **Name** text element to edit it.

2. At the top of the **Inspector**, where **Normal** is currently shown, choose **Save Format Attributes** from the drop-down menu.

3. In the dialog that appears, name the style as **Big Avenir Bold**.

4. Double-click on the smaller **Description** text element to edit it.

5. At the top of the **Inspector**, choose **Save Format Attributes** from the drop-down menu, and name the style as **Smaller Avenir Regular**.

These styles can be used again any time you want them. While it's pretty easy to duplicate titles with a quick ⌥-drag, saving styles makes it easier to apply the same look to other kinds of titles. Here are a few I prepared earlier:

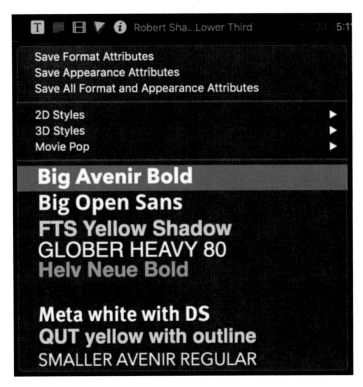

Figure 15.12: Saving text styles lets you reuse common settings across multiple jobs – Repetition

Now, it's time to reposition the two elements a little closer to the edges of the screen. You'll want to keep them lined up with one another (**Alignment**) and make sure they're still close to one another and not too close to the edges of the screen (**Proximity**). Here, I'll position the text in the upper third of the screen rather than the lower third, though either can work. Here's how to do it:

1. Drag the upper **Name** text element to just inside the left edge of the outer **Action Safe** line, and position the top edge to the edge of the inner **Title Safe** line.

2. Drag the larger **Description** text element to just below the **Name** element, aligned vertically:

Figure 15.13: Alignment and Proximity are both important settings

3. Turn off the **Action/Title Safe Zones** setting with the **View** menu in the **Viewer**.

You'll be able to see the overall composition much more clearly without the safe zones, so reposition the text elements if you need to. If you're using closed captions (and you should be!), remember that captions might obscure the titles. Consider using a higher "upper third" text placement if you expect your video to be shown on small screens, and especially if it's an advertisement.

The **Basic** text properties can be seen in the following screenshot:

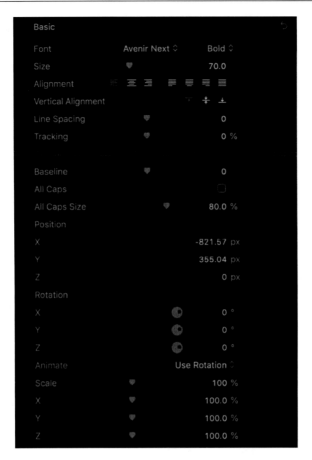

Figure 15.14: Use the numbers in the Position section
for repeatable text element placement

While you can always position text with a drag in the **Viewer**, the **Position**, **Rotation**, and **Scale** properties in the **Inspector** (just below the other options) allow you to be as precise as you want to be. And there's more to come.

EDITING OTHER TEXT PROPERTIES

Underneath the **Basic** text properties, you'll find five more categories full of properties: **3D Text**, **Face**, **Outline**, **Glow**, and **Drop Shadow**. Each of these categories is hidden by default, so hover over the name to see the word **Show** appear, and then click on the word itself. Here's a quick explanation of what these options cover:

- **3D Text** — A huge amount of power with some subtle tricks hiding there, and we'll return to this one in the next section. Let's leave it off for now, though.

- **Face** — Important controls over the color or gradient that fills the text, along with blur and opacity controls.

- **Outline** — An outline can be added to the text, with a variable width, color, and blur.

- **Glow** — An even blurrier outline that can be pushed well beyond the text.

- **Drop Shadow** — A dark shadow behind the text that has come in and out of fashion over the past few years, and is due for a resurgence. A subtle shadow can be important when separating white text from a lighter background (remember **Contrast**), but don't overdo it.

These text appearance options can be seen here:

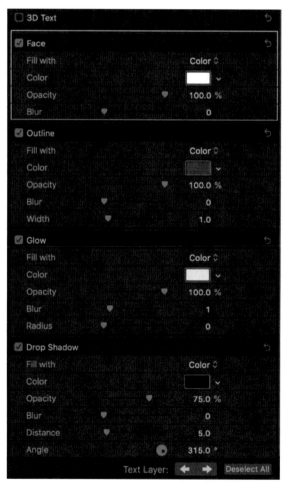

Figure 15.15: Text appearance options, active and set
to their defaults – remember to change them!

Face is obviously critical to control the color of text, and while you might not need to use all the other controls for every title, it's great that the options are there. An important use for these controls is to animate them so that the text can, for example, appear transparent and blurry at first, but then come into focus. Luckily, there are title templates that can do that for you, and you may not need to play directly with these settings very often.

The 2D Styles presets can be seen here:

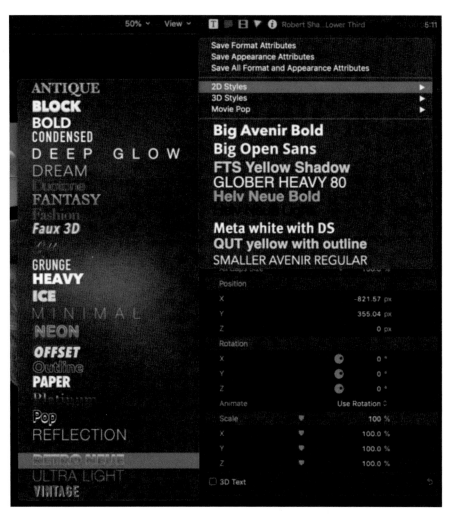

Figure 15.16: Use the 2D Styles for inspiration if you're stuck

To see a few of these extended properties in action, check out a few of the presets at the top of the Inspector, just underneath the tabs. From the menu there, choose **2D Styles**, then:

- **Block** — to see how the glow can be used to create a blocky, pseudo-3D effect
- **Retro Neue** — to add a gradient and crazy colors to that same look:

Figure 15.17: When too much is never enough

- **Neon** — to see gradients, outlines, and shadows all used at once with a rounded font
- **Outline** — to see that you don't always have to use a fill
- **Paper** — to see one of the built-in textures used as a fill (normally, you'd use a **Blend Mode** for this effect)

There are many more, and you can of course make your own. When you get the settings right and want to save a new preset text style, use **Save All Format and Appearance Attributes** from the drop-down menu to preserve the extended settings (collectively, **Appearance**), as well as the font settings (**Format**).

But what's that **3D** option in the presets? Let's take a look.

EDITING 3D TEXT PARAMETERS

If you check the **3D Text** option in the text properties for any title, the **Face** and **Outline** sections disappear, replaced by:

- **3D Text** — Depth, weight, and bevel controls to change how thick the letters are in all three dimensions.
- **Lighting** — To redirect the light source and its intensity.
- **Material** — Offering a huge variety of fabrics, woods, stones, and metals, among others. Pick from the **Appearance** drop-down list, then (depending on your choice) finesse the **Options**, **Finish**, **Paint**, and **Substance** settings.

Here's an example of the Redwood preset:

Figure 15.18: There's an extensive library of materials that will let you go crazy here

To explore the **3D Text** settings, you can look through the **Materials** library, or try the **3D Styles** presets from the menu at the top of the **Inspector**, as illustrated:

Figure 15.19: The 3D Styles only scratch the surface of what's possible here

Probably the most important control is to be found in the Viewer, where the old position control has made way for a 3D position and rotation widget. Clicking once on a 3D text element displays three arrows, for movement, and three circles, for rotation. Each arrow is shown in a color (red, green, and blue) that corresponds to movement in the x, y, and z axis respectively. Understanding the arrows and circles is important for careful movement, so let's take a look by doing the following:

- Click and drag on any arrow to move the 3D text along that axis — red = x, green = y, and blue = z. The arrows can be seen in the following screenshot:

Figure 15.20: The R/G/B arrows allow for movement in the x/y/z axes

Each circle is white, but shows red, green, or blue when you hover over it. Which is which?

- Click and drag the top (red) circle to rotate around x (tilt, or pitch)
- Click and drag the left (green) circle to rotate around y (pan, or yaw)
- Click and drag the right (blue) circle to rotate around z (roll)

The green circle is being dragged in the following screenshot:

Figure 15.21: The three R/G/B circles allow rotation around the x/y/z axes

It's quite powerful to be able to place editable 3D text on your timeline without thinking about it, and the only issue is that a 3D title could be overkill when used in the wrong situations. Use with restraint.

IMPORTANT NOTE

If you're looking for 3D controls, but you've already double-clicked and the text is selected for editing, you've gone too far. Press **Escape** and click just once on the text element to see its 3D controls. If you ever get stuck editing text and you can't access the controls you're looking for, click elsewhere in the timeline to select nothing, then **⌥-click** once on the title and start over.

As well as the universal 2D and 3D text controls, each title allows access to unique properties that can completely change how they look and how they animate on or off the screen. Understanding how these controls work is crucial, and that's next.

EDITING UNIQUE PARAMETERS AND ADDING ANIMATION

Some animated titles have quite a distinctive look, and while this can be effective, if you use a title style that viewers have seen many times before, it'll feel stale. It's therefore important to add your own stamp on a title by changing its unique parameters, at least a little. To the left of the **Text** icon at the top of the **Inspector**, you'll find the **Title** icon, a **T** in a box, and the **Title** section is where you'll make changes to the specific options that each title allows. This blue icon is what you're looking for:

Figure 15.22: Select the Title tab to examine unique
settings and any built-in animation

The **Basic Title** and **Basic Lower Third** titles don't actually include any settings here, so you'll need to add in something else. While many titles do include some settings, the **Custom** title is the king of them all. As it only includes a single text element, if you want two independent lines with different styles you can add two titles one above the other, or type two lines of text, and select and format each line independently. We'll add it now, as follows:

1. Click on the **Build In/Out** title category.

2. Drag the **Custom** title to a spot above the primary storyline.

3. In the **Viewer**, double-click on the word **Title** to edit it, then overtype with your own title.

4. Click on the **Text** icon in the **Inspector** (the small lines), then choose one of the text presets you saved earlier, such as **Big Avenir Bold**.

5. Click on the **Title** icon in the **Inspector** (the **T** in a box) to see all the other controls.

The **Custom** title exposes far more controls than most other titles, with more flexibility than most. The **In** settings here govern the initial state of the text as it builds in, animating to a "normal" appearance. After a short period of normality for viewers to read the text, the **Out** settings then govern the final state of the text as it builds out. Right now, though, the In and Out settings aren't doing anything at all.

1. Change **In Opacity** to 0, **In Scale** to 60, and **In Blur** to 20.

   Because the **Blur** slider has a limit of 10, that last change can only be done by dragging on the numbers directly, or selecting the number and typing in a new value. Always drag on the numbers for quickest results.

   The settings can be seen here:

Figure 15.23: During playback, the "h" is now unblurring as it grows and fades in

2. In the **Timeline**, click above the start of this title and press the **spacebar** to start playback.

   You'll see that the text fades in as it grows and unblurs. You could use any of these settings on their own, but they also look good together. Currently, only one letter animates at a time, though, and we can soften that.

3. Make sure the title is still selected, and click back to the **Title** tab if necessary.

4. Change **In Spread** to 5.

The **In Spread** value controls how many elements animate onto the screen at once, and you can change the **In Unit Size** parameter to fade words, lines, or everything rather than just characters.

You can see the change here:

Figure 15.24: Now, several characters animate at the same time

You can tweak this title all day to produce unique results, and it's a great way to add your own touch to a simple title. While the **Out** controls do work, you may need to experiment with the **Custom** title's duration to get the fade out to happen in exactly the right place. Often, I'll build a title in to grab attention, but then just hard cut it out with a shot change underneath:

Figure 15.25: Often, a shot change is a good opportunity to hard cut away from a title

While **Custom** can be a little complicated to fade out, most animated titles offer simple checkboxes for **Build In** and **Build Out** that make this easy, as seen here:

Figure 15.26: Here's Pixie Dust, with optional Build In and Build Out parameters

Another option is to use a transition to build it away; after all, there's a huge range of unusual transitions included. It's possible to add a transition (⌘T for the default **Cross Dissolve**) to build it in and out, but you'll see that the title gets much taller, as it will be placed in a connected storyline. (Transitions can only be added within a storyline, so one will always be created if you add a transition to a connected title.) You'll see this:

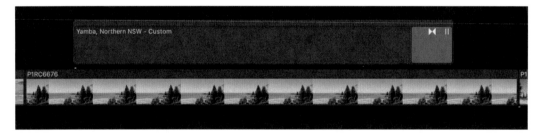

Figure 15.27: To fade this title out earlier, use the Title controls, or perhaps add a transition

If you'd prefer to keep the original small height of a connected title, you could use the Opacity fade handles found in **Video Animation** (^V) instead, as seen here:

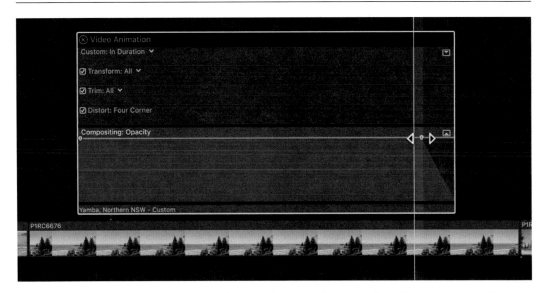

Figure 15.28: If you use the Video Animation Opacity fade handles, the clip stays at a regular height

Of course, this will only help you to fade a title as a single unit, and as you're about to find out, there are more exciting ways to transition text. Here are some of the best included title templates.

THE BEST TITLES

In this section, you'll find out about some of the hidden gems of the built-in titles. Remember to customize all these titles to see their true potential, and as you're trying out new titles, here's a shortcut:

- Select an existing title, then double-click a replacement in the **Title** browser.

The existing title will be replaced with a new one, and any text previously entered will be copied across.

3D

If a 3D title is appropriate for your Project, start here. The **Basic 3D** title isn't entirely bare-bones like its 2D equivalent; it includes several different animation styles such as slides, zooms, swivels, and tumbles:

Figure 15.29: A Custom 3D example with different formatting for the first and second lines

For more control, go for **Custom 3D**, starting from scratch but letting you add anything you want to the **In** or **Out** builds. For simpler controls over a single type of animation, use **Fade 3D**, **Rotate 3D**, **Scale 3D**, **Text Spacing 3D**, or **Tumble 3D**, and the **Lower Third 3D** provides two lines and a blurry gray bar. These are all good.

3D CINEMATIC

Less flexible than the regular **3D** category, these effects are quite distinctive and should be used sparingly. Here's Graphical:

Figure 15.30: This Graphical title punches the text through from the background, with shadows

The **Shadow** title has some versatile options, as does the **Graphical** title.

BUILD IN/OUT

Probably one of the most versatile categories, including several simple yet effective options. Try **Blur**, to unblur the text in then blur it away; **Continuous**, with several persistent options under the **Style** drop-down option; and **Custom**, which we have already explored. Here's **Knock Out**:

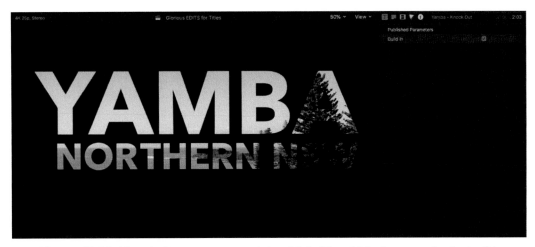

Figure 15.31: Knock Out repeats a trick which Blend Modes can do, but with some useful animation too

Fade is a simplified version of **Custom** with only opacity controls; **Highlight** provides a passing sparkle; and **Knock Out** shows the video behind it. **Soft Edge** provides a paragraph of text with a little movement, and **Tracking** stretches the text in and out as it fades. Here's an example of **Tracking** in action:

Figure 15.32: Tracking, in mid-animation, is a popular style

While there are several other options here, they're quite distinctive, so be sure not to overuse them.

BUMPER/OPENER

Many of these options bring a lot of their own style, but you can make them your own. Try **Ink**, then change the font, the background, and the **Ink Dab Width**. Here's an example of that:

Figure 15.33: The Slate background on Ink looks very different from the defaults

Look to the themed collections below the standalone Titles to see related options, such as the **Data** theme's **Reveal** and **Endpage** options, and the **Event** theme's **List**, **Push** and **Ribbon** options. All of these options are changeable.

CREDITS

If you want to add scrolling credits to your piece, **Scrolling** will automatically retime the text you provide to the duration you allow. Below this, several themes here can manipulate everything in the timeline under the title, allowing the camera to zoom out with a **Push**, **Turn**, or **Slide** to reveal that you've been watching a **Comic Book**, or a **Photo Album**, or a **Scrapbook**. These are best used as connected titles to include the Primary Storyline within them. An example of the **Turn** option can be seen in the following screenshot:

Figure 15.34: Your video can become a postcard if you use Bulletin Board's Turn title

If you do find a title that includes the background as this does, be sure to avoid using its **Transform** controls, as they will affect not just the text but the entire image. This occurs because they make use of the same background-controlling feature that enables Adjustment Layers, as discussed in *Chapter 11, Play with Light: Color Correction and Grading*.

ELEMENTS

The **Instant Replay, Score**, and **Stats** options are all useful for sports, while **Speech Bubbles** can be handy to present a character's idea in a comic book style. Here's another:

Figure 15.35: The Stamp can work well; just remember to tweak the settings

Stamp can introduce a new location quite effectively.

LOWER THIRDS

This section is probably the most useful, because the primary use for these titles is to give your subjects a name and a caption. **Gradient – Edge** and **Gradient – Center** are useful, simple options with controls over the size and position of a gradient bar:

Figure 15.36: Gradient – Edge includes two lines and built-in fades, and can work on any background

Looseleaf, **Snap – Left**, and many of the themed options such as **Bulletin Board** and **Data** include backgrounds behind the text, and more lively animations in and out.

Here's something sneaky:

Figure 15.37: Date/Time automatically extracts the date and time of recording from the clip it's connected to

The preceding screenshot shows the **Date/Time** title, a special title that defaults to the actual date and time that the clip below it was created — very handy for home movies.

SOCIAL

This new and useful category of titles is a great choice if you're creating movies that will change aspect ratio: these titles will adapt if your project changes shape, from wide to tall or square. Several of these titles also include a spot for a logo by utilizing Drop Zones, which you'll learn about soon, and others include a "bump," pushing in the underlying video for emphasis.

Figure 15.38: This Lower Third Basic title, like the others here, will adapt to different aspect ratios

Though the built-in titles are good, **Motion** makes it easy to build new titles for use within FCP, defining the animation while allowing you to type in your own text and control text properties during the edit. While you can certainly make your own complex titles in **Motion**, many professional motion designers have done so already, creating packs of titles and other effects for every occasion imaginable. Here's just one such title, with the free font Barrio:

Figure 15.39: Here's a custom third-party title from LenoFX that includes fancy animations

There are many, many titles available for purchase or for free, so fire up a search engine and go on the hunt.

REVIEW — ADDING AND EDITING TITLES

That probably felt like a lot of information, but it should have made sense. As well as understanding the full range of titles available, you know how to find the Titles Browser, then preview a title and add it to your timeline. You also know how to set the text properties, and how to save or recall formatting presets. With the formatting out of the way, you can attack the specific animation properties of that particular title, make it unique, and make sure it stands out for the right reasons.

What next? Some advanced techniques that will get you out of a jam someday.

ADVANCED TITLE TECHNIQUES

In this section, you'll learn how to find and replace text across all titles, how to retime titles to insert pauses or control speed, and how to reuse a complex composite of several titles and other elements. While you won't use these techniques in every Project, if you ever have to incorporate bullet points or correct a typo in someone's name, these are the tools you'll need. You'll also discover how to use Drop Zones to include a clip as part of a title. First up, replacing text.

REPLACING TEXT IN TITLES

Text replacement is quite easy, but it's still worth mentioning. To replace one word with another in a Project (or all Projects), follow these steps:

1. Choose **Edit > Find and Replace Title Text** to see this:

Figure 15.40: Here, I'm searching for an abbreviation and replacing it

2. In the dialog that appears, type in the word(s) to search for and the replacement.

3. Click **Next** to move to the first instance, to confirm that it's been found correctly.

4. Click **Replace & Find** to replace one instance and move to the next, **Replace** to replace and not move on, or **Replace All** to make all replacements. (If only one instance is found, you can only select **Replace All**).

If the new text is longer than the old text, it's possible that not all the new text will fit. If this is the case, use **Replace** and check that it's good before moving on to the next instance. There's another way to search that can be useful, but it only finds text in the first text element within a title. To search with the Timeline Index:

1. Press ⌘F to open the search field in the **Timeline Index**.

2. Click **Clips** at the top of the panel.

   Optionally, you could click **Titles** at the bottom of the panel to limit the search further.

3. Click in the search field at the top, then type the word(s) you want to search for.

If you have already replaced these same words in the titles (or they're in the second Description line in a lower third), you shouldn't find anything. However, you can search for more than just text in titles here: names of clips and text in captions can both be found this way, as illustrated:

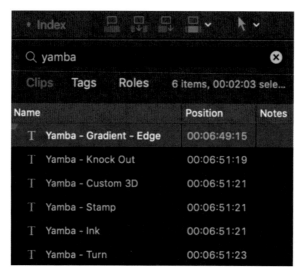

Figure 15.41: Trying out a few titles? They'll all be here

Of these two options, **Find and Replace Title Text** is more powerful because it searches through multiple text elements within titles, and also because you can replace text across multiple Projects at once. The **Find** feature searches only the current Project, and you may need to replace text in more than one Project. But it's important: remember that if you're correcting a misspelled title, that same text may appear in captions too, and you should fix both. (If you haven't added captions, no problem — they're coming up soon!)

Now that typos are under control, how can you present a bulleted list properly?

RETIMING TITLES WITH COMPOUND CLIPS

Bulleted lists aren't the most exciting way to present information, but they can be a necessary evil. If a Project demands that you retime multiple bullet points to match a voiceover or a presenter on screen, here's how to do it:

1. Create a **Custom** title with all the bullet points included.

2. Adjust the **Custom** title's animation to animate in a character at a time, with **Spread** at 1, **In Opacity** at 0, and **In Blur** at 10.

   You could use **In Fade**, **In Position**, or anything else you like, but make sure that only one element is animating at any one time. Animation by line or character is OK.

3. Select that title in a timeline.

4. Press ⌥G to create a Compound Clip, then name it.

   Creating a Compound Clip is the key here. While a title can't be paused and will stretch out to the time given, a Compound Clip is fixed and can be retimed easily. The following screenshot shows how to create one:

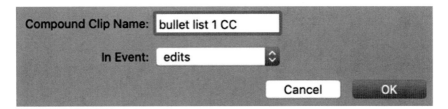

Figure 15.42: I like to use "CC" in the name of Compound Clips

5. Skim to the frame immediately after the first bullet point has fully appeared. Make sure the second bullet point isn't visible yet.

6. Press ⇧H to create a **Hold Frame** at that point.

The **Retime Editor** now appears above the clip with a red area to indicate the Hold Frame.

7. Skim to a frame at the end of each subsequent bullet point, and press ⇧H to create a **Hold Frame** at each one, as shown:

Figure 15.43: With all the Hold Frames in position, you'll see this

8. Drag the single-line handle at the right of each red area (from left to right) to change the duration of each Hold Frame:

Figure 15.44: After extending the length of each Hold Frame, you'll see this

The length of time that each bullet point stays fixed on screen is up to you: adjust the timing to fit a voiceover or an onscreen presenter. The single-line handle can be dragged as far to the left or right as you need to adjust the length of the pause before the next bullet animates on.

What if you've been given a video recording of a presentation rather than titles you created? The same ⇧H technique for adding Hold Frames lets you pause in the same way, but you won't need to make a compound clip first.

IMPORTANT NOTE

For these pre-recorded presentations, an additional trick can help to remove the background easily. If your presentation uses white text on a black background, the **Screen** blend mode will remove the background, leaving only the white text. This means that rather than placing a presentation in a box next to your presenter, you can integrate the two in the same frame.

Bulleted lists are one thing, but are Compound Clips good for any other title-related tasks? I'm glad you asked.

CREATING COMPLEX TITLES WITH COMPOUND CLIPS

Compound Clips can turn any number of titles into a single unit that can be reused and retimed, and the most common workflow they enable is easy reuse of common title elements across different Projects in a series.

Some titles, such as an introductory bumper title, will be used unchanged in a series of different videos, and wrapping a common bumper in a compound clip is sensible: if the bumper needs to change late in the process, you only need to edit that one Compound Clip, not a loose title (or several layered clips) at the start of every edit. This simplifies your timeline too:

Figure 15.45: Here's a composite of a few clips and a title in a compound below, with a changing title above

A hybrid approach can also work, involving a composite of several elements you expect to remain the same, and one or more titles on top that will change each time. To reuse only some elements of a complex multilayered title, a good approach is to create a "base" Compound Clip with all the common elements, then change additional elements on top of each instance. A background generator with a fixed logo and two different text elements would be a good candidate for this — you could put the logo and background together in a compound, then add two independent titles on top. When you reuse it, copy the entire chunk, then double-click each title and change them.

Remember: editing any underlying Compound Clip causes changes to ripple through to all instances of it. Compound Clips are therefore a sensible choice if you expect there to be changes, such as when you just haven't had time to design a background behind a title yet, and you're going with something basic for now.

While you'll mostly want to use reuse a compound clip across multiple Projects, it's also possible for each instance of a compound clip to be independent of other instances. One way to do this is to duplicate your Compound Clip a few times in the Browser, then place each independent duplicate where you want them. You'll see something like this:

Figure 15.46: Three different versions of a title can all
be used and edited separately if needed

Another way to create independent Compound Clips is to select a single Compound Clip instance in a timeline, then choose **Clip > Reference New Parent Clip**, which creates a duplicate compound clip in the Browser for you, then points the selected timeline copy at the new duplicate. Neat.

Either way, you'll find it easy enough to use Compound Clips as a wrapper for one or more titles. They enable easy reuse of one or more assets, and can be duplicated and edited independently if you want something more complicated.

Another way to manage complexity within a title or generator is to incorporate another element (a regular clip or a compound clip) inside it, and allow the editor to scale and reposition that element. That magic happens through **Drop Zones**.

USING DROP ZONES

Drop Zones allow you to include one or more additional clips within a title — or, indeed, within a generator, or even a transition. Titles can already include the clip below them, though: in the **Bumper/Opener** category, there's a title called **Keynote** that moves whatever's placed underneath it to the left, and then introduces text to the right with a gradient background. Drop Zones allow you to bring in another clip entirely, and you'll find one in **Bold Fin**, also in the **Bumper/Opener** category. Let's explore it through an exercise, as follows:

1. Add the **Bold Fin** title above an existing clip in your timeline.

2. Double-click the title to select it and move the Playhead to its center.

3. Overtype the selected text element, then double-click and change the other elements. (Type a space if you want an element left blank.)

4. Click on the **Title** tab (the **T** in a box) at the top of the **Inspector**.

   You'll see several controls, including a **Media Well Inset** control, currently set to *No source*. This is a Drop Zone that you'll add your own clip to:

Figure 15.47: Here's a title you could use just before a commercial break

5. Click in the **Image Well** next to **Media Well Inset**, where the downward-pointing arrow is shown.

6. Click on the **Library** icon in the top left of the **Browser** to access your clips.

7. Click on the filmstrip of a clip (not just its name) to load it into the Image Well.

   It's possible to use a Browser clip or a timeline clip as the source. Importantly, the frame you click on is the first frame that will be used in the Drop Zone, so be sure to click on the section of the clip that you want to see first. If you click late in a clip, you could see a still frame at the end if the clip isn't long enough. At this stage, you should see something like this:

Figure 15.48: Click on a clip in the Browser to see it play in this Viewer split screen

8. Click **Apply Clip** to the lower left of the **Viewer** to confirm the choice.

   Note that if several Drop Zones are present, you can click on each one, then click on a source clip each time, and finally click **Apply Clip** once to approve them all.

9. Play back the title in the timeline to see (but not hear) the clip in the Drop Zone.

10. Pause, then double-click the Drop Zone in the **Viewer** to select it.

11. Scale the clip up by dragging the corners of the Drop Zone, and reposition it by dragging it, as seen here:

Figure 15.49: Content in a Drop Zone can be scaled and repositioned

If you can see a Drop Zone, you should be able to double-click it, change its scale, and re-crop it easily. However, in some complex titles with overlapping elements, double-clicking on the right element can be difficult, and you might prefer to use Inspector-based **Pan** and **Scale** controls, like these:

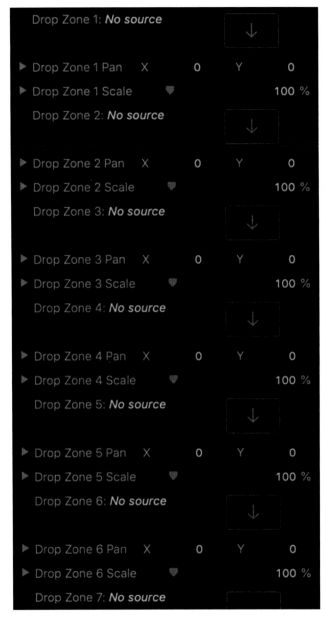

Figure 15.50: A third-party "gallery" Generator might use many Drop Zones
and Inspector parameters

A trickier issue is timing. Sometimes, it can be difficult to put exactly the right region
of a clip in a Drop Zone, and this can happen for subtle reasons. Firstly, the clip will
always play at normal speed, while other elements in the clip will retime themselves

to match the duration of the clip. Secondly, the Drop Zone may start to play before it is visible, so you may see content in the clip that appears some time after the exact frame you clicked on.

A nice workaround is to create a Compound Clip from the source clip that you place inside a Drop Zone. That way, you can Slip the content of the Compound Clip in time (or even retime it) to make sure that exactly the right part of the clip is used. This strategy can be important with dealing with long, complex animations such as this:

Figure 15.51: This is only part of a long animated sequence
with 20+ Drop Zones, from motionVFX

Drop Zones are more frequently used in third-party Titles (and Generators) but you'll also find them in the **Build In/Out** category's **Fold**, in the **Bumper/Opener** category's **Stacked**, and elsewhere in the **Sports** theme. They're worth using, though the innate ability of Titles to repurpose the content beneath them means that you won't always have to.

Time for a quick look back.

REVIEW — ADVANCED TITLE TECHNIQUES

Find and Replace Title Text is one of the boring but necessary features that will save your bacon at some point, and Compound Clips are too. Bulleted lists are one occasion you'll need them, but a bigger reason is to ensure that you deliver consistent titles and bumpers over time.

Many jobs are repeat jobs, either multiple videos in a single larger job or multiple similar videos for a single client. For any repeat jobs, consider creating Compound Clips to ensure consistency. If you'll be working with a client for many years, also consider making a dedicated library to hold those Compound Clips, to make it easier to reuse them across multiple libraries.

Now that you know how to replace text, how to use Compound Clips for retiming and reuse, and how to place, size, crop, and retime Drop Zones, you're all set. And yet, titles aren't always enough, so you'll also want to be across **Generators**, up next.

ADDING AND EDITING GENERATORS

While titles generally add text, Generators generally add background elements: images, generated graphics, patterns, or something else. Here, you'll learn how to add and edit Generators, including some of the fancier controls accessible in the Inspector and the Viewer. Finally, you'll find out about some of the best Generators included with the app, remembering of course that there are plenty of free and cheap third-party Generators out there too.

The most common uses for Generators are to stand in for other content (such as the Placeholder generator, which you learned about back in *Chapter 6*, *Build the Spine of the Story: Quick Assembly*) or to act as a background behind other elements such as titles or keyed green-screen shots. But some types of videos, such as slideshows, might be built entirely from Generators — they can do quite a bit.

> **IMPORTANT NOTE**
>
> An alternative to Generators is to use real still images or video instead — possibly stock photos or stock footage. Before you do, consider if it's projecting the right message; the generic, staged look that many stock shots and clips share can feel dated. You can find good imagery at free stock libraries such as <u>pexels.com</u>, <u>unsplash.com</u>, and <u>pixabay.com</u>, though paid stock libraries offer a wider range of choices.
>
> However, always remember that anyone can access the same clips that you can. Shooting your own stills or video will always ensure a unique result.

You'll find Generators to be largely similar to Titles, but with some key differences. Some are animated while others are static; some offer many controls while others offer none. We'll start by adding some Generators, then move on to editing them.

ADDING AND EDITING A SIMPLE GENERATOR

The simplest way to get started with Generators is to add one of the most useful ones, and here's how:

1. If it's not already visible, click on the **Titles and Generators** icon at the top of the **Browser** (the third icon), as illustrated here:

Figure 15.52: Once more to Titles and Generators

2. In the **Browser**, click the small disclosure triangle next to the word **Generators**, to expose the categories within.

3. Click on the **Solids** category.

    As with titles, all these Generators can be previewed by hovering over them, though only their default state will be visible:

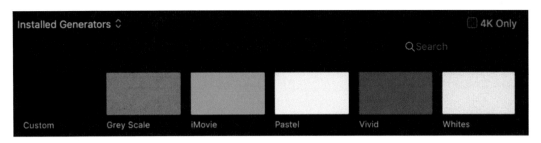

Figure 15.53: The Solids generators aren't flashy, but they are useful

4. Drag **Custom** to a spot in the Primary Storyline.

   Custom defaults to a black background, but we can change that now.

5. **⌥-click** on the new **Custom** clip in the timeline to select the clip and move the Playhead to that point.

6. In the **Inspector**, click on the first icon to the left — the **Generator** tab.

   There's only one item here: the color of the background. You can click on the **Color** box to bring up the macOS color picker, or the small arrow to the right to bring up a small color-picking spectrum. Both are shown here:

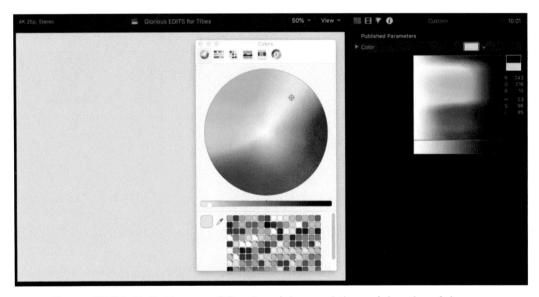

Figure 15.54: Both the macOS color picker and the quick color picker are shown here

7. Click on the box (not the arrow) to bring up the macOS color picker.

8. Click on the small eyedropper icon in the macOS color picker to activate the system eyedropper.

9. Click on any color anywhere on the screen to sample it.

This technique allows you to use any color you like behind a title. Of course, if you prefer, you could use a still image or a low-contrast video, or a video with a blur effect applied instead — but a solid color is still a popular choice. Still, there are many more complex generators with many more settings to change.

CHANGING ADVANCED GENERATOR SETTINGS

Just as with titles, each Generator offers its own set of controls. You'll find them in the **Generator** tab at the top left of the Inspector, and as this process is very similar to how you would change the Title properties on a title, I won't go into too much detail. Briefly, you'll need to do the following:

1. **⌥-click** on a Generator clip in the timeline to select the clip and move the Playhead to that point.

2. In the **Inspector**, click on the first icon to the left — the **Generator** tab. The following screenshot shows an example of the **Clouds** Generator:

Figure 15.55: The Clouds Generator offers a partly transparent background, just visible here as a checkerboard

3. To change a Generator's settings, drag on a property's numbers, choose new items from drop-down menus, and choose new colors from the macOS color picker or the built-in square color picker.

4. If a Drop Zone is present, click the image well, then click on a frame in a filmstrip of a browser clip and click on **Apply Clip**.

5. If desired, add color correction or video effects to change how the clip appears.

There's really nothing difficult here, and if you've played with effects and titles, you shouldn't have any trouble. It's the Inspector; you know what to do. Now, should you always put a Generator on the Primary Storyline? No.

POSITIONING A GENERATOR

While in most circumstances you *would* simply place a Generator on the Primary Storyline and connect a title above it, that's not always the case. One exception is if you're adding a background behind a green-screen shot that now has (thanks to the **Keyer** effect) a transparent background, as shown here:

Figure 15.56: This checkerboard background (indicating transparency) can be shown in Preferences > Player under Player Background

As this transparent-background shot should be the main clip driving the edit, it should be on the Primary Storyline, and the Generator should be connected underneath it. That way, you can safely edit the main shots without worrying about creating gaps, like this:

Figure 15.57: A green-screen clip in the primary and two Generators
to create a stripy background

An exception to this strategy occurs if you need to transition between keyed clips. Sometimes, it's safe to transition between two background elements (in a connected Storyline) at the same time as you transition between two keyed foreground elements (in the primary storyline).

This usually works, but for technical reasons some transitions can look strange, as they're expecting to manipulate the entire frame, not just a keyed element. In those cases, create Compound Clips from each foreground-background set, then transition between the two resulting Compound Clips.

Now that you know where to put Generators and how to integrate them with Compound Clips, here's a list of the best of them.

THE BEST GENERATORS

While there aren't that many Generators included with FCP, the options here are more flexible than you'd expect. Remember that you can scale, rotate, color-correct, and add effects to any of these to change their look totally, and even animate these properties with keyframes.

Most Generators are fast to work with, but some can be a little complex and might slow down your Project on a slower Mac. If that happens to you, consider exporting a Generator on its own, then re-importing the resulting movie and using it instead.

360°

These Generators are useful if you're working with 360° Projects, but not otherwise.

BACKGROUNDS

This category has plenty of useful options: some organic, some real-world, some abstract, and many themed options. Of the abstract Generators, **Lines** is extremely flexible, generating animated stripes with several controls, and **Beam** is surprisingly flexible too. **Lines** is shown here:

Figure 15.58: Lines can be configured in many different ways

Blobs, **Clouds**, **Curtain**, **Organic**, and **Underwater** are all useful in the right context, but be sure to add your own touches with effects or color:

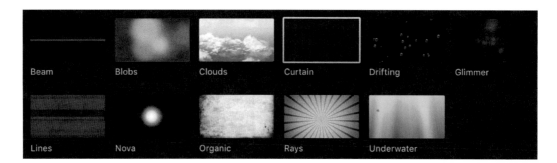

Figure 15.59: Useful in context, but change the settings

If you've made use of some of the themed transitions (including **Bulletin Board**, **Comic Book**, and **Event**), then consider using their matching backgrounds behind a title.

ELEMENTS

The familiar **Placeholder** lives here, but it's still quicker to add it with ⌥⌘W. You'll also find **Counting**, a great way to create numbers that count up or down; **Timecode**, to display the Project or clip timecode for technical purposes; and **Shapes**, to create one of several kinds of shapes with controllable fill, outline, and shadow:

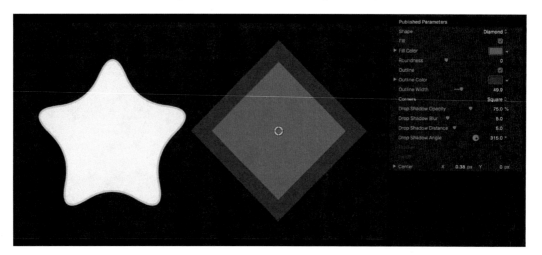

Figure 15.60: Two Shapes above some purple Curtains

When used with blend modes inside a Compound Clip, the **Shapes** Generator is perfect for placing video inside a random shape.

SOLIDS

You know about the **Custom** Generator already, and it's the best option here. The others (**Whites**, **Pastel**, **Vivid**, and so on) offer solid colors from drop-down menus, but the macOS color picker is more useful.

TEXTURES

Gradient is a good option when a flat color is too boring, but you want to stay with a simple, synthetic look. Most of the other options (**Fabric**, **Grunge**, **Metal**, **Natural**, **Paper**, **Stone**, **Wood**) follow the same template, offering a menu with several themed background choices and an optional tint. Pretty pictures at your fingertips:

Figure 15.61: One of many images in the Natural generator

The remaining Generators here are essentially a single still image, and of course there's an entire world of high-quality free and paid still images out there you could be using instead.

That's it for the built-in Generators, but of course you'll find third-party ones for purchase and for free online. Note that Generators are sometimes packaged as Titles to gain access to their background-manipulating powers, so check in the Titles Browser if you can't find what you're looking for in the Generators Browser.

REVIEW — ADDING AND EDITING GENERATORS

Backgrounds are important behind many opening titles, and if video's not appropriate, generators are often a good answer. The **Placeholder** Generator is especially useful when you haven't shot the video yet, but there are plenty of other ways to fill in a gap. As with titles and effects, be sure to change the default settings so that you aren't using exactly the same Generators as everyone else.

You're very nearly finished with your edit, and it's time to explore captions.

CAPTIONING AND SUBTITLES

In this section, you'll learn how to put words at the bottom of the screen, for people who either can't hear the audio, choose not to hear the audio, or don't understand the audio. This isn't a small audience either; a huge number (around 90%!) of social media viewers watch videos without sound, at least initially, and captions can fill the gap:

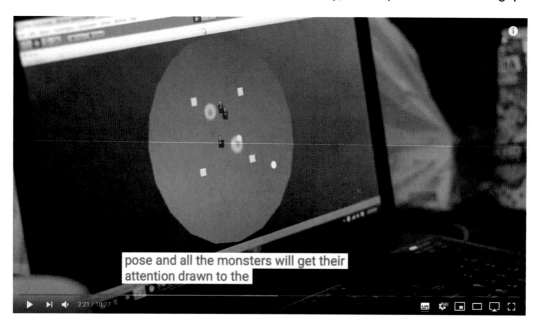

Figure 15.62: Automatically generated captions aren't terribly accurate or pretty

Captioning is therefore incredibly important if you're creating videos that people didn't ask to see, and of course captions are important for accessibility. Before we continue, it's important to understand that captions aren't quite the same as subtitles, though they do have a lot in common. Have a look at the following description:

- **Subtitles** are usually intended for a hearing audience, to provide a translation from another language.

- **Captions** are usually intended for a deaf or hard-of-hearing audience, or for any audience who chooses to watch a video without the audio. Captions may therefore include audio descriptions to indicate music or sound effects, while subtitles would not.

Therefore, the difference between subtitles and captions comes down to content. Both of them are "words on screen", but if you're providing a text version of the audio in the same language, you're probably providing captions rather than subtitles.

First, you'll learn about caption formats, then how to import them, how to make them from scratch, and then how to edit them, including splitting and joining. Exporting will be covered in *Chapter 16, You're Done: Exporting Your Edit and Finishing Up*, but there's plenty to learn before we get there. Some groundwork first.

UNDERSTANDING CAPTION FORMATS

In practical terms, your choice of delivery method is more important to the finished product than the type — subtitles or captions — of the text you're adding. You can create optional Closed Captions, or permanently burned-in Open Captions, as detailed here:

- **Closed Captions** are provided in addition to the video, and can be turned on or off by the viewer. These captions could be in one of several formats and will be delivered in a separate file, or embedded as part of the video container. The playback mechanism (an app, a website, a TV) has to be able to understand the closed caption format to be able to display them. Because the playback device or app generates the captions itself, you have little control over formatting. In fact, the user may be able to change the size and font they prefer, and closed captions will automatically move out of the way of playback controls. As they are text-based, Closed Captions can be indexed by search engines, and even automatically translated to other languages. Here's an example of Closed Captions:

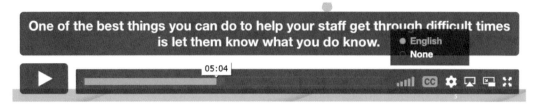

Figure 15.63: These Closed Captions (on Vimeo) can be disabled and moved up and down with the playback controls

- **Open Captions** are burned in to the video, just like regular titles, and cannot be turned on or off by the viewer. However, you have total control over formatting and positioning, just as with any title. Unfortunately, Open Captions placed at the traditional lower third of the screen are likely to be covered up by playback controls. As they are no longer text, Open Captions cannot be indexed by search engines or automatically translated. Here's an example of Open Captions:

Figure 15.64: Burned-in Open Captions such as these may be obscured by controls, and they cannot be moved or disabled

For the widest use and greatest accessibility, I recommend creating Closed Captions. At export time, you can burn these in to create Open Captions if it's absolutely necessary, but today, more and more playback environments can accept Closed Captions. It's the more accessible choice; they're easier to correct if an error is found after exporting; and they return control over the appearance of captions to the user.

In technical terms, you can choose to create Closed Captions in one of the following formats:

- **iTT — iTunes Timed Text**, used for iTunes Store deliverables. Allows a degree of flexibility with regard to placement and color, but not widely accepted online.

- **CEA-608** — A broadcast standard (**CEA** stands for **Consumer Electronics Association**) with a wide degree of control over color and placement, though it appears in a monospaced font in the Viewer. Limited acceptance online, but this is the only caption format that can be embedded as part of an exported file and viewed on an iOS device. It can also be exported independently as an `.scc` file.

- **SRT** — A common standard online (**SRT** stands for **Secure Reliable Transport**), and though some formatting controls are available, many delivery platforms don't recognize those formatting options. This is the format you want to use for delivery to most online video sharing platforms such as YouTube and Vimeo.

Note also that that you may need to deliver captions to other standards (including **WebVTT**, which stands for **Web Video Text Tracks**), and conversion services are available.

For a new **Project**, the **iTT** format will be active, and **SRT** will be an option. To use **CEA-608** captions, you'll need to edit the **Caption Roles** setting for your Project by choosing **Modify > Assign Caption Roles > Edit Roles** and then pressing the **plus** to the top right. (Note that switching to **CEA-608** won't be necessary unless that format has been specifically requested by a client, or you want captions to be embedded directly in video files.) Here's an illustration:

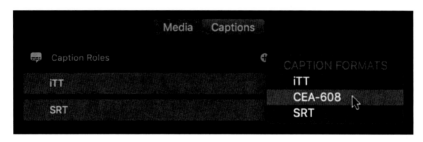

Figure 15.65: Three caption formats are available; activate any format (and language) you need in Roles

Multiple languages are supported in the same dialog. Just as a Project can use Subroles within Roles, a Caption Role can include several languages within that format. For now, we'll assume that you're working in English, but of course if you translate your work to other languages, you'll widen its reach.

While multiple languages can be accommodated in a single Project, if any changes are needed to other elements (such as visual effects or titles) you may prefer to duplicate the Project instead of juggling Roles or Subroles. Another option is to consider creating an *audio description* track so that blind users can understand the visual component of your video.

It's important to know that the capabilities of video sharing services and social media platforms vary, and not all of them support Closed Captioning. Therefore, you won't always be able to deliver Closed Captions but will sometimes have to burn them in to create "always on" Open Captions. This list will become outdated as these services and apps become more accessible, but at the time of publication, the following information was accurate:

- **YouTube** — accepts SRT; can create captions automatically through audio transcription; allows caption editing online:

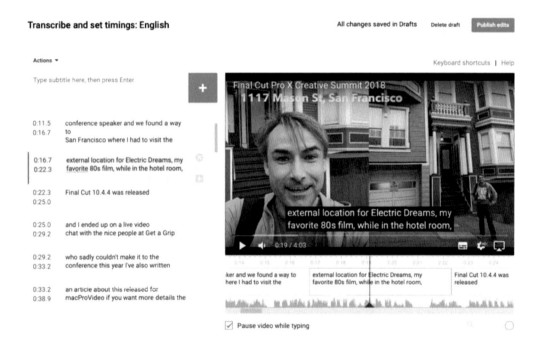

Figure 15.66: Captions on YouTube can be edited and retimed (note that this interface will change soon)

- **Vimeo** — accepts SRT:

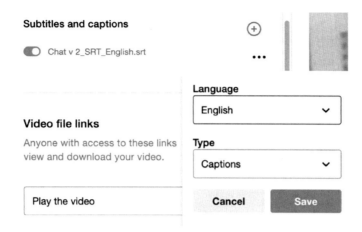

Figure 15.67: In the Distribution tab on Vimeo, you can add one or more caption files

- **Twitter** — accepts SRT, but in the app, captions are only shown if audio is muted
- **Facebook** — accepts SRT
- **LinkedIn** — accepts SRT
- **Instagram** — doesn't currently accept SRT captions; Open Captions only
- **TikTok** — doesn't currently accept SRT captions; Open Captions only

The bottom line right now is that if you plan to put your videos online, you'll need to make SRT captions, and if you're going to use Instagram or TikTok, you'll need to burn them in.

Social media videos often include more titles than other types of videos, and they can happily co-exist with captions. There's no need to duplicate your titles in caption form, but do position your titles so that they won't be hidden by captions, and check how they look on a few different devices to make sure.

With that in mind, how do you actually create your captions? You have a few options.

CREATING CAPTIONS

Captions can be created one at a time by hand, but a third-party captioning service can enable a much faster workflow. Here, we'll just add a few captions by hand, but if your Project runs for more than a few minutes, you'll probably want to use a third party to create the captions as they'll be much more efficient. While most captioning services use **artificial intelligence** (**AI**)-powered voice-to-text conversion, you can pay a higher rate for humans to do it instead. Some AI-based options today include **Simon Says**, **SpeedScriber**, and **Scribeomatic**, while **Rev** offers human translation for a higher cost.

IMPORTANT NOTE

Some transcription services are designed to be involved earlier in the editing process, to allow a rough cut to be created by editing a transcribed text file. While these workflows go beyond the scope of this book, they could save a significant amount of time earlier in the editing process, especially for large-scale documentary work. Third-party services from Lumberjack and Scribeomatic can both enable this workflow.

Another way to use captions is to use them to make note of client feedback, as you would use **To Do Markers**. The advantage of captions is that they're shown in the Viewer during playback, while Markers are less visible.

As I personally prefer to have the final say over the captions on my work, I use an automated service for the first pass, but check and edit every caption by hand to make sure that even industry jargon is correctly spelled. Computer-powered dictation is improving all the time but won't ever be 100% accurate, and even a human can make mistakes if they're not aware of all the specialist terms and acronyms used in a particular video. As an editor, you should probably be aware of those specialist terms and can fix any problems yourself.

To get started creating captions, you'll need a video where someone talks; try with a short video first. Here's how:

1. In the **Timeline**, click to place the Playhead when a person starts to speak.

2. Type ⌥C or choose **Edit** > **Captions** > **Add Caption**.

A new light-blue caption will be added at the top of the timeline, connected to whatever clip is below it. You'll also see an empty box in which you can type. (Captions should be on by default, but if they're off, choose **Show Captions** in the **View** drop-down menu in the **Viewer**.)

3. Type the words that the person speaks into this box.

It's also possible to use the Inspector to enter text, but I prefer to stay on the timeline for this. If you have an untimed transcript of your video, you can paste the text here instead of typing it, and if the box disappears, double-clicking will bring it back, ready for editing. This is what it will look like:

Figure 15.68: Editing a caption on the timeline is a convenient way to position and trim it

4. Trim the duration of the caption clip to match the length of the words spoken, up to two lines of text.

   Accurate placement and duration are important, for viewers and for standards compliance, and two lines of text is a regularly accepted amount of text to include in a single caption.

   As this is the first caption you've added, you'll also need to set the format from **iTT** to **SRT**, easily done at the top of the caption box on the timeline.

5. From the small menu at the top of the caption, choose **English** just under **SRT**:

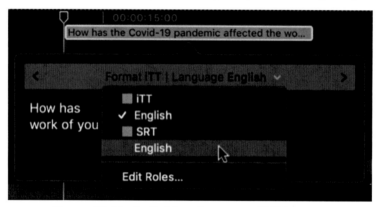

Figure 15.69: Switching format to SRT is easy

A warning pops up, as shown, to let you know that you're changing between formats. That's OK, as we won't be using formatting in SRT captions:

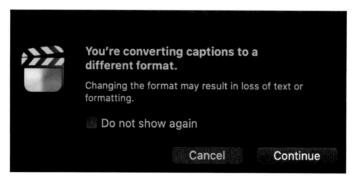

Figure 15.70: Formatting isn't as important as accessibility, so this is OK

6. Click on **Continue** in the warning dialog that appears.

As only one caption format can be used at one time, new captions will automatically be placed into the **SRT** format.

7. Repeat *Steps 2–4* to add, edit, and correct duration of captions for all other speech in your video.

Captioning by hand isn't painful for a short video but can take a while for a longer video. If you've decided to use an online service to create your captions, the workflow (and cost) can vary widely, but it'll probably go something like this:

1. Export a low-resolution video or audio file from your Project.
2. Upload the file to the conversion service.
3. Process the file.
4. Download an SRT file.

Some applications are more tightly integrated with FCP, and you may be able to obtain captions without leaving the app at all. A free way to obtain (not very good) captions is to upload your video to YouTube, then download its automatically generated captions file. However, I won't document the workflow here as it is expected to change soon, and accuracy is better with inexpensive paid services.

IMPORTANT NOTE

An SRT file, as with most other caption formats, is a text file, and that makes it easy to edit the actual captions with a text editor. Feel free to edit the caption text with TextEdit or another text editor of your choice before importing it to FCP. Changing the existing text is easy, but the specific numbered formatting can make it difficult to insert new captions or to delete existing captions this way.

Whichever method you've used to obtain an SRT file for your Project, you can easily import it with **File** > **Import** > **Captions** and then locate the file, with these options:

Figure 15.71: Importing generated captions, even if they aren't perfect, is a big time saver

One final alternative is that if you're given media with embedded CEA-608 captions, you can extract them to make changes or convert them to other formats. Select the clip, then right-click and choose **Extract Captions**.

With all your captions in place, you'll need to fix up any mistakes, and here's how.

EDITING CAPTIONS

Editing captions isn't just about editing the text of a caption but will also involve splitting long captions and potentially joining shorter captions, as well as adding formatting if you're using a format that supports it.

Typing and editing text is straightforward, but beware: some text shortcuts you might be used to are already assigned to operations in FCP. For example, **forward delete** will always delete an entire caption, not the character to the right of the text insertion point. The handiest shortcuts are ⌘← and ⌘→ to move between captions; they're the standard shortcuts to jump between clips using the same role, and they'll save you a lot of double-clicking.

To split a long caption into multiple smaller captions, follow these steps:

1. Double-click the caption to edit it.

2. Click at the point you want to start a new caption, and press the **return** key once to create a new paragraph, as illustrated here:

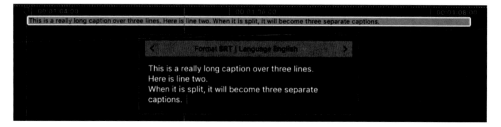

Figure 15.72: Longer captions will be split where the line breaks are placed

3. Repeat this step to create three lines rather than two.

4. Right-click the caption and choose **Split Captions**, as shown here:

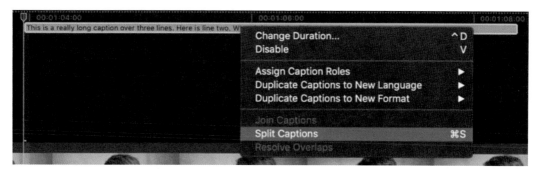

Figure 15.73: If you end up splitting captions often, assign
a more convenient custom keyboard shortcut, as I have here

You will now see three captions taking up an equal amount of space on the
timeline.

5. Trim the duration of each caption to make sure they correspond to the correct
   audio, something like this:

Figure 15.74: Trimming captions so that they start and finish at the correct
time is important

The opposite operation is also important: sometimes, you may prefer to combine
multiple short statements into a single caption. To join two or more captions, follow
these steps:

1. Drag a selection box around multiple neighboring captions to select them
   all at once.

2. Right-click any of the captions and choose **Join Captions**:

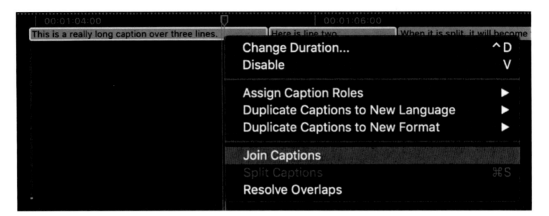

Figure 15.75: Joining captions is easy, but remember to remove extra return characters if you want lines to run together

The captions will now become one, taking up all the space covered by the previous captions and any gaps between them.

3. Edit the new caption and remove any unwanted return characters by pressing **delete**, as illustrated here:

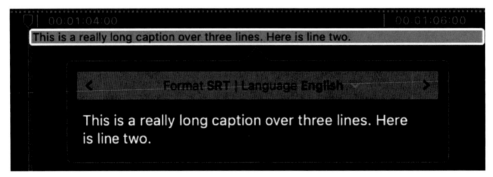

Figure 15.76: The first two captions have now been rejoined and the extra line break removed

The **Join Captions** command doesn't have a shortcut by default, so if you'll be doing this regularly, add a shortcut (to **Join Clips or Captions**) using **Final Cut Pro > Commands > Customize**.

Positioning captions accurately is important: make sure that each caption is correctly timed, appearing with and lasting for the same length as its matching speech. While you won't always get it right the first time, moving and trimming captions is straightforward. Captions can be moved with the mouse just as with any other clips, and trimmed by dragging their edges. You can also nudge them with the **comma** and **period** shortcuts, use **Trim Start** and **Trim End**, and so on.

Normally, captioning is a job done just before final delivery, and so it's unlikely that the edit will change after captioning. But if you do need to edit, you can — even major editing changes can still be made after captioning, due to the magic of the Magnetic Timeline. As you can see in the timeline, captions are connected and will move if their underlying clips move. But crucially, captions can be connected to *connected clips*, not just clips on the Primary Storyline, so moving *any* clip will move any captions connected to it. To reconnect a caption to another clip, or another point on another clip, simply select the caption, then **⌥⌘-click** where you want the connection point to be placed, like this:

Figure 15.77: The first two captions here are connected to the voiceover, making edits easy

Moving underlying clips can sometimes cause captions to overlap, and this can also happen with an incorrectly formatted SRT file. Overlapping captions will change from blue to red to indicate that they are invalid, because only a single caption can be shown at one time:

Figure 15.78: The two red captions here are invalid and should be edited

To fix this automatically, select both captions together, then right-click and choose **Resolve Overlaps**. You can also fix it manually by dragging or moving the edge of one caption so that it no longer overlaps another, or joining the two captions together if that would be appropriate.

UNDERSTANDING STANDARDS AND FORMATTING

Some standards are more restrictive than others. SRT is fairly loose, but with CEA-608, if you use more than four lines of text in the default monospaced font, you'll fail validation and your captions will switch to red, as illustrated here:

Figure 15.79: These captions will need a bit of editing to be valid in CEA-608

Other limits apply to how close your captions can be to the start of the Project or to each other — it's easy for most of your captions to go red if you're not careful, as you can see here:

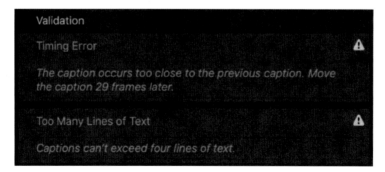

Figure 15.80: Just a couple of the errors you might see listed in the Inspector under an invalid caption

Even without that *four lines of monospaced text* restriction in SRT, try to keep captions to — at most — two lines in the default font in the Viewer. This is only a rough rule of thumb; different players will render the text at different sizes, so your captions can easily spill out over a larger area.

Also, make sure to add in captions for music or sound effects. During a conversation, use a dash preceding a line of dialogue, to indicate that the active speaker has changed. Unwanted sounds such as *um*, *ah*, and breaths can be omitted, as can any obvious minor mistakes or repetitions in what was said.

Depending on delivery requirements, you may have to abridge the text if speech is especially quick and/or complex. If you're not sure, check your delivery requirements, which can be quite specific for larger distributors, or simply outsource this job to a professional service.

You may have noticed a number of formatting options in the Inspector, but unfortunately, many jobs can't make use of them:

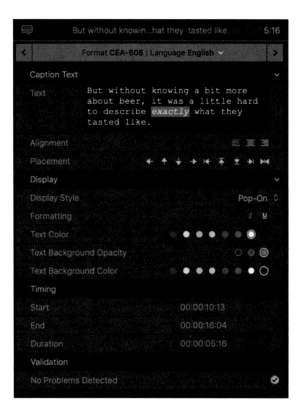

Figure 15.81: SRT offers italic, underline, placement, and color, but you can't always use them

If you're using the CEA-608 format, formatting can be helpful, and this section will let you use different colors for different speakers or position the captions at the top of the screen to avoid a lower third title. But SRT, the most widely understood option online, doesn't offer the same functionality. YouTube, for example, doesn't display color information in SRT files correctly, and positioning information (top, bottom, and so on) can't even be stored in the format. Sadly, the formatting section is best left alone if you're going to export to SRT.

Exporting captions is covered in the next and final chapter, so let's take a quick look back.

REVIEW — CAPTIONING AND SUBTITLES

You've learned about caption formats and that SRT is probably the way to go if you're distributing your video online. You know how to create captions from scratch, but you'll probably have realized that you're better off purchasing your captions for anything over a few minutes, and then editing them.

You know that formatting captions is possible but not always useful, and how to edit, reposition, trim, join, and split captions to get good results. Various kinds of deliverables have standards to follow, and for the most particular clients, captions may be something you outsource entirely. But that's OK. The majority of captioning jobs for many people can indeed be handled on your own timeline, and I've certainly handled captions myself on many larger jobs over the last few years.

SUMMARY

You've learned about a number of ways to augment your videos with words, and backgrounds behind or between those words. Any time there's speech there should be captions, not just because it's a legal requirement in many countries but because it's the right thing to do. And besides captions, good titles can bring so much life to a video that it's simply disappointing to see so many videos that don't do titling well. This is largely because many other NLEs don't have the controls or integration that you can enjoy here, and if a fancy title means outsourcing or juggling another application, many editors don't bother.

Do bother! Clients will appreciate that extra effort, and, if used well, a few changes to the **Custom** title are enough to lift your lower thirds and bumpers way above the norm. Generators, especially if you explore the wild third-party world out there, allow you to perform all kinds of tricks with animated split screens and galleries, so don't overlook them either. A little animation goes a long way:

Figure 15.82: I buy third-party titles as well as making my own — they can be a massive time saver

But you're nearly done! You've finished your edit, corrected the color, enhanced with effects, sweetened the audio, and added a few words. Time to share with the world, in the final chapter.

REVIEW QUESTIONS

1. What's the easiest way to stop editing a text element?
2. Which four principles are important in title design?
3. Which command lets you save text properties for reuse?
4. If you drag on the green circle on 3D text, which axis are you rotating around?
5. Which 2D title lets you apply your own blur, position, scaling, and opacity animations to text?
6. What happens when you add a transition to a connected title?
7. Which title extracts date information from the clip it's connected to?
8. Which generator creates a black background by default?
9. Which closed caption format is popular online?
10. If the delivery destination doesn't support closed captions, what can you do to include captions?

REVIEW ANSWERS

1. Press **Escape**.
2. **Contrast**, **Repetition**, **Alignment**, and **Proximity**.
3. **Save Format Attributes**.
4. The *y* axis.
5. **Custom**.
6. It gets taller and is placed in a storyline.
7. **Date/Time**.
8. **Custom**.
9. **SRT**.
10. Burn in the Closed Captions, converting them to Open Captions.

16 YOU'RE DONE: EXPORTING YOUR EDIT AND FINISHING UP

"I enjoy using FCP X so much I wanted to let the world know about it. So, I made a documentary."
— Brad Olsen, Director, Off The Tracks: *offthetracksmovie.com*

Once you've exported your video, that's it, right? Well, probably not. You (or more likely your client) might decide to rethink a color treatment, or trim a few frames, or fix an unfortunate typo. Unless you're very lucky, the first export is rarely the last, but it's OK to loop back around, tweak a few edits, change a few settings, and send out a version 2, 3, or 14. (Just don't send anything called "final", because it won't be.)

Once the review process is over and the finished Project is ready to show to the world, some of you will want to give away your work for free to as many people as possible, and many others will need to deliver it quietly, to a private audience. Either way is fine, and we'll cover many ways to share (or export) here.

As well as showing you the quickest and easiest ways to prepare and then share your Projects with the world, this chapter will also show you how to share high-quality masters for archiving or further production, how to send your Project to other applications for collaboration purposes, and how to safely archive your work for future use. Lastly, you'll discover a few ways in which you can extend your skills, because media production is forever changing.

This last chapter covers the following topics:

- Preparing for sharing
- Exporting, uploading, and distributing your video

- Exporting for further production
- Archiving your work
- What's next?

Excited? I am, and I hope you are too. It's been a long journey, and we're nearing its end.

PREPARING FOR SHARING

One of the two main ways to finish off a video is to export the final file yourself, and that's what you'll learn to do in this section. First, you'll prepare your file for sharing by making sure the video and audio are within legal bounds. Next, you'll actually share out a file suitable for uploading. Finally, you'll drag it into a browser (or use an app) and upload it to whatever sharing services or other apps you want to send it to. There are other workflows, too, and you'll discover them on the way.

PERFORMING FINAL CHECKS

Before you share your video more widely, it's an excellent idea to take one last look over it. You'll have seen your timeline many times by now, and if you have any spare time before your deadline, spending some of that time on an entirely different Project (or away from the computer altogether) will buy you a fresh perspective. With eyes and ears open, watch your timeline and judge whether every edit is as good as it could be, every shot is as bright and shiny as it should be, and everyone's skin tones look the same from one shot to the next.

And then fix all the things you suddenly noticed.

With your final viewing out of the way, some more automated effects can save you, and if you're going to be making changes to your master Project, right-click on that Project in the **Browser** and then duplicate it before you go any further:

Figure 16.1: This is modern version control, isn't it?

If there's a space before a number at the end, that number will increment, and you just need to double-click on that new Project to make sure you're editing the latest (and hopefully, final) version.

LIMITING THE AUDIO LEVELS

If you've followed the audio workflow from *Chapter 14*, *Boost the Signal: Audio Sweetening*, you've probably already turned everything into a Compound Clip, and monitored the audio levels to make sure no levels peaked too high. If you haven't followed that workflow and audio is important, please do so.

Of course, if your destination isn't fussy about these things and you're out of time, you can skip these steps.

When your edit is contained within a Compound Clip, you can add additional effects to it, making sure that nothing goes too high:

Figure 16.2: Here's a Limiter applied to a Project-wide Compound Clip, to make sure nothing can peak

The **Compressor**, **Limiter**, and **AUDynamicsProcessor** are all good options that can keep audio from getting too loud and, of course, you can control the overall volume manually, with or without keyframes.

LIMITING THE VIDEO LEVELS

While excessive video levels are less likely to create problems for viewers than excessive audio levels, it's still something that some delivery mechanisms can be fussy about, and it's easy to fix. So, if your destination specifies that video levels need to be "broadcast legal," all you need to do is throw on a **Broadcast Safe** video effect from the **Color** category:

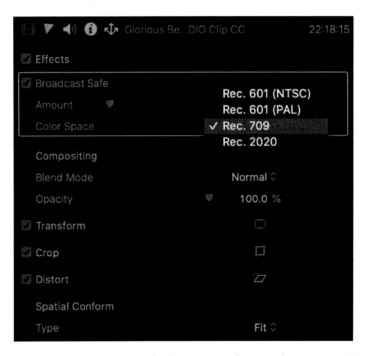

Figure 16.3: The Broadcast Safe filter has a few options, tweakable for broadcast or HDR output

You can verify that the **Broadcast Safe** effect has done its job by activating the Viewer's **Range Check** setting. Head to the **View** menu in the Viewer, then choose **All** from the **Range Check** section near the bottom. With those "zebra" lines active, flick the effect on and off in the Inspector to see the difference, if any. However, if your destination isn't fussy about these things, you can skip all these steps.

If you've created a Compound Clip for audio mixing, you can add it to that Compound Clip. If you haven't, you can add an adjustment layer on top of the whole timeline and then add the effect there. The default settings in the effect should be fine, but tweak them to follow whatever specs you've been given.

CREATING DUPLICATE PROJECTS FOR DIFFERENT ASPECT RATIOS

With the audio and video sounding and looking good, it's time to create any additional versions you might need to produce for alternative aspect ratios. For example, you might have a primary deliverable at 16:9 for regular computers and TVs, plus a shorter square version and/or a vertical version for other platforms. This is now much easier to configure thanks to *new features in 10.4.9*.

And once more, if you only need to deliver to a single aspect ratio, you can skip these steps.

For each alternative aspect ratio, follow these steps:

1. Click once in the **Browser** to give focus to that interface pane.

2. Right-click on your **Project** in the **Browser** and choose **Duplicate Project As...**:

Figure 16.4: Duplicating your Project is a great safeguard and a way to create alternative aspect ratios

3. In the **Project Properties** panel that appears, give the new Project a name that includes the aspect ratio, such as `square` or `vertical`.

4. Change the **Video Format** and **Resolution** properties to fit your new aspect ratio, using the built-in presets or typing your own values into **Custom** to suit the provided specifications.

5. Check the **Smart Conform** option, then press **OK**, as shown:

Figure 16.5: If the main deliverable is approved in 16:9 aspect, you'll need to get this square version approved too

When used automatically like this, **Smart Conform** here applies to every clip on the timeline, so you'll have to wait for a short while as the clips are analyzed. (If you don't check this box now, you can later select all the clips and then choose **Modify** > **Smart Conform**). Either way, you'll see this:

Figure 16.6: Smart Conform will take a short time to figure out what the best framing is for each shot

Smart Conform should help a lot, but you may still find that some shots need to be reframed manually, as discussed in *Chapter 12*, *Refine and Smooth: Video Properties and Effects*. Head through the timeline shot by shot, repositioning and scaling each one as needed, using **Transform Overscan** so that you can check that you're choosing the best part of each shot. With any luck, you've planned for this by shooting wider than you needed with a high-resolution camera, but if a shot just doesn't work, you might have to replace it with an alternative shot, or two shots in a split-screen.

Figure 16.7: Smart Conform was a good start, but the X position still needed a tweak here

In each different version of your Project, the audio can stay the same, the color will be fine, and any captions should still work. Most effects will work properly too, but some transitions (especially third-party complex ones) might look a little odd. If a transition assumes that the frame is 16:9, you could see some glitches around the edges, but most of the built-in transitions look fine.

Another thing that's likely to need work is titles. With **Motion**, titles can be designed to work automatically with multiple aspect ratios, but many older titles were not. If your titles weren't designed to work in multiple aspect ratios, they may need to be scaled down, repositioned, or replaced entirely. (You'll probably have to scale them down, then copy them, then find all the other titles with the **Timeline Index**, and then **Paste Attributes** to fix them. And if those titles are in Compound Clips, remember to use **Reference New Parent Clip** to avoid destroying the original versions).

With regard to lower thirds and bumpers, you can avoid problems by choosing aspect-adaptable third-party titles, or use a style that's more square than rectangular to help it work in more contexts.

> IMPORTANT NOTE
>
> Another use for titles is to control how burned-in captions appear. As you'll see soon, the built-in options for burning in are very basic, so if you have to control font and appearance, you'll have to convert them to titles instead. Look at **X-Title Extractor** from spherico.com/filmtools for more on this.

Some clients have alternative forms of their logos available for different aspect ratios, so check the style guide and replace the logo if you need to. If you've wrapped the logo in a Compound Clip, duplicate that Compound Clip so you don't mess up the original version.

With the aspect ratio(s) taken care of, it's time to make use of all that work you put into roles way back at the start of the Project.

LIMITING ROLE VISIBILITY

If you've used Roles to separate different languages (or anything else) for titles or audio, this is the time to turn them on or off, so as to make sure the right clips are active. **Timeline Index** is the place to check and fix this; just turn on the things you want and any extra languages off:

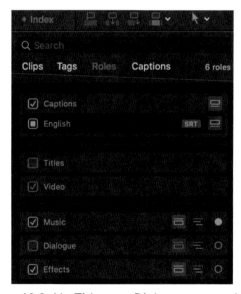

Figure 16.8: No Titles, no Dialogue, no problem

OK, you're ready. Video, audio, aspect ratio all checked. Nearly time to export.

SETTING UP A SHARING PRESET

Standards will change over time, but today, H.264 is the most commonly used standard codec for exporting compressed video. H.265 (HEVC) is another option, and while it can produce similar quality at lower data rates, it currently takes much longer to export and requires Apple's Compressor application; for now, we'll stay with H.264. Before we jump into the process, we'll quickly set up a couple of presets to make things easier. It's a good idea to set up your presets first and then stick to them, and here's how you do it:

1. Choose **Final Cut Pro** > **Preferences**.

2. Click **Destinations**, and then **Add Destination** at the bottom left.

   This pane lets you change the export presets. If you own Apple's Compressor app, you'll be able to add extra options here, but most users can get by with the built-in options.

3. Drag **Export File** from the area on the right to the menu on the left:

Figure 16.9: When you drag from the right to the left, a new destination is created

4. Set **Format** to **Computer**.

5. Set **Resolution** to the largest setting possible, **4096×2160**.

6. Change **Action** to **QuickTime Player**. (If **QuickTime Player** isn't an option, choose **Other**, and then find **QuickTime Player** in the **Applications** menu.)

7. Double-click on **Export File** and rename it Computer:

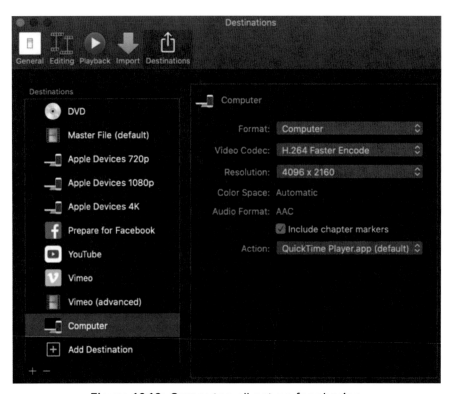

Figure 16.10: Computer, all set up for sharing

This is a one-time operation that creates a new high-quality preset for almost any kind of online sharing service. But what do the format options mean? All these options use the H.264 codec, but with different container formats and at different data rates:

- **Apple Devices** uses a .m4v container at a lower data rate (~10 Mbps for 1080p, ~20 Mbps for 4K)

- **Web Hosting** uses a .mov container at a low to moderate data rate (~15 Mbps for 1080p, ~20 Mbps for 4K)

- **Computer** uses a .mp4 container at a high data rate (~20 Mbps for 1080p, ~30 Mbps for 4K)

Don't worry too much about data rates. When you upload a video to an online sharing service such as YouTube or Vimeo, that service compresses it down to a much smaller data rate (as little as 2.5 Mbps for 1080p), so your job is simply to provide a file that looks good to them, so that their recompression looks good too. Reducing the data rate will make your upload go faster, but greatly increases the chance that compression artifacts will be visible after it's recompressed — and there's no way to avoid that final recompression process.

> IMPORTANT NOTE
>
> There's one exception: if a client will be distributing your final videos directly on their own network, you might need to directly produce files at a lower data rate than any of these options. For this, I recommend the free Handbrake app (handbrake.fr) because it produces acceptable quality at a much lower data rate (under 4 Mbps for 1080p) than Final Cut Pro or even Compressor can.

While dedicated compression apps such as Compressor and Handbrake can offer a wide range of options, you don't need to worry about them if the final destination is any kind of video sharing site or social media platform — just keep the data rate high and let the site take care of the rest:

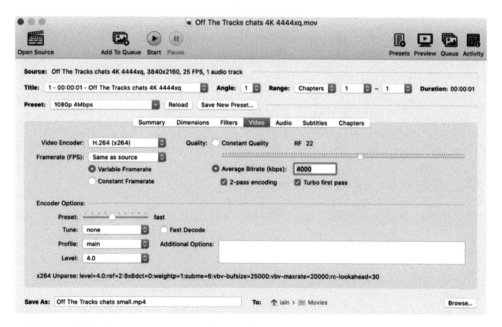

Figure 16.11: Most people won't need to mess with Handbrake, although it works and is free

Computer has a high enough data rate to avoid compression artifacts, but not so large that it's hard to work with. Another reason to choose **Computer** is its container format. The MPEG-4 container (.mp4) is widely recognized as a video format, and plays on many kinds of devices. While you can rename .m4v and .mov to .mp4 and most players will still function correctly, they're not quite the same internally. Just pick **Computer**.

REVIEW — PREPARING FOR SHARING

You've done a few things here. You fixed the audio and video to valid limits, and made it look and sound as good as you could. If you needed to make any duplicates for alternative aspect ratios, you made them — or at least, you did once the edit was signed off. And you've set up a preset that you can use to export to just about anyone. Sorted! Let's get something out there.

EXPORTING, UPLOADING, AND DISTRIBUTING YOUR VIDEO

In this section, you'll learn how to turn your timeline into a finished video, and then how to get it in front of people. You'll want to show your client first, get their feedback, and make their changes in an efficient way. When everyone's finally happy, you'll want to put it on any number of video sites and social media platforms. But it all starts with a file, and that file will be compressed.

EXPORTING A COMPRESSED VIDEO

There are several easy ways to export a high-quality file, including direct-to-site exports and master files, but we'll go for the one that works every time. For a complete experience, you'll want to find a Project that includes captions, in either 1080p or 4K resolution. To get started, perform the following steps:

1. Double-click the **Project** you want to export.

    This step isn't strictly necessary, as you can export a selected Project you're not currently working on, but it's a good confirmation that you're exporting the correct timeline.

2. If you want to select only part of the video, switch to the **Range Selection** tool **(R)** and drag a range, or press **I** at the start and **O** at the end.

   This step is entirely optional, and is only needed for partial exports.

3. Choose **File** > **Share** > **Computer...** or choose **Computer...** from the **Share** drop-down menu in the top-right corner:

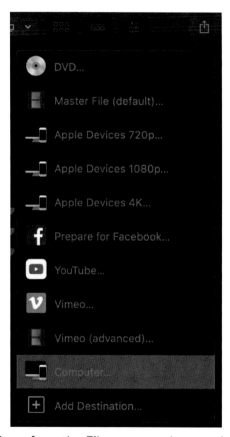

Figure 16.12: Share from the File menu or the top-right Share menu

In the dialog that appears, you'll see a preview of the video to the left, information at the bottom, and three tabs at the top. The information at the bottom left tells you the resolution, frame rate, and audio type, with the duration on the left and the file extension (container) on the right, along with an estimated file size.

4. If desired, change the **Name**, **Creator**, and **Tags** fields.

The name of the Project becomes the name here and, in turn, it will be used to generate the filename:

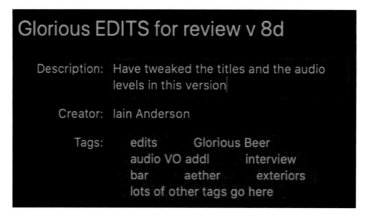

Figure 16.13: The name, description, and tags will all be exposed in QuickTime Player's Info window

Note that this name will be visible in **QuickTime Player** even if you change the filename later, so use a sensible name here as it might be seen.

5. Click on **Roles** to examine the options.

If you have used captions in this Project, you'll see additional options here.

6. To export Closed Captions, check the box in the bottom captions section to **Export each language as a separate file**.

If you're exporting SRT captions, don't include formatting as it doesn't work everywhere and may cause issues:

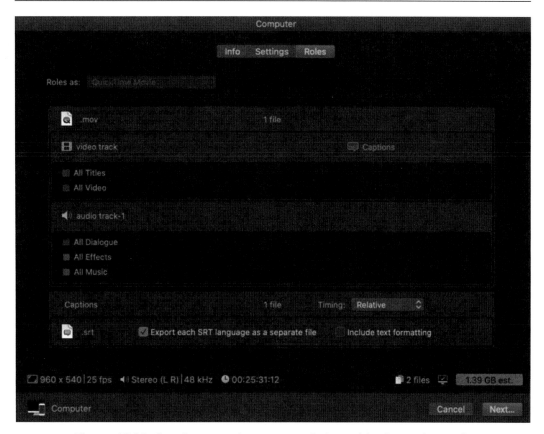

Figure 16.14: Captions can be exported alongside the main movie

7. To export embedded CEA-608 or Open (burned-in) Captions, click the word **Captions** in the video section above and then pick the appropriate options from the menus.

Remember that Open Captions should only be used if your delivery mechanism doesn't support Closed Captions:

Figure 16.15: To embed captions, click Captions and then choose a format to burn in, or embed CEA-608

If you want to burn in captions with more control than is possible here, you'll need to convert them to titles with a third-party app, as noted in the earlier section in this chapter.

8. Click on **Settings** and check that the format options are correct.

These should be the same as the **Computer** preset you saved earlier. If you make changes here, the preset will also change, so don't! Instead, create fresh presets for each export type. It should still look like this:

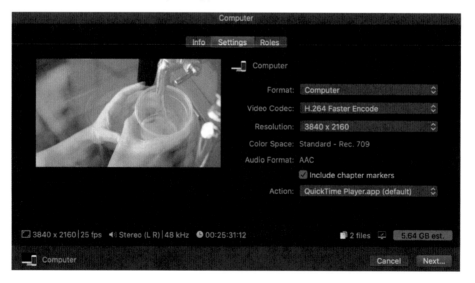

Figure 16.16: Double-check that the Resolution setting is correct, but don't tweak it

9. Click **Next**, and then choose where to save the file.

    If you only see a very small **Save** panel, press the small arrow to the right of the drop-down menu to expand to the full dialog.

10. Press **Save**.

In the top left of the interface, you'll now see a clock-style progress display:

Figure 16.17: The progress indicator should wipe around pretty quickly — exports are quick here

11. Click this progress display to show the **Background Tasks** window.

    This optional window will display the progress of any task in more detail:

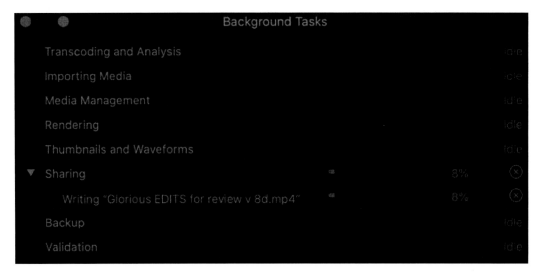

Figure 16.18: If you're on a deadline, you might prefer the extra information from this window

12. When the timeline finishes exporting, play the output file in **QuickTime Player** and make sure it's as you expect.

13. If you've exported captions, make sure the `.srt` captions file is next to the video file.

With each export, you'll just want to check the name and that the caption settings are correct — it's easy once you know how. And finally, if the Closed Captions are the only thing that's changed (or you forgot about them during the first export!), another option is to use **File** > **Export Captions**.

Importantly, if you have several edits to export, you can do that easily. Just select them all at once in the Browser (don't double-click) and then share them all in a single operation:

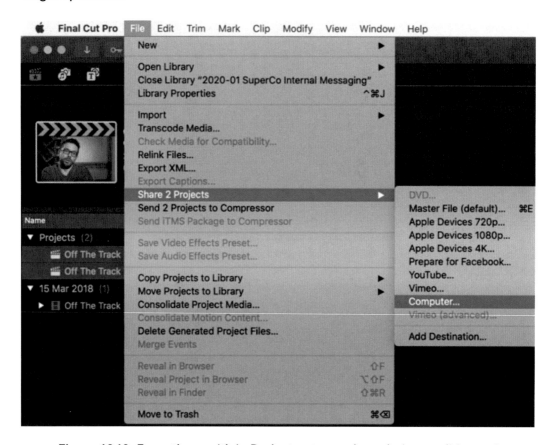

Figure 16.19: Exporting multiple Projects at once is entirely possible, and very useful

In a multi-Project export, you won't be able to select only part of a timeline, and you can't change the names, descriptions, or settings for individual Projects, but that's likely not a problem — it's a big time saver. Though you may not need to, it's also possible to export Compound Clips or regular clips in the same way.

IMPORTANT NOTE

My preferred workflow is always to export a file, and then to upload it in a separate step. While it is possible to upload directly to YouTube or Vimeo using the built-in export presets, I avoid these direct-upload options for a few reasons.

Firstly, Final Cut Pro must be kept running for the entire upload process, and while that's usually quick, a slow network connection or a large file can make it take much longer. It's also not easy to find and keep a copy of the video file made as part of this process, and I always want to archive that file with the rest of the job.

These methods don't allow SRT captions to be uploaded automatically, so you'll need to add captions manually. Similarly, other site-specific video settings aren't always supported. For example, direct Vimeo uploads can't be set to "Anyone with the private link", a common sharing option. And when the video is finished uploading, you'll have to visit the site to get a link for a client review anyway.

By all means, use the instant-upload Share presets if you have a very fast upload speed and don't care about keeping your exported video files — those features do work. But at some point, you'll need to visit the website.

With a compressed video and caption file in hand, you can upload it to the video site of choice through a browser, through a dedicated uploading app, or give it to the client via a file sharing service such as iCloud Drive, Dropbox, OneDrive, Google Drive, or something else. But there are a few fancy options too, so let's take this to the next step.

UPLOADING FOR CLIENT REVIEW

To upload a compressed file, you might use a browser, third-party integrated service, or an uploading app — but using a website through a browser is the universal option. If you're using a browser to upload a draft, the rough process is something like the following:

1. Open a browser (Safari, Chrome, Firefox, and so on) and head to the site you want to post your video to.

2. Log in and click the **Upload** or **Create** button.

3. Drag your compressed video file into the browser.

4. While the video uploads, apply privacy settings, keeping it private for now.

5. Upload your captions.

6. Send your client a link for review.

The review loop will involve receiving feedback, duplicating your Project, making the changes, and repeating all these aforementioned steps. While captions may not be completed until the final version, the client will need to check them at some point before distribution.

Which site(s) are good for review? Most video professionals today use Vimeo or Frame.io, though other options exist. YouTube is very popular for final delivery, but it's less commonly used for client review:

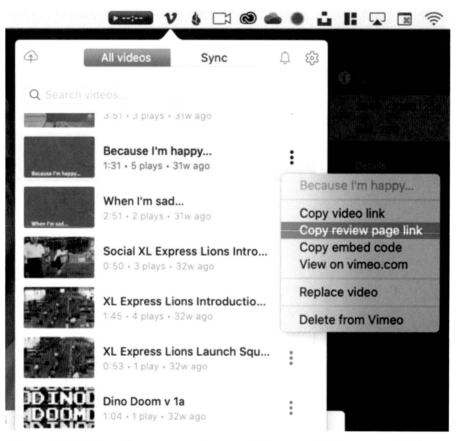

Figure 16.20: The Vimeo menu bar app lets you quickly copy a link to a review page

Unlike YouTube, both Vimeo and Frame.io offer dedicated apps that can make the upload process faster and more efficient. Their review and commenting workflows allow clients to leave notes at specific moments in the video, security is tighter, and Frame.io even allows client comments to be reimported to your timeline through an extension.

There's a lot to both of these services, but I don't want to get into much detail as these are both paid subscriptions, they'll change over time, and they have competitors. If you're exchanging videos with clients, look into the options currently available as they could save you serious time in the review process.

A less useful alternative is to share videos through a file storage service such as Dropbox, Google Drive, OneDrive, or iCloud Drive. These all include Finder integration with their apps, so the upload process is as simple as putting the file into a folder and waiting for it to sync. However, file storage sites aren't great at client review, don't always deliver video in a reliable way to all platforms, and can't be used to deliver the final video to a wider audience — important if the client wants to simply flick a switch and make it live. As a halfway house, integrations exist between some video sharing sites and online storage services (for example, you could upload a file to Google Drive and then instantly transfer it to Vimeo), so look into what your services can offer if you want to speed up the upload process.

You may wish to check the final video quality after that site's recompression, but be ready to be disappointed. If you look for flaws, you'll see compression artifacts even on paid streaming services, with the worst picture quality to be found in features shot on film. All that lovely grain doesn't compress well, and you'll often see blocky noise in the shadows. Weirdly, a clean video shot on a modern camera will suffer a lot less from these issues.

If you're unhappy with your final video quality online, you'll probably find that reducing image complexity and noise will help a lot more than increasing the data rate of the file you send them. The best version of any movie is always the one you see in the edit bay, and nobody else can see it in the same way.

UPLOADING FOR DISTRIBUTION

At the end of the review process, when everything is signed off, you'll probably want to send your video somewhere. For many editors, that means putting it up for free online, and that's what this section is about. If that's not what you're about, no problem — skip down to the next section:

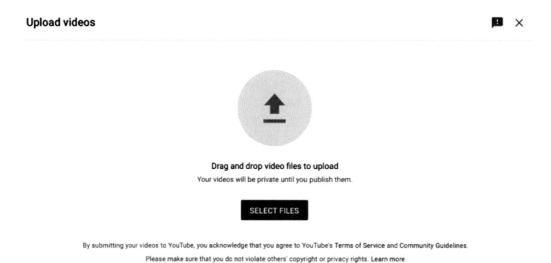

Figure 16.21: Make sure not to close the window during the upload process

YouTube is currently the king of free video distribution online. The website is very good, offering extensive auto-captioning and translation, caption editing, commenting, monetization, and much more. It's extremely popular, with apps on almost every platform, and can really bring an audience:

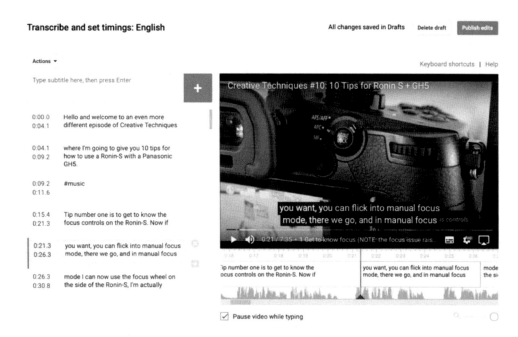

Figure 16.22: Caption editing is comprehensive, and begins with automatically generated captions

Video-focused competitors such as Vimeo focus more on embedded and paid distribution, while social platforms such as Twitter, Facebook, Instagram, LinkedIn, and others distribute short, free videos to millions of viewers a day. Many more social media platforms are waiting to be launched and will have failed before you read this, so I won't go into too many specifics about your final video distribution.

If the target platform has a website, you can probably use that, but if not, you may need to send the final video file to your phone, and upload from the dedicated app. (AirDrop is a great way to move files from your Mac to an iPhone or iPad.)

For distribution through YouTube, Vimeo, or another site, just follow the upload process from the preceding client review. You'll need your final video file, your captions, and also the following:

- Thumbnail images that are intriguing but not annoying
- A full description that appeals to people and algorithms
- A plan for advertising and promotion

Don't underestimate the power of promotion, or your very good video will go unsung and unnoticed. Expectation management is also important. While no views at all is bad, small numbers can be pretty normal. Remember that most videos are intended for a very specific audience — whatever niche your clients are trying to reach — and that the vast majority of videos will never see the millions of views in a day that every popular music video gets:

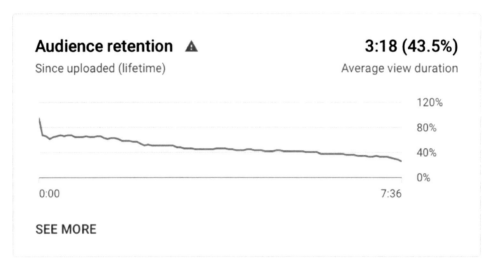

Figure 16.23: So... most people don't actually watch a whole video?

Every site counts views differently, and you can stare deep into the abyss of analytics if you really want to, but you'd be surprised how little of a video has to be seen to count as a "view." Consistency over time will help you build an audience, but if there was a magic formula for success, everyone would follow it.

IMPORTANT NOTE

Recently, YouTube allowed videos to be segmented into chapters by entering timestamps in the description, which is a good way to break up longer videos. While it's unfortunate that no services currently recognize the built-in **Chapter Markers**, the app **Creator's Best Friend** (in the Mac App Store) can convert timeline-based Chapter Markers into the right format for YouTube, saving you effort. This is very useful if you'd like to distribute longer videos, but something you'd have to do by hand on Vimeo.

Each platform has its own style and its own set of restrictions, so you'll need to play by the local rules regarding duration and aspect ratios. You'll want to experiment to find out whether short or long videos work best (short, usually) and what kinds of videos each platform's audience prefers.

REVIEW — EXPORTING, UPLOADING, AND DISTRIBUTING YOUR VIDEO

You can now export a high-quality compressed file and a caption file, and then upload them. Websites are easy, and you know about apps too. You've been along the review path, received feedback, made changes, and done it all again. You've also considered distribution, and you're OK with your video not getting a million views in its first week.

But wait a minute. If you're not the last link in the production chain, you won't be the one who distributes the final file, and you may well not care about this online stuff at all. Instead, you might need to collaborate with other professionals who will edit and finesse color, audio, or visual effects in a way you can't. And that's coming up next.

EXPORTING FOR FURTHER PRODUCTION

While the last section focused on compressed output, in this section, you'll learn all about high-quality output, for delivering the final product, or just your part of a larger job. You'll learn about ProRes, about audio stems, about the wonders of XML and the workflows it enables, and even how to work with other editors.

In some cases, you'll export high-quality finished files (in some flavor of ProRes) and in others you'll provide your original media files along with an XML file, or some kind of compressed version. It's even possible that you might send an entire Library and everything inside it. The wider world of production uses a variety of different applications for audio and for video, and if you want to work with others, you'll need to be able to send them something they can work with.

High-quality files are a good place to start. We've mentioned it before, but let's take a deep dive into ProRes.

UNDERSTANDING PRORES

ProRes is a family of intermediate or "mezzanine" codecs that are ideal for high-quality exports. While it's easy to export to this popular Apple-made format, first let's understand why you might want to do this.

You may remember an earlier discussion about optimized media, way back in *Chapter 3, Bring It In: Importing Your Footage*. Optimizing a clip means converting it to ProRes 422 to make it easier to edit than the original compressed video formats. Some compressed formats are easier to work with and don't require any optimization, while other formats are difficult or impossible and must be converted to ProRes 422 first. Not all files are equal, and not all H.264 files are the same; some may need to be optimized:

Figure 16.24: Use one or both of these if you're working with difficult media, but neither if your footage is easy to work with

As ProRes is a widely accepted format in the industry, it's a sensible choice for sending high-quality files to other professionals for further editing or production. The codec is designed to make decoding as quick as possible, even in Multicam workflows, and can be recompressed into the same codec many times over without visual degradation. ProRes is an intra-frame codec in which each frame is independently compressed, and while not all intra-frame codecs are easy to work with, ProRes definitely is:

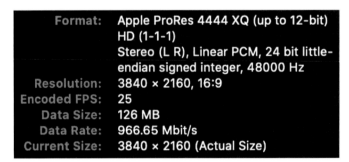

Figure 16.25: This one-second ProRes 4444 XQ movie has a huge data rate, but it does play back well

Data rates are variable, jumping up to accommodate more detail, and also vary depending on the frame rate and frame size chosen. Refer to the Apple ProRes White Paper (https://www.apple.com/final-cut-pro/docs/Apple_ProRes_White_Paper.pdf) for all the fine details.

Optimized always means the "regular" ProRes 422, though there are other members of the codec family that you might choose to use for exporting. While visible quality loss is unlikely with regular ProRes 422, you can choose to use a lower-quality version (to save space) or higher-quality version (for the most demanding post-production applications) if you prefer. Including the approximate target data rate for 1080p @ 29.97 fps, here are your ProRes choices:

- **ProRes 422 Proxy** — 45 Mbps, low quality, usually shows visible artifacts and so should not be used for exporting
- **ProRes 422 LT** — 102 Mbps, medium quality, sometimes shows visible artifacts and so should be used only if space or bandwidth are restricted
- **ProRes 422** — 147 Mbps, high quality, good for high-quality exports
- **ProRes 422 HQ** — 220 Mbps, very high quality, good for high-quality exports for footage from high-end cameras
- **ProRes 4444** — 330 Mbps, very high quality with $4:4:4$ color space and transparency support, good for high-quality exports for footage from high-end cameras where full color information or transparency is required
- **ProRes 4444 XQ** — 500 Mbps, extremely high quality with $4:4:4$ color space and transparency support, good for the absolute best exports for footage from the very best cameras where full color information or transparency is required

While it's tempting just to turn every setting up to maximum, you'll hit some real-world limits at the incredibly high data rates of 4K. For example, a UHD Computer export to H.264 takes up 30 Mbps, but ProRes 422 is far higher at 492 Mbps, or 221 GB per hour, and ProRes 422 HQ adds 50% on top of that! While those numbers might not seem such a big deal for a single file delivered on a hard drive, if your internet connection is less than top-tier, you'll find it takes a while to upload high-quality files.

Though a single file is unlikely to fill up your hard drive, if you're using ProRes as a codec throughout production (for example, with an external recorder), then you'll need a lot more of it. While many professionals are used to this, if you're planning to send high-quality files around in post-production, make sure you have enough storage, and enough time to move it around. Only use the 4444 versions of ProRes if you're working with VFX houses or need to support transparency, as they're almost certainly overkill otherwise.

Now that you know what the different kinds of ProRes are for, how do you export them? That depends on whether you're exporting a simple movie, or if you have more complex requirements. Simple stuff first.

EXPORTING A SIMPLE PROJECT

Assuming you've already prepared your Project for sharing by following the earlier steps, this process is very similar to exporting a compressed file:

1. Select a **Project**, a **Compound Clip**, a **clip**, or **part of a Project** using the **Range Selection** tool, or **I** and **O**:

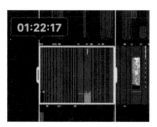

Figure 16.26: If you only want to export part of a longer Project, select it first

2. Choose **File** > **Share** > **Master File** or choose **Master File** from the **Share** drop-down menu at the top right.

3. If desired, change the name, creator, and tags.

4. Click **Settings** at the top, and make sure **Format** is set to **Video and Audio**:

Figure 16.27: Master File exports cannot change the resolution, but will always match the Project

5. Under **Video Codec**, choose the variant of ProRes you're looking for, or use the default for your Project by choosing **Source**.

6. If you need to send captions, click on **Roles** and make sure the correct options are checked.

7. Click **Next**, choose where to save the file, and then click **Save**.

That file can now be sent on for further post-production or even distribution. And yes, it is possible (though usually overkill) to upload ProRes or ProRes LT files to sites such as YouTube. Some people swear that it gives better quality, but I'm yet to see that myself. Always remember that every video platform will mercilessly crush whatever you send it, and pushing up the data rate too far just makes it take longer to get it there.

It's also worth noting that the **Video Codec** menu hides a few non-ProRes options, too. The uncompressed options shouldn't be used unless absolutely necessary as the files are absolutely colossal: more than 3x the data rate of ProRes 4444 XQ. Truly uncompressed video is something rarely seen today, as it's difficult to work with and transport:

Figure 16.28: Codec options include a lot of ProRes, plus H.264 and Uncompressed

But there's a far more compressed option in the same menu. If you choose **H.264**, it will export at the frame size of the Project, to an approximate data rate of 12.5 Mbps in 1080p (lower than the **Computer** export preset's 20 Mbps) or 50 Mbps in 4K (much higher than **Computer**'s 30 Mbps). If you ever notice that a 4K Project has visible artifacts when using the **Computer** export preset, remember this as an option, but don't use it for 1080p Projects.

The movie you've just made functions like a single file, and can be used like one. But you can do a whole lot more if you need to keep the different parts of your Project separate for further post-production. The best way to keep those components apart is with Roles, and here's how to take best advantage of their power.

EXPORTING SEPARATE ELEMENTS WITH ROLES

For a multi-element export, find a more complex Project, one with a few titles (using the Title role) and different kinds of audio (Effects, Music). When you're ready, start the export process again:

1. Select a **Project**, or **part of a Project** using the **Range Selection** tool, or **I** and **O**.

2. Choose **File** > **Share** > **Master File** or choose **Master File** from the **Share** drop-down menu at the top right.

3. Click **Settings** at the top, and make sure **Format** is set to **Video and Audio**.

4. Under **Video Codec**, choose **Source**.

5. Click on **Roles**, and then click the drop-down menu in the top-left corner and choose **Multitrack QuickTime Movie**.

   The **Roles** section now offers new controls, and in the main part of this window you'll see one video track and multiple audio tracks:

Figure 16.29: The Multitrack QuickTime options allow you to include separated audio

6. Click **Remove x** next to one of your video roles to turn it off.

7. From the **Add Role** menu to the right of the video track, select the role you just deleted to add it back in.

   Only a single video track will be produced from all active video roles. However, each audio role will be rendered to a separate track within the QuickTime movie, which means each one can be controlled separately by someone down the line. You can turn off extra roles if you don't want them.

8. Click **Next**, choose where to save the file, and then click on **Save**.

To test that this workflow was successful, you can reimport the file back into one of your Libraries. If you add it to a timeline and then **⌥-double-click** the audio waveform, you'll see multiple channels, with different content on each. They won't have the correct role names, but that can be easily communicated:

Figure 16.30: After re-importing the multitrack QuickTime movie, you'll see a channel for each role

Some applications can't deal with a multitrack QuickTime movie, and need entirely separate files. Repeat steps 1–4 above, then click on **Roles**, and then click the drop-down menu in the top-left corner and choose **Separate Files**. Very similar controls allow you to add not just extra tracks, but extra `.aiff` files for audio. (AIFF is an uncompressed format that's very similar to `.wav`, and widely readable.) The audio files created this way, known as *stems*, are named for their Roles and will be straightforward for an audio post-production specialist to deal with:

Figure 16.31: Exporting to separate files is another option from the same menu

While it's tempting to create separate files for video and for titles, there's an issue. Only a single format can be chosen for both of these files, and while you'll need to use a larger 4444 format to maintain transparency in the titles, you don't need such a heavy format for the video. If you would prefer to export the titles to ProRes 4444 and the regular video to ProRes 422, you'll have to do that in two operations.

You can choose to export only video or audio as separate files from the same top-left menu, and, to make repeated tasks easier, you can save export presets there too:

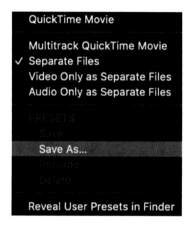

Figure 16.32: Doing this a lot? Save a preset!

Depending on requirements, you might end up exporting a few different versions:

- A regular QuickTime movie for reference (everything active, one Video, and one Audio track)

- A multitrack text-free QuickTime movie for translation purposes (Video on, Titles off, all audio tracks on, but Dialogue will be replaced)

- A separate files version with a Video only file, a Video + Titles file, and all Audio Roles separated

Whether you go for separate files or multitrack QuickTime movies will depend on who you're collaborating with. Ask them what they'd prefer, and try the different options out. Still, an audio professional might reply with a request such as "Can you send me an OMF?". Well, OMF is a dead format, but it's been replaced by AAF, and that's just one of many formats you can deliver with the help of XML.

EXPORTING TO XML

To enable various advanced workflows, you'll often need to export to XML, an interchange format supported by many applications. **XML** stands for **eXtensible Markup Language**, and while it is text-based and human-readable, it's not a fixed format like JPEG or AIFF. Each application that uses XML does so in a different way, so it's not enough for an application to just *support XML*, it has to *support a particular version of XML from FCP*.

The process involves exporting an XML file from Final Cut Pro, and then passing that along to a third-party app that then re-interprets it. Creating an XML file is easy, but it's also flexible, so you have to make sure you have the right thing selected first. As you can export a Project, an Event, and even an entire Library to XML, you must select whatever you want to export and then choose **File** > **Export XML**. The only clue is the name you'll see when saving the file, as it will reflect the name of the Project, Event, or Library you have selected:

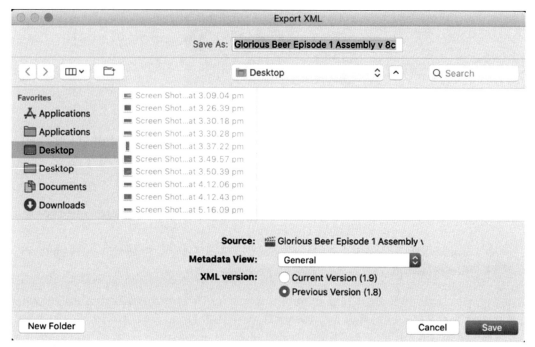

Figure 16.33: I'm exporting a Project here, and the name is the only clue

Importantly, an XML file does not include any media, it just describes the files and/ or edits. If you're using XML, you should be following an external media workflow, and you'll need to provide the media as well as the XML file. For more details, refer to *Chapter 3, Bring It In: Importing Your Footage*.

With the XML and media handy, a third-party app called **X2Pro** can handle the conversion to AAF, so an audio engineer using ProTools has full flexibility. If you don't have X2Pro, you might be able to use DaVinci Resolve as a conversion tool of sorts, and it does lots more too. With limits, Resolve and other conversion tools can send timelines to or from other editing applications via XML, which is very handy if you need to finish a job someone else has started.

Many other apps can do useful things with XML too. One interesting option is **Producer's Best Friend**, which can create spreadsheets to report on the exact durations of clips, keywords, roles, and lots more besides. This could be vital if you have to pay royalties for stock footage or audio. In general, if you find an external app that can usefully interpret the data on a timeline, it's probably using XML:

Figure 16.34: XML can be imported and exported, and it's a useful transfer mechanism

You could even periodically export an XML from your timeline to function as a backup of sorts, because you can import an XML file with **File** > **Import** > **XML...**. However, because there are some pieces of information that XML doesn't correctly store (or which aren't correctly read on import), data can be lost in translation. Some text styling and Drop Zone assignments may be set to defaults, but basic edits should be fine. The .fcpxml format changes regularly, so be sure that all the applications in the mix are up to date.

If XML's shortcomings mean it doesn't work for you, that's no problem. You need to learn about transfer Libraries.

COLLABORATING USING LIBRARIES

To work with a small team, a common workflow is to keep matched copies of your media on local, duplicate drives, and share small Libraries between editors. A *lean* Library is one that uses external media, and a *transfer* Library is a small, lean Library used to transport a single Project in an Event. Depending on your needs, you may choose to use a lean Library (including all clips and Projects) or a transfer Library (just one Project) to work collaboratively.

In each case, your editors will need a copy of the media — original, optimized, or some flavor of proxy. If media is kept (as is likely) external to the Library, each editor should place it in the same location, on a hard drive with the same name (or indeed, access the same network-based storage system in an edit facility). That way, relinking may not be needed at all.

At a high level, here's the collaboration process:

1. Share your entire Library (a small file) and your media (large if original, small if proxy) with another editor.

2. The other editor opens their copy of your "lean" Library.

3. If that Library has no media, they may need to relink to their copy of the media (original, optimized, or proxy).

4. The other editor makes duplicates of your Project and makes editing changes.

5. They send a copy of their new Library back, but they don't need to send the media — you already have it.

6. You open this lean Library and move the new Project back into your original Library without copying media.

7. The media should now automatically relink, but you can relink manually if needed.

This workflow works no matter where the editors are; they could be on different machines in the same office and connected to the same storage system, or on different sides of the planet. There is the possibility that you might see some duplication of containers, such as Compound Clips or Multicam Clips, so be careful.

How do you share a Library, with or without the media? The 10.4.9 release added a new feature that lets you create a new Library containing some or all of the contents of an existing Library, and 10.5 improved on this, allowing on-the-fly transcoding. Even better, since proxy files can now be really small (H.264 at 12.5% of original size), it's also possible to send a self-contained Library including only proxy media, rather than a totally lean Library. Either way, it's easy:

1. Select your Library (or Project, or Event) in the Browser sidebar.

2. Choose **File** > **Copy to Library** > **New Library** (this command will change its name slightly if you select a Project or Event).

3. Give the Library a name and click **Save**.

4. In the next dialog, choose to include media or send a Library without media (for example, if you plan to send it separately, or they have it already).

5. If you choose to include media, pick which kind(s) of media you wish to include:

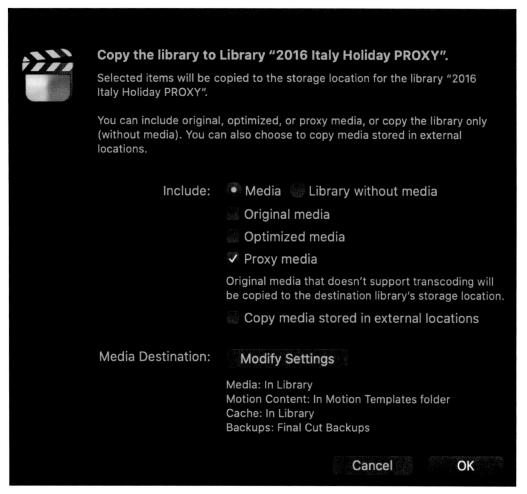

Figure 16.35: Here, I've chosen to include only proxy media, but I could have chosen to include no media at all

6. If you wish, you can also choose to store the media in an external location using **Media Destination**, but the default is **In Library**.

This new Library is entirely independent of the original, and much, much smaller. If you'll be sending Libraries backward and forward between editors many times, or want to maximize the image quality for all involved, sending the full media at least once — and storing it externally — is still a good idea. However, sometimes that original media is just too big for a limited internet connection, or the original media is too sensitive to share. In those cases, proxy files can be shared instead, and you can store them inside a Library if you wish.

Note that you will see a variation of the preceding dialog when dragging Projects or Clips between Libraries. If the same media clips exist in both Libraries, choose **Project without media** to try to avoid duplication. Note that if you pass around a Project or a Clip then Library-level organizational niceties, such as folders for Smart Collections, will be lost, so share full Libraries if you need to keep them.

If you are using external media, you should double-check that media storage locations are as you want them after each transfer. If possible, to minimize relinking issues while collaborating with external media, make sure to use identical copies of your media, on identically named drives, with strict copying and storage practices. For the official word on media management and collaboration, here's Apple's White Paper: http:// images.apple.com/final-cut-pro/docs/Media_Management.pdf.

Manual collaboration isn't hard — and it's certainly been made easier — but it does have the potential for version control issues should both editors work on their own copies of the same Project at the same time. There are more refined ways to collaborate, and probably the best at present is **Postlab**.

In the server-based Postlab system, you can check a Library out when you want to work on it and check it back in when you're done. In-built version control means that you can roll back to any previous version of a Library, and comments will tell you what has changed in each version. If you're working in even a moderately sized group, look into a professional collaboration solution like this to stay sane.

Exporting to ProRes, to multiple separate files, to XML, collaborating, phew. Let's recap.

REVIEW — EXPORTING FOR FURTHER PRODUCTION

Post-production requires high-quality files, to make sure that your video and audio data moves through all the stages with minimal quality loss. ProRes is an important codec in that process, and you now know more about how to export to it, as a single high-quality file or in separate files. You also know about XML, and its potential for interfacing with other applications and people, and possibly, you might have decided to use transfer Libraries or something more automated if you want to collaborate.

With all those exports under your belt, you might actually be done now. Time to clean up.

ARCHIVING YOUR WORK

Here, you'll discover a workflow for making sure your work is accessible months or years after a job is completed, with no media or effects missing. The archiving process might not be exciting, but it's definitely important. If a client comes back to you in six months wanting an urgent re-edit on a past Project, you'll win kudos if you can get the job done quickly and easily. While it would be nice if storage was unlimited, you can't keep every past job on your active storage forever; video is big, and expands to fill hard drives of any size.

Specifically, you'll find out how to make sure everything's in one place by consolidating the media and everything else you need. Then you'll figure out how to throw things away, first a little, and then a lot. Finally, you'll establish how to manage your archives, and recover from a backup.

In a few words? Consolidate your old jobs, and then move them somewhere else. Let's start.

CONSOLIDATING MEDIA

Consolidation is the process of moving all the files you need for a job into one place, to make it easier to copy everything needed to pick up the job again in the future. This is certainly made easier if you store your media inside a Library, as it's just a single item in the Finder, but there are other considerations, too. Let's go over what you'll need to do:

Glorious Beer Episode 1 Assembly v 9 COMPLETE

Figure 16.36: Including an exported copy of the final Project in the Library itself

First, it's a great idea to import a final, finished copy of your video to the Library itself. A ProRes file is ideal, but an H.264 copy will do in a pinch, and including the finished movie guards against the possibility that the Library itself is unreadable at some point in the future. How do we peek inside? Libraries are really just fancy folders:

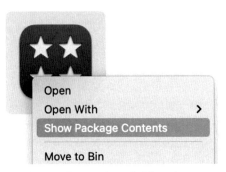

Figure 16.37: Every Library is really a folder that you can peek inside
(but don't move anything!)

Even without a copy of Final Cut Pro, anyone can open up a Library to extract the movie files within. All it takes is a quick right-click on the Library, and to choose **Show Package Contents**:

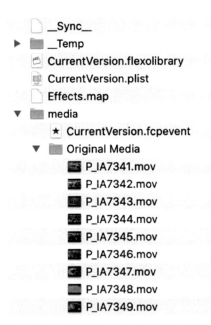

Figure 16.38: My Event is called "media," and inside the Original Media
folder you'll see all its files

Inside the package, each Event has a folder with a matching name, and inside that, there's a subfolder called **Original Media**. The Event's video files are all inside.

> **IMPORTANT NOTE**
>
> As well as storing this final exported file inside the Library itself, it's a great idea to keep another Library (ideally on another drive) to act as a collection of all your work with which you could build a showreel or simply a private folio. This builds over time, and if your archive drives are somehow lost, you can do a lot with a high-quality export in an emergency.

Next, decide whether you'd like to store your media inside the Library or externally. Select your Library in the browser's sidebar, click **Modify Settings** in the **Inspector** window, next to **Storage Locations**, and make your choice there:

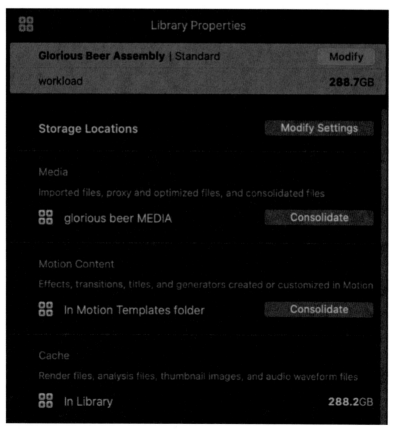

Figure 16.39: Modify Settings is the button you're looking for

You can stick with the decision you made way back when you made the Library in the first place, or change your mind. As discussed, some advanced workflows require external media, but if you're working alone, internal media is easier to manage. Either can be fine, but when you finally move this Library to archive storage, you'll have two things to move with external media, and you may have to reconnect media after reopening:

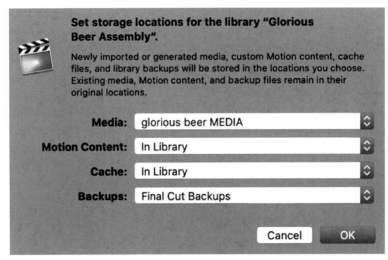

Figure 16.40: Currently, this Library uses external media, but I might switch to internal for archiving

This time around though, do store your **Motion Content** in the Library, rather than in the **Motion Templates** folder on your Mac. This way, any custom titles, generators, effects, and transitions you've used will be stored inside the Library, and if you open this Library on another Mac, they won't be missing:

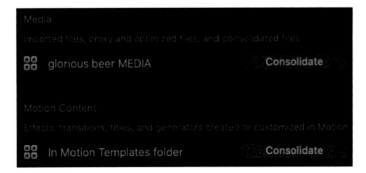

Figure 16.41: The Inspector has these Consolidate buttons, and you can find menu items under File that do the same thing

With the locations confirmed, look again in **Inspector** and click on **Consolidate** next to **Media** and next to **Motion Content**, confirming each one. Now, nearly everything you need will be copied into the Library, or into the Library and the external media location. What's potentially missing? Additional elements that you'll need in order to back up manually include the following:

- **Color LUTs** loaded from your hard drive
- **Non-standard fonts** used in titles
- **Third-party effects, titles, generators, transitions, and other plug-ins that use copy protection** — they'll need to be installed on any other Mac that opens your Library

Your Library is going to be the main focus, though. It's likely to be pretty big, but you can recover some of that space.

REDUCING THE SIZE OF LIBRARIES

The easiest way to save space is to select the **Library**, and then choose **File > Delete Generated Library Files**. (New in 10.4.9: you can also delete generated files for only selected clips.) The dialog that appears lets you throw away render files that have been created during the lifetime of the Library, which could be significant. You can use this command any time you want to save some space during your edit, but if you have **Background Rendering** turned on in preferences, they'll just be recreated. At this point, you might as well delete not just **Unused** render files, but **All** of them.

The other kind of file you can throw away is any of your **Optimized** or **Proxy** files. Since they're intended to speed up the editing process, and you're done with editing, you don't need them anymore. That'll save a ton of space too:

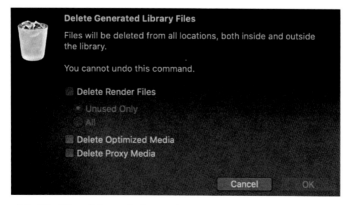

Figure 16.42: Checking all these boxes can save significant space

Without the optimized or proxy files, you'll still have the original media to fall back on; at worst, it'll be a bit slow. Mind you, even the original media can be big, and you can throw more away if you need to.

DELETING UNUSED MEDIA

If your Library is still too big, there's one more lever you can pull. The last step here is definitely optional, and not everyone will want to do it. If a number of files were never used, you can throw the unused clips away, creating a new Library that only includes the clips you need. The process is as follows:

1. Create a new Library with a new name, and set **Motion Content** to **In Library**.

2. Drag the final version of any Project(s) you want to keep from your existing full Library into the new Library.

When you copy a Project into a new Library, it copies all the clips used in that Project, but nothing else. Other clips don't make the journey, though keywords on used clips will come across. Obviously, if there are amusing behind-the-scenes moments that might be needed later, don't do this. Also know that this technique doesn't trim any media — if you use 10 frames of an hour-long clip, you'll have to keep the entire hour-long clip. But for most jobs, it's still going to save a lot of space.

Now that you've saved as much storage space as possible, let's get that thing off your main working drive.

COPYING TO AN ARCHIVE DRIVE

If the final destination is a regular drive, there's nothing fancy here. Just use the **Finder** to copy the Library (and your external media folder, if you used one) to a large hard drive, and then another one. Label the drives so you know what's on them, and on your main Mac, and make a record of the names of the drives so you know where the Library is. There's a nice third-party app called **Final Cut Library Manager** that will record where your Libraries live, and much more:

Figure 16.43: Final Cut Library Manager can show you what's missing, where space can be saved, and even where Libraries are on disconnected drives

Hard drives will die eventually, and sooner than you'd think if they aren't powered up every few months. Set some periodic reminders to power up your drives and make sure they're OK, and if they're ever not, duplicate a new copy from the remaining good drive. Of your two copies, move at least one drive offsite to guard against natural disasters.

If all of that sounds unworkable, consider other solutions. Larger facilities that need longer-term archives might use a tape drive, so if you have one, put your archival Library on a tape. You could also upload your old Libraries to archival storage online. There are options, and the march of technology drives down the cost of storage. It's entirely possible that the situation will have changed in just a few years, so keep an eye on this.

However you archive your work, it's sensible to test your archives. Eject your main media drive, and then load up the archival copy of the Library. For extra bonus points, open the new archive copy on a different Mac and make sure everything's there. Normally, you'll see an error on opening a Project, and warning symbols in the browser. Most often, it's from a file that wasn't consolidated or an old effect that's been deleted from your system. Either way, if something goes wrong, you can remount your original drive and then consolidate the new Library one more time.

When you know the archive is OK, the original copy is safe to delete, but I tend not to delete it straight away. Instead, I keep three folders on my working drive: 1 ACTIVE, 2 COMPLETED, and 3 ARCHIVED:

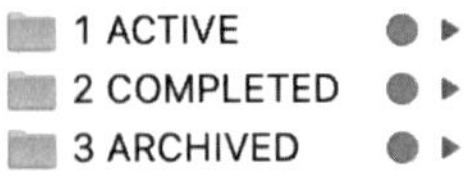

1 ACTIVE ● ▶
2 COMPLETED ● ▶
3 ARCHIVED ● ▶

Figure 16.44: All my video work moves through these folders in order

Active is for working jobs, **Completed** is for finished jobs that haven't yet been archived, and **Archived** is for jobs that are now safe to delete. I don't actually delete them from working storage until I run a little low on space, and this has saved me more than once when a client has had a late thought about a recently completed job.

Oh, and remember — archiving is not backup! You'll still need a backup strategy in place while you work. Online backup is a terrific option, and a local backup through something like Carbon Copy Cloner will help you to sleep at night. And guess what — FCP has a backup function built-in already. You probably won't need it often, but it's worth knowing about.

RESTORING FROM A BACKUP

First, if you're restoring an archived Project, that's pretty straightforward. Copy the Library back to your working drive, then open it up, do whatever you need to, and archive it again when you're done. But what if you accidentally destroy something important, and you quit FCP before you can undo? That's usually easy too, because FCP regularly makes backups of every Library it opens:

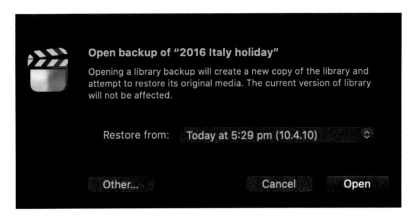

Open backup of "2016 Italy holiday"

Opening a library backup will create a new copy of the library and attempt to restore its original media. The current version of library will not be affected.

Restore from: Today at 5:29 pm (10.4.10) ⬍

Other...   Cancel   Open

Figure 16.45: It's easy to step back in time if something goes wrong

To roll back a Library to an older version of itself, choose **File** > **Open Library** > **From Backup**. A dialog appears with a selection of previous versions of the Library in a menu. Choose one, click **Open**, and it'll open up with a timestamp in its name. Drag whatever you need from the old Library to the new one, and then close the old one down again — done.

If your Library won't open at all, you can still recover. The default backup location is in your home directory, in Movies, in Final Cut Backups, so open that folder up now. (As an aside, if you're using cloud backups, this is a great folder to include.) In there, you'll find a subfolder for each Library you've ever worked on, and inside each of those, you'll see a collection of timestamped Libraries. None of these backups include media, so you'll need to locate the media from a backup of the media, either in a full copy of the Library with internal media, or an external media folder. Without media, backups don't take up a heap of space, but eventually, you might want to throw away the oldest ones:

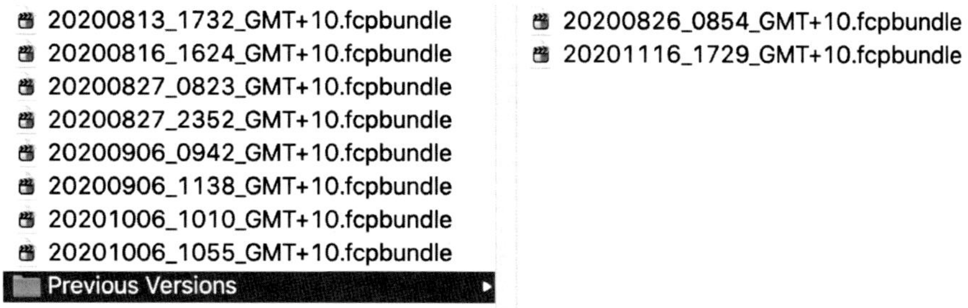

🗃 20200813_1732_GMT+10.fcpbundle	🗃 20200826_0854_GMT+10.fcpbundle
🗃 20200816_1624_GMT+10.fcpbundle	🗃 20201116_1729_GMT+10.fcpbundle
🗃 20200827_0823_GMT+10.fcpbundle	
🗃 20200827_2352_GMT+10.fcpbundle	
🗃 20200906_0942_GMT+10.fcpbundle	
🗃 20200906_1138_GMT+10.fcpbundle	
🗃 20201006_1010_GMT+10.fcpbundle	
🗃 20201006_1055_GMT+10.fcpbundle	
📁 Previous Versions ▶	

Figure 16.46: These backups can still be double-clicked
if the original Library can't be opened

Double-click any Library to open it up, and then reconnect media if you need to. But don't work in that backup Library. It's a bad idea to make changes to a timestamped Library in the backups folder, not just because it's the wrong place to save a Library, but because the names will become very confusing. Instead, create a new Library and copy anything you want to that new Library.

All that works very well, but there's no easy way to force a backup to be made in the first place. It'll happen from time to time in the background, but you don't have any control over it. For such control, look to a third-party app named simply **Backups for Final Cut Pro**. Let's hope you never need to use it.

REVIEW — ARCHIVING YOUR WORK

It's all done. You've exported, reimported, consolidated (even the Motion Templates!), and then trimmed down to save some space. You've safely copied it to a couple of archives, and then opened up an archive while the main drive was ejected to make sure it's fully self-contained. Maybe you've deleted it from your main storage already. Finally, maybe at some point you've had to restore an older version of your Library, from archive, or from your own system, but you figured it out.

Finally, that's it. What's next?

WHAT'S NEXT?

Indeed, what *is* next? Though there's been so much in this book already that your brain may have exploded, this section will give you a few jumping off points to consider what the editing experience might be like for you a few years from now. While the core editing experience is likely to remain the same, there's always going to be something new on the horizon, and it's good to keep an eye on what's possible.

In this section you'll find out where you can learn even more about editing and discuss the issues with other editors. You'll find out a few places to discover and download new plug-ins, play with new technologies such as 360° editing — a really fun thing that hasn't quite taken off yet — and also learn about helper apps to make the editing process even more fun.

The future's bright, and while it might not be evenly distributed, it's good to know what's coming next.

PREDICTING FUTURE DEVELOPMENTS

A book is written at a point in time, and it's good to look ahead to what came recently, and what's coming soon. Video editing keeps changing, and you shouldn't expect to do one job for the rest of your life. Smartphones didn't really exist 20 years ago, and though we'll still be viewing moving images in another 20, who knows what we'll be viewing them on?

AUGMENTED REALITY (AR)

It's been long-rumored that Apple will introduce a set of AR glasses, and while that sounds interesting, it's unclear what part video will play. Maybe 3D video will have a comeback? Certainly, it might be worth considering how your video could be placed within a 3D environment.

WIDE GAMUT COLOR AND HDR

This is absolutely going to become more of a focus in the next few years; it's already here today. New iPhones and Macs support Dolby Vision, Wide Gamut colors and HDR luminance ranges, and support will only improve as time goes on. Today, most productions destined for online distribution just ignore these newer technologies, and while that's OK when most of the audience can't display them, that will change. Suddenly, your clients will want to show their work in brighter and more vivid colors than their competitors can, and then you'll want to be across it. High-end production is already there, the software is there, the hardware is there, and we humans will get there eventually.

NEW CODECS

H.264 is the most popular standard today, but HEVC supports HDR and makes smaller files; if it was quicker to encode HEVC then more people would use it, and in the future they will. H.266 and others are waiting in the wings, and change is certain — eventually.

APPLE SILICON MACS

Apple recently announced that its entire range of Macs will transition from Intel chips to Apple-made chips over the next 2 years, and some low-end Macs made the move in late 2020. Final Cut Pro 10.5 is the first release to support the new chips natively, and is a flagship app to show off the potential of the new systems. It's a fascinating time to be an editor on a Mac, and a lot could change eventually.

COLLABORATION

It remains to be seen whether Apple will introduce an official collaboration workflow (as they already do with iCloud for iWork documents) but so far, this hasn't happened. Third parties have filled the gap for now, others may follow, and maybe we'll see more on this front.

3D MODELS MAY BECOME MORE IMPORTANT

The latest version of Motion supports USDZ-based 3D models, and so there's the potential for a whole new world of 3D integration in video editing. These same models are usable in Apple's **Augmented Reality (AR)** applications, so you'll potentially be able to share assets between videos and AR experiences.

360° VIDEO MIGHT TAKE OFF

Working with 360° video is not just possible in FCP, it's also a heap of fun. The first step is always to process your footage into equirectangular format, a 2:1 view that represents the entire sphere around the viewer. You can import those clips like any others, and work with them in a regular flat Project, or in a dedicated 360° Project — even a 3D 360° Project *since the 10.4.9 release*.

If you're delivering to a flat screen, you're in charge of where the viewer looks, but if you're delivering to a VR headset, the viewer is, and that's a challenge for many kinds of products. Your decision has consequences:

- In a regular Project, you'll choose which way to look, using dedicated 360° controls in **Viewer** and **Inspector**.
- In a 360° Project, the viewer chooses where to look, but you can simulate that process in a window or in a connected VR headset.

Unfortunately, 360° video just hasn't taken off — yet? — as a delivery platform. Though it's really fun to shoot casual video with a 360° camera, as everything around the camera is captured, it's difficult to hide lights, to hide crew, and to direct. It's also hard to edit, to deliver, and to view, and is affected by issues such as bandwidth limitations, the limited distribution of headsets, and the basic difficulty of figuring out where people might be looking. Probably the biggest limitation is that if the camera moves, half of the audience in headsets will become nauseous:

Figure 16.47: Across from Apple Park, as you might see it in a headset on the left, and the whole equirectangular view on the right

Most of those limitations go away when you use 360° footage in a regular Project because you can choose which way to look as you edit — and this is fun to work with:

Figure 16.48: The same clip in a regular Project, forcing the viewer to look the other way

Used this way, a 360° camera is just an action camera you don't have to aim, but unfortunately this hasn't been a world-beating revolution. The lesser known 180° video (half the view, but in 3D) doesn't look like it's taking off either. Fingers crossed that a popular future piece of hardware changes things, because 360° video really is something new, but not enough people can experience it just yet.

CAMERAS WILL GET BETTER

Right now, most new TVs and cameras are 4K, but a lot of lower end production still ends up at 1080p, mostly viewed on phones. Eventually that will shift, and when it does, camera manufacturers will be ready with far higher resolutions than anyone needs, like the newest 12K(!) camera from Blackmagic Design. We'll also see higher frame rates, increased dynamic range, and more besides. Computers will get faster, cameras will get better, and eventually, some of your audience will see better images.

FURTHER LEARNING

In any creative field, looking back on your old work can be bittersweet, first with nostalgia for times past, and then horror at how bad your work was back then. There's always more to learn, about how best to place that edit, or those lights, or that sound effect, and it's never been easier to find out information. Here are a few places to look.

THE OFFICIAL FCP USER GUIDE

In Final Cut Pro, choose **Help** > **Final Cut Pro Help** to make the official **User Guide** pop up in a small window that's always on top.

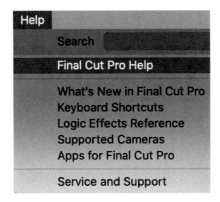

Figure 16.49: The built-in help will answer any remaining questions you might have

It's extremely informative, written by very nice people, and should always serve as the canonical source of information. If something you've read here disagrees with something written there, trust it. The search field at the top of the **Help** menu is also a great way to locate a menu item.

ONLINE VIDEO TRAINING

I can't pretend to remain impartial here, as I've created many training courses for macProVideo.com, but you'll find plenty of great paid video training courses for Final Cut Pro and for Motion out there. While there's good free training out there too, the quality is more variable. While a book definitely has advantages — the information density here is far higher and you don't need to keep pausing — sometimes it's nice to see things in motion. We can all get along together.

ONLINE COMMUNITIES

Facebook has several Final Cut Pro groups full of friendly, awesome people, Twitter has the #fcpx hashtag that's worth a search, and FCP.co (run by Peter Wiggins) is the biggest independent news site. Keep in touch with all of these to stay up to date with the current news, for opinions, user stories, and more.

PODCASTS AND LIVE STREAMS

Final Cut Pro Radio (by Richard Taylor) and the **FCP.co Live Show** are (at the time of publication) the biggest regular shows where editors and other members of the community chat about the app, editing, and more. **FCPX Grill** (by Chris Fenwick) is on hiatus for now, but may return.

CONFERENCES

For the last few years, I've been a regular speaker at the excellent **FCP X Creative Summit**, held in Cupertino, California, organized by FMC and usually hosted by Jeff Greenberg, famous for his "inside voice." It's the best chance to hear what the world's best Final Cut editors have to say, meet up with the community, and talk directly to the development team at Apple. In 2020 it went virtual — see you there?

COMPLEMENTARY TOOLS, PLUG-INS, AND EFFECTS

There are many great products in the wider Final Cut Pro world, and this is not by any means an exhaustive list. None of these companies have paid for these listings, but I have used their products and can recommend them:

- **Motion** (from Apple) is a fantastic complement to Final Cut Pro, and the biggest bargain out there. It's the tool used to create the vast majority of the included and third-party transitions, effects, titles, and generators, so if you can get your head around it, you'll be able to explore a whole new world. Even if you never master all the depths of this great app, you'll easily be able to modify third-party content to put your own spin on it — and now with 3D models too! Awesome stuff.

- **Compressor** (also from Apple) is a great app if you need to deliver content to a fussier audience with H.265, in specific data rates and containers, with watermarking, or simply to the iTunes Store. If you just put your content online, you probably won't need it, but it's a magic toolbox for everyone else.

- CommandPost, a genius open source app from Chris Hocking and David Peterson, is the first thing you should install If you like to tinker. It extends Final Cut Pro in all kinds of ways, enabling advanced workflows, automation, and even integration with external hardware such as MIDI controllers. If you've ever wanted to color correct using a hardware controller, here's how. Fantastic stuff, so send the developers a donation if you can:

Figure 16.50: Color correction with a MIDI hardware controller — yes please!

- Intelligent Assistance makes a suite of helper apps that integrate with Final Cut Pro, and if you're at the higher end of the market, you'll want to run straight to their translation and reporting solutions as they'll save you a ton of time and money. For live logging and transcription that ties into the edit, take a look at their **Lumberjack System**.

- Hedge offers software designed to import footage safely, but now also offers **Postlab**, the best collaboration solution to date. Definitely a great solution to remote editing as it lets you handle jobs for anyone on the planet, potentially a revolution in the making.

- CoreMelt offers a suite of plug-ins for Final Cut Pro, but I have to admit that I'm not impartial as I've made a lot of their training materials. If you want to track something around the screen, they have a great toolset available, and I've been using their **Scribeomatic** for automatic captioning too. CoreMelt also runs fcpxfree.com, a massive free directory of FCP downloadables.

- motionVFX offers not just a huge range of stylish bumper title designs, transitions, and color solutions, but also powerful custom plug-ins such as mO2 for 3D animation and other options for tracking. I've used many motionVFX templates to make clients happy over the years.

- LenoFX offers many packs of titles, generators, and transitions that can add pizzazz to your edits without being cheesy. When your clients demand more transitions or titles, head here for a pack or two.

- FxFactory is a marketplace where many smaller developers sell their own effects and other plug-ins, and there's a huge variety of things here. Take a really good look around, but especially at the superb, genius **Nodes** by **Yanobox** and the quite excellent **Hawaiki Keyer**.

REVIEW — WHAT'S NEXT?

At this point, it would seem foolish to predict anything but change. At least you should now have an idea of the kinds of changes coming soon, of where you can learn more, and where you can go when you want to extend the capabilities of the software. Final Cut Pro isn't going anywhere. Over time, it will add new features and continue to be the most efficient way to edit.

SUMMARY

You've exported a compressed file, then many more, and finally had your edit approved. Maybe you did that many times today. Maybe you exported a higher quality version for someone else to work on, or collaborated with someone on another continent. Maybe you archived an older job, or brought one back to make a change, or used a third-party app to transcribe an interview or create a wild and crazy background.

These might be the final steps in one edit, but they aren't your last. You've chosen a crazy industry with many niches to fall into, one which can make people happy or change minds, not just sell sugar water. Editing can be one of the most interesting challenges a creative mind can tackle, so get out there and make something amazing. You can.

FINAL WORDS

Thank you so much for reading this far. What seemed at first like a good idea during a global pandemic has become a monster, far larger and more detailed than I'd thought. While my first real editing gig was a Senior Video at school in 1991, and I've been teaching editing in Final Cut Pro since before it had an X, I'm still discovering features even now. There's always something new to learn, a new technique to conquer, a new effect to create.

Video is becoming an ever-more important aspect of our lives, and we editors must adapt, delivering fresh kinds of moving images to a voracious audience on evolving devices and platforms. Simple shots and straight cuts have their place, but when they're not enough, they don't have to be.

Final Cut Pro is a key part of my creative toolkit. It's expanded what I'm able to do and how easily I'm able to do it, letting me edit at the speed of thought and have fun at the same time. It really is a great app, and I hope this book opens it up to you too. Get out there and edit!

REVIEW QUESTIONS

1. If you have to deliver a piece for broadcast, which effect should you apply to the whole timeline?

2. Where can you control clip visibility with Roles to change your timeline?

3. Where can you control clip visibility with Roles for exporting?

4. What are two methods for exporting an SRT file?

5. What export option produces a file with a .mp4 container?

6. What's the name of the window where you can see export progress?

7. If you're exporting a final file for further production, would you use H.264 or ProRes 422 for highest quality?

8. What's the highest quality and highest data rate ProRes codec?

9. What is an AIFF file?

10. What command lets you open a previous version of your Library?

REVIEW ANSWERS

1. **Broadcast Safe**
2. The **Timeline Index**
3. In the **Roles** tab of the **Share** window
4. **File** > **Export Captions** and in the **Roles** tab of the **Share** window
5. **Computer**
6. **Background Tasks**
7. For highest quality, ProRes 422
8. ProRes 4444 XQ
9. A high-quality audio format
10. **File** > **Open Library** > **From Backup**

ACKNOWLEDGEMENTS

This book could not have happened without the contributions of many amazing people. Many thanks go to my editors at Packt (Sofi, Rakhi, and others) and technical reviewers (Chris Hocking and Kevin Luk) who all spotted several embarrassing errors. Any remaining mistakes are my responsibility; apologies in advance. Massive hugs and thanks go to my family, who've had to tolerate many late nights of writing over the last few months.

It almost (but not quite) goes without saying that the entire team behind FCP needs a huge round of applause too — kudos to you all. Much gratitude also to those who let me share screenshots of their work (or work I created for them) within this book. A special shout out goes to the music artist Ky, for whom I created a music video, and you can check out his audio track here: https://gyro.lnk.to/Gravitate.

Finally, thanks also to the talented editors who contributed quotes to open each chapter. They're all fantastic and worth tracking down online, but an extra thank you to Bradley Olsen, who created the awesome documentary *Off The Tracks*, and to Steve Bayes, who looked after Final Cut Pro and ProRes from launch and for several years afterward — we're all in your debt.

See you all online!

— Iain Anderson (@funwithstuff / iain-anderson.com)

INDEX

OTHER BOOKS YOU MAY ENJOY

If you enjoyed this book, you may be interested in these other books by Packt:

BLENDER 3D BY EXAMPLE - SECOND EDITION

Oscar Baechler, Xury Greer

ISBN: 978-1-78961-256-1

- Explore core 3D modeling tools in Blender such as extrude, bevel, and loop cut
- Understand Blender's Outliner hierarchy, collections, and modifiers
- Find solutions to common problems in modeling 3D characters and designs
- Implement lighting and probes to liven up an architectural scene using EEVEE
- Produce a final rendered image complete with lighting and post-processing effects
- Learn character concept art workflows and how to use the basics of Grease Pencil
- Learn how to use Blender's built-in texture painting tools

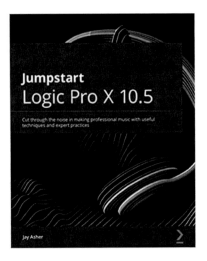

JUMPSTART LOGIC PRO X 10.5

Jay Asher

ISBN: 978-1-80056-277-6

- Get to grips with Audio and MIDI and how they are different, along with covering Apple Loops
- Record and edit audio, such as your voice or guitar
- Create and edit MIDI parts, using Logic Pro X's software instruments
- Develop realistic drums and electronic drums with Logic Pro X 10.5's amazing Drummer
- Explore the new Step Sequencer, Live Loops, and Quick Sampler that are now included with version 10.5
- Edit your arrangement and prepare the parts for mixing
- Discover the principles of good mixing, including automation, pre-mastering, and final bouncingss

LEAVE A REVIEW - LET OTHER READERS KNOW WHAT YOU THINK

Please share your thoughts on this book with others by leaving a review on the site that you bought it from. If you purchased the book from Amazon, please leave us an honest review on this book's Amazon page. This is vital so that other potential readers can see and use your unbiased opinion to make purchasing decisions, we can understand what our customers think about our products, and our authors can see your feedback on the title that they have worked with Packt to create. It will only take a few minutes of your time, but is valuable to other potential customers, our authors, and Packt. Thank you!

PACKT IS SEARCHING FOR AUTHORS LIKE YOU

If you're interested in becoming an author for Packt, please visit authors.packtpub.com and apply today. We have worked with thousands of developers and tech professionals, just like you, to help them share their insight with the global tech community. You can make a general application, apply for a specific hot topic that we are recruiting an author for, or submit your own idea.

Made in the USA
Middletown, DE
21 March 2021